NO SHAME IN MY GAME

The Working Poor in the Inner City

KATHERINE S. NEWMAN

Katherine S. Newman is an anthropologist who has carried out extensive and highly respected research on poverty and urban life. Previously at Columbia University, she is currently Ford Foundation Professor of Urban Studies at the Kennedy School of Government at Harvard University. She is the author of *Declining Fortunes: The Withering of the American Dream* and *Falling from Grace: Downward Mobility in the Age of Affluence.*

No Shame
in My Game

NO SHAME
IN MY GAME

NO SHAME IN MY GAME

The Working Poor in the Inner City

KATHERINE S. NEWMAN

WITHDRAWN

VINTAGE BOOKS

A Division of Random House, Inc.

and

RUSSELL SAGE FOUNDATION

New York

FUP

FIRST VINTAGE BOOKS / RUSSELL SAGE
FOUNDATION EDITION, APRIL 2000

The Library of Congress has cataloged
the Knopf/Russell Sage Foundation edition as follows:
Newman, Katherine S.
No shame in my game: the working poor in the inner city /
Katherine S. Newman. — 1st ed.
p.   cm.
Includes index.
ISBN 0-375-40254-3
1. Urban poor—United States.
2. Urban poor—Employment—United States.
3. Inner cities—United States.
I. Title.
HV4045 IN PROCESS
362.5'0973'091732—dc21
98-38244
CIP

Vintage ISBN: 0-375-70379-9

Author photograph © Martha Stewart
Book design by Robert C. Olsson

www.vintagebooks.com
www.russellsage.org

Printed in the United States of America
18 17 16 15 14 13 12

For my very special friends and
colleagues at Columbia University:

Elaine Combs-Schilling
Caroline Bynum
Herbert Gans
Donald Hood
Nancy Epstein
Norma Graham
Wayne Wickelgren
Kathleen McDermott
Roger Lancaster
Helen Benedict
Stephen O'Connor

and my wonderful students:

Catherine Ellis
Chauncy Lennon
Ana Ramos-Zayas
Eric Clemons
Travis Jackson
John Jackson
James Edell
Bill Hawkeswood
Kathryn Dudley
Nandini Sundar
Sarah Mahler
Jean Scandlyn
Bill Peace
Doug Slater
Rose Williams
Catherine Wanner

Contents

Preface

SOME OF MY BEST IDEAS have come to me while riding around in the backseat of New York City cabs. The drivers themselves are often the source of inspiration, but the seeds of this particular volume were planted while gazing out the window of a yellow cab as it tried to weave its way through central Harlem on an early Monday morning in 1989. I was on my way from my home on Harlem's far west side to La Guardia Airport, headed for a meeting, and late as usual. No one crosses Manhattan on 125th Street at eight on a workday morning expecting a fast ride. This trip was proving no exception. It took nearly forty minutes to crawl twenty blocks, but since I was still half asleep it didn't matter.

The car's slow creep gave me time to ponder a fast-approaching deadline. I had promised to write a paper for a conference on urban poverty at Northwestern University that was to focus especially on jobless neighborhoods. Mulling over what I might contribute, I was staring out the window at the streets of central Harlem, a ghetto not unlike the inner-city enclaves my colleagues were describing as locked in downward spirals of unemployment and despair.

Mired in traffic, my cab passed slowly down the main thoroughfare of Harlem, inching past one bus stop after another. Standing at the bus shelters were lines of men and women dressed for work, holding the hands of their children on their way to day care and the local schools. Black men in mechanic's overalls, women in suits—drinking coffee from Dunkin' Donuts cups, reading the *New York Post*, fussing with their children's backpacks—tapped their feet on the ground, waiting for the buses trying to maneuver toward them, caught in the same maddening traffic. The portals of the subways were swallowing up hordes of commuters who had given up on the buses. Meanwhile, people walking purposefully to work were moving down the sidewalks, flowing around the bus shelters, avoiding the outstretched arm of the occasional beggar, and ignoring the insistent calls of the street vendors selling clothing and videotapes from tables set up along the edge of the sidewalk. It was Monday morning in Harlem, and as far as the eye could see, thousands of people were on their way to work.

The driver finally gave up on the main boulevard and turned off onto a parallel street, hoping to gain some advantage. Here the shops of 125th Street gave way to burned-out, bombed-out brownstones, once Harlem's pride and joy, now decorated with graffiti and littered with crack vials. Stairs and stoops were broken down, windows were covered in iron bars. At least one building on every block was boarded up altogether, plastered with large notices announcing evictions or health hazards. 126th Street looks the part of the hard, broken-down ghetto. Yet upstairs, in dozens of second-floor windows, hand-lettered signs advertise the Pentecostal churches within. I had walked through this neighborhood on the occasional Sunday. Little girls in patent-leather shoes and their best pink coats could be seen on their way to services, stepping gingerly over the drunks passed out on the sidewalk and the broken glass sprayed in the gutters. These storefront churches have a lively following. Harlem Pentecostalists still host big-tent preachers who roll into town to spread the gospel on summer nights, and open-air crowds in the hundreds gather underneath awnings erected over parking lots to hear the traveling ministers, just as their grandparents did in the southern towns from which so many of Harlem's older residents hail.[1]

Remembering those Sunday walks through Harlem's back streets on that Monday morning, I kept thinking that this place was a far cry from the jobless ghettos described in the literature on the "urban underclass." It was teeming with impatient people trying to get to work. The social institutions that stabilize most communities—churches, stores, schools—were visible to anyone who bothered to look out the window. True, they were surrounded by the physical hallmarks of a poor community: graffiti on the walls, trash in the streets. No one would confuse 125th Street with Park Avenue. But it was hard to see how central Harlem could be mistaken for the complete wasteland my colleagues were describing either.

What accounts for the difference? Is it just that Harlem is a different kind of ghetto from Chicago's South Side or East St. Louis, with a different history and a more prosperous present? Certainly this is part of the answer, but it occurred to me that another part derives from the preoccupations of social scientists. When colleagues concerned about unemployment looked at those ghettos, they saw the families destroyed by the flight of manufacturing jobs from so many of the nation's urban centers. When I looked at Harlem that Monday morning, I saw the working poor people who were still in the community, soldiering on, even though Harlem too has lost much of its job base and has suffered many of the same problems of crime, poor city services, depopulation, and the loss of employers that other ghettos have endured.

It seemed to me that social scientists eager to put the urban poverty problem back on the national agenda had focused almost all their attention on people who were outside of the labor market, sitting on the welfare sidelines. What do we know about the others, the hardworking people of communities like Harlem struggling to get to work on time that Monday morning? Not much, I thought.

This focus on the jobless poor has created a gap in our understanding of inner-city economies. The preoccupation with ghetto dwellers who don't work has convinced policy-makers and most Americans that no one else is left in places like Harlem. Sixty-nine percent of the families living in central Harlem have at least one worker.[2] Yet in surveying most books on poverty over the last two decades or so, one would have to dig pretty deep before finding very much information about the working poor, people who toil year-round and either fail to pull above the poverty line or struggle to make ends meet just above it. Having convinced ourselves that welfare dependency and joblessness represent the true face of American poverty, the policy agenda of the 1990s as pressed by conservative politicians became very easy to sell. If the inner city is a mess because no one wants to work, we need to aim all our efforts at making it much harder to get on welfare and much easier to push people off of state support.

What has this kind of thinking got to do with the lives of the working people of communities like central Harlem?[3] Should we not learn something about these people, whose strengths we might be able to build on, before we consign our whole poverty policy to the ups and downs of the welfare system? This, at any rate, was the idea that began percolating in my mind as my cab finally made it across Manhattan and hit the approach to the Triborough Bridge. By the time I reached La Guardia Airport, the outlines of this book had formed in my head.

Because I was wrapped up in other research at the time, it took nearly four years before the ideas I presented at that Northwestern conference yielded a research project. By the time the fieldwork discussed in this book was underway, the problems of the working poor in the nation's inner cities had become even more urgent. For they are at continuing risk of being left behind in an economy that is now booming along,[4] the envy of the western world. Inflation seems to have gone the way of the dinosaurs. The stock market reached new high-water marks virtually every week throughout most of the nineties. With unemployment below 5 percent, a low not seen for over thirty years, Americans of all ages and races are being pulled back into the labor market.[5] For well-educated, highly skilled workers, these truly are the glory days. They have prospered in the last two decades, reaping higher wages, greater employment growth, and far more stability—downsizing notwithstanding—than any other group of employees.[6]

Yet the economy is generating relatively few good jobs, jobs that pay well and come with full benefits. Between 1994 and 1997, 19,000 jobs were created in high-wage fields like manufacturing. More than 400,000 jobs were created in retail stores during the same period, and they typically paid poorly.[7] This shift to a service economy[8] has seen a gulf the size of the Grand Canyon open up between the educated, skilled "haves" and the high school dropouts in the labor force. Hence even though more Americans are working, those in the middle are working for less, and those at the bottom of the occupational pyramid face a bleak future.[9] Young workers in today's job market who lack a high school diploma are at least four times more likely to be out of work than those with college degrees.[10] Their wages continue to fall.[11] High school graduates are only marginally better off—they too have lost much ground.[12]

These trends are bad news for the nation's poor, both children and adults. In 1974, 10.2 million American children lived below the poverty line. By 1994, the number had risen to well over fifteen million. The proportion of all American children classified as poor grew from 15.4 percent to almost 22 percent.[13] According to the Annie E. Casey Foundation, one of the most respected nonprofit organizations in this field, a quarter of the nation's children under the age of six now live in poverty, making the United States one of the worst offenders among the advanced nations of the world.[14] *More than five million of these poor children live in families in which one or both parents worked all year, an increase of nearly 100 percent since 1989.*

What forces lie behind these unfortunate trends? Why, in a nation marked by prosperity unknown in most other societies, do we see an increasing number of people who work but are still poor? The labor market has shifted drastically in favor of the well-educated, leaving those who attend bad schools (or drop out of them) in trouble. Once upon a time, not so long ago, poorly educated job-seekers might have found refuge in high-wage work in the auto factories or the steel mills. Those days are history now. Where manufacturing retains a foothold, manual workers are now expected to gather statistical quality-control data, organize problem-solving groups to develop innovative solutions based upon their own research, and implement changes in the organization of assembly lines.[15] The average high school dropout, and many an inner-city grad, cannot compete against more advantaged job-seekers when it comes to the written tests manufacturers now routinely employ to find people who can fit into the new, high-tech factory. And in many communities, manufacturing jobs hardly exist anymore anyway.

Racial segregation and the increasing concentration of poverty have made the consequences of trends that disadvantage the poorly educated all the more problematic. Between 1970 and 1990, the number of poor people in high-poverty neighborhoods nearly doubled—even though overall poverty changed little.[16] And those neighborhoods were largely black and Latino. Concentrated poverty often translates into poor schools and high dropout rates, thus reducing the chance that employers will look upon ghettos as fertile trolling ground for new employees. The giant sucking sound Ross Perot once spoke of in describing his worst fears about NAFTA was loud and clear many decades before, as good jobs drained out of ghetto neighborhoods. The nation's urbanized poor—African-Americans, Puerto Ricans, and Dominicans in New York, Mexicans in Los Angeles or El Paso—took the brunt of the collapsing demand for low-wage labor.

What was left behind, however, was millions of poor workers occupying the lowest rungs of the occupational ladder. They were ensnared by marginal jobs that pay poorly and offer little hope of significant advancement. Their jobs are often part-time, though we have seen a steady increase in the proportion of the poor who work full-time and year-round. For the most part, they do not have access to private health insurance, but they earn too much to qualify for Medicaid. Child care is a permanent headache for them, and those who do not have family members they can rely upon to help are forced into substandard arrangements for their children. Nonetheless, they work.

Perhaps because the nation's working poor are so busy trying to make ends meet, they have attracted very little attention. They do not impinge upon the national conscience; they do not provoke political outrage as welfare recipients do; they are not represented by organized labor, and few public figures (save, perhaps, Jesse Jackson or Hugh Price) take the time to dramatize their problems; and they are too tired to take to the streets to demand a larger part of the national pie. As far as most Americans are concerned, the working poor are not a social problem.

Yet we ignore these people at our peril: their children are at risk for a host of problems that ramify throughout the life span. As the Annie E. Casey Foundation has reported, children in working poor families are

> less likely to be fully immunized; less likely to enter school ready to learn; and far more likely to experience academic failure and to drop out. As teens they are more liable to delinquency and pregnancy; if they do graduate, they are less likely to go to college; and finally, like other poor kids, they face a reduced chance of being economically successful as adults.

The working poor are perpetually at risk for becoming the poor of the other kind: they are one paycheck away from what is left of welfare, one sick child away from getting fired, one missed rent payment short of eviction. They may want nothing more than additional work hours to increase their earnings and cushion themselves against these hazards, but they can easily be reduced to indigence.

To appreciate what the lives of the working poor in the inner city are like and why we ought to focus more public and policy attention on them, I undertook a two-year study intended to explore how young (and not-so-young) adults in the Latino and black neighborhoods of central and west Harlem go about finding jobs in the first place. Where do they look? How are they greeted by employers when they come knocking? I wanted to know what kind of social price they pay among their peers when they stoop to seeking "hamburger-flipping" jobs that have become the butt of countless parodies and sarcastic asides. How do they summon the personal strength to blast past that stigma? What do other workers on the shop floor do to help them live with the ostracism that may follow? Who sticks with the grind and who folds, losing whatever attachment he or she might have cultivated to the world of work?

I wanted to know whether the popular epithets directed at these "no skill" jobs are deserved. Do people enhance their "human capital" when they take a McJob, or are they wasting their time? What can a worker learn from a minimum-wage job that would make a difference to the next employer? Can those skills, whatever they may be, translate into upward mobility, or is the ghetto worker stuck permanently in employment that will never pull his family above the poverty line?

Finally, this work was driven by an abiding concern with family—with understanding how low-wage workers make a place for themselves in households and among extended kin who are poor. For if we hear little about the working poor, we hear even less about what "family values" might mean in the inner city. The common assumption is that the family has disintegrated behind ghetto walls—end of story. Yet the work ethic I found in central Harlem did not emerge from thin air. It has been incubated inside families, often by mothers on welfare who wanted something better for their children. Without painting a saintly portrait of struggling heroes, I nonetheless wanted to ask how family life is organized when working a low-wage job is central to its survival.

SECULAR FORCES and special circumstances have combined to make life particularly difficult for the working people of America's inner cities. Yet there is reason to believe that the efforts we make on the poverty policy frontier would have the greatest payoff if we focused attention on this large and growing population of poor workers. One of their greatest assets is the commitment they share with more affluent Americans to the importance of the work ethic. These are not people whose values need reengineering. They work hard at jobs the rest of us would not want because they believe in the dignity of work. In many instances they are not only not better off, they are actually worse off from a financial perspective for having eschewed welfare and stayed on the job.[17] It costs them—in child care, in transportation, in clothing costs—to remain in the labor force. But it also benefits them, as it benefits their middle-class counterparts, because working keeps them on the right side of American culture. Nonetheless, they are poor, and because of this unhappy truth, they are subjected to many of the same forces that the nonworking poor must contend with: decaying housing, poor diet, lack of medical attention, lousy schools, and persistent insecurity.

To understand what might be done to reverse this scenario, to build upon the advantages that a life on the job confers, we have to delve deeply into the lives and experiences of the working poor. We cannot understand the obstacles they face and the achievements they have earned just by looking at numbers and tables. Anthropologists like me find it more illuminating to spend time with poor workers and their children and parents, employers, friends, schoolteachers, and ministers in order to appreciate the nuances of working poverty.

MORE THAN THREE HUNDRED New Yorkers—African-American residents of Harlem, Dominicans and Puerto Ricans from Washington Heights, business owners and managers—gave generously of their time in order to contribute answers to my questions. They permitted me and my research team to plague them with surveys and interviews. They tolerated our presence as we tagged along with them to their jobs and to meet their families, teachers, and preachers. The project they participated in went on long enough for new children to be born, new marriages to take root, painful divorces to unfold, promotions and graduations to be celebrated, and disappointment to take its toll. I would like to thank these good people but promised I would never use their real names or the names of their friends and family members. Moreover, I have altered some biographical details to further obscure the identities of everyone who participated in this project. Still, I hope they will consider this book an accurate reflection of their lives, and I am most grateful to them for making this research possible.

It takes a prodigious amount of support to mount a project of this complexity. Indeed, the whole enterprise would never have happened without the devotion of a large group of doctoral students at Columbia University. I have listed their names on the dedication page, but must say a few words about them and how they contributed to this book. Eric Clemons, Catherine Ellis, Travis Jackson, and Ana Ramos-Zayas were the members of my core research team, responsible for the interviews, the shop floor research, and the intensive fieldwork in the homes and among the peers of our working poor "informants." This remarkable group of students—African-American, Puerto Rican, and white—crisscrossed color and class lines to learn about people who lived near our Columbia neighborhood but were a world apart, their life chances circumscribed by poverty. There is no thanks sufficient to convey my appreciation to these four students.

Without the cooperation of business owners and shop floor managers in Harlem's fast food industry, this project would have been dead on arrival. They took valuable time away from their jobs to talk with me about their views of the inner-city labor force. Having promised them and their firms complete anonymity, I cannot name them here. They know who they are, however, and I offer my thanks to them. There is much more to be learned from minority business people in the inner city than I have presented here. Suffice it to say that Harlem business owners are unsung heroes. They could undoubtedly find easier places to make a living, but most have chosen to locate in this community because they are committed to providing employment for its residents (as well as to making a profit). We need millions more of these entrepreneurs to help solve the employment problems of urban ghettos.

Sometime during the middle of this project, colleagues at the University of Michigan and the University of Chicago raised the objection that the research design was too limiting, that we were going to end up finding out only about the "diamonds in the rough," the hardworking people who might or might not be representative of central Harlem. Because they were right, we added a whole phase of research that would not have existed without their criticism—a study of people looking for work, largely without success, in Harlem. John Jackson, Anthony Browne, and Neal Savishinsky, all Columbia doctoral students, and Laura Ortiz at the City University Graduate Center, took this project on, becoming at once detectives and sympathetic interviewers. They tracked down applicants for fast food jobs, looking for them all over New York City so that we could claim a representative sample.

The waves of data that poured into my office were quite overwhelming at times. Without the help of Chauncy Lennon and Doug Slater, it would have proved impossible to organize, order, and analyze our results. Chauncy worked on virtually every phase of the analysis, staying up through the night in order to finish enough of it to make our results available to the Department of Health and Human Services as it prepared for the hearings on the welfare reform bills of 1996. Doug went over every line and did much of the background research that is reflected in the notes. I am deeply grateful to them both.

Many of my colleagues have spent their lives, from graduate school to retirement, studying the problem of poverty. I have not followed this consistent a pathway. Although I have long been interested in the local, personal consequences of large-scale economic trends, much of my writing has been about America's troubled middle classes. I came late to the question of poverty and have depended on the generosity of a remarkable national community of scholars to learn about the poor and to help me think through what an anthropologist might contribute to a literature that is primarily the province of economists and sociologists.

For me, the greatest benefit of having entered this intellectual territory has been the chance to learn from these colleagues and to repay their confidence in my approach with this book.

In addition to personal friends at Columbia whom I have listed in the dedication, I am particularly grateful to Sheldon Danziger and Mary Corcoran at the University of Michigan; Greg Duncan at Northwestern; William Julius Wilson, Christopher Jencks, David Ellwood, Mary Jo Bane, Jane Mansbridge, Julie Boatright Wilson, and Pamela Metz, my colleagues now at Harvard; Frank Levy and Paul Osterman at MIT; Barry Bluestone at the University of Massachusetts; Harry Holzer at Michigan State University; Frank Furstenberg and Kathy Edin at the University of Pennsylvania; Jeanne Brooks-Gunn, Larry Aber, and Tom Bailey at Columbia; Diane Hughes and Richard Sennett at New York University; Marta Tienda and Michele Lamont at Princeton; Rick Shweder and Lindsay Chase-Landsdale at the University of Chicago; and my longtime colleagues in Berkeley, Arlene and Jerry Skolnick, Philip Selznick and Doris Fine, Hank and Lillian Rubin, Jim Stockinger, Bob Fitzgerald, and Judy Small.

Perhaps the greatest unanticipated consequence of a year-long residency at the Russell Sage Foundation was the opportunity to work with Robert Merton. His encyclopedic understanding of the social sciences owes mainly to the fact that he developed so many of our most fundamental concepts in the first place. Besides, Bob let me share a wonderful assistant, Camille Yezzi, a luxury from which I have yet to fully recover. My agent at the Garamond Agency, Lisa Adams, and my wonderful editor at Knopf, Ash Green, have improved this book in countless ways. David Haproff, who runs the publication program at The Russell Sage Foundation, has also been generous with his time and attention.

I must reserve special thanks for Professor Carol Stack at the School of Education, University of California, Berkeley. The work discussed in this book began as a comparative study of Harlem and Oakland, California, with Carol at the lead in the west. She and I worked closely together for a number of years, and being able to tack back and forth between New York and Berkeley as the data unfolded was a special pleasure for both of us. Her own writings on Oakland's low-wage workers will add greatly to our understanding of the urban poor.

It takes more than people to pull off a project of this magnitude. Financial support is critical, for without it research teams like the one I was so lucky to have cannot be assembled. Yet if all that the foundations who underwrote this project did was pay for it, the relationship would be limited and instrumental. It wasn't. My intellectual debts to the foundation leaders who encouraged this research are much deeper than dollars. Eric Wanner, President of the Russell Sage Foundation, was an essential partner in this enterprise from the very beginning. He was the first person to push me forward in the direction of a real research agenda when I first began thinking about the working poor. From that point forward, he has been my chief critic, interlocutor, and supporter. Like so many social scientists working on labor market issues, I owe him greatly.

Eric, however, was not alone in this arena. Julia Lopez and Aida Rodriguez at the Rockefeller Foundation were steadfast in their belief in the value of learning about the working poor and rescued me from various commitments so that I could get the book done. Betty Hamburg and Lonnie Sherrod at the William T. Grant Foundation also had faith in the importance of this work. The Ford Foundation and Spencer Foundation contributed generously to the project. The Academic Dean's Faculty Research Fund at the Kennedy School of Government provided a small grant at the last minute that helped see the volume off to the publisher on time; I thank my colleagues, Deans Fred Schauer and Joseph Nye, for their interest in this work and their contagious congeniality. Malcolm Wiener has helped to support research on social policy conducted at the Kennedy School. As a member of two MacArthur Foundation research networks, I have benefited from many opportunities to discuss the project with colleagues around the United States. Bert Brim and Nancy Adler, the directors of those networks, have made these conversations possible and have supported other aspects of my research generously.

I have dedicated all my other books to members of my family, leaving this one for colleagues and students who worked with me during the fifteen years I spent teaching in the Anthropology Department at Columbia University. However, nothing much happens in my life that doesn't have a major impact on my husband, Paul Attewell, Professor of Sociology at the City University of New York Graduate School. His contributions to this project began at the conceptual phase and have carried through to the final writing. Steven (fifteen) and David (nine) have cheered me on from the sidelines and kept the grumbling to a bare (though audible) minimum.

Cambridge, Massachusetts
November 1998

No Shame
in My Game

No Shame
IN MY GAME

CHAPTER ONE

Working Lives

JAMAL'S WORLD

From the outside, Jamal's building looks like an ordinary house that has seen better days. Shingles are strewn about the foundation and the cement steps are cracked and broken, but it is not hard to imagine that with a little bit of paint and a thorough sweeping, the place might not be too bad. A family—like Jamal's family—could live in a home like this and be comfortable.

But once you walk through the front door, all resemblance to a real home disappears. For at least a decade, the building has been broken up into separate living quarters, a rooming house with whole families squeezed into spaces that would not even qualify as bedrooms in most homes. Toilets, such as they are, sit at the end of a dark hallway. Six families take turns cooking their meals in the only kitchen and argue with one another about the provisions they have squirreled away in the refrigerator they share.

The plumbing breaks down without warning—the bane of everyone's existence. Most rooms sport windows that are cracked and broken, pieced together by duct tape that barely blocks the steady, freezing draft blowing through on a winter evening. Jamal is of the opinion that for the princely sum of $300 per month, he ought to be able to get more heat. But the landlord isn't buying his argument, so a feeble electric space heater hums away in the corner of his room, providing just enough warmth to get through the night, if you huddle under the covers and wear a lot of clothes.

Jamal's room, which he shares with his common-law wife, Kathy, is big enough for their bed, the television (tuned, always, to a shoot-'em-up western or a kung fu video), and a few shelves that hold canned goods and pasta. The walls are covered with posters of their favorite stars—Michael Jackson, Tupac Shakur—which is just as well, because the wallpaper is peeling underneath, an unsightly mess that resists any attempt to smooth the surface. The room is a major step up from the basement they used to occupy in the same building; its only windows were up near the ceiling, making fresh air scarce.

A hot plate in the corner of the room gives Kathy the freedom to cook in her "own space," even though the super would throw a fit if he knew she uses it. Fires have erupted in the past when hot plates were left on, so they have been banned for some time. Still, Jamal and Kathy are hungry for a modicum of privacy, the illusion that they live in a real home where an ordinary family can cook a meal without the hovering intrusions of neighbors who live on the other side of the bedroom wall.

Despite Kathy's best efforts to keep their clothes in good order, Jamal hates to put his things away; she gets tired of picking up after him, and they argue, a lot, about whose job it is to clean up the room. It is important to clean thoroughly, they have discovered, because among their unwanted roommates is a pack of rats. Especially in the dead of winter, when the pickings are slim outside, the rats make their way through the cracks and holes in the walls to Jamal's and Kathy's floor. Finding a rat among the shoes, Kathy notes, is among life's most repulsive experiences.

Peace and quiet are rare in the rooming house. Little kids, like two-year-old Amara next door, have nowhere to play. So they roam around and visit the families who live in the rooms nearby until their mothers, momentarily distracted from their cooking chores, come to find out where their charges have wandered. Arguments are constantly breaking out among the tenants in the house, loud voices spilling out into the hallways and through the thin walls. Close quarters breed discord, for no one has the privacy or mental space to cool off when tempers flare.

Jamal feels the walls closing in on him, on his relations with Kathy, because they are so cramped. They can barely turn around at the same time without running into each other. Jamal would like to be able to do separate things at home, like watch his favorite TV show, without getting on Kathy's nerves. He even thought about getting a divider for their room, but rejected the idea because it would simply accentuate the confinement. It does not help his temper, which has its explosive side, to be stuck in such a dump.

And he needs his rest, because at the age of twenty-two, he does a full shift whenever Burger Barn,* the fast food joint where he works, will give him the hours. In the winter of 1993, when I first came to know him, Jamal was having a good run, piling up many an eight-hour shift. At the minimum wage—then $4.25 an hour—he was earning only $34 on a good day. But if he could get enough days like that, he could keep the family's head just above water. Trouble was, he was usually only able to persuade the manager to put him on for five hours and then he'd be sent home. "Everyone wants more hours," the boss told him, "but this is all I got to give you." So Jamal would board the bus for the hour-long journey across the Bronx, glad to get off his feet, but worried about how they were going to pay this month's rent, much less the back rent he already owed.

In some ways, he was glad to leave work early. For in order to get to the job on time, he had to wake up at 4:30 a.m. and board the bus by 5:00. That was a struggle in winter when it was dark and bitter outside. Tired and freezing-cold in his thin maintenance uniform and his green khaki duffel coat, Jamal had to struggle against his own exhaustion just to make it to work. He was usually late, but not late enough to rankle the manager, a Jamaican woman who, truth be told, was often a bit late herself. Still, there were many days when all he wanted to do was jump back under the covers and forget about the job. There were all too many people in the neighborhood, God knows, who thought he was crazy to work so hard, travel so far, for the grand sum of $25 on a typical short-hour workday. Why bother?

Jamal can see their point of view. "I hate this damn job," he complains, "but it's a job. The people at [Burger Barn] are real jerks, always acting like they're better than me. But it's hard when you have no real good work experience." He allows that he'd like to find a job "where I can really be somebody who has something." If his experience of the past three or four years is any indication of what he can look forward to, this dream is a very long way off. Having pounded the pavement all over Manhattan, Queens, and the Bronx, Jamal has never been able to do better than a minimum-wage job in the fast food business.

Even these opportunities have come to him because of his "associates," young men he has encountered on the job who have helped him find new positions. Without their help, Jamal would not have done as well as he has. He would be out on the street in no time. Knowing this, he makes it his business to get to meet people. "You never know when you might

*Burger Barn is a pseudonym for a national chain of fast food restaurants.

need them," he points out, and in a high-turnover industry, where people are always losing hours and then losing jobs, you have to stay on your toes and keep the lines of information open.

The need for "associates" is especially strong for a young man like Jamal because employers don't exactly rush to open the door and let him in. His very physical presence is intimidating, especially to those who don't know him. The day we first met, on the campus of Columbia University where I was teaching, it was easy to pick him out from a distance. The sea of young white students parted right down the middle of the stately brick walkway to let him pass. At six feet and 220 pounds, he had the look of a pro football linebacker. With the hood of his gray sweatshirt pulled down low over his brow and a slight scowl on his face, he probably looked dangerous to this crowd. And that is exactly what most employers see coming in the door: a young black man with an attitude. What they don't see is Jamal's rounded face, almost a child's face, his luminous brown eyes, and the doting love he has for his young wife.

Over the two years that I got to know him, the Jamal I came to see was bright, perceptive beyond his years about the motives and ambitions of the people around him, and very, very depressed. At twenty-two, about the same age as many of my effervescent, optimistic undergraduate students, he was sure that he knew what his future would hold: an endless series of dead-end jobs that would condemn him, and Kathy, to life in a rat-infested tenement. He had the brains to be one of those college students, but he knew he would never, ever have that kind of chance. Instead, he was going to have to slog it out on the crosstown bus at 5:00 a.m. and spend his days cleaning out french-fry vats, catching hell from a manager "who acts better than other people." Yet the fact that he could speak so articulately and forcefully about the world he lives in and write his heart out in the diary he kept for me for over a year, told me that such a fate was a waste of a young man who could have switched places with any number of my students had his biography been different.

Still, Jamal realizes that he has a lot to be grateful for. He has a woman who loves him, even though they fight a lot over nothing. She takes care of him, fusses over him, and waits for him to come home from his job so they can share some popcorn and watch C-grade movies from the local video shop. Kathy ran away from her home in Florida, at the age of sixteen, just to be with Jamal. Her white mother was none too keen on her daughter's marrying a black man, so Kathy severed all ties to her family, save for the occasional heartbreaking call to her little brother from a pay phone. She is given to staring down at her long, shiny red fingernails when she talks about leaving her brother behind. But Kathy hardens when she talks about her mother, not just because she disapproved of Jamal but because she has been appropriating the money Social Security has sent every month since her father died. Kathy figures that money belongs to her; Mama down in Tallahassee sees the situation differently.

The money would be a big help. Kathy especially could have used it when she found out she was pregnant with Jamal's child. When their daughter was born, about six months before I met them both, the young couple had nothing to live on besides Jamal's part-time wages from Burger Barn. Kathy worked at the Barn too, for a time, but finally gave it up when the baby was born. They wedged the crib into their single room in a Brooklyn tenement and struggled to manage the piles of Pampers and a squalling child in this tiny, claustrophobic space. But Tammy developed colic and became difficult to handle. Neither Jamal nor Kathy had ever taken care of an infant before, and they didn't know what to do to make her stop crying. To his eternal regret, Jamal lost his temper one day and lashed out at the helpless child, an incident he never did quite confess to. He insisted that he had accidentally pushed the baby's crib and the little one fell out. Social Services didn't buy this, though, and they removed Tammy from her home, charging Jamal with abuse and Kathy with neglect.

When I first began spending time with the couple, you could tell that there was a hole in their hearts, a kind of grief and nervousness. They were absolutely determined to get their baby back. Every week they visited her in a family center run by the city Social Welfare Department, supervised closely by the foster mother who had temporary custody of Tammy. They attended parenting classes, trying to learn how to take better care of the little girl—how to change diapers, hold a bottle, and tolerate the mind-numbing cries of a newborn. Just the sight of Tammy, now six months old, turned them emotionally inside out. Jamal marveled at "how big she is getting to be." Kathy just wanted to hold her, give her toys to play with, make sure she remembered what her real mother looks like.

Indeed, one of the saddest days in Jamal and Kathy's lives came about because it was Tammy's first birthday. The couple had brought me a handwritten invitation to her party and clearly wanted me to come. But the baby's birthday was a teaching day for me and I could not break free, so I asked a member of my research team, Travis Jackson (now a professor at the University of Michigan), to go to the party on my behalf, loaded down with presents for Tammy and her parents. Travis had spent much more time with Jamal and Kathy than I had; indeed, he was almost a member of the family by now. He traveled to the family center in Brooklyn, the only place where the court would allow supervised visits between parent and child. Later on, Travis recalled for me how the party had gone:

> *When I got there, Jamal was standing inside waiting. I asked whether he was waiting for me. He told me no and said that he was waiting for the baby to get there. He went over and said something to one of the women at the desk and then took me to the room where they were going to have the party. . . . Kathy and Jamal had decorated it with a banner that said "Happy Birthday," and a few other colorful things. The table was filled with gifts and a cake, sodas, and ice cream. I could tell that they had taken some time to prepare this party setting. Unfortunately, at that moment, I was the only party guest who had arrived. Jamal said that they had invited other people, but that I was the only one who had showed up. Kathy then went out to wait for the baby and her foster mother to show up.*
>
> *She came back a few minutes later with the news that Tammy wasn't coming. Apparently, she was sick, maybe with a cold, and her foster mother didn't think it wise to bring her outside, especially because the weather was so cold—temperatures in the teens. . . . The disappointment was literally too much for Kathy. She started to cry, and Jamal did his best to comfort her, telling her that the baby would be back in little more than a week. Kathy said she understood, but at least had wanted to spend the baby's first birthday with her.*

Jamal had a hard time convincing Kathy that it mattered to him, deeply, that they regain custody of their child. "It's hard for her," he would say, "not having the baby at home. She thinks that I don't care, but I do. It's just hard to show my deepest feelings." The biggest problem, though, was that they couldn't meet the court's conditions for the return of Tammy. Somehow on his Burger Barn salary, Jamal was supposed to provide an apartment with a separate bedroom for Tammy. Kathy was forbidden to work, since the law's position was that she had neglected the baby's care. The cheapest place they had seen that met these conditions, deep in the heart of the South Bronx, a place known nationwide for its mean streets, was still $600 a month. And that would get them only a one-bedroom apartment. Landlords were asking for a security deposit as well, a reservoir of cash that was completely beyond the family's means.

In the very best month Jamal had ever had, he earned only $680 before taxes—and that meant working full-time, something he could never count on.

Young couples in this predicament often turn to their parents for help, but it was not a real option for this couple. Kathy's mother was ready to charge Jamal with kidnapping a minor, even though Kathy had willingly joined him in New York. Jamal remembers meeting his father in the dim recesses of his childhood, but hadn't seen him in many years and had no idea where he was. In fact, he was pretty sure his dad was dead, a rumor he heard from one of his half sisters (by another mother) who lives in Queens. His mother, Jacqueline, used to have a good job working for the Postal Service on a military base near Tallahassee, but she has been drug-addicted since Jamal was in his early teens.

When I was thirteen, it was real good, 'cause she was working at the Post Office. And you know, she would do a lot of good things and we'd go hang out. But she started fucking up her life, and it's like we just got more distant. I never really had a father. My father is like . . . who knows where he's at. And that's how it is, [fathers] don't want to be bothered with nobody. And my mother, too. They could really care less. So I had nobody.

The worse Jacqueline's drug habit became, the more she pressured fifteen-year-old Jamal for money. In the beginning she just wanted him to provide for himself so that she could use her own money on herself. But as time went on, she wanted him to give up his Burger Barn earnings, or else:

She'd say, "Gimme money," and I'd argue, and she threw me out a couple of times. You know, it was just wild. I don't see how I can even see her. I seen her a week ago; hadn't seen her for like a month and a half. I can't be around her 'cause every time I see her she just wants money. I know she has problems, but I can't live with that because I have my own problems. I'm struggling myself.

Jacqueline inhabits a devastated block in the middle of Harlem, a street overrun by drug dealers and crack addicts, even though it borders a Catholic high school, filled with orderly children in uniforms. Nearly as tall as Jamal himself, Jacqueline is now a spectacle of emaciation, with sunken cheeks sporting streaks of rouge that no longer camouflage her parchment skin.

The stoop of the building where Jacqueline lives provides the visitor a front-row seat from which to watch the local trade in drugs, guns, and women. Boarded windows in the houses nearby are dimly lit to let even a casual observer know that someone is open for business. Lookouts stationed in the doorways stop buyers from bringing in bags or anything else that could contain a weapon, but this is the only real restraint of trade. It is a busy drug supermarket.

But it is not a place devoid of the human spirit. Jamal is clearly known and loved in these parts. Many people in the neighborhood recognize him, even though he hasn't lived here for four or five years. Women coming home from shopping climb out of taxis with their arms full of grocery bags, and greet him warmly. Two girls who looked to be about fourteen or so walked up and down the block and stopped to chat with Jamal. One, the sister of the drug dealer plying his trade in front of the building next door, wanted to know what was happening with Tammy.

Yet Jamal takes little pleasure in spending time in his mother's neighborhood. Sitting on the stoop, waiting for her to resolve the latest raging argument with her boyfriend, he cannot escape the savage consequences of her drug problem. Its impact is written all over her. Why a woman with a good job at the Post Office would get herself strung out on crack is really beyond him. And how could his mother's boyfriend, who brings home a king's ransom of $10 an hour from a perfectly legitimate job, throw it all away for a momentary high?

Jamal finds it hard to cultivate a detached attitude, for his mother's habits have cost him dearly. He was forced out on his own at an age when other children are navigating junior high school:

> She lost a good job, a job at the Post Office, 'cause of that shit [crack]. She went to rehab and she backtracked. And she would call in for work for a week, and wouldn't come to work and just get high. She did it to herself, you know, she can't blame anybody. You know, she'd always blame other people. "Well, I never had anybody to help me. You never helped me."
>
> I tell her, "I couldn't help you." What was I gonna do? I didn't even understand [the drugs] myself. You know, I was trying to get away from it. So I couldn't help her. All she had to do was go to work, I mean nine to five! That wasn't so hard. She was making twelve, thirteen, fourteen dollars an hour.
>
> Man, I could have had a BMW, my own apartment, be in school. My

girl [wife] could be in school. I would be living nice . . . if [my mother]
would just have [gone to work]. And I would have been a better-rounded
person instead of going from here to here to here, and doing this and that.

Jamal is all too aware that his mother's downward spiral destabilized his
life as well and set him on a path that leads, at best, to the kind of working
poverty that is his lot right now.

In years past, his grandmother in Virginia did what she could to help
him out, but she was so far away that the only time he could see her was
when he ran away from home—which he began doing regularly at the age
of thirteen. These days she has tired of Jamal's branch of the family tree,
convinced they are a blot on the reputation of the rest. Jamal knows his
grandmother has written him off.

There is nothing he can do to prevent the same fate from befalling
his five-year-old half brother, Jacqueline's son by another man who came
before the boyfriend of the moment. Already tall for his age, the little guy
very much resembles Jamal. And he looks up to Jamal, waiting for his
infrequent visits, and cracking a wide smile when his big brother comes
up the steps. But while Jamal knew some stability in his early years—
as the son of a working mother—his brother is growing up under much
harder, more debilitating circumstances. He is the young, vulnerable
child of a strung-out addict who worries more about where the next hit is
coming from than whether he gets to school in the morning. Jamal does
what he can to cheer the little guy up, but it is a depressing rerun of his
own later life experience, one that fuels a simmering anger inside.

Still, the same anger is responsible, at least to some degree, for Jamal's
belief that he must not fall into the same trap.

I had to find something to do with my spare time other than just go to
school and come home and listen to my mother, you know, do crack all
night. So I found a job and then once I found a job, it really changed a lot
of things that I did and do.

Even at the age of thirteen, when he first started working (at a corner
store, bagging groceries), Jamal was determined to find a different path
for himself, to keep himself away from the influences that led his mother
downhill. He has been working ever since.

Unfortunately, the kind of money he earns at Burger Barn puts him
into tempting situations. He too lives in a blasted ghetto neighborhood,
where many young men on the block are dealing drugs. Some are selling

guns. Only a few are working at the kind of dreary job Jamal has. The rest are perplexed about why he continues to kill himself for "chump change."

His "associates" from the neighborhood like him and invite him along on their escapades, but Jamal resists because he knows that is the road to trouble with the law. His willpower isn't always perfect, though. Last summer he started drinking and taking the occasional hit of cocaine. But he pulled himself out of it by sheer force of character. Still, the episode scared him into thinking he could lose control over everything. So he is in a panic about the need to get out of New York and move back to Tallahassee, to a less crazy way of life.

In the meantime, Jamal continues to do what no one really thinks he is capable of doing: work for a living, every day and for as many hours as his Burger Barn manager will give him. He dons his maintenance uniform, scrubs and sweeps, cleans and polishes, and takes whatever abuse (imagined or real) is dished out to this low man on the workplace totem pole. In his off-hours, he looks for better jobs. Years ago, when he lived with his grandmother, he had a temporary position in a car factory in Virginia. He earned twice as much money at that job as at anything he had found before or has encountered since, but he was laid off and was never able to recoup from the loss. Any chance Jamal gets to apply for a position in a car plant he jumps for, but thus far he has had no luck. So the string of fast food jobs he has taken instead—three in the time I have known him—are all he has to make ends meet.

It is easy to imagine a young person—a twenty-two-year-old black man with a crack-addicted mother—giving up under these circumstances. There are surely many cases like his where the effort required to keep going simply becomes overwhelming. Jamal, however, is different. He takes his responsibilities seriously, worries about Kathy's safety during the hours he is gone, and does what he can to make their lives together as comfortable as they can be. He hopes for the return of his baby girl and hustles Social Services to help him find a suitable apartment, one that the judge will accept as an adequate home for his fledgling family. He dotes on Kathy, and there is a great deal of affection binding them together. After all they have been through, they never speak of leaving each other or giving up hope for a better life.

He is far from a perfect human being, as he would be the first to admit. More dedication to his education would have made a difference, he thinks. The deck is stacked against a young man who scraped through with a GED. Good jobs are basically out of reach. And he knows he has not always been able to avoid the seamier side of life in the neighborhood where he lives. He is not proud of his temper and is deeply ashamed of the pain he has caused his wife by the loss, temporary as it may be, of their daughter. No one else is to blame for the times he has "messed up."

What is, however, most notable about Jamal is his commitment to work, to the importance of trying to make it on his own. It is this work ethic that keeps him boarding that bus, that compels him to track down whatever job leads come his way. He is not an optimistic person; he has no confidence that this drive will actually pay off in a much better life someday. But he believes, nonetheless, that people who have taken the other available paths in life are fools, and he does not plan to be one of them.

CARMEN'S WORLD

The number "1" subway line snakes up the spine of Manhattan's Upper West Side, smack through neighborhoods that once teemed with Jewish immigrants from Eastern Europe. Way up the line, far past the stops where students disembark for Columbia University and City College, riders find themselves in the midst of a bustling *colonia*, a new immigrant enclave where Spanish is the language of choice.

The train station near Carmen's home fronts Dyckman Street in Inwood, home to what seems like a thousand bodegas and *colmados*, and a myriad small shops offering tailoring and sewing services. Dominican bakeries can be found on every block, tantalizing smells pouring out the door, enticing customers. Cramped for space, the shopkeepers set up outdoor displays—cosmetics, laundry soap, fruits and vegetables familiar to Caribbean shoppers—spilling out onto the sidewalks. Every store has a young man perched atop a ladder or chair watching the display so that nothing leaves without being paid for. Mothers shop with children tugging at their sleeves, asking for a sweet or a plastic toy. On a nice day, it seems as though the whole population of Santo Domingo has descended on Washington Heights.

As you turn the corner onto the residential streets that crisscross Dyckman, the stores fade away save for one or two small bodegas. Gypsy cabs clog the choice parking spots, since their drivers live in the neighborhood. In the early mornings, street vendors set up their wares, hoping to snag customers before they get to the proper stores near the subway station. Maintenance men who manage the boilers and the plumbing crises in crowded apartment buildings come out in the early-morning sun to greet the vendors. In this neighborhood everyone knows everyone, and many have been friends since their days in the Dominican Republic.

The apartment house where Carmen lives is not a Manhattan sky-scraper. Like most of the other buildings along the curving boulevards of this immigrant enclave, it is six stories high and has about sixty apartments. These apartments almost never rent on the open market but are passed among family members and friends from back home; housing is a precious commodity in an expensive city like New York. Their scarcity bears no relationship to opulence; accommodations are quite bare, services are minimal, complaints are constant about landlords who neglect their property, and the threadbare rugs and dim lightbulbs in hallways express the landlords' attitude. Visitors can press the buzzer downstairs and wait in vain for someone to answer; most of the time, the intercom is out of commission. Still, in a city with high rents and a shortage of living spaces, immigrant families take what they can find, and they almost always find it through family connections.

That is exactly how Carmen and the majority of her extended family came to be living in Winston House, a building whose name memorializes the desire of the original Jewish immigrants to blend into the American scene in the 1920s and '30s. Carmen's grandmother—her father's mother and the undisputed matriarch of her enormous Dominican family—was the first to set foot in New York. Grandma married a Puerto Rican with automatic residence rights on the mainland. He, in turn, registered her and gave her that most precious of commodities: a green card. Though he has long since died, Grandpa's green card was enough to launch Carmen's family on an odyssey that has now lasted three generations, and continues to pull additional members back and forth from Santo Domingo to Inwood. Carmen's grandmother worked in a clothing factory, ironing, and on her very modest income managed to send for each of her eight children—including Carmen's father—one by one.

The sign on the door of Grandma's apartment reads (in Spanish), "Child care available here. Person with experience." A thousand children seem to be in the living room already, but that is only because they are running around at such high speed that their numbers multiply before your very eyes. None of the kids are paying customers; all are cousins, children of Carmen's many aunts and uncles who immigrated after the grandmother they have in common established herself in Inwood. They congregate at Grandma's place because their mothers are out to work or to doctor's appointments and because Grandma has that rare luxury, cable TV. All the best shows, including many Spanish-language soap operas, are piped in through cable, providing continuous entertainment or background noise for the multitudes who pass the day in the family's hub.

Aunts, uncles, cousins, grandparents, step-relatives, and close friends who pass for relations live in adjacent apartments, connected by fire doors that can be opened to make a continuous living space. Carmen's father, Jorge, divorced from her mother for many years now, was among the first of the "uncles" to leave Santo Domingo and follow his mother to New York. Carmen had not lived with her father since she was a little girl, having grown up with her mother in the old country. Still, even with the estrangement divorce creates, Jorge sent for two of his daughters—Carmen and her sister Rena—as soon as he could, and arranged for them to live with his mother until he had a place of his own, in the same building, of course.

Since the day Carmen arrived at the age of fourteen, she has hardly had a moment to herself. Her "rosary of aunts" surrounded her with cousins to take care of, a constant coming-and-going of people. Eight adults and twelve children live together in the three apartments that connect through the fire doors. There are others as well. Carmen's twenty-eight-year-old aunt lives next door with her (sometime) husband and three children. Carmen's uncle, a construction worker whose employment fluctuates with the industry, lives on the fourth floor. Another aunt is down on the second floor. Yet another aunt, and her three children, are on the third floor. A fourth aunt works as a home attendant and lives with her two girls in the building next to Carmen's.

Carmen's father and stepmother, with whom she was living when we first met in the fall of 1994, have a one-room apartment; her father works two jobs to pay the rent.

> *My dad works at night. Well, night and day, because now he has two jobs. We are living in a studio. There's a room, a kitchen, and a bathroom, and there's five of us in it. It costs seven hundred dollars and something for that studio. My dad starts working at six in the afternoon and works until about three a.m. He gets home at five and goes to sleep. Then he gets up and does his other job. His wife works during the day and gets off at about four.*

Carmen was never entirely comfortable in this house. Neither she nor her sister Rena was particularly fond of their stepmother, and the feeling appeared to be mutual. Conditions were very crowded, forcing these somewhat distant parties into one another's faces. Rena finally found things so bad that she up and got married, a common escape route from a bad situation.

In doing so, however, Rena seems only to have gone from one dubious predicament to another. She and her new husband moved in with his family not more than a couple of blocks from the rest of Rena's clan. Rena, her husband, their baby, and his father, mother, sister, and the sister's three children share a three-bedroom basement apartment with a small kitchen and a minuscule living room. Each family in this extended group has one small room to themselves, brimming with cots, mattresses, clothes hanging on the walls, and toys filling in all the cracks. The home is meticulously clean and orderly, but it is a long way from anyone's dream apartment. In fact, the whole building is a disaster. The most recent plumbing repairs left several large holes in the raw cement floor of the living room, holes that reach right down into the soil. Legal Aid is now the agency of last resort, summoned to force the landlord to attend to the gaping spaces in the floor.

Rena married and moved in part to avoid the fate that Carmen willingly elected when she completed high school: going to work. Rena preferred to remain in school while starting her family and has been a continuing student at Bronx Community College, a popular choice for Dominican immigrants intent on getting an American degree. Carmen has also doggedly stuck to her plans for securing a college diploma, and when we first met was enrolled part-time in the same college. But unlike Rena, Carmen was also working full-time for Burger Barn.

From the day she arrived in the United States, Carmen was determined not to be dependent upon her grandmother and to find a way, as soon as possible, to begin sending money back to her mother in Santo Domingo. But how to find a job at the age of sixteen, with a limited command of English? Her first efforts were to ask around her neighborhood in the shops. This got her nowhere, though. Carmen needed some help.

I was in high school and I was desperately looking for a job. I'd always call my grandmother—"Grandmother, someone told me about a job. I'm gonna go check it out." Then she'd tell me, "Okay, but don't be home late. Don't go by yourself." I'd never go with anyone, though, because I didn't know anyone at school.

One day I was in a counselor's office. She heard me talking to my sister, telling her that I had walked all over the place, that I had gotten home at six-thirty and hadn't found any [work]. That's been going on for days. The counselor said, "You want to work?" I told her, "Ay, yes, I've been crazy looking for work." And then she told me, "Well, look, I'm gonna give you these letters. Go to that Burger Barn that's [around the corner] and tell them to get this letter to Mr. Benito."

They're friends. So I took the letter. The man wasn't there, but another manager took it and read it. And he then told me, "Okay, I'll give it to Benito tomorrow, but I've already read it, and I'm the one who does the hiring. Come tomorrow with your passport and residence papers, if you want."

Carmen was so elated to have found a job that she rushed home and brought the papers back in fifteen minutes. She thanked the school counselor the next day, who shook her hand and reminded her that "God is always there."

Carmen had been working for Burger Barn for three years when we met. Her schedule was a killer. She would go to high school at 8:00 a.m., her work uniform tucked into her backpack. When school ended at 3:30, she would change into the uniform in the bathroom and walk to Burger Barn without stopping for a break. Arriving at 4:00, she would put in a full shift, finally leaving at about 2:00 a.m. Exhausted, but determined to manage the demands of schoolwork and the job, she would put in an hour or so on her homework and fall asleep over her open books. She was always worried her teachers would catch her out and penalize her for not doing enough homework, but Carmen is a quick study, a smart student, and she made up for the lack of time with her brains.

It was, and still is, very important to Carmen to do well in school. Her mother is a teacher in the Dominican Republic, and her maternal grandmother was a teacher as well. They instilled in her a love of ideas, respect for educated people, and the desire to become a white-collar professional. She came to the United States to pursue exactly these ambitions, believing that the education she could get here would take her farther than the schooling she would have had in Santo Domingo. Yet the only way to realize this dream has caused her enormous stress. She had to balance her desire to do well in high school with the need to earn enough money to help both her grandmother and her mother. For even though Carmen's mother was a teacher, her salary was never enough to keep the family afloat. To be sure, they did better than the average single-parent family in Santo Domingo, but their aspirations were more middle-class than that. Carmen's remittances—carved out of her minimum-wage job at Burger

Barn—made the difference and freed her from being a burden on her grandmother or her father. But it hasn't been easy.

> My homework started to go down. I'd do all of it. I'd always do all of it. But I was so tired that, even if I wanted to . . . I'd leave [an assignment] undone. Something inside would tell me, "You have to do [this work]." But I would just fall asleep. I would be so tired.

She debated the problem with her grandmother, but never found a solution, for both spheres, school and work, were critical.

> I would tell my grandmother, "Ay, Grandma. I don't wanna leave school. But I'm too stressed out." And she'd tell me, "Well, you are the one who knows what she's doing. Leave one of the two." I had the idea she meant leave work. And I'd say, "No, not work. I don't wanna leave work." Then she'd tell me, "Well, then leave school." But I'd say, "No, that neither." So she'd say, "So what are you gonna do?" And I'd say, "Oh, tough it out." You see, one always has to make sacrifices, so I'd think, if others can do it, why can't I?

Her uncles spoke up, adding in their two cents, telling Carmen that she was kidding herself—that she would burn out or flunk out, or both. But the more they admonished her, the more determined Carmen became to stick to her plan.

> Never in all that time did I fail a class. I always passed with the grades they wanted me to get. In my house, my grandmother would say, "I want this grade and this grade." And I had to get those grades. . . . So I'd learn the lesson and fall asleep in half an hour. The next day I'd wake up and take the book to the bathroom with me. I'd put it on the towel holder and I'd shower looking at the book. And in the subway, I'd start dozing off into sleep, but would wake up and say, "No, I have to study. . . ."

Part of Carmen's hesitation, or confusion over the best direction to take, had to do with her ambivalence toward the job itself. She began working as an ordinary crew member, cooking hamburgers and french fries and cleaning the grill. Mechanically adept, she learned how to break down the milk-shake machine and put it back together. In fact, over time she learned how to repair virtually every piece of mechanical equipment in the store, a talent Burger Barn encourages, in part to avoid the expense of calling in outside repair people. Slowly, Carmen moved up the ranks and learned how to operate the cash register. And finally, because she is attractive, well-groomed, and personable, management put her in charge of the birthday party business.

She loved it. Little children gravitate toward Carmen. The many years she has devoted to her cousins, nephews, and nieces have left her with a natural herding instinct, the ability to corral and entertain a rowdy bunch of kids with good humor. But she also discovered that she is a whiz with adult customers, good at sensing their needs, good at managing their tempers when the birthday parties threaten to disrupt the rest of the restaurant. They are invariably pleased with her work, and this, plus the contact with children, affords Carmen a sense of enjoyment that would otherwise be missing from a low-status job.

Burger Barn had other merits as well. The managers were supportive of Carmen's educational ambitions and did whatever they could to make her work schedule compatible with her school hours. Beginning with her high school years and continuing on as she entered Bronx Community College, her boss adjusted her hours around her classroom obligations. Never once did Burger Barn insist that she come to work when she had to go to school, and Carmen was grateful for that support.

Of course, this meant that she worked late into the night in order to keep her hours up. In her neighborhood, that is risky. Young women on the street alone after dark are easy targets, and the *tigres*—Dominican parlance for street-corner men—let Carmen know that she was not safe. One night she found out firsthand how vulnerable she really was, and although she escaped the robbery with her life, she was one shaken woman. In fact, she was terrified. For a time she refused to go anywhere alone and timed every moment of her schedule so that Rena could always accompany her. After months of reactive anxiety, and some costly therapy sessions, Carmen began to reconstruct her life, leaning upon her boyfriend, Salvador, for help in keeping her job.

> *When you walk at night, you see the* tigres *out there. That makes me so scared. I go by there with phobia whenever I'm on my way home after work. Sometimes when I get out at midnight, I call my boyfriend. He works at night and gets out at midnight too. I call him and tell him, "Hey, Salvador, come pick me up because I don't want to go by myself." And he says, "Okay, wait for me at the subway station." And I say, "No, no, no. Come pick me up at [Burger Barn]. Knock on the door. I'll tell security to open the door for you." Because I'm afraid.*

Grateful as she was to find her job, Carmen had grown tired of it by the time I had known her for six months. She had worked at the Barn for three and half years by then. The restaurant had acquired a new swing manager, Diana, whom Carmen didn't like very much, and the feeling was mutual. It seems they had both had their eyes on the same man— Salvador, also a Burger Barn employee—and it was Carmen who had won his heart. This did not sit too well with Diana, and now they were thrown together in an authority relationship that rubbed Carmen the wrong way. These extraneous circumstances twisted Carmen's perspective on her job, throwing its negative aspects into higher relief.

I only earn four-fifty an hour, and that's not enough, considering how one is exploited there. In this type of job, they only know how to boss around, as if one were an animal. While one works, the other people boss around and humiliate with the authority of an owner over his pet. It's because of that that many of us want to seek the possibility of a better future for ourselves and our children.

"Our children" had a lot to do with Carmen's decision one day to leave Burger Barn, without warning. By the winter of 1994, she had married Salvador, and, in keeping with traditional expectations, she had gotten pregnant almost immediately after the wedding. They moved into an apartment in Carmen's family building, one vacated by an aunt who had returned to the Dominican Republic, and began living the usual life of a young couple. Carmen now had something to think about besides school and work; she had a baby on the way and a future to plan with her husband. That future was supposed to include a job as a travel agent or a clothing designer, not as a hamburger flipper. Salvador was opposed to Carmen's working at all; he certainly did not favor her continuing at Burger Barn, even though he himself had worked there for more than a year.

Hence, Carmen "allowed" the conflict with Diana to be the last straw and she walked out of the job and set about becoming a housewife. This, however, proved much easier said than done. For one thing, Salvador's earnings were really insufficient to support the two of them. He now had a job stocking the shelves at a twenty-four-hour drugstore, which he had found through a new friend who had recently landed a position there. When Salvador mentioned that he too was ready to move on from Burger Barn, his new buddy referred him to the drugstore manager. Now

Salvador had something a little cleaner, a little less frantic; he no longer came home from work covered with grease from the french fry station at Burger Barn. Still, he wasn't earning any more money, and now Carmen was broke.

The way Salvador saw things, money was *his* problem. At twenty-two, he was now the man of the house, and Carmen's "job" should be to cook, clean, and wait for the baby to come. That is how things are done in *La Republica*, and that was good enough for Salvador. Unfortunately, his earnings didn't measure up. After the rent was paid, he had no money left to give Carmen. In fact, in order to make ends meet, Salvador was eating most of the time at his mother's house nearby. He told Carmen that they "each had to find their own solutions," meaning that she ought to eat whenever possible with her grandmother so as to lighten expenses in their own household. There was no money to pay the utility bills either, and Con Edison was on their case. Cable TV refused them service. They were really down to the bare bones and yet still owed money on the furniture they'd bought when they married. On a single stock-clerk salary, they just weren't going to make it.

Carmen was partially persuaded by Salvador's traditionalism and was genuinely happy the baby was on the way. But the whole arrangement was a far cry from the expectations she had had only a few months before when she was practically killing herself trying to manage the demands of school and a full shift at work. Back then, before Carmen got married, she knew what she wanted, and had plenty of moral support for her vision from her best friend, Carla.

Carla and I, we like to work. We had the same ideals and goals. We want to be something first and then try to be part of a couple. I want to be someone in life, and I want my boyfriend, assuming we get married, to be someone too. . . . [Carla's] boyfriend was going to school—well, her husband. He left to start working. My boyfriend [Salvador] did too. The two of us were insisting that they go back to school. None of them wants to. . . . She calls me and tells me, "Oh, Carmen, now Martin doesn't wanna go to school because he wants to work. And I tell her the same thing's happening with Salvador. . . . These men are crazy.

I think first in having my career, get my diploma and later have kids. After I have my diploma. So, first I want to finish college and then have kids. It's too difficult to be able to maintain the responsibilities of the home, the kids, and school on top of that.

Carmen's ambitions, recorded in this interview in September, were on hold by the following February.

Still, she had not bargained for the kind of dependence and genuine hardship she faced now. Carmen could no longer send money to her mother in the Dominican Republic, and she worried constantly about how Mama would manage without those weekly infusions of American dollars. Salvador gave her almost none of his money, save a few dollars to take care of some of the overdue utility bills so that their services wouldn't be cut off. In fact, she had no idea how much money Salvador actually made. What was worse, she could not afford to see the doctor, and that was proving to be a serious matter. Rather than gaining weight, Carmen was losing it at a steady clip—not the ideal state for a pregnant woman. Her appetite had dwindled to almost nothing; her only desire was for fatty foods, and anything else repulsed her. By her third month of pregnancy, Carmen was down to about ninety pounds, and counting. She knew she needed to get to a doctor, but there was no money for it.

Salvador realized that the situation was pretty grim, and Carmen could see he was worried. He had taken to pacing the apartment nervously, pounding on a calculator every night trying to figure out how to pay rent and the other bills on a weekly salary of $184. Their rent was $530 a month, and utilities ate up the rest. Clearly, something had to change. Finally, Salvador set about looking for a second job. He tried a delivery company on 14th Street, a broad commercial boulevard in downtown Manhattan that is still dotted by "Spanish" clothing stores. Carmen wasn't very keen on this prospect, because it would have meant that between the two jobs her husband would be working from 8:00 a.m. through to 1:00 a.m.

Salvador didn't get that position anyway, but his desperation convinced Carmen that she was going to have to do something she had always wanted to avoid: go on welfare. She needed to qualify for Medicaid so she could get to a doctor. She had to find a way to get some more money into the house. Several of her aunts, who had been abandoned by their husbands not long after arriving in the U.S., had gone on welfare when they found they couldn't support three children on a single salary from the factory where they worked. They volunteered to show Carmen the ropes.

The whole experience was a frustrating, time-consuming bureaucratic nightmare. Everything Carmen had been told to expect about "the welfare" turned out to be true, but she persisted because she could see no other option. While the effort finally paid off and Carmen got some regular prenatal care, it took weeks. During that time, Salvador managed to find a second job after all, handing out food to homeless people for a church-based organization that was stepping up its charitable activities in the wake of big budget cuts in the city. This second job—which was "off the books" and therefore did not pose a threat to Carmen's welfare benefits—meant that the newly married couple hardly saw each other, but between the state assistance and the two jobs, the negative cash flow started to taper off. They were hardly living in the lap of luxury, and Salvador still urged Carmen to eat as often as possible with her grandmother. But they were not facing those dreaded FINAL NOTICE alerts plastered over their electric bill anymore.

In her fifth month of pregnancy, Carmen came down with some kind of virus or infection that sent her temperature soaring. She was vomiting constantly, unable to keep any food down, and was terrified that she might lose her baby. Thanking God for Medicaid, Carmen went to the clinic, where doctors slapped fetal monitors across her stomach. Carmen had never been so scared and never so relieved to be able to see a doctor. Having spent most of her time in New York without any medical care— and having experienced the agony of a hernia that she could not afford to have treated the year before—Carmen was well aware that she could have ended up on her own with this crisis. In the end, the doctors were able to treat her with antibiotics, and they thought the baby would be all right.

Carmen was sent home to bed. Salvador cut back his work hours so he could take care of her at least a little bit. Their finances were ragged, and without the continuous support of their extended families, the whole enterprise would have been impossible. Unlike Jamal and Kathy, who were all alone with their problems, Carmen and Salvador had a huge network of people to come to their aid. With their help, some of the rougher bumps of life at the bottom of the economic heap could at least be weathered. But the bumps never stopped, and without better jobs—and more education—in sight, Carmen was beginning to lose her confidence in the white-collar future she had hoped for only a year before.

KYESHA'S WORLD

Tyron Hamilton makes his way to Burger Barn once or twice a week when the weather is decent, spare change in hand and hunger in his belly. He is one of the regulars, one of the disconnected men who come around the restaurant hoping for a handout on the many days when they lack the wherewithal to buy the fries. Tyron skulks a bit, drawing the hood of his sweatshirt down over his forehead—a look that seems menacing to the more welcome customers. He figures that the slight fear he inspires as he moves across the street, under the shadow of the elevated subway tracks, is useful. It keeps some of the troublemakers away, men who might like to take what little money is in his pocket. But the more compelling reason for the hood is to minimize the need to make eye contact with Kyesha Smith, the young woman behind the counter at Burger Barn who is nearly always there when Tyron comes in for his semiregular infusion of fast food.

Kyesha and Tyron grew up in the same housing project, not far from the Barn where their paths cross these days. They played together when they were little, but long ago lost touch. By the time Tyron resurfaced as a street-corner man, Kyesha had forgotten all about him. She recognized him, though, the first day he came into the restaurant and ordered a meal. His history was written all over his face and tattered clothes. Kyesha was stunned by the transformation. "He begs outside the door of the restaurant, right in front of me," she says in amazement. "I cannot believe it. He don't even look at my face—he can't." But they recognize each other, for sure.

Encounters like this happen all the time in Kyesha's world. She stumbles over drug addicts on the stoop of her housing project and in the elevators that form the treacherous obstacle course inside her building. She can see the young men lingering together on the corner, cell phones in hand, waiting for instructions from the more powerful dealers who control the trade. None of these people are strangers. She has known them since their playground days. Many are acquaintances of her older brother, a well-heeled dealer who has moved up to the interstate drug trade—a regular captain of this particular industry.

For Kyesha, these chance meetings are filled with lessons. They are daily reminders of the ease with which she could have found herself on the other side of the counter, waiting for a handout. Had she not found her job at Burger Barn, at the age of fourteen, she might well have zeroed out and dumped herself onto the welfare rolls. Instead, she has a steady job, one she had kept for five years by the time we met. Kyesha has to remind herself that Tyron's fate is not hers and won't be as long as she stays on the job, because some days she does feel the world closing in on her. On those days, she worries that she won't be able to walk the straight and narrow forever, not because she is tempted by the streets—she isn't—but because she can see many examples of failure in her neighborhood, people going down. She cannot help but panic, sometimes, about whether this might be her fate too.

Kyesha lied about her age when she first applied to Burger Barn, knowing that they wouldn't give her the job if they knew how old she really was. Then a sophomore in high school, and not doing terribly well, Kyesha's main focus was on getting enough money together to pay for the clothes she wanted, clothes her mother had no intention of buying (and no money to spare to buy, even if she had been more sympathetic to Kyesha's teenage desires).

My mother, she limit the money for clothes. I wanted more things that everybody had and it cost a little too much for her, so I had to get a job and get it myself. . . . My family was like, "Ah, Kyesha's becoming independent. I'm proud of her. Starting to get things on her own now." So I felt good. I didn't have to ask my mother for money.

This is still an important motivation for Kyesha, for now that she is twenty-one, it is her turn to contribute to the support of her mother's household, and she expects and receives no financial help from anyone else. But the job has become far more important, far more dominating as an anchor for her life, than her original material purpose. It has become the center of her social universe, the place she spends nearly all of her time, the source of all of her closest friends and romantic attachments. Burger Barn is really Kyesha's preferred home.

Under the tutelage of the original owner of her restaurant and the managers she worked for, Kyesha earned her keep and graduated from high school with a respectable average. Never a very good student and always a bit of a discipline problem, she was what researchers call a "high risk" student, one deemed likely to drop out and disappear. Kyesha would not disagree with this assessment, for she knows she was never very focused on achievement in school. What's more, many of her friends in the projects were dropping out, getting pregnant, and hooking onto the welfare rolls—fulfilling every conservative stereotype of irresponsible "dependency culture." It is a miracle, some would say, that Kyesha avoided the same fate. She had, in fact, gotten pregnant twice during her high school years.

The difference between Kyesha and her less successful friends can be credited to Burger Barn, citadel of the low-paid hamburger flipper, the one place most Americans would not think to look for positive inspirations, role models, or any other source of salvation for a poor girl from Harlem's housing projects. Working every day after school, Kyesha developed the kind of discipline and sense of order in her life that she had utterly lacked before she started earning a living. The structure spread into her school life and pushed her to finish what she started. Although she has been an inveterate diarist, a scribbler of major proportions, Kyesha's grammar and spelling are far from faultless. But she did develop a backbone, a sense of direction that got her over a hurdle thousands of inner-city kids never leap: the high school diploma.

Her mother, a longtime welfare recipient, encouraged this progress from the sidelines. It was Dana who insisted that Kyesha get two abortions and finish school. Dana's first child was born when she was fifteen and the last during the years of our fieldwork—a span of twenty-six years. But Dana had learned from her own experience what a mistake Kyesha would have been making had she in fact had a child the first time she got pregnant, at age sixteen. Besides, Dana wanted Kyesha to keep her job and continue contributing to the cost of running the house, and that was not likely to happen if Kyesha dropped out to become a mother.

Still, this young woman is strong-willed. She doesn't take direction easily and rarely bends to the demands of others unless they happen to coincide with her own wishes. No amount of persuasion on Dana's part would have been sufficient to deter her from having a baby at sixteen if that had been what she wanted. But it wasn't. Her desire was to stick around Burger Barn, around her friends, around the social life that the workplace provided her. By that time she had been working and going to school for two years, and that was what she wanted to continue doing. The choice she made, to terminate the pregnancies, resulted directly from the desire she had to hold on to the one part of her life that really worked: her job. And that is what distinguishes Kyesha from the many young women she knows who have walked down the other fork in the road and are now burdened by children they cannot support; it is what separates her from the fated young men who gather around Burger Barn in the early hours of the morning hoping to score a hot cup of coffee and a sweet roll. She has a structure, a place, an income, and a source of identity that matters to her. She is a working woman.

Now that she is twenty-one years old, it has become even more important to her to hold on to that job. For now she *does* have a child to take care of—little Anthony, the apple of her eye, a "love child" who came into the world as the consequence of a serious relationship that began when Kyesha was eighteen. The baby's father, Juan, works at Burger Barn as well, and their romance was the talk of the place for the first six months. Although the African-Americans and the Puerto Ricans who work behind the counter are often at loggerheads with one another,

Kyesha and Juan crossed the race barrier and began seeing each other after work. Both had grown up in housing projects in west Harlem, both live with their mothers and siblings, and both have large extended families all around them—though many of Juan's relatives live in Puerto Rico. The families were all for the marriage, and the two lovebirds were happy about it as well.

Unfortunately, what married life, or even steady courtship, meant to Juan and what it meant to Kyesha turned out to be two different things. Steeped in a Latin culture that confines women, especially married women, to the home while leaving the men free to enjoy themselves in the wider world, Juan expected Kyesha to settle down and become more circumspect in her social relations. She was not to go out, not to party, not to stay up all hours of the night; she was to be a good girl, Puerto Rican–style. Kyesha found it hard to cope with the tightening noose.

My son's father and I were engaged and the whole nine yards. But then he got to be very boring to me. Always wanted me in the house and I couldn't go anywhere. He didn't like my friends or nothing. He'd tell me things like "If you hang out with that person, I will leave you." At the time, I was pregnant. When you're having a baby, you will do anything for the man, because you don't want him to leave you stranded with the total responsibility.

She acceded to Juan's demands for a time, but eventually the relationship broke down over her unwillingness to live a cloistered existence, and she was, indeed, left with the "love child." Many a young woman in her position would have collapsed onto the welfare system at that point. After all, on $4.25 an hour, there was no way that Kyesha could afford child care on the open market. But she really loved her job and had no desire whatsoever to leave it behind for the joys of full-time motherhood. She knew from her mother's experience that becoming a housebound baby-sitter was a ticket to claustrophobia, even when you love your child.

Fortunately for Kyesha, and for her employer (who did not want to lose her), she had resources in the form of family members who could and did step in to help so she could continue to work. Dana, technically on welfare but actually a full-time child-minder for her own kids and a collection of neighbor children, could always add one more. So from the very beginning of Anthony's life, Grandma was in charge. Kyesha went to work every day and Dana went to work too—courtesy of Aid to Families with Dependent Children.

Virtually overnight, Kyesha went from living as a child in her mother's home to being a transitional adult, expected not only to pay for her own expenses but to contribute to the central coffers as well. This was only fair, as all parties saw it, because Dana was performing an important service for Kyesha, and the Burger Barn salary, while hardly generous, could at least be tapped for a regular tithe. The situation worked out well from Kyesha's point of view, because she had child care and did not have to face the insupportable burden of paying rent: her mother's housing subsidies, provided because of her low income, took care of the apartment. No one was living well. Kyesha had one room, which had to accommodate her and the baby, and the tithe cut into her resources. Still, the situation was workable as long as Kyesha and Dana could get along well enough to live under the same roof.

They don't always get along, however. The longer Kyesha leaves her son in her mother's care, the more he comes to see Grandma as the authority figure in his life.

My mom says two grown people can't live in the same house, so right now she pretty much want me to find my own place, and I really do too. The problem that I have is she minds my son, so when I'm trying to teach him things that I want him to know, it's like he'll look at Grandma, like "Gram said." She trying to raise my son like she raised us, but I wanna try [my own way]. I might do some things similar, but I wanna do some things different.

Sometimes these tensions get so bad that Kyesha loses her cool and storms around trying to figure out how she can get out of that house. "Today," Kyesha tells me, "I am thinking that I should prepare myself to move out." The weekend has been rough on everyone's nerves, she explains, "because me and my mother fight a little too much." She starts to fantasize about how she is going to take the situation in hand and move herself and her little boy.

I should just take a [cardboard] box from [Burger Barn], fill it with household goods, and just chill. So when I move, everything will be ready. . . . I just wanta have my own nest, that's all.

Kyesha is dying to have her own space, her own adult station in life. But there is no way she could pull this off on her current salary of $5 an hour, the princely sum she earns after five steady years on the job at Burger Barn. "It's easier said than done," she sighs.

The tensions that divide a twenty-one-year-old woman from her mother are not unfamiliar in middle-class households. The pressures building in the nation's economy have forced many a better-educated young adult back into the arms of parents. These "incompletely launched adults" or "boomerang kids" are growing in number,[1] and they too find it hard to return to the subordinate status of "child." Still, these young adults in the middle class can hope their situation is temporary. Kyesha has no reason to believe hers will change, ever.

Dana often feels the same way. In fact, she gets to feeling trapped now and again, being in charge of all these kids. She is not the world's greatest day care teacher, either. In truth, the television set is the prime baby-sitter in her house. But the kids are safe, clothed, and fed, and this is no small accomplishment in the midst of poverty.

It helps Kyesha to know that Anthony is not her responsibility alone. From one perspective, he is the child of a single parent. As it happens, however, Anthony has two parents who are regularly involved in his care. Despite the breakdown in Kyesha's relationship with Juan, he has maintained a consistent interest in his son's life. He and his female kin—principally his own mother—take care of the little boy almost every weekend. Dad takes Anthony for his haircuts, even when Kyesha objects that he should wait until winter is over. He berates Kyesha for spending time with men that he does not approve of, on the grounds that their influence will not be good for his son. He buys the boy Pampers when he can afford it and decks him out in an occasional outfit, picked by his sisters. When Dana miscarried, he dutifully went to the hospital (at Kyesha's request) and helped to look after her, much the way a favored son-in-law would do. Juan is an attentive father and a significant partner, doing what he can for his son from the distance of another household.

Juan's ability to partake in the rearing of his son is made possible by two things. First there is his continued work at Burger Barn, a job that pays enough for him to contribute to his own family's household and have something left over for his son. Secondly, Juan's mother's willingness to help him with child care, to be a real grandmother to Anthony, encourages the father to remain a part of his son's life, a rather big part as it happens.

There is little hope that Kyesha and Juan will ever marry, settle down, and give their son a home of his own. Given their low earnings, this was always an unlikely prospect. They never had the money to make a go of it as an independent family, even when they were getting along. Still, they are responsible parents who work for a living, whose contributions to their mothers' coffers help them all get by when no single person in either family makes much. Without those jobs, they would constitute one more statistic in the long litany of problems in the welfare system.

But the jobs alone are hardly enough. "In-kind" contributions from mothers, sisters, and aunts are essential parts of the picture. No one can make it on such a low wage alone. Hillary Clinton may believe that it "takes a village" to raise a child. In central Harlem, it takes a network composed of people with access to jobs and to state subsidies. Kyesha can see what happens to women who don't have these resources. Tanisha, one of her coworkers at Burger Barn, is a single mother like Kyesha. But Tanisha has no one to help her and is close to destitute: she works for as many hours as Burger Barn will give her, lives in a homeless shelter with her daughter, and is now expecting another child by a man who promised her a life and left her with nothing. Kyesha has little sympathy for Tanisha, because she is always having to borrow money and never seems able to pay it back.

> Tanisha only makes a hundred dollars a week now because she don't know how to come to work and she don't pay her bills. She's broke and she wants people to feel sorry for her. I don't, 'cause she should know better. The only reason people pity her is because she has a baby and another on the way.

Critical as she may sound, however, Kyesha is also terrified by the thought that she might end up in Tanisha's situation.

At one level, Kyesha's life constitutes a success story. She is working, she is raising her child, she does not depend upon the welfare system in any direct fashion. But at another level, her family is very vulnerable. "Welfare," the catch-all phrase she uses to describe the myriad of public bureaucracies that intersect her life, has denied her access to Medicaid. This has left Kyesha scrambling to find a way to afford birth control pills, something she knows she needs if she is to avoid adding to her problems in the future. She is a diabetic who needs insulin treatment, but cannot afford to see the doctor. Knowing full well that she has to watch her sugar, Kyesha still occasionally binges on candy. A familiar feeling in her stomach and an elevated temperature tell her that she has overdone it. Her only recourse is the emergency room of Harlem Hospital and a seven-hour wait for a shot of insulin in her upper arm. Bills pile up whenever she has to see a doctor—bills she has no hope of being able to pay. "I can't afford to be sick," she explains, " 'cause I have no medical insurance and it really hurts your pocketbook."

Kyesha has been to the emergency room dozens of times, for herself and for Anthony's periodic ear infections. There is nothing quite like a screaming baby with a high fever to motivate Mom to push through on the paperwork for Medicaid. At least then you can get to a doctor and don't have to suffer through the endless wait in the ER.

I just got Medicaid for my son. They said that I made too much at [Burger Barn] to get Medicaid. I said, "one-fifty a week . . . shit." I guess I have to be completely broke to get medical assistance. This world is cheap . . . 'cause if I wanted to build a missile I'd get over ten billion!

"Welfare" is threatening other intrusions that are likely to prove far more devastating over the long run. Juan's mother, also an AFDC recipient, has been told she must seek employment, probably a workfare job. Since she has to work, she can no longer provide child care for her grandson on weekends. This wreaks havoc with Kyesha's work schedule, because she cannot prevail upon Dana to add the weekends to her already overburdened life as a baby-sitter. Juan too needs to work, so it is uncertain what will happen if they cannot persuade some other member of his family to step in and help.

What really worries Kyesha, though, is that "Welfare" is coming after Dana as well. For years now, her mother has been exempt from these demands because she has continued to have babies. Her youngest child is almost the same age as her grandson. But Dana has also had a number of miscarriages in recent years, hence her youngest is now about four and "Welfare" wants her to find a job. If this comes to pass, it would be a monumental crisis for Kyesha. Where is she going to get child care for Anthony if her mom ends up working for the same minimum wage as Kyesha? These are not idle threats; Kyesha has had experience with the way the welfare bureaucracy makes life harder. For the first year that she worked, "Welfare" was none the wiser. When "they" found out, they raised the rent on Dana's apartment and made her pay the city back for the excess stipend she had received.

Dilemmas of this kind always get Kyesha ruminating about how much easier life would be if only her current boyfriend, Kevin, would marry her. Kevin works in a pharmacy, down the street from the Burger Barn, where he has a nice white-collar job managing the store. He's an "older man," about nine years Kyesha's senior, with a son by a previous common-law relationship whom Kyesha likes to fuss over on the weekends when the boy comes to visit his dad. Kevin has come up the hard way, and he was headed for trouble in his early twenties when a chance encounter with the owner of the drugstore gave him an option he thought he'd never see: a trainee job, learning the cash register in the store. Over the years, the store had had its share of trouble with street punks coming in and harassing customers. Putting a young man up front, someone able to handle himself in a confrontation, made good business sense. This was the opportunity of a lifetime for Kevin, and he knew it. Ten years later, he has moved up to the general manager's job, a rank and status unknown in his family. He earns about $30,000 a year, enough to live a comfortable existence for the first time in his life.

Kyesha doesn't know how much Kevin earns, but she has spent plenty of time at his house—which is a far sight more desirable than the projects where she lives. There are plenty of crackheads in his neighborhood too, but Kevin at least has his own place, and he wears a tie to work. Anyhow, in Kevin's house, Kyesha feels like a grown-up and not Dana's daughter. There she can escape the pressure her mother brings to bear, the demands for ever-larger contributions to the family budget, and the sinking feeling—which grows perceptibly every day—that there is no end in sight to her dependent condition. It is only natural that she dreams about becoming Kevin's wife, whisking little Anthony off to a real home where they could live together as people are supposed to do when they hit adulthood.

Unfortunately, Kevin doesn't buy into this scenario. He has had relationships before, one of which brought his son into the world, and is leery of settling down to life with one woman. He might feel differently if he thought Kyesha was going to make something more of herself over the long run—move up, maybe, to a managerial job at Burger Barn. It's not as if he hasn't encouraged her to do just that, as have many other people at the Barn itself. But Kyesha doesn't seem to be inclined toward a job with much more responsibility than the one she has. And Kevin is not sure that he ought to marry at all, much less marry someone who may never amount to anything more than a hamburger flipper.

Kevin and Kyesha met because he patronizes her restaurant almost every day at lunch. They had been an item for about three months when I first met Kyesha. Throughout the six or seven months that she spent time with me and my research group, Kevin was always on her mind and in her diary. She thought about him all the time, worried about their relationship in all its aspects, and even listed the names of the children she hoped she might have with him when they got married. But as time wore on, she began to realize—with heart-wrenching bitterness—that Kevin was not going to be her salvation. Kyesha began to resent her own longing, began to berate herself for the ways in which she had twined herself around his little finger and sold herself short.

And she was right. By late spring, just about the time that "welfare" began to nag Dana to get a job, Kevin stopped calling and broke it off. Kyesha was left to stew in frustration, having lost not only the love of her life but the one man she knew who actually had the wherewithal to give her a future beyond the endless sameness of life as a single mom in a low-wage job.

By her own admission, Kyesha would have gone crazy had she not had a group of friends to comfort her and entertain her when she felt desperate. Those friendships—especially with two half sisters, Latoya and Natasha—came about because of Burger Barn. They joined the crew the year that Kyesha turned eighteen: her fourth year on the job. Together they have weathered the ups and downs of boyfriend troubles, problems raising little kids, and the hassles of working a hard job for low pay. They have forged a tight sorority, with many a satellite in the form of other women (and men) who work behind the counter. When the shifts end, they go out together for a beer. On days off, they take in a movie or go downtown to a strip joint to laugh and ogle the hunky young men who strut the runways. Holidays are often spent in one another's company, and tough times—when money runs out or the boss is breathing down their necks—are much easier to take because they have one another.

In fact, these friends are so important to Kyesha that she spends most of her days off going in to Burger Barn, even though she doesn't have to. Kyesha has more fun and feels better about life when she is at work than almost any other place. That was true even when Kevin was in her life. Now that he is fading from view, the job looms as the one orderly, consistent, and welcoming activity in Kyesha's life.

It's like a part of me that's in that store. Burger Barn is like my house. I couldn't leave it because I'd miss it. I come in there every day. [The manager] would be like, "Don't you got something better to do?" It's just this thing. So I just, I'm in there all the time. Even if I come in there on my day off and they need help, I'll just take over the fries station or help somebody in the grill.

This is not because the job itself is so great. Kyesha is well aware that there is no real future at Burger Barn, that she will never amount to anything in society's eyes if she stays put. With her son in tow, she feels a nagging pressure to become something more than a fast food worker. She wants to make him happy and do things for him that were not done for her. Even when she's exhausted from having worked a night shift, she tells herself, "I gotta stay up" for him. "Just looking at him makes me want to do more." To do more, to get a job that would move her up and out of the low-wage world she inhabits, would require a whole different strategy.

Today I was just looking in the help wanted ads so I could get another job. I really need one because it's so many things I could be getting. . . . If it don't work out for me this year, I guess I will take my ass back to college, 'cause to me I am not being all I could be. I could be so much better. And then I have my son. So I got to get where the money rolling and that's really in a bachelor's, master's, etc. The higher the degree, the bigger the fee. So my goal is to be all I can be, and that's not where I am working now.

Once upon a time, not so long ago, Kyesha would not have had to enter college to craft a more promising future. She knows that because when she thinks about her older relatives, her grandmother and great-aunts (Dana's mother and her sisters), she can see living, breathing examples of a much better life. For Kyesha does not quite fit the stereotype of the multigenerational welfare family. Her mother, who worked when she was very young, has been "on aid" for a quarter century. But her grandmother is a hardworking woman who has had a job in the Postal Service forever. In fact, in her mid-fifties, Kyesha's grandmother is just now beginning to contemplate retirement, with a federal pension and the prospect of a Social Security check in her old age.

The Post Office gave her a good life, far better than Kyesha has ever known. On the strength of that job, Grandma Evie was able to leave Harlem when the going got rough and move her family out to Wyandanch, a mostly black suburb on Long Island, where she bought a little house with a garden. The house is still in the family; it now belongs to one of Kyesha's aunts, Beth, who also has a good job, working for the corrections department. It got to be too much for Evie and her common-law husband, Harry, who is older and now retired from his job parking cars in a Manhattan garage. Evie figured that as long as she held on to that house, her less fortunate grown kids would expect to be able to live free under her roof, so she sold it to her daughter. She has not been entirely successful at cutting the apron strings: one of her daughters and her husband have moved into her new (much smaller) apartment with their kids because they've had job troubles. It seems the burdens never end for Evie, who has sometimes found her good fortune—steady job, nice housing—a mixed blessing.

For Kyesha, however, the existence of this extended clan out on Long Island has meant a keen awareness of what is lacking in her life in Harlem. She knows all too well what a better life looks like; she's visited her relatives hundreds of times. There is nothing in this world she wouldn't like more than to join them out there on the Island where the streets are quieter and the drug problem less severe, and a person can breathe the air from the ocean. She also knows, because you'd be a fool not to notice, how Evie managed to do so well. She got herself a good job working for the government, as have a number of other relatives in her generation.

Kyesha is no fool, so she pursues this path herself. She has taken endless civil service exams, and applied to a host of places like the Postal Service and the Metropolitan Transit Authority. The trouble is, they aren't hiring. When Evie was Kyesha's age, back in the early sixties, those jobs were multiplying. What's more, the government was looking over the shoulders of public employers, paying more attention to minority hiring. In the 1990s, those same employers have been shedding jobs in record numbers. With every budget crisis in New York City, the number of good jobs like Evie's goes down. And the chances that a young woman from Harlem could land one are just about nil.

This does not stop Kyesha from trying. And because the same history runs through many of the family trees of her fellow workers at Burger Barn, there is a collective culture behind the counter that sends hamburger flippers down to the civil service exams whenever they are held. Everyone wants to do better than minimum-wage.

For now, Kyesha sticks with her job at Burger Barn and thanks God she has friends there who help pass the days. In the summer, she asks for the night shift so she can take on a second job, cleaning the grounds around her housing project. Dana hooked her up to that opportunity, because Dana is an active participant in the tenant organization and is tight with the president of the housing project. The two jobs taken together wear Kyesha out, but they do improve the cash flow. What they don't do, and will never do, is give her a way out of her mother's house. And while that's no fun at the age of twenty-one, Kyesha cannot bear to think what it might be like if it keeps up and she hits thirty, at home with Dana and Anthony.

JAMAL, CARMEN, and Kyesha do not inhabit the very bottom of America's social order. They are not the targets of the nation's fixation on welfare and its successor forms of public aid. Indeed, they are barely on the national radar screen at all. All three have been, and continue to be (with occasional interruptions), hardworking, taxpaying citizens. They are also poor. They do not earn enough money, on their own, to take care of the basic necessities of life. Without the support of others in their families, forthcoming to various degrees, they would not be able to manage at all. Those relatives are often able to help only because they've found a way to tap into the social welfare system that provides housing support, food stamps, medical care, and the like for those who have not done as well as these three young people.

I got to know them in the course of a research project that ultimately involved three hundred New Yorkers. Two hundred of them were employed in four large, successful fast food restaurants in Harlem, while the rest were unsuccessful job-seekers who had come knocking on the door at two of those establishments during the same period. All three hundred of these people completed surveys administered by my multiethnic research team, and 150 of them gave us their complete life histories in interviews that took three or four hours to complete.

Once those interviews were done, my research team put aside the paperwork and their tape recorders and themselves donned the crew uniform to work behind the counters of the restaurants for four months. Day in, day out, my graduate students worked the french fry machines, struggled to learn the tricks that are second nature for veteran workers in preparing burgers and shakes, gave up in frustration while trying to manage the "drive-through" lane, and engaged in the daily banter that makes a boring job palatable. I spent time alone with the owners and managers of the same restaurants, learning about the ups and downs of small business, finding out what brought them to Harlem in the first place, and absorbing the admirable blend of profit motives and missionary zeal that led them to establish their firms in a community where the costs of doing business—financial and psychic—are far higher than they are in comfortable suburbs.

Working in the restaurants gave us a chance to observe the on-the-job learning process firsthand, a better purchase on how managers decide whom to hire, and some understanding of the racial dynamics of a workplace that is both a production line and a competitive fishbowl of people angling for promotion. Fieldwork of this kind gave us a chance to compare what our interviewees told us about their work lives and what we could see for ourselves. And because we were on hand for a long time, we could explore questions about the skills embodied in low-wage jobs of this kind that might be invisible to survey researchers.

Twelve workers—men and women, black and brown, teenagers and adults—let us invade their lives for almost a year. We shadowed these twelve fast food employees at close range, spent many hours around their kitchen tables, joined them for holiday celebrations, went out with them to clubs and movies after hours, sat with them while they helped their kids with homework, hung around on street corners in Harlem and Washington Heights watching the occasional drug deal go down, attended their high school and junior college classes, and went to church with them in our Sunday best. We interviewed their friends, and followed them to new jobs when they left Burger Barn. All of them kept personal daily diaries for the year, which gave me another, more intimate way of understanding their point of view.

The rich, detailed data that poured in from all sides are the basis for this portrait of minimum-wage workers employed in the fast food industry in the historical capital of Black America. In the chapter that follows, I will consider how representative these workers are of the large number of Americans who might be defined as working poor and make the case that they ought to be a larger concern in the public debate on poverty than they have been. Chapter 3 will take us back into the lives of the workers themselves and explain how they go about getting jobs in a community where work is scarce. I then explore the cultural challenges and moral dilemmas that attend low-wage work, the confrontation with stigma, and the slow but steady ways in which working for a living pulls ghetto dwellers away from street culture and into the mainstream. Chapter 5 looks at the strategies young people like Carmen use to balance the competing demands of school and work and examines in some detail the potentially valuable skills they learn in their "no skill" jobs.

Most Americans are introduced to the work world through a low-wage job, but it is no one's idea of a glorious long-range future. Middle-class kids generally graduate from this end of the labor market into better jobs as they get older. What about inner-city workers? Who gets to leave the minimum wage behind and who gets stuck? This is the subject of Chapter 6.

No study of workers would be complete if we failed to consider the families and neighborhoods that surround them. Chapter 7 explores the values that emerge among working poor families, the delicate social negotiations they must engage in when confronted by the symptoms of poverty we hear about all the time: drug dealers and violence in the neighborhood. But we will also explore how they take care of their elders and kids, how they develop crucial friendships with neighbors and coworkers that help them handle a constant flow of emergencies and still hold down a job. We will also explore in some detail the intimate connections between welfare and work, the inseparability of low-wage earnings from state subsidies, and hence the looming crisis that welfare reform presents for low-wage earners trying to get by in the inner city.

There are many more people looking for work in poor communities like Harlem than there are jobs for them to find, even when the rest of the nation enjoys low unemployment. What makes the difference between the people who crack that barrier in the first place and those who are left behind, the jobless job-seekers? We will look at the characteristics and the culture of failed job-seekers in Chapter 8. Finally, I close by asking what we could do that would make a difference for the working poor, that would enable more of them to support their families, find better jobs in the long run, and reap the benefits that participation in the labor market—that most mainstream of institutions—is supposed to confer.

CHAPTER TWO

The Invisible Poor

FORTY YEARS AGO, when it first began to dawn on this prosperous nation that the end of the Great Depression had not cured widespread poverty, popular representations of the poor focused on Kentucky hollows where Appalachian children sat on wooden stoops, their bellies swollen and faces blank. Miners whose livelihoods had disappeared with the end of the coal boom were left behind like refugees from another era, their families consigned to a threadbare existence. We understood that these were working folk who had fallen on hard times. The whole country reeled at the thought that such desperate conditions existed in the heartland—among good (white) people—and the war on poverty was born in order to lift up the downtrodden.

In the intervening years, however, as many writers have noted, poverty has been racialized. Even though the majority of the poor are still white and working—as they were in the 1930s and thereafter—the public impression is quite clearly the reverse: poverty wears a black face and is presumed to follow from an unwillingness to enter the labor force. As Herbert Gans explains in his compelling book *The War Against the Poor*,[1] the tendency to racialize the undeserving, the objects of society's contempt, is of long standing. The English poor laws of the mid-nineteenth century distinguished sharply between the shiftless and the working poor, associating the former with the Irish, who were regarded as an undesirable racial caste.[2] In the United States, successive waves of immigrants have taken their place in the unholy category of the undeserving poor, including the Italians, the Slavs, and the Eastern European Jews who filled the boweries of the eastern seaboard in the early twentieth century.

But the Great Migration of African-Americans out of the rural South to the industrialized cities of the North in the twentieth century altered forever the racial dynamics of urban poverty. And urban poverty has long been far more visible, to the media and hence to the public at large, than its rural counterpart, however devastating the latter may be.[3] Initially pulled by war-related job opportunities and pushed by agricultural mechanization that put a damper on southern demands for labor, blacks flooded into cities like Chicago, Milwaukee, Akron, New York, Pittsburgh, and elsewhere, only to be met by intense white hostility and overt policies of containment.[4] They were confined in segregated communities that rapidly became overcrowded. Nicholas Lemann's history of the migration's consequences in Chicago[5] shows clearly that the official policy of the Democratic machine was to contain this enormous population of African-Americans in spaces that would keep them far from the white working class. High-rise public housing projects were born, institutions that could house the poor up to the sky and prevent spillage into white neighborhoods hell-bent on preventing blacks from moving in. The endless blocks of bleak, monolithic buildings that lined the Dan Ryan Expressway on Chicago's South Side were the visible legacy of deliberate segregation.

As the jobs that initially sustained the northern migrants began to dry up, the consequences of extreme segregation became all too evident: places like the Cabrini-Green housing project were devastated and volatile. The underground economy and the welfare system were all that remained as forms of subsistence in some projects, and the association of African-Americans who were not gainfully employed with the damning label of "undeserving poor" took root. It was an easy linkage to make in a country obsessed by race.

It is also misleading because in fact the largest group of poor people in the United States are not those on welfare. They are the working poor whose earnings are so meager that despite their best efforts, they cannot afford decent housing, diets, health care, or child care.[6] The debilitating conditions that impinge upon the working poor—substandard housing, crumbling schools, inaccessible health care—are hardly different from those that surround their nonworking counterparts.[7] For many, indeed, these difficulties are measurably worse because so many of the working poor lack access to government supports that cushion those out of the labor force: subsidized housing,[8] medical care,[9] and food stamps.[10]

DEFINING WORKING POVERTY

Debates over how to define poverty have raged for many years now, and not just because scholars love to argue: federal dollars ebb and flow depending on the definition. The technicalities of these debates need not concern us,[11] but some of the principles that underlie them are relevant because they determine whose lives we are talking about when we use the term "working poor."

In 1996, about 7.4 million Americans worked or looked for work and lived in households whose annual income put them below the official poverty line, and 58 percent of them worked full-time.[12] Compared to the 1980s, the 1990s have seen an increase in the number of people who are defined as working poor, no doubt because the economy has lost many of its high-paying jobs (particularly for the less educated) and has gained poorly paid jobs (especially in the retail end of the service sector, but elsewhere as well).

TABLE 2.1
PERCENT OF THE WORKING POPULATION WHO ARE POOR, 1990–96

	1990	1991	1992	1994	1995	1996
% of all workers	5.5	6.1	6.3	6.2	5.9	5.8
% of working families*	6.4	7.0	7.3	7.2	7.0	7.0

Source: From Table A, "Poverty Status of Persons, Primary Families, and Unrelated Individuals in the Labor Force for More than Half of the Year, Selected Years, 1987–92," in Earl Mellor, "A Profile of the Working Poor," Report 869 (Bureau of Labor Statistics, March 1994), p. 1; and from Table A, "Poverty Status of Persons, Primary Families and Unrelated Individuals in the Labor Force for 27 Weeks or More 1994–96," Report 918 (Bureau of Labor Statistics, December 1997), p. 1.

* A working family is one in which at least one member works.

We might want to think of the working poor as those employees who receive the minimum wage. This is hardly a perfect measure, for many of these minimum-wage earners are young people who live with their middle-class families. While their earnings are low, they do not live in poor households. Still, this is not universally true: only 36 percent of minimum-wage workers are teenagers; 42 percent are adults twenty-five years old and older.[13] Some scholars dismiss the problems of minimum-wage workers because so many of them are women who work part-time (and are therefore presumed to be bringing in "pin money" rather than the necessities of life).[14] While 65 percent of the nation's low-wage workers are women, the gender picture changes dramatically when we examine only *full-time*, year-round minimum wage workers: about 60 percent of them are men.[15]

Congress recently raised the minimum wage, providing the first real boost to the standard of living of these low-wage workers in many years.[16] Yet we have a long way to go to correct the slide in the value of the minimum wage, which fell steadily for many years before this latest rise. By the mid-1990s, about seventeen million workers worked for wages at or below the real value of the 1979 minimum.[17]

No matter which of these definitions of working-poor adults we choose, we might agree that the children who grow up among them will be burdened by special problems. The families not only have low incomes, they have to find ways to care for the children when the adults are at work. How many children are we talking about?[18] In 1995, 4 percent of all American children lived in poor households in which there was at least one full-time, year-round worker. Seven million children (10 percent of all children) lived in poor families receiving in-kind assistance (e.g., food stamps) but no welfare. As expected, the number of working-poor children rises as criteria for defining the working poor are relaxed.[19]

When readers picture this low-wage workforce, they are likely to imagine hamburger flippers. Service workers of this kind are indeed among the working poor. Yet a surprisingly varied group of American employees take home wages low enough to pull their households below the poverty line. Household service workers (housekeepers, child care workers, and cooks) had a poverty rate of 21.8 percent during 1996. The rate for dental assistants, bartenders, hairdressers, and waitresses was 13.2 percent, and that for operators, fabricators, and laborers was 8 percent.[20]

AGE, FAMILY STATUS, EDUCATION, AND RACE

With these definitions of the working poor in mind, we might ask who they are in a sociological sense: what kinds of people find themselves in this category? The short answer is that the nation's young, its single parents, the poorly educated, and minorities are more likely than other workers to be poor.

As America's youth enter an increasingly inhospitable labor market, they have found themselves at a disadvantage over those who preceded them in better years.[21] Poverty rates for young workers have nearly doubled in the last twenty years.[22] Family status has a powerful impact on the working poor as well. Not surprisingly, families in which both husband and wife work are the least likely to be poor. Working single mothers, on the other hand, are the most likely to be poor—the poverty rate of families supported by single mothers is almost four times that of married-couple families with at least one worker. Single-parent families with mothers at the helm are almost twice as likely to be poor as families maintained solely by men, a reflection of the weak position of women in the labor market. But the predicament for single men should not be understated: 10 percent of America's working men who maintain families without a wife suffer poverty as well.[23] Clearly, lacking a second earner—male or female—a low-wage worker is at great risk for falling below the poverty line.

We know that our changing economy favors the well-educated. Their incomes have risen while high school dropouts have seen a precipitous loss in their wages and their employment rates and a concomitant increase in their poverty. Sixteen percent of workers who dropped out of high school are poor; less than 2 percent of our college-educated workers are poor.[24] This is a departure from the past.[25] In 1974, 20 percent of our full-time workers with less than a high school diploma earned low wages. By 1990 this figure had jumped to 36 percent, a big leap in the space of a decade. High school graduates in the full-time labor force did a bit better, but they too saw a near doubling of their poverty rates.

Race complicates this picture.[26] In an all-too-familiar story of America's racial divide, we discover that the white population has a significantly lower proportion of working poor (5.4 percent using the BLS definition) than either African-Americans (13.3 percent) or Hispanics (14.6 percent).[27] This is not just a matter of educational disadvantage concentrated among minorities: African-Americans in the labor force are more likely to be poor than their white counterparts at all levels of the educational continuum. For example, about 6 percent of the nation's white high school graduates are poor, but the rate is 15 percent among black high school graduates.[28]

The intersection of age, race, and gender has proven particularly troublesome. Young black women have the highest rate of poverty of any group in the labor force, but the racial disparity persists as they age: black women aged fifty-five to sixty-four in the labor force are almost three times more likely to be poor than white women of the same age.[29] Black and Latina women workers who head families are about twice as likely as white women to be members of the working poor. This already dismal number jumps to three times the rate for white women among those minority women who have young children.[30]

Scholars who have factored out other possible explanations for these disparate findings by race—including experience and educational credentials—have come to the conclusion that discrimination remains a potent force pushing the country's minority workers down the income scale.[31] But it is not the only explanation for the wage pattern. People with the same educational credentials (e.g., a high school diploma) may still perform differently on tests, a reflection perhaps of the mediocre quality of many high schools in segregated neighborhoods.[32]

TABLE 2.2
PERCENT OF WORKERS WITH LOW EARNINGS, BY GENDER AND RACE

Race/Gender Category	Percent with Low Earnings*
White men	13
Black men	22
Hispanic men	28
White women	24
Black women	29
Hispanic women	37

Source: U.S. Bureau of the Census, "Workers with Low Earnings 1964–1990," *Current Population Reports,* Series P-60, No. 12 (U.S. Government Printing Office, 1992).

* Workers have low earnings if their annual earnings are less than the poverty level for a four-person family. The 1990 threshold for low earnings was therefore an annual income of $12,195.

Why have the numbers of working-poor Americans increased when the country overall seems to be doing so well economically? Economists point to a number of forces, all of which contribute to the widening gap between the haves and those that have less in the labor market. The flight of manufacturing jobs is an important part of the story: the closure of auto plants, steel mills, and other blue-collar employers has reduced the availability of jobs that paid well but demanded little skill. These days the good jobs that have evolved in the manufacturing sector tend to demand greater skill and are therefore out of reach for those who bring fewer credentials to the labor market. Declining union representation has taken its toll as well. Less than 17 percent of the nation's workers are covered by collective bargaining agreements, and the rest are in a weaker position to exact wage increases, even when unemployment declines.

In most of the nation's high-poverty neighborhoods, saturated labor markets make it much harder to push wages up. With so many people searching for work, those who are already employed dare not ask for more. That this situation persists, even as the nation as a whole has experienced tightening labor markets, attests to the difficulty of increasing the wages of the working poor under conditions of segregation and concentrated poverty. Indeed, the only force pushing wages up in central Harlem has been the mandated increase in the minimum wage. Without this legislative intervention, wage stagnation would have persisted even longer, since there is a labor surplus in the ghetto.

Debates over the role of international competition are both persistent and inconclusive. Some analysts have argued that we have entered the age of globalization, and along with it greater competition with low-wage workforces overseas. On this account, American firms that want to stay in business have to lower wages if they are to compete successfully with companies in the Philippines or China.[33] Others claim that although global trade has increased, the United States' economy is still dominated by internal trade.[34] These arguments grew particularly strident when the NAFTA treaty was on the table. Early returns suggest that the United States has indeed lost a large number of jobs to Mexico, but the long-range consequences are hard to forecast. International trade aside, we do know that American employers came under greater shareholder pressure to increase profits, and responded by shrinking the size of their core workforce. Downsizing, outsourcing, and the growth of "contingent work" followed. Few of the urban poor were caught in these trends; middle-class white collar workers were the more likely victims. Yet I found more than one fast food worker in Harlem who had been pushed out by Citibank when it outsourced its janitorial services.

The computer has been blamed for much of the bad news. As employers have increasingly turned to new technologies, they have looked for workers who have the skills to use them. When this happens on a large scale, demand for low-skilled workers falls and the wages for those who are on the job decline as well. "Skill-biased technological change" clearly contributes to the problems of low-wage labor, but economists argue over how powerful an explanation this is. Undoubtedly all of the forces discussed here are playing a role in increasing the size of the working-poor population.

Writers such as Charles Murray and Larry Mead have raised the volume on discussions of poverty by focusing mainly on the nonworking poor who receive Aid to Families with Dependent Children. The clamor over welfare reform that crested in 1996 further tightened the linkage in the public mind between the indigent poor and the whole concept of poverty. The forest of data presented here suggests that this is a relatively minor part of the problem. More important by far are the trends that have increased the size of the *working* population that cannot make ends meet and the millions of children growing up in their households.

The Working Poor in Harlem

Central Harlem is one of the poorest parts of New York City. Nearly 30 percent of its households were on public assistance in 1990. Poverty stands at 40 percent.[35] Harlem's walls are laden with graffiti, windows are frequently shattered, and housing projects—magnets for troublemakers—rise above the skyline and dominate the once-elegant brownstones that are now boarded up, their stoops crumbling in decay. Running through the middle of this enclave is a bustling commercial strip, 125th Street (Martin Luther King, Jr. Boulevard), that has a long and glorious history as the crucible of the Harlem Renaissance. The Apollo Theatre, still the grand center of Harlem culture, is on 125th Street, as is a large state office building, named after one of the most famous of the community's native sons, Adam Clayton Powell, Jr.

Harlem residents do much of their shopping along 125th Street, for it is there that the most accessible drugstores, clothing shops, furniture marts, and fast food restaurants are to be found. To buy anything at a fancier store requires a subway trip or bus ride to another neighborhood. Shopping is therefore a community ritual, a constant public parade through the heart of America's best-known African-American enclave.

The main thoroughfare is also the place many Harlem residents turn to when they try to find work. Hence it is also the place where I began to look for the working-poor families who are the centerpiece of this book. I found them by way of four fast food restaurants that cater to the African-American and Latino clientele in the center of Harlem and on its periphery, where immigrant families from the Dominican Republic and Puerto Rico cluster. Beginning with fast food eateries was not an accident, for the stereotype of hamburger-flipping as the emblematic low-wage job turns out to be quite accurate. *More than one in every fifteen Americans has worked in the fast food industry.* Minority youth are a big part of this labor force: some one in eight of them has worked in the business. Hence the public image of the "McJob" accords fairly well with reality, for the fast food industry is a critical gateway into the labor market for thousands of people who live in inner-city neighborhoods. It is from this starting point that they hope to launch careers that will take them out of the minimum-wage bracket into a job that pays enough to sustain a family.

As is true in any study of a particular occupational group, fast food workers do not necessarily represent the entire universe of low-wage workers. One could just as usefully study people who scan in groceries and supermarkets or clerks in low-priced clothing shops. The question naturally arises, then, how far we can generalize from the experience of Harlem's fast food workers to the working poor elsewhere in the country. This is another way of asking just who, in the sociological sense, are the workers whose lives are chronicled here?

Race/Ethnicity

Nearly all of the residents of central Harlem are African-American.[36] But the workforce we encountered in Harlem's fast food establishments was far more diverse: only slightly over half of its workers are black. A large group, nearly one-quarter, are immigrants who were either born in the Dominican Republic and immigrated to New York as children or first-generation Americans of Dominican parentage.[37] They are members of one of the fastest growing groups of newcomers to New York: the population of Dominicans in the city grew by 165 percent between 1980 and 1990, to well over 300,000—the largest concentration of Dominicans outside of the Republic itself.[38]

TABLE 2.3

AGE AND RACE OF EMPLOYEES IN CENTRAL HARLEM BURGER BARN RESTAURANTS

| Age group | Race Group | | | | |
	African-American	Dominican	Other Latino	Other	Total
15–18	25 45.5%	19 34.5%	10 18.2%	1 1.8%	55
19–22	25 41.7%	17 28.3%	10 16.7%	8 13.3%	60
23–32	39 76.5%	3 5.9%	7 13.7%	2 3.9%	51
33–50	9 50.0%	4 22.2%	2 11.1%	3 16.7%	18
Total	98 53.3%	43 23.4%	29 15.8%	14 7.6%	184 100%

Sons and daughters of Dominican immigrants tend to live in enclaves dominated by friends, family members, and other co-ethnics, communities where most children begin life as monolingual speakers of Spanish. Eventually, of course, they learn the English language and American ways as they move through New York's school system and rub shoulders with outsiders who do not share their culture. Nonetheless, the identification they feel with their fellow immigrants—an identity reinforced by frequent visits and long stays in their "homeland"—is so strong that they think of themselves as Dominican even though many were born in New York.

Sixteen percent of the people whom we encountered in the restaurant workforce were Latinos from elsewhere in the Caribbean, principally Puerto Rico, which has for decades sent workers to the U.S. mainland for jobs, and pulled them back with family ties that run deep. Return migration, or, rather, circular patterns of migration, are so common in this community that a hybrid culture has developed: the Nuyoricans. Puerto Ricans are the largest Hispanic group in New York; one-half of all the Latinos in the city are of Puerto Rican origin. In fact, they are among the largest ethnic groups of any kind, numbering nearly a million and increasing at a rapid rate.

In the 1940s, the older generation of Puerto Ricans were lured by the factory and service jobs that were then plentiful in New York City.[39] Wages were high and the income could go a very long way back home, the destination of many older workers who always planned to retire to the island on the strength of their mainland earnings. Succeeding generations have found many of the factory doors shut tight[40] and have had to make do with low-wage jobs in the Nuyorican enclave economy of bodegas and clothing stores, or have turned to the burgeoning service sector.[41] The poorest of them have been absorbed into the welfare system—an option foreclosed to Dominicans, who do not arrive as U.S. citizens and so lack automatic work rights or social welfare benefits.

Puerto Ricans and Dominicans represent the two largest groups of Latino immigrants in New York City.[42] They are also among the poorest of the city's residents: Hispanics have median household incomes that are two-thirds of the median for whites or less, and their poverty rates are at least one and a half times greater than those for whites. Nuyoricans and Dominicans, who are important entrants to Harlem's low-wage economy, are also among the poorest of the city's Hispanics,[43] falling well behind the smaller and more prosperous groups of Argentines, Panamanians, and Peruvians.

This is hardly surprising, for given the connection between human capital and labor market success, Puerto Ricans and Dominicans are decidedly disadvantaged in the credential race.[44] This is especially true for the city's Dominicans, less than 40 percent of whom are high school graduates. They lag well behind their Puerto Rican counterparts in English proficiency, reflecting the comparatively shorter duration of their immigration experience.

Both Latino communities have high rates of poverty among married couples, and a significantly higher proportion of female-headed households than do their white counterparts. Men and women in the Puerto Rican and Dominican communities suffer much higher unemployment rates—one and a half times as great—than whites. Within this general profile, however, Puerto Ricans are likely to be better off than their Dominican counterparts. Puerto Ricans are more likely to be white;[45] black Dominicans encounter some of the same racial barriers in the labor market that native-born African-Americans contend with, which depresses employment and earnings for Dominicans as a whole.

Puerto Ricans' U.S. citizenship and greater English proficiency give them advantages in terms of access to employment, health care, public housing, Social Security, and a wide range of other benefits available only to citizens. Thus, although the two groups of Latinos are comparable in many respects (age, fertility, family structure), Puerto Ricans tend to have higher earnings. Dominicans in New York—and in my study—tend to make up for this disadvantage by increasing the number of people per household who are in the labor market. Both groups, however, are at great risk for joining the ranks of the working poor. In this they resemble the native-born African-Americans in Harlem, whose options are similarly limited by the pressures of racial discrimination, an imploding labor market, and a weak educational system that does little to position New York's poverty population for the good jobs that remain.

Age

We usually think of a fast food job as a youngster's first stepping-stone into the labor market, a part-time foray for pocket money and a foretaste of an adult lifetime of full-time employment. In most of the nation's suburbs, and in some of its more affluent cities, that is exactly who occupies this employment niche. Not so in central Harlem: Table 2.3 tells us that while a significant number of high-school-age kids are working in these restaurants, most of the employees are considerably older. Seventy percent of the workers we interviewed are over nineteen. Thirty-five percent are well into adulthood, twenty-three years old and older. This stands in marked contrast to national figures on the fast food workforce. Nationwide, nearly three-quarters of the workers in this industry are twenty years old or younger, with more than one-quarter in the high-school-age group.[46] No doubt the differences reflect the relative paucity of opportunities in a depressed economy like that of central Harlem. Older people have fewer better-paying prospects and are therefore "pushing down" into jobs that would qualify as entry-level way stations elsewhere.

When we look at the local age figures for African-Americans, the contrast with the national average-aged worker grows sharper.[47] As Table 2.3 shows, one-half of the African-Americans in this workforce are twenty-three years old and older, reflecting once again the more restricted nature of the labor market opportunities open to them. Dominicans, by contrast, look more like the stereotypical young worker in a hamburger flipping job: half of them are in the youngest age group and only 16 percent are as old as the majority of black fast food workers.

Education

Fast food jobs are often thought to act as magnets, pulling young people away from school, distracting their attention from the kind of "human capital" investment that will pay off in the long run. In a later chapter I will argue the opposite—that working while in school increases attachment to education. For the moment, however, it is worth noting that—contrary to prevailing stereotypes of fast food workers as high school dropouts—these inner-city workers are both quite strongly attached to the educational enterprise and better educated as a group than we might have expected.[48] About 70 percent of the youngest workers (fifteen-to-eighteen-year-olds) are in a regular high school program, and another 10 percent are enrolled in an alternative high school. Eight percent are going to college. Less than 10 percent, most of whom are immigrant workers who completed their schooling in Latin America, are completely detached from the world of education.

As we move up the age groups, involvement in education declines, but not as much as I expected. Among the nineteen-to-twenty-two-year-olds, for example, more than half (56 percent) have a high school diploma or its equivalent. About one-fourth of these people were high school dropouts, but the remaining 18 percent had some education beyond high school.[49] These numbers compare quite favorably to national studies of America's youth.[50]

For many people in these age groups, education is an ongoing process that will continue for many years into adulthood. It is instructive, then, to consider what they hope to accomplish over the long run—what the *aspirations* of these low-wage workers look like. Perhaps in part because of their encounter with the raw world of low-wage employment and their desire to find something better over the long run, Burger Barn employees have very high expectations for their educational futures.[51] Over half of the youngest workers expect to go on to college.[52] African-Americans have higher educational goals than do their Latino counterparts, and part-time workers (many of whom are taking courses while working) expect to do better than those who work full-time.[53]

Whether these aspirations will be realized or not is hard to forecast, but the data on the actual enrollment patterns of these fast food workers are not particularly encouraging. The older the workers, the less likely they are to be enrolled in courses of any kind, and most of those who are in school are taking vocational, technical, or para-professional courses, rather than liberal arts courses of the kind that is typical for the four-year institutions they aspire to attend. Older workers with adult responsibilities may find higher education out of reach.

Still, we see an extraordinary commitment to higher education in aspiration if not in practice, even among those fast food employees who are already quite a bit older than the normal middle-class college student. The numbers reflect what we found in the course of many months of conversation with Harlem's low-wage workers: an enduring belief in education as an essential credential for mobility in the labor market. This portrait could not possibly be farther from the stereotypical picture of the inner-city minority (usually described as a high school dropout with no appreciation of the value of education).

Gender

We have known for some time that low-wage work is often women's work. Nationally, women are concentrated in the jobs that cluster at the bottom of the income distribution.[54] Fast food jobs, prototypical examples of low-wage work, are overwhelmingly held by females in the United States: in 1984, two-thirds of this labor force was female.[55] Not so in Harlem. Nearly half of the workers in these ghetto restaurants were men. This suggests that men face a steeper uphill battle in finding better jobs in communities like Harlem, ultimately "slipping down" into sectors that, elsewhere, would be largely women's employment preserves.

Family/Household Structure

There are many ways to describe the "sociological identity" of Harlem's fast food labor force, and we have already encountered some—race, gender, and age being among the most common demographic descriptors. One other needs to be added, however, if we are to understand who these people are: family structure. In suburban America, we would expect to find that the fast food labor force was composed mainly of young people who are living at home with their parents and passing through this work experience as a way station to a more remunerative future. We already know that Harlem's restaurant workers are older. But what kinds of families do these low-wage workers come from, or more particularly, what do the households they live in look like?

Almost one-third of these Harlem workers live with a single parent (overwhelmingly a mother).[56] Only 13 percent of these workers are children living in a nuclear household (with both parents). Over half of the workers we studied are over the age of eighteen, but still live with their parents or other relatives. These are young adults who cannot earn enough money to launch independent lives and are therefore forced to remain at home, where resources can be pooled and poverty managed collaboratively in the family.

More than one-third of these Harlem workers were parents trying to support families on the strength of these minimum-wage positions. Very few had children under the age of six, most likely because it is so hard to pay for child care out of wages this low. Those who did have young children were older (twenty-five to thirty-four) and worked full-time; one-third were trying to make ends meet alone, as single parents.[57]

The literature on the urban underclass posits a physical separation of welfare recipients and working people, a separation that supposedly underwrites divergent cultures. Aid to Families with Dependent Children, we are told, spawned negative socialization patterns, most especially an unfamiliarity with (or lack of appreciation for) the world of work. When we look at real families, though, we find that what look like separate worlds to the Bureau of Labor Statistics are whole family units that combine work and welfare, and always have.

Twenty-nine percent of central Harlem's households received support from the welfare system in 1995. However, many of the same families also contained members who were in the labor force. Indeed, among restaurant workers, about one-quarter were living in households where someone was receiving AFDC income, though wages remain the overwhelming source of family support for virtually all of these households.[58] Two in five of the Burger Barn workers are the only formally employed person in their household. This is more than designer sneakers and gold chains: the income these young workers receive is a critical source of support in poor households in Harlem.

Rather than paint welfare and work as different worlds, it makes far more sense to describe them as two halves of a single coin, as an integrated economic system at the very bottom of our social structure.[59] Kyesha's family is a clear example of this fusion. Her mother needs the income her working child brings into the house; Kyesha needs the subsidies (housing, medical care, etc.) that state aid provides to her mother. Only because the two domains are linked can this family manage to make ends meet, and then just barely. Of course, many of these restaurant workers are in families that have no contact with the state welfare system at all. Instead, they are wage workers whose family members are also working for a living. Our understanding of their parents' occupational situations is complicated by the fractured family structure that so many are embedded in: 27 percent of their fathers are deceased, and 14 percent of their mothers as well.[60] Since very few of the people we studied were over the age of forty, this suggests a pattern of early mortality among their parents, with all the difficulties this brings about in the lives of young people.[61] Divorce and the incidence of never-married mothers produce enough distance between children and their fathers that many know only that their fathers are alive, and are not aware of what they do for a living.

Still, we do know something about the employment patterns of the parents of our restaurant workers. Over half of their mothers are working, with medical services[62]—hospitals, home care agencies, and nursing homes—providing by far the largest source of employment.[63] The health care industry was one of the few sectors that continued to grow in New York City throughout the relentless recession of the early 1990s;[64] it absorbed many of the inner city's working poor.

What we know about the fathers of these fast food workers is probably less reliable than the information about mothers, simply because the ties between children and their fathers are more tenuous. Nonetheless, 46 percent of the fathers are reported by their sons and daughters to be employed. For many of them, we have no information about their occupation at all because their children do not know where they work. Those for whom we have information are employed as skilled craftsmen and transportation workers. The rest are scattered in janitorial services, factory labor, and retail trades. A number of them are retired and 10 percent are presently unemployed but once worked.

HARLEM'S WORKING POOR are perpetually one paycheck away from disaster. This would probably be the case even if we did not face a new policy climate brought about by the failures of health insurance reform and the continued fiscal instability of major cities. To appreciate why we ought to give special attention to the nation's low-wage workers right now, we have to detour into these arenas to see how they are being affected by these problems.

Almost half of Americans who work under the poverty line lack health insurance of any kind.[65] While the Clinton administration has focused some long-needed attention on uninsured children,[66] their parents (whose wages are essential to household survival) are still unprotected from medical catastrophes, since even at $6 or $7 per hour they earn too much for Medicaid and too little to afford private insurance.[67] Bankruptcy is often their only practical option when health bills mount.[68]

For those who do qualify for Medicaid, the news is not much better. Medicaid has been targeted for major budget reductions at both the federal and state levels. In New York, health-related cuts from both sources were estimated at $2–2.3 billion in 1996. While many of the working poor are ineligible for Medicaid to begin with, they have virtually all been affected by these cuts where access to health care itself is concerned. Doctors and clinics have become harder to find in poor neighborhoods, where many of the hospitals targeted for closure in the wake of Medicaid reform are to be found. Yet the need for health care among the poor continues to grow. Chronic asthma rates are rising at alarming rates among ghetto residents;[69] diabetes is also far higher among African-Americans.[70] There is virtually no aspect of the country's health profile that looks encouraging when we consider the inner-city poor.[71]

This is a national disgrace in its own right, but the health problems of the poor also set the stage for employment instability as parents struggle to cope with the endless rounds of hospitalization and doctor visits that treatment for chronic asthma requires. Many a mother has found herself on the welfare rolls because she could no longer manage these demands within the strictures of a low-wage job. Recall Carmen's experience: her first and only spell on the welfare rolls came about because she had no health care and was experiencing difficulties in her pregnancy. Having to travel a long distance to take a child to a doctor is an annoyance for anyone. For a poor worker, with an employer who does not give time off for medical needs, it can mean the end of a job as the two domains—work and family—collide.[72]

Children are not the only dependents that working-poor families are responsible for. Elderly relatives are often an even more problematic burden for workers who lack the resources for nursing homes. The same is true for many middle-class families, of course, but they often do have some supports to rely upon, including pension benefits, insurance policies, and, among the more fortunate, the free labor of (mainly) women who can afford to stand outside the labor market and take care of elderly relatives because their husbands or children earn enough to support the family. Among Harlem's poor, those resources are hard to come by. People who have worked seasonally (as many of Harlem's elderly did in their southern youth), in low-wage jobs, or under the table (as most domestics, for example, have done for decades) may be entitled to only minimal social security. Their children and grandchildren are therefore left to care for them in their sunset years without the financial resources to cushion the burden, even if these younger relatives are themselves working away in the low-wage world.

Federal and state resources for home health care, widely regarded as a cost-efficient means of caring for the elderly (especially when compared to the expensive alternative of nursing home placements), have been slashed. Twenty-five percent of the dollars directed at noninstitutional care, approximately $577 million, was subtracted from New York City's 1996 budget, a move that was estimated to place nearly twenty thousand home care patients in need of nursing home placements.[73] These facilities are already oversubscribed and not particularly anxious to inherit a population that cannot contribute financially, owing to its poverty, especially in the face of declining government support for reasonable reimbursement rates. We can expect the waiting lists to grow,[74] but in the meantime, many a working-poor adult is going to face the demand to take care of an elderly relative while maintaining his or her working hours.

Cuts in home care budgets and hospital closings create heavy losses in health care positions, one of the few sectors that have been growing in recent years. About one of every eight jobs in New York's metropolitan region are found in the health care field. The budget cuts enacted by the state and the city are projected to cost New York City alone as many as 61,000 positions.[75] Doctors, nurses, and other skilled specialists are affected, but the largest numbers of job losses are felt at the bottom end, where minimum-wage workers who empty bedpans and change the linen are to be found. As Howard Berliner, professor of health policy at the New School for Social Research, has noted:

Health care will still be a large employer with a large economic presence . . . but as a mass employer of people on the lower economic rungs—

low-wage, low-skill workers in 24-hour-a-day hospitals—its best days
are probably already a memory. Demand for such workers will decline
along with the length of hospital stays and the shift to outpatient
treatment.[76]

Columbia-Presbyterian Hospital and Harlem Hospital are both located
near the neighborhoods where the workers appearing in this book live.
They are the largest employers for miles around, and their presence gen-
erates tertiary industries (restaurants, grocery stores, and other shops
that cater to workers on their lunch hours). As these giant institutions
shed workers in large numbers, the shock waves are felt by the workers
and then by the families who run businesses in the area. While we might
expect to see growth in home health care jobs, they are more likely to be
organized into managed-care groups that will not be hiring the same
people as those who worked in the lower tiers of the hospital labor force.
Positions in managed-care organizations usually go to those who are
better-educated, because supervision is minimal compared to the old-
style hospital hierarchy. If the city's budget cuts are fully enacted, the consequences will be significant, since this is the sector where the heads of
households in these Burger Barn families have been most successful at
finding work.[77]

PROBLEMATIC TRENDS in the low-wage labor market have been with us
for some time now. Their impact is compounded by new pressures on the
working poor arising from the introduction of welfare reform in 1996.
The real consequences of this reform will not be known for some time.[78]
But it does not take a rocket scientist—or even a trained economist—to
know that pushing thousands of low-skilled women with little recent job
experience into a labor market that already has a surplus of would-be
workers will worsen conditions for everyone. As I document elsewhere in
this volume, job-seekers now confront an even more competitive situation in communities like central Harlem where thousands of AFDC
recipients are approaching their time limits. Even in a robust economy,
it is hard to believe that these women will all find employment. Many
would be considered unemployable because they lack even the most
minimal qualifications of literacy and numeracy. Others would be able to
find work if they either lived in communities that were not so depressed
or could travel to places that were job-rich.[79]

The combination of these forces—poor preparation for the labor market and transportation difficulties—will create a new population of poor people who have lost access to all government support and have no realistic hope of employment. But to the extent that they make the effort to try to find work, all arrows lead into the same labor market that Harlem's working poor have been in for years, not to mention the thousands of would-be workers who have been knocking at employers' doors, only to be turned away.

What does this mean for the working poor, the people who have been standing on their own two feet while the nation abolishes public assistance? Absent further mandated increases in the minimum wage,[80] those lucky enough to get work confront downward wage pressure: with hundreds of people waiting in line for their jobs, there is no incentive for employers to raise wages.[81] While unemployment remains at record lows across the nation, the deep pockets of poverty in the country's inner cities sport numbers that look a lot less cheery since they are home to populations that sustain much higher rates of unemployment than the national average. African-Americans, especially the men (and teens) among them, nearly always have been unemployed at rates 5–7 percent above whites and Hispanics. In the communities where they live in large numbers—like central Harlem, with its 18 percent official unemployment rate—this translates into a surplus labor pool, *without* welfare reform. Policy changes that result in a flood of new entrants to this overcrowded system hurt the chances of those already hard at work inside it.[82]

This alone would alter the life chances of the working poor in the inner city for the worse. New pressures are building that are curtailing vital social services that the working poor depend upon in order to stay on the job. Subsidized child care, which is chronically oversubscribed, is a case in point.[83] Working families at the bottom of the income distribution spend more than 20 percent of their monthly income on child care, and for that they tend to receive low-quality care. The availability of Head Start makes an enormous difference for the better, but it reaches only a fraction of the children who need it and as a part-day program cannot suffice to meet the needs of families with full-time workers who cannot quit in the middle of the day to rush home.

Poor parents cannot stay in the labor market[84] without access to child care and city-funded day care centers, which provide affordable, reliable, and comparatively high-quality supervision for families whose only other options include "family care" or unlicensed operators who may be bad bets.[85] Now comes the pressure to put AFDC mothers into the labor force. How are cities like New York to respond to the demands they must make on the child care system? Because there is a powerful fiscal incentive to push former welfare recipients into the labor market,[86] the city gives them highest priority for coveted child care slots.[87] This leaves the working poor, whose lives have little impact on the city's bottom line, out in the cold, or potentially taking their place on the welfare lines.

Without a massive buildup of capacity in the child care system as a whole, it is the working poor who are likely to bear the brunt of welfare reform. And instead of a vast increase, we are seeing the opposite: competition between the working poor and AFDC recipients coming off the rolls for the modest number of slots available in the publicly subsidized system, the only institutional day care most poor people can afford.

Welfare reform is also removing from the underground labor force private baby-sitters. Women like Dana, Kyesha's mother, have long supplemented their grants with underground earnings caring for the children of the working poor. These women are now expected to get a job "above ground," which removes them as an inexpensive source of child care in families and neighborhoods with a mix of workers, welfare recipients, and young children.[88]

For most young workers at the bottom of the occupational pyramid, the best chance for upward mobility lies in getting more education. Employers favor better-educated workers—even in fast food restaurants and in home health care, to name two low-wage domains that are demanding high school diplomas these days, credentials they never used to require. Poor workers are well aware of this credential premium. Indeed, I argue in Chapter 5, one of the most compelling forces pushing minority youth into the low-wage labor market in the first place is the need to fund further education. Although the advantages of higher education are known to all, access is becoming more problematic with every passing year.

The City University of New York, for decades the main educational gateway into the world of good jobs for the city's minority and immigrant populations,[89] was tuition-free for 129 years. That policy ended for good in 1976 during New York City's financial crisis, when modest tuition charges were instituted. The costs of higher education for the most needy of the city's students have risen beyond their ability to pay.[90] In recent years, tuition rates have become a political football, as governors intent on reducing the state's deficits have sought to slash and burn their way through the City University budget, leaving the institution little fiscal recourse but to raise tuition. CUNY's community college students, the majority from households with annual incomes of $20,000 or less, now pay $2,500 per year in tuition alone.[91] Ironically, tuition increases which pushed many poor students out of college coincided with the results of new studies showing tremendous gains in employment and wages for students who completed their degrees under CUNY's controversial program of "open admissions," which began in 1970.[92] Over the succeeding twenty-five years, these students—who would most likely never have been able to go to college without this special dispensation—found their way into professions, benefiting not only their families but the city tax coffers as well.

This will surprise no one familiar with the GI Bill, which had a similar impact nationwide some fifty years ago. Designed to dampen the consequences of mass military demobilization, the GI Bill produced the largest increase in first-generation college graduates the nation has ever seen. Their contribution to America's prosperity, not to mention their own, has been substantial ever since. For the working poor of our own age, however, these kinds of social supports have been deemed luxuries we can no longer afford (or worse, policies that created unwarranted subsidies or lower-quality graduates). Hence the opportunity ladders extended in the past, often as recently as a few years ago, are being rolled up.

Upward mobility is an important goal, of course, for anyone working in a poorly paid job. Yet for millions of entry-level workers, that is a dream deferred if not foregone. Surviving the moment has to take precedence over getting ahead, and here the food stamp assistance program plays a critical role. In 1994, some 2.3 million food stamp households included at least one worker. For these families, food stamps make the difference between being able to eat and having to go without when low wages cannot stretch to the end of the month or, worse, a job loss occurs.[93] Yet the food stamp reductions in the welfare reform bill of 1996 cut deeply into this part of the safety net for poor workers. While some of the cutbacks were reinstated, the current law eliminates food stamps after ninety days in any three-year period for able-bodied men and women aged eighteen to fifty working fewer than twenty hours per week and not raising minor children. Job-seeking does not fulfill the work requirements, and though workfare does fulfill eligibility requirements, many poor food stamp recipients were never on AFDC and do not have workfare programs available to them. These cuts were so severe that at least forty states have received waivers to continue federal food stamp coverage in those areas where few jobs are available.

Immigrants face particularly difficult conditions today, owing to changes in federal policy that aim specifically to discourage entry into the

United States, particularly from countries with large populations of low-skilled workers.[94] Under the 1996 welfare law and subsequent legislation, many legal immigrants began losing federal food stamp benefits in 1997.[95] And while the Balanced Budget Act reestablished Supplemental Security Income eligibility for many legal immigrants who were disqualified from that program in 1996,[96] most future legal immigrants will not be eligible for it. SSI and food stamps are major forms of support for elderly immigrants. There is ferocious debate over the costs to the tax coffers of the nation and particular border states of immigration policies that foster family reunification over those that would select newcomers on the basis of the skills they could contribute. It is clear that immigration shifted markedly toward poorer countries and poorer entrants with the legislative changes of 1965, with Mexicans being the biggest beneficiaries of the change. Some states (notably California, Florida, New York, and Texas) have borne high costs as a result, especially where public expenditures for education and health care are concerned. They have also reaped important benefits as immigrant communities spend money on goods and services and, more to the point, pay taxes.

Nonetheless, the ire directed at immigrants—legal and illegal—has translated into legislative assaults on entitlements that form an important income stream into immigrant households, including those of the working poor who rely on them to make up the difference between the low wages they earn and the real cost of living. Dominican families in Washington Heights, a Latino immigrant enclave on Manhattan's Upper West Side, have responded to the high cost of living by putting as many of their members into the labor market as they can spare. Elderly relatives supervise the youngest children so that all the other, able-bodied adults can go to work. No one can afford to pay the grandparents for their labor. In a sense, the state pays through the SSI and food stamp system, and with these additional "earnings," the family as a whole can make a go of things. Food stamps are critical to the equation.

Legal immigrants' access to food assistance and SSI coverage is being reduced and eliminated, even though they pay the same taxes as the rest of us.[97] Clearly the policy is aimed at making the United States a less attractive destination[98] or, alternatively, making the cost of maintaining a low-wage labor force even less than it has been thus far. Hence while high-income earners gain from the availability of inexpensive child care, waiters, hospital orderlies, and the many other labor-intensive contributions made by immigrants to our economy (and our productivity), the benefits we extend to these legal residents have been greatly reduced.

·   ·   ·

ONGOING CHANGES in the American economy have pulled the rug out from under the low-wage labor market. The continued fiscal instability of cities like New York is spurring cuts in public employment and critical services. Federal government retrenchment has reduced funding for everything from housing subsidies to Medicaid. These trends conspire to make the problems of the working poor more severe than they used to be. That's the bad news. The good news is that despite all of these difficulties, the nation's working poor continue to seek their salvation in the labor market. That such a commitment persists when the economic rewards are so minimal is testimony to the durability of the work ethic, to the powerful reach of mainstream American culture, which has always placed work at the center of our collective moral existence. As we shall see in the next chapter, that culture does not stop at the gates of the ghetto.

CHAPTER THREE

Getting a Job in the Inner City

IF YOU DRIVE around the suburban neighborhoods of Long Island or Westchester County, you cannot miss the bright orange "Help Wanted" signs hanging in the windows of fast food restaurants. Teenagers who have the time to work can walk into most of these shops and land a job before they finish filling out the application form. In fact, labor scarcity (for these entry-level jobs) is a problem for employers in these highly competitive businesses. Therefore, though it cuts into their profits, suburban and small-town employers in the more affluent parts of the country are forced to raise wages and redouble their efforts to recruit new employees, often turning to the retiree labor force when the supply of willing youths has run out.

From the vantage point of central Harlem, this "seller's market" sounds like a news bulletin from another planet. Jobs, even lousy jobs, are in such short supply that inner-city teenagers are all but barred from the market, crowded out by adults who are desperate to find work. Burger Barn managers rarely display those orange signs; some have never, in the entire history of their restaurants, advertised for employees. They can depend upon a steady flow of willing applicants coming in the door—and they can be very choosy about whom they sign up. In fact, my research shows that among central Harlem's fast food establishments, the ratio of applicants to available jobs is 14:1. For every fortunate person who lands one of these minimum-wage jobs, there are thirteen others who walk away empty-handed. Since these applicants are also applying to other jobs, we should assume that the overall gap between the supply and demand of workers is not this large. Nonetheless, almost three-quarters of the unsuccessful job-seekers we interviewed were unemployed a year after they applied to Burger Barn, suggesting that the majority were no more successful with their other applications.

Statewide estimates of the gap between the number of people who need jobs (the unemployed plus the welfare recipients) and the number of available jobs in New York approach almost one million.[1] This is a staggering number—which may indeed be an exaggeration, since it includes many people who are unemployed for only a short time, but it should draw our attention to the acute nature of the job problem, especially for low-skilled workers from the inner city.[2]

Long lines of job-seekers depress the wages of those lucky enough to pass through the initial barriers and find a job. Hamburger flippers in central Harlem generally do not break the minimum wage. Longtime workers, like Kyesha Smith, do not see much of a financial reward for their loyalty. After five years on the job, she was earning $5 an hour, only 60 cents more than the minimum wage at the time. Carmen and Jamal had done no better. And this is not because they are not valued; indeed, they are. It is because the supply-and-demand curves familiar to students of Economics 101 are operating with a vengeance in poor communities, as they are on Long Island or in Madison, Wisconsin, where the same jobs are paying more than $7 an hour.

The long odds of landing a job do not stop thousands of inner-city residents from trying. When Disneyland took applications after the Rodney King riot in South-Central Los Angeles, some six thousand neatly dressed young people—largely black and Latino—waited in line to apply. In January 1992, when a new Sheraton hotel complex opened in Chicago, three thousand applicants spent the better part of a day in blowing snow, huddled along the north bank of the Chicago River, hoping for an interview. Four thousand anxious job-seekers stood in lines that wrapped around the block in March 1997 when the Roosevelt Hotel in Manhattan announced it would take applications for seven hundred jobs.

Why do people seek low-wage jobs in places like Burger Barn? How do they go about the task in labor markets that are saturated with willing workers? What separates the success stories, the applicants who actually get jobs, from those who are rejected from these entry-level openings? These are questions that require answers if we are to have a clear picture of how the job market operates in poverty-stricken neighborhoods like Harlem.

WHY WORK?

You know, when I was out, when I wasn't working, I used to get into fights. Well, it wasn't really fights, it was like really arguments. . . . [Now, my friends] ask me, "Why don't we see you anymore?" Like, I can't. I don't have time. But, you know, I don't really wanna hang around my block anymore 'cuz it's like getting real bad. You know, it's a lot of people fighting around there for no reason. And they shootin' and stuff like that.

Jessica has worked at a fast food restaurant in the middle of Harlem since she was seventeen, her first private-sector job following several summers as a city employee in a youth program. During her junior and senior year, Jessie commuted forty-five minutes each way to school, put in a full day at school, and then donned her work uniform for an eight-hour afternoon/evening shift. Exhausted by the regimen, she took a brief break from work toward the end of her senior year, but returned when she graduated from high school. Now, at the age of twenty-one, she is a veteran fast food employee with an unbroken work record of about three years.

Jessica had several motivations for joining the workforce when she was a teenager, principal among them the desire to be independent of her mother and provide for her own material needs. No less important, however, was her desire to escape the pressures of street violence and what appeared to be a fast track to nowhere among her peers. For in Jessica's neighborhood, many a young person never sees the other side of age twenty. Her own brother was shot in the chest, a victim of mistaken identity. Jessie's mother narrowly escaped a similar fate.

It had to have been like twelve or one o'clock. My mother was in her room and I was in my room. . . . I sleep on the top bunk. We started hearing gunshots, so first thing I did, I jumped from my bed to the floor. I got up after the gunshots stopped and went into my mother's room. She was on the floor. . . . "Are you all right, are you all right?" she said. "Yeah, yeah." The next morning we woke up and it was like a bullet hole in the window in her room. Her bed is like the level of the window. Lucky thing she jumped, I mean went to the floor, because it could have come in through the window.

Incidents of this kind happen every day in Jessica's neighborhood, but contrary to popular opinion, they never become routine, something to be shrugged off as "business as usual." They are the unwelcome and unnatural consequence of a community plagued by a few very troublesome drug dealers, often the only thriving, growth area of the local economy.

Street violence, drive-by shootings, and other sources of terror are obstacles that Jessica and other working-poor people in her community have to navigate around. But Jessica knows that troubles of this kind strike more often among young people who have nothing to do but spend time on the street. Going to work was, for her, a deliberate act of disengagement from such a future.

William, who has worked in the same Burger Barn as Jessica, had the same motivation. A short, stocky African-American, who was "a fat, pudgy kid" in his teen years, Will was often the butt of jokes and the object of bullying in the neighborhood. Tougher characters were always giving him a hard time, snatching his belongings, pushing him around. They took a special delight in tormenting the "fat boy." William's ego took a pounding.

As he crested into his teenage years, he wanted some way to occupy his time that would keep him clear of the tensions cropping up in his South Bronx housing project. Lots of boys his age were getting into drugs, but Will says, "Fortunately I was never really into that type of thing." After a stint with a summer youth corps job, he found his "own thing": working for Burger Barn. Having a job took him out of the street and into a safe space.

The job was good. . . . Just having fun that was unadulterated fun. There was no drugs. It was no pretenses, nobody givin' you a hard time. It was just being ourselves. That was cool.

For Stephanie, the trouble wasn't just in the streets, it was in her house. When she was in her teens, Stephanie's mother began taking in boarders in their apartment, young men and their girlfriends who did not always get along with her. The home scene was tense and occasionally violent, with knives flashing. The worse it got, the more Stephanie turned her attention to her job. She focused on what her earnings could do to rescue her from this unholy home life. Because she had her own salary, she was able to put her foot down and insist that her mother get rid of the troublemakers.

By the end of the month, I told my mother, if [that guy's] not gone, I'm not never coming home. You don't even have to worry about me. I have

*this little job, I can pay for myself. I'll get my cousin [to join me] and we'll
get a room. . . . Ever since then, my mother, she trying to do the right
thing. She says he's supposed to be out by the end of the month. So by
[then] hopefully he'll be gone.*

Living where she does, Stephanie is an expert on what happens to people who do not follow the path she has chosen into the legitimate labor
market. People she has grown up with, neighbors, and the boyfriends of
some of her closest friends have all had brushes with violence and run-ins
with the police. It happens alarmingly often in her neighborhood.

*[Gary], my girlfriend's boyfriend, just got shot. Gary and his friends . . .
always used to stand on this corner. Always, it was their hangout spot.
Some other friends was hustlin' [drugs] on our block and they went up to
Gary, gave him a high five and just passed by. Some other guys came up
to Gary and shot him. Shot him right in the leg. They told him, "Ya'll
can't hustle on my block." He's lucky because the bullet grazed him, but it
was a hollow-tip bullet, so them bullets explode. Blown off a chunk of his
knee.*

One of the only positive outcomes of these encounters is the resolution
Stephanie feels about taking a completely different approach to her own
life. She is hardly ignorant of the consequences of getting too close to the
drug trade. The knowledge has given her confidence, in the face of many
obstacles (not the least of which is a chaotic home life), that an honest
job for low pay is preferable to getting mixed up with people in the illegal
sector.[3]

Because the working poor have little choice but to live in neighborhoods where rents are low, they often find themselves in social settings
like Stephanie's. They have lots of friends and neighbors who are working
at real jobs for little income, but they also rub shoulders with criminals
who headquarter their enterprises in these poor neighborhoods. Exposure to folks who have taken the wrong fork in the road provides good
reason for seeking a safe haven like Burger Barn.

There are many "push factors" that prod Harlem youth to look for
work. Yet there are many positive inducements as well. Even as young
teens, Jessica, William, and Stephanie were anxious to pay their own way,
to free their families from the obligation to take care of all their needs. In
this, they are typical of the two hundred Burger Barn workers I tracked,
the majority of whom began their work lives when they were thirteen to

fifteen years old. This early experience in the labor force usually involves bagging groceries or working off the books in a local bodega, a menial job under the watchful eye of an adult who, more often than not, was a friend of the family or a relative who happened to have a shop.

Taking a job at the age of thirteen is a familiar path for anyone who lived through or has read about the Great Depression of the 1930s, when working-class families fallen on hard times often sent out their young people to find jobs. It stands in sharp contrast to the prevailing expectations of today's middle-class world, in which young teens are told to concentrate on their homework and their soccer leagues and leave the world of work for later in life.[4]

Yet most of the working poor come from homes where the struggles of the 1930s are all too familiar. Poor parents cannot stretch their resources to take care of their children's needs, much less the demands they make when their better-off peers are buying a new CD or a special kind of jacket—the kinds of frills that middle-class families routinely provide for their teens (along with the second telephone line, access to a car, and many other expensive items). Inner-city kids cannot even dream of such luxuries. Even finding the funds to pay for transportation, basic clothing, books, and other necessary expenses is hard for these families.

While middle-class parents would feel they had abrogated a parental responsibility if they demanded that their kids handle these basic costs (not to mention the frills), many poor parents consider the "demand" perfectly normal. Whether American-born or recent immigrants, these parents often began working at an early age themselves and consequently believe that a "good" kid should not be goofing off in his or her free time—summers, after school, and vacations—but should be bringing in some cash to the family.

Burger Barn earnings will not stretch to cover a poor family's larger items like food and shelter, and in this respect entry-level jobs do not underwrite any real independence. They do make it possible for kids like Kyesha and Carmen to participate in youth culture. Many writers have dismissed teenage workers on these grounds, complaining that their sole (read "trivial") motivation for working (and neglecting school) is to satisfy childish desires for "gold chains and designer sneakers."[5] Jessie and Will do want to look good and be cool. But most of their wages are spent providing for basic expenses. When she was still in high school, Jessica paid for her own books, school transportation, lunches, and basic clothing expenses. Now that she has graduated, she has assumed even more of the cost of keeping herself. Her mother takes care of the roof over their

heads, but Jessie is responsible for the rest, as well as for a consistent contribution toward the expense of running a home with other dependent
children in it.

Minimum-wage jobs cannot buy real economic independence; they
cannot cover the full cost of living, including rent, food, and the rest of
an adult's monthly needs. What Jessica can do with her earnings is cover
the marginal cost of her presence in the household, leaving something
over every week to contribute to the core cost of maintaining the household. Youth workers, particularly those who are parents themselves, generally do turn over part of their pay to the head of the household as a kind
of rent. In this fashion, working-poor youth participate in a pooled-
income strategy that makes it possible for households—as opposed to
individuals—to sustain themselves. Without their contributions, this
would become increasingly untenable, especially in families where Mom
is receiving public assistance.[6]

This pattern is even more striking among immigrants and native-born
minorities who are not incorporated into the state welfare system. In
working-poor households with no connection to the state system, survival depends upon multiple workers pooling their resources.[7] Pressures
build early for the older children in these communities to take jobs, no
matter what the wages, in order to help their parents make ends meet.
Ana Gonzales is a case in point. Having reached twenty-one years old, she
had been working since she was fifteen. Originally from Ecuador, Ana
followed her parents, who emigrated a number of years before and presently work in a factory in New Jersey. Ana completed her education in her
home country and got a clerical job. She emigrated at eighteen, joining
two younger brothers and a twelve-year-old sister already in New York.
Ana has ambitions for going back to college, but for the moment she
works full-time in a fast food restaurant in Harlem, as does her sixteen-
year-old brother. Her sister is responsible for cooking and caring for their
five-year-old-brother, a responsibility Ana assumes when she is not at
work or attending her English as a Second Language class.

The Gonzales family is typical of the immigrant households that participate in the low-wage economy of Harlem and Washington Heights,
and it bears a strong resemblance to the Puerto Rican families in other
parts of the city.[8] Parents work, adolescent children work, and only the
youngest of the children are able to invest themselves in U.S. schooling.
Indeed, it is often the littlest who is deputized to master the English language on behalf of the whole family. Children as young as five or six are
designated as interpreters responsible for negotiations between parents

and landlords, parents and teachers, parents and the whole English-speaking world beyond the barrio.[9]

The social structure of these households is one that relies upon the contributions of multiple earners for cash earnings, child care, and house-work.[10] Parents with limited language skills (and often illegal status) are rarely in a position to support their children without substantial contributions from the children themselves. Jobs that come their way rarely pay enough to organize a "child-centered" household in which education and leisure are the predominant activities of the youth until the age of eighteen. Instead, they must rely upon their children and, at most, can look forward to the eventual upward mobility of the youngest of their kids, who may be able to remain in school long enough to move to better occupations in the future.

Older workers, especially women with children to support, have other motives for entering the low-wage labor market. Like most parents, they have financial obligations: rent, clothes, food, and all the associated burdens of raising kids. Among the single mothers working at Burger Barn, however, the options for better-paying jobs are few and the desire to avoid welfare is powerful.[11] This is particularly true for women who had children when they were in their teens and dropped out of school to take care of them.

Latoya, one of Kyesha Smith's closest friends at Burger Barn, had her first child when she was sixteen. She was married at seventeen and then had another. But the marriage was shaky; her husband was abusive and is in jail now. Latoya learned about being vulnerable, and has made sure she will never become dependent again. She lives with Jason, her common-law husband, a man who is a skilled carpenter, and they have a child between them. Jason makes a good living, a lot more money than Latoya can earn on her own. Now that she has three kids, plus Jason's daughter by his first marriage, she has occasionally been tempted to quit work and just look after them. After all, it is hard to take care of four kids, even with Jason's help, and work a full-time job at the same time. She barely has the energy to crawl into bed at night, and crumbles at the thought of the overnight shifts she is obliged to take.

But Latoya's experience with her first husband taught her that no man is worth the sacrifice of her independence.

> *This was my first real job. . . . I take it seriously, you know. . . . It means a lot to me. It give you—what's the word I'm lookin' for? Security blanket. 'Cuz, a lot of married women, like when I was married to my husband,*

when he left, the burden was left on me. If [Jason] leave now, I can deal
with the load because I work. [Jason] help me—we split the bills half and
half. But if he leaves, I'm not gonna be, well, "Oh my God, I'm stranded.
I have no money." No. I have a little bank account; I got my little nest
egg. You know, so it does mean a lot to me. I wouldn't just up and leave
my job.

For Latoya, as for many other working mothers, working is an insurance
policy against dependence on men who may not be around for the long
haul.[12]

FINDING A WAY IN

Tiffany was little more than ten years old when she first tried to find work.
She was still living with her mother in the Bedford-Stuyvesant area of
Brooklyn at that time, but they were in trouble. "Things were bad," she
remembers. "Checks weren't coming in. And what would happen is we
needed food. . . . So I would pack bags and stuff [in a local store] for spare
change. And after a full day, I would make enough to buy groceries." Little
Tiffany wasn't saving for gold chains, she was trying to help make ends
meet in a family that was falling apart.

But the bagging job wasn't a real, legitimate job. In fact, it was pretty
dicey.

We was at the whim of the cashiers. Discretion was with the store owner.
'Cause they would run us out sometimes. It was almost like how you see
on a larger scale, big-time [crime] organizations. . . . It was like a little
gang thing going on with the packers. There was a lead packer and even
he would extort money from the other packers. One time I got beat up by
a guy 'cause I was the only female. I was not gonna give none of my
money. And he bullied me around. I was scared. I didn't go back for a
while.

Still, Tiffany felt she was doing something useful, something important.
When customers gave her a tip, she thought she had earned it, and it was
more money than she had ever seen. But the whole day might yield no
more than fifty cents.

By the time she was thirteen, Tiffany's mother had given her up to a
group home in New York's foster care system. In some ways, she had
more stability in her life, facing less pressure to provide the food for the
table. Yet group homes are regimented, Spartan places, with many rules

and regulations. Once school was out for the summer, Tiffany wanted to escape the military atmosphere—the system of infractions and privileges withdrawn, the searches of personal belongings, the single phone call on the weekends—and find something useful to do. She also wanted to earn some money, since her group home was lean on what it deemed "extras," like funds to take in an occasional movie.

Ironically, because she was in foster care, Tiffany had direct access to the city's employment programs for young minorities, collectively known as "summer youth" by most inner-city kids. Through the good offices of her caseworker, she found a job as a clerical assistant in an office that provided assistance to victims of domestic violence. At the age of thirteen, Tiffany was answering the office phone, taking down information from women who had been battered and were seeking shelter. The job gave Tiffany an appreciation for white-collar work: the clean environment, the comfort of air-conditioning (while her friends working for the parks department were outside sweating the hot summer), and the feeling of importance that comes with a little prestige and the ability to help someone in trouble. It focused her desire to work in a social service agency someday.

Working for summer youth, Tiffany discovered one of the liabilities of a paycheck delivered by the government. Like Social Security checks, these salaries were delivered biweekly, on the same Friday, to thousands of kids working throughout the city. Everyone in her neighborhood knew when those checks would be available.

There was a real element of fear involved. Hundreds of other people were getting their checks. There were many people who would steal your check. People would follow you to the check-cashing place and take your money. Waiting on line, you'd usually take a friend with you to pick up your check. If you were smart, you wouldn't cash it right away. You'd go home. You'd wait and go to a check-cashing place in your neighborhood. But you know the young, they wanted their money right away. They wanted to go shopping. So they'd cash it right there and they get hit.

Despite these problems, Tiffany learned a lot from this job that she could apply to other jobs as she got older. She discovered that work involved taking care of responsibilities that were delegated to her and no one else, that it wasn't always fun but had to be done anyway. It taught her that she had to be on time and that completing her work in a defined period of time was an expectation she had to meet. "I had to stay on top of my duties!" Public employment of the kind Tiffany had is often the first gateway into the full-time labor force that inner-city kids experience.[13] They graduate from bagging groceries for tips into these more regular jobs and learn firsthand what it means to report to work daily, handle responsibilities, and be part of an organization.

Job corps initiatives, like the one Tiffany participated in, were born out of a desire to give inner-city kids something constructive to do in the months between school terms, a prophylactic against petty crime during the long hot summers of the War on Poverty years. But they have a much more important, albeit latent, purpose: they are a proving ground for poor youth who need an introduction to the culture of regular (salaried) work. A summer youth position is often the first regular, on-the-books job that an inner-city kid can find, the first refuge from the temporary, irregular, off-the-books employment that kids find on their own.

Larry's first experience with work was handing out advertising flyers on the sidewalk in front of a drugstore. It wasn't a popular occupation in the wintertime; Larry had to stand outside in the freezing slush, waiting for infrequent customers to come by and reluctantly accept the broadsheet thrust at them. It lasted for only a couple of weeks, for the employer decided it wasn't bringing in much business. So Larry followed the advice of his older friends and applied for a summer youth job. He landed one working for the New York City Parks Council, a jack-of-all trades position. "I basically did everything for them," he noted. "Fixed benches, cleaned the park, helped old people. You know, all kinds of things. Paint. Plant. Mop, sweep, all that. Whatever they needed done, I'd do it."[14]

Working for the parks and recreation department, Larry learned some basic carpentry skills. He also learned what all newcomers to the world of work must absorb: how to cooperate with other people, show up on time, take directions, and demonstrate initiative. Most important of all, the job gave Larry a track record he could use when he went out to look for a new job when summer was over.

> That Park job did get me my job at [Burger Barn], 'cause they could see that I had work experience, you know. They called and they got good reviews on me. I'm a very hard worker and I'm patient. All of the stuff that they was looking for, you know.

Many of the Burger Barn workers in central Harlem got their start in the public sector. They were able to build on this experience: they could prove to the next employer that they had some experience and drive. This alone put them ahead of many other job-seekers who cannot bring these credentials to bear on the task of finding employment.

The experience also gave them a fount of cultural wisdom about what employers are looking for when they make their choices. Much of the literature on the nation's urban ghetto dwellers tells us that this kind of knowledge has disappeared in high-poverty neighborhoods: young people are said to be ignorant of what work is like, of what the managers on the other side of the counter "see" when job-seekers from communities like Harlem or the South Bronx walk in the door.[15] Do they see a willing worker who should be given a chance, or do they see a street-smart kid in shades and funky clothes who looks like trouble?

High schools in Harlem and elsewhere in New York have turned some attention to this problem, by trying to educate young people about the realities of a tough job market. They pound information into the heads of their students: that they have to dress right, speak right, behave with respect and a certain amount of deference. They have to park all the symbolic baggage of their peer culture at home. Later in this book, we will consider just how much of an impact this message has had, for whether we consider the success stories, people who have crossed the barrier of finding a job, or the ones who haven't been so fortunate, we find evidence of widespread knowledge of these stylistic hurdles, and recognition that employers hold the upper hand. Decisions will be theirs to make in a highly competitive market, and one must be prepared to meet their expectations.

These very mainstream attitudes are particularly clear in the voices of Harlem youth who have had some experience with youth employment programs. Larry's days in the parks department gave him a chance to see what management's position was.

> *If you come to an interview talking that street slang, you lost your chances of getting that job. I think if you want a job, you gotta speak appropriately to the owner, to the employer.*

These are not particularly easy lessons to swallow, especially in a youth milieu which celebrates macho independence and rejects deference. Scholars who come no closer to daily life in communities like Harlem may be tempted to conclude that rap records and videos that display this "oppositional culture" represent a lived reality. Youth everywhere are attracted to music and films that glorify a separate culture. But this does not mean that they apply these "lessons" in everyday life. Even those who have been raised in poor homes, where welfare has been the major source of income, are aware of what it takes to "play the game" when you are trying to get a job. As William, whose mother is on welfare, explains, you have to learn to subordinate yourself to the demands of an organization that simply isn't interested in your individuality.

> *Unfortunately, when you get to corporate America, you have to talk their language. That's part of life. When you try to get into something, you have to become a part of that organism. You can't go into it being who you are. Once you are in it you can be what you wanna be. But in order to be in it . . . you gotta become a part of it. How you dress, how you speak, how you present yourself.*

If you aren't willing to pay attention to how your image will "hit" an employer, you won't get the job. The expectations that count are the ones held by the person who has the power to say yes or no to a job-seeker. And that person is probably going to have different tastes in clothing, hairstyles, and diction than the average youth looking for work. These are the unwritten rules of job-hunting that William absorbed a long time ago.

He didn't need to adhere to them too closely when he was in the summer youth program, because he did not have to squeeze through a bottleneck of job-seekers. But he heard a lot about the demands employers can make for conformity, the expectations they have and insist on, and when he finally did go out into the marketplace, Will was prepared. Indeed, he is baffled by the thought that anyone could be ignorant of this screening process, and of the consequences of projecting an oppositional or uncooperative "attitude."

Once on the job at Burger Barn, William recognized how important this "cultural knowledge" was, because he saw many people flunk the test. He knows that his current boss has a whole image in her head of what she wants in an employee and that the "package" makes sense in the business she is in.

> *What [my boss] looks for . . . she looks at character. She looks at how they present themselves. She looks at how they view things, you know, life, themselves, other people. 'Cause that's important, 'specially if you are*

dealing with a public-orientated atmosphere. So you have to be able to get along with people, whether you get along with them or not.

Burger Barn's operations depend on close timing and cooperation; there are lots of competitors in Harlem, and the success of William's restaurant, amid the range of consumer choices, rides in part on the crew's ability to show people a good time. He knows that the expectations his boss has of incoming workers make good sense.

Helena, the child of Dominican immigrants who has grown up in the immigrant enclave of the Upper West Side, has worked at a Burger Barn in the neighborhood for several years while going to high school. Job-seekers who don't know the unwritten rules simply amaze her.

Some people act stupid. They don't show responsibility or interest, even in the job interview. Even if you just go to apply, you should act, you know, like a normal person. Even if you're just picking up the application. Because, even from picking up the application, they'll know who you are. Don't wear an earring in your nose. That looks disgusting. Don't wear big earrings. If you can't wear them when you're working, why would you wear them to go to apply for a job? You have to look neat, not all bummed out.

Helena knows that employers read surface signals of demeanor, dress, and language as snapshots of underlying qualities they are seeking, or, more to the point, characteristics they are careful to avoid. She knows, as does William, that you have only one chance to sculpt the impression an employer will be left with, one chance to put your best foot forward. Helena has seen people her own age fail to get jobs because—inexplicably—they seem not to know or care about how to make a good impression, not to understand that they have to "display" or perform their motivation. Helena has little sympathy for these "rejects," since she believes these rules are common knowledge—anyone who doesn't abide by them is a fool.

Of course, it is not enough for job-seekers to know how to present themselves to employers. It is not enough to look good. Once kids have exceeded the age boundaries of the city summer youth programs and begin searching for a real job, they have to have a plan, a way of figuring out what kinds of employers are likely to receive them. Having seen few people like themselves in expensive boutiques on Manhattan's East Side or in the midtown banks, most Burger Barn workers we met focused their efforts on more likely prospects: inexpensive clothing shops, grocery stores, variety stores (like the Woolworth's of yesteryear), pharmacies, cosmetic or sport clothing shops, and private security firms that provide shop guards.

Entry-level jobs in local family businesses or low-cost chains look like good targets for the "walk-in trade," or so many would-be workers believe. Acting on this hunch, Harlem residents anxious for employment stop by the shops near where they live, or the shopping areas they know well outside their neighborhoods. It takes a certain amount of courage to put your ego on the line and face the prospect of rejection many times over, especially when looking for work in white neighborhoods. And while few of the job-seekers we knew ventured to the high-couture zones of Madison Avenue, many had gone to the Upper West Side boutique strips and the midtown areas dominated by the big department stores like Macy's to apply for jobs in the less tony stores as cashiers, waiters, shop assistants, or clerks.

Given the stress involved, many choose to look for work in small packs. When Kyesha's friends Latoya and her half sister Natasha went to apply, they combed the city together. Small groups of Dominican and Puerto Rican youths—a few friends—now working in the immigrant enclave follow suit. This is not always a wise approach. It can be intimidating to employers who may worry about whether it is sensible to hire concentrated groups of young people who are friends. Managers worry that it will be difficult for them to get the attention of too large a group of people during the training process, and too problematic to keep them in line on the shop floor. Young people, for their part, often sense these concerns on the part of prospective employers, and so refrain from arriving at the same time when they apply; instead, they follow one another through the door, appearing to be independent.

It is certainly more fun to go out on a job-hunting expedition in the company of friends, and it lessens some of the pain of being rejected. Friends who are looking for work together may also be able to rely upon one another when it comes time for management to call them back. Many people in Harlem have no phone and no functioning mailbox (since landlords often take mailboxes out when drug dealers try to use them for nefarious purposes). This can make it hard for a would-be worker to give employers a way to contact them, something a better-positioned friend in a job-hunting "pack" can help with.

But the main reason groups seek jobs together, or try to land in the same workplace even when they are looking on their own, is that they want to end up working side by side when they finally land something. Having friends on the job, and making new ones once there, is a major goal for most people working at the low-wage end of the market. Entry-level positions are rarely intrinsically interesting or well rewarded. They are often routinized, are boring once mastered, and offer little variety—a daily grind not unlike an assembly-line job in a car factory. What makes them worth holding, apart from the obvious importance of the money they provide, is the opportunity to socialize, to spend pleasant hours with friends during the time when one must work anyway.

Reynaldo, an eighteen-year-old Latino, worked for about a year in Burger Barn as a senior in high school. It was his first formal position, beyond the odd jobs he had around the neighborhood, and the regimentation took some getting used to. What made it all worthwhile was the fun he could have while still getting the job done.

> It is hectic working at Burger Barn. 'Cause it's not like you do your own hours. Over there, you got to do now, until things slow down. You got to work constantly—like clockwork. But there are good aspects of working at Burger Barn. The food! You eat. There's that. Sometimes you have fun. You play around. I would have a good time when two of my friends were there. We used to play around, tried to make it fun. 'Cause it was boring. If you don't try to make it fun, forget it. You do things a little slower, 'cause you be playing around. But it's better than working constantly, 'cause you feel like a robot.

Having friends on the job helped Reynaldo pass the time and kept him on the job for a longer stretch than he would have managed if "all work and no play" had been an enforced policy. Besides, having friends along gave Rey some "cover" when he needed it—on the occasions when he was late to work or when something went wrong at the grill. Everyone needs that kind of help from time to time, and Rey could reciprocate when his friends got into a similar bind.

IT'S NOT WHAT YOU KNOW, IT'S WHO YOU KNOW

Walking all over town, calling in at every place that looks likely, can indeed produce job possibilities—but as it turns out, not as many as most job-seekers hope. Harlem's Burger Barn owners have whole closets full of applications completed by the walk-in trade, so many in fact that they cannot review more than a fraction of them, even when they are hiring.

As we will see, employers tend to cut the costs and nuisance of looking for new workers by using the social networks of the workers they already have.[16]

What this means is that a job-seeker's greatest asset is the chain of friends and acquaintances who are already working somewhere, people who can provide a personal connection to an employer.[17] Carmen, whom we met in Chapter 1, found that first connection in the form of her high school guidance counselor who happened to be a friend of the Burger Barn manager in the neighborhood. Carmen's new husband, Salvador, got his pharmacy job through an acquaintance he met at the same Burger Barn. When he wanted to move on from the Barn, Salvador knew whom to call, and the connection clicked.

Parents and grandparents who have made it their business to get to know shop managers often serve as intermediaries for their kids when they get old enough to want a private-sector job. Tamara is particularly blessed in this regard. A young African-American woman who grew up in a tough public housing project, she has well-placed contacts in the form of her grandmother and her mother.

> People in my family find jobs mostly through my grandmother. My grandmother is like the one source. . . . "Grandma, we need a job," we say. She goes to this place, she knows that person, she knows about this job, that thing. I think she knows so many people because of her job. She's been there for maybe seventeen, nineteen years. She works at the Simmons Day Care Center. She knows, it seems she knows everybody in the world.

Through her grandmother, Tamara has been able to put together a complete work biography that began at the age of eleven. Her grandmother knew the elderly man who sold newspapers in her neighborhood and helped Tamara get her first job assisting him (when he could no longer stand up to serve his customers). "I used to sit there and people used to come and pick up the papers and give me the dollars," Tammy remembers. "Rudy was very old; he couldn't walk very well. I was something like his helper. As his health started getting worse, he needed somebody just to do the hard work for him. He was always a good friend of the family."

When Tamara got a little older and needed a more regular income, she found a summer youth position and built up a record as a reliable worker. That alone, however, would not have been enough to obtain a job at the age of fourteen. Fortunately, her mother knew the manager of the local

Burger Barn, and without a hitch, she slotted Tammy into the job she has now held for five years. The manager who hired her originally has now moved on to another fast food franchise, and Tamara knows that if she needed to make a switch, she could follow him.

Being a member of a large family is a big help if those relatives have been out in the working world for a few years. Latoya has a younger sister who works as a home attendant, having moved on from the Burger Barn where Latoya works. Her stepsister's boyfriend works in a fish market. Her Uncle Scott works as a housekeeper in a large hospital. Jason, the father of Latoya's two-year-old, has a good job working for a unionized construction company, a godsend of a job his sister's boyfriend hooked him up to several years ago.

Latoya and her siblings are the children of working parents, but were not raised in what most readers would recognize as stable economic circumstances. Her father, who was a truck driver until his drinking got the better of him, was around only on occasion during most of Latoya's upbringing. He comes around more often these days because he really needs the financial and emotional support of his family, now that he is elderly and in poor health. For the sake of blood and family, he is accepted into the fold. For the most part, however, Latoya's stepmother was on her own raising her two daughters. A hardworking, churchgoing woman, Lizzy has spent her whole adult life working as a domestic for wealthy families on Manhattan's East Side. She migrated to Harlem from the South as a teenager and almost immediately began her career as a housekeeper; she has been at it ever since.

What this family tree has done for Latoya is to give her access to an ever-expanding set of contacts who act as a remote sensing system for job opportunities. Few of these positions, save Jason's, will pull a family above the poverty line. There is no real prospect of upward mobility in most of them, although Latoya now occupies the lowest rung of management at Burger Barn and could move up over time. She depends upon food stamps to get through the month and worries a lot about how she is going to pay medical bills now that she has been cut off Medicaid. Latoya remains, by all measurements, poor. Still, the mere fact that she is connected to so many people who have jobs at all gives Latoya advantages in a competitive marketplace. She hears about openings; she has people who can vouch for her when she applies for work and are critical sources of support, and, even more, essential contacts in a world where the employer has the upper hand.

From her relations, Latoya has learned a thing or two about the art of job-seeking, about the expectations of employers, not to mention some sobering messages about the limitations of entry-level jobs: the low wages, the high turnover, the difficulty of moving up to something better. For a single mother who dropped out of high school, and therefore faces some formidable barriers in the job-seeking game, this family-based social network is crucial.

Once a job-seeker has found success, he or she quickly becomes an important resource for others in the friendship circle. It is hardly a secret that everybody needs "contacts" to make it in the work world. Hence, a fresh success story, a newly minted employee, also acquires a position of privilege in central Harlem: he or she becomes someone worth knowing. Not long after Latoya and Natasha found their jobs at Burger Barn, they were able to bring their sister Stephanie and a cousin, Crystal, into the restaurant workforce as well. In earlier years, Crystal had helped Natasha get a job at a local Woolworth's. The contacts were crucial, for management has its pick of willing applicants. Since Stephanie and Crystal have worked out well as new employees, their performance helped to establish Latoya and Natasha as workers with good judgment, as assets to the firm beyond the contribution of their daily work effort. For the families, however, Latoya and Natasha represent an entirely different kind of asset: they are connections, even though they only earn $5 an hour.

Everyone in the labor force, working or searching for work, is aware that these connections spell the difference between having a serious shot at a job and wasting your time. Young people in the inner city, even those who have grown up in "welfare households," know the value of networking, of meeting new people in order to extend their reach. They learn how to network from their older siblings, from their parents, from teachers and friends, and they cultivate anyone they can who might be able to help.

Advantage clearly flows to those who are born into families where those connections are already in place, where older people are working themselves and can foster their children's access to the stream of opportunity. As William explained, he was blessed by "strong ties,"[18] who were willing to do this for him.

People in my family find jobs through my momma. Momma is that kind of individual where she can stay at a job for nineteen years. That's the kind of woman she is. Whether she like it, whether she loved it. She's there at the job. She'll ask around. She got most of her jobs through knowing people. My brother, he got his job from people knowing people . . . people

who know people. That's the best. Because nowadays, it's not what you
know, it's who you know.

As William points out, having an effective network will open a crack in
the door, even when you don't have the skills the employer is looking for.
You can learn on the job, once you work your way through the barriers.

*At certain times, you might not know anything [about the job demands].
But if you know that right person, they can pull you in and hook you up
with a job, a title, and you're in there. And you are getting paid and you
don't have to go through the procedures [of formal testing].*

He knows as well that the more education you have, the better the quality
of your network, the more its participants can do for you. That is at least
as important a reason to go to college as the formal learning opportunities that reside there.

*You network in college and these people graduate and they become the
success. And when you are down and out or need an extra little something, call these people up. "Yeah, remember me?" "Oh yeah, I remember
you. How the hell are you doin'?" And the next thing you know, "Well,
look, I'm kind of in a bind right now." "Say no more, I see what I got. Get
back to you." Two days later, boom! Now I'm sittin' pretty with them. So
yes, contacts are very important, very important.*

The job-seeking task is not generally this easy, and William himself has
not actually solved all of his employment problems in two days. But he
recognizes the importance of this personal resource and values the fact
that his friends and family can "hook him up" when he asks them to
do so.

While advantage falls to those blessed with lots of working relatives
and friends, women on welfare can also be an important asset, because
they too may have a wide range of contacts, particularly in public housing. Project administrators and counselors, teachers in day care centers
who work nearby—these are people who get to know the stay-at-home
moms that live in the projects. This network too can be an important
resource, particularly in a poor community where jobs funded by the
public sector are at least as important and numerous as private-sector
opportunities. Dana, Kyesha Smith's mother, was able to get Kyesha a
summer job working as a groundskeeper in their housing project, a job

she now reclaims every summer, added on top of her regular stint at Burger Barn. Dana controlled that vital link even though she has not held a formal job of her own in more than twenty years.

Because networks are so valuable, their members must be careful to use them wisely. Workers like Larry know very well that they have to be careful about the people they refer to the boss. A bad call can jeopardize a good worker's reputation and damage his credibility should he want to foster another friend's chances someday.

> I've tried to help friends, but they wouldn't go when I'd tell 'em to go, you know, when it was the best time to go. They're lazy, so . . . I can't be up there, putting myself on the line always. That's bringing myself down. I don't need that.

Larry trains a critical eye on the people in his own family and realizes that though he loves them, they are not always good bets as referrals. He thinks his sister is lazy and doesn't want to work. His mother doesn't work either and hasn't for as long as Larry can remember. The nose-to-the-grindstone types are rarer than they should be.

> My aunt and myself are the only stable persons out of my whole entire family. We know to keep a job. She had her job like twenty-something years. I don't think she loves it, but it's her job, and she knows how to keep it. And myself, I know I want to keep my job; I want to keep it as long as I possibly can. My [cousins] they get jobs. Then they find out there's another job somewhere else, they quit their job to go to that other job and don't have the job when they get there. They don't think before they do.

Larry would take a long, deep breath before recommending his cousins for a job at Burger Barn, because he would not want to be responsible for a "fair-weather" employee, someone bound to disappoint the boss.[19]

Michelle is an older woman, born in North Carolina, who migrated to New York as a teenager. She has had a lifetime of poorly paid jobs, scraping by as a domestic on Long Island for much of the time. For the past thirteen years or so, however, she has had steady work at Burger Barn, where she occupies a matronly role, looking after the rest of the workers, who tend to be a good twenty years younger. Over the years, Michelle has been approached by many neighbors and acquaintances for help in finding a job. She used to comply most of the time, weeding out and turning down only those whom she knew to be hopeless cases, irresponsible types who wouldn't be able to keep a job. Then she got burned by a cousin she thought she could trust.

> *Had a cousin who asked me for a job. . . . She got fired after two months. She just couldn't stay to herself; she was taking money. The general manager fired her in a way that nobody but me, him, and her knew. I said [to the boss], "Excuse me. Do what you have to do. I'm not gonna lose my job because of my family. If [firing her] is necessary, you have to do it."*

The experience taught Michelle that she had to be more cautious, that it was risky for her to vouch for someone, even someone she had some confidence in. Nowadays, she lets people try on their own.

> *Any of my people ask me for a job, I tell them, "Look, all I can do is tell you to come fill out an application. If they accept you, fine. Don't do anything wrong. Because this is where I work. Don't come here acting like a crazy and try to pretend like you don't understand anything someone tell you. Whatever they tell you, you do it."*

Taking this attitude is a risk for Michelle, because her kin expect her to help them.[20] She is dodging some unwritten rules in poor families that say you must help your own when you have a resource they need, like the ability to wield a bit of influence over a manager's decision. Michelle subscribes to this code of reciprocity to a degree and will give family and friends money if they need it, or a place to stay if they are hard up. What she won't do is risk losing her hard-earned reputation at Burger Barn, the only long-term, stable job she has ever had. If this costs her friends, so be it. And it does. By her own admission, Michelle only has two or three friends in this world. She keeps to her own a bit more because to become more expansive is to open herself to demands she cannot afford to meet.

Folk wisdom on the subject of connections is rich throughout American society. Almost everyone, of whatever social standing, realizes that the ability to marshal some "pull" affects one's life chances. It takes connections to get into the right schools or to find an apartment. There is very little in our social system that doesn't depend upon these contextual factors. Popular images of the job market rely somewhat more on the meritocratic ideal that what really matters is human capital: the skills, knowledge, and formal credentials that an individual brings to the job market. Individual qualities of this kind, we believe, guide managerial hiring decisions, particularly at the high-wage end of the employment universe, since technical abilities and professional knowledge matter so much.

At the low-wage end, the assumption has been that these things matter far less.[21] Little skill is involved. What matters is simply the ability to show up on time, be neat and clean, and to know how to work with others. Surely employers can make judgments about these qualities based upon what they see in a job application, what they can learn from a reference, or what they see for themselves in employment interviews. This is true to a degree, but the room for error (at both the high-wage and low-wage end of the continuum) is substantial. Hence employers use the information that networks contain—the opinions of workers they already trust—to cut down on the risk of a mistake and to lower the hassle factor in finding new workers. With a flood tide of applications filling up their filing cabinets, life is simpler if they can turn to someone like Larry and ask him who he knows that might work out.

The importance of social networks as a vital resource for job-seekers has long been recognized by sociologists who study the "matching process," the machinations of the market that link employers to workers. Mark Granovetter's *Getting a Job* was among the first to show in a systematic fashion that the "market" is a social system that advantages some and disadvantages others. Granovetter aimed to recast a more purely economic, market-man image of the employment system, with its relentless emphasis on human capital, with one more sensitive to the power of social context, to the importance of connections in determining who (among the many who have the right qualifications) actually gets a job. Ever since his seminal work, sociologists have accepted the idea that networks are crucial filters in the matching process, particularly for technical and managerial labor. The same principle operates with a vengeance in Harlem, because it is a buyer's market. Employers can be very choosy, and they use social networks, among other things, as a mechanism for streamlining the choice-making process.

FROM THE VANTAGE POINT of the inner-city dweller, getting a job is no simple matter, even when the national economy is humming along, graced by thirty-year lows in unemployment rates. As it happens, New York City has not seen the tight labor markets that have blessed the rest of the country. Even in 1998, when the national unemployment rate was well below 5 percent, the Big Apple labored under 9 percent, and that did not include "discouraged workers" who had stopped looking and dropped out of the labor force altogether. Central Harlem routinely posts unemployment rates that are more than double the citywide average. And although its inhabitants routinely search beyond the boundaries of the ghetto for jobs, the saturation of the local labor market can hardly be good news.

Despite these odds, Harlem job-seekers work their networks, turn in applications wherever they find an open door, and take civil service exams in hopes of landing a plum opportunity. While many come away empty-handed, thousands join their middle-class counterparts in the work world.

CHAPTER FOUR

No Shame in (This) Game

IN THE EARLY 1990S, the McDonald's Corporation launched a television ad campaign featuring a young black man named Calvin, who was portrayed sitting atop a Brooklyn stoop in his Golden Arches uniform while his friends down on the sidewalk passed by, giving him a hard time about holding down a "McJob." After brushing off their teasing with good humor, Calvin is approached furtively by one young black man who asks, *sotto voce*, whether Calvin might help him get a job too. He allows that he could use some earnings and that despite the ragging he has just given Calvin, he thinks the uniform is really pretty cool—or at least that having a job is pretty cool.

Every fast food worker we interviewed for this book knew the Calvin series by heart: Calvin on the job, Calvin in the streets, Calvin helping an elderly woman cross the street on his way to work, Calvin getting promoted to management. And they knew what McDonald's was trying to communicate to young people by producing the series in the first place: that the stigma clings to fast food jobs, that it can be overcome, and that even your best friends will come to admire you if you stick with it—after they've finished dissing you in public.

Americans have always been committed to the moral maxim that work defines the person. We carry around in our heads a rough tally that tells us what kinds of jobs are worthy of respect and what kinds are to be disdained, a pyramid organized by the income a job carries, the sort of credentials it takes to secure a particular position, the qualities of an occupation's incumbents—and we use this system of stratification (ruthlessly at times) to boost the status of some and humiliate others. This penchant for ranking by occupation is more pervasive in the United

States than in other societies, where there are different ways of evaluating the personal worth of individuals. In these societies, coming from a "good family" counts heavily in the calculus of social standing. Here in America, there is no other metric that matters as much as the kind of job you hold.

Given our tradition of equating moral value with employment, it stands to reason that the most profound dividing line in our culture is that separating the working person from the unemployed.[1] Only after this canyon has been crossed do we begin to make the finer gradations that distinguish white-collar worker from blue-collar worker, CEO from secretary. We attribute a whole host of moral virtues—self-discipline, personal responsibility, maturity—to those who have found and kept a job, almost any job, and dismiss those who haven't as slothful or irresponsible.

We inhabit an unforgiving culture that is blind to the many reasons why some people cross that employment barrier and others are left behind. While we may remember, for a time, that unemployment rates are high, or that particular industries have downsized millions of workers right out of a job, or that racial barriers or negative attitudes toward teenagers make it harder to get a job at some times and for some people, in the end American culture wipes these background truths out in favor of a simpler dichotomy: the worthy and the unworthy, the working stiff and the lazy sloth.

These days, our puritanical attitudes owe some of their force to the resentment the employed bear toward the taxes they must pay to support those who cannot earn on their own. But it has deeper cultural dimensions. From the earliest beginnings of the nation, work has been the *sine qua non* of membership in this society. Adults who work are full-fledged citizens in the truest sense of the term—complete participants in the social world that is most highly valued. No other dimension of life—community, family, religion, voluntary organizations—qualifies Americans for this designation of citizen in the same way.

We express this view in a variety of ways in our social policies. Virtually all our benefits (especially health care but including unemployment insurance, life insurance, child care tax credits, etc.) are provided through the employment system. In Western Europe this is often not the case: health care is provided directly through the tax system and benefits come to people who are political "citizens" whether they work or not. In the United States, however, those outside the employment system are categorized as unworthy and made to feel it by excluding them from these systems of support. To varying degrees, we "take care" of the socially excluded by creating stigmatized categories for their benefits—welfare and Medicaid being prime examples. Yet we never confuse the approved, acceptable Americans with the undeserving, and we underscore the difference by separating them into different bureaucratic worlds.

For those on the positive side of the divide, those who work for a living, the rewards are far greater than a paycheck. The employed enter a social world in which their identities as mainstream Americans are shaped, structured, and reinforced. The workplace is the main institutional setting in which individuals become part of the collective American enterprise that lies at the heart of our culture: the market. We are so divided in other domains—race, geography, family organization, gender roles, and the like—that common ground along almost any other lines is difficult to achieve. Indeed, only in wartime do Americans tend to cleave to their national origins as a major feature of their self-concept. The French, by contrast, are French whether they work or not. But for our more diverse and divided society, participation in the world of work is the most powerful source of social integration.

It is in the workplace that we are most likely to mix with those who come from different backgrounds, are under the greatest pressure to subordinate individual idiosyncrasy to the requirements of an organization, and are called upon to contribute to goals that eclipse the personal. All workers have these experiences in common; even as segregation constrains the real mix of workers, conformity is expected to a greater degree for people who work in some kinds of jobs than in others, and the organizational goals to which they must subscribe are often elusive, unreachable, or at odds with personal desire.

The creation of an identity as a worker is never achieved by individuals moving along some preordained path. It is a transformation worked by organizations, firms, supervisors, fellow workers, and the whole long search that leads from the desire to find a job to the end point of landing one. This is a particularly dramatic transformation for ghetto youth and adults, for they face a difficult job market, high hurdles in convincing employers to take a chance on them, and relatively poor rewards—from a financial point of view—for their successes. But the crafting of an identity is an important developmental process for them, just as it is for their more privileged counterparts.

Powerful forces work to exclude minorities from full participation in American society. From a school system that provides a substandard education for millions of inner city kids, to an employment system rife with discrimination, to a housing market that segregates minority families, there is almost no truth to the notion that we all begin from the same starting line. Precisely because this is the case, blasting one's way through the job barrier and starting down that road of acquiring a common identity as a mainstream worker is of the greatest importance for the young. It may be one of the few available pipelines into the core of American society, and the one with the greatest payoff, symbolic and material.

THE SOCIAL COSTS OF ACCEPTING LOW-WAGE WORK

Even though we honor the gainfully employed over the unemployed, all jobs are not created equal. Fast food jobs, in particular, are notoriously stigmatized and denigrated. "McJob" has become a common epithet for work without much redeeming value. The reasons for this are worth studying, for the minority workers who figure in this book have a mountain of stigma to overcome if they are to maintain their self-respect. Indeed, the organizational culture they join when they finally land a job at Burger Barn is instrumental in generating conditions and experiences that challenge a worker's self-esteem.[2]

As Robin Leidner has argued,[3] fast food jobs epitomize the assembly-line structure of de-skilled service positions: they are highly routinized and appear to the casual observer to be entirely lacking in discretion—almost military in their scripted nature. The symbolic capital of these assembly-line jobs can be measured in negative numbers. They represent the opposite of the autonomous entrepreneur who is lionized in the popular culture, from *Business Week* to hip-hop.

Burger Barn workers are told that they must, at whatever cost to their own dignity, defer to the public. Customers can be unreasonably demanding, rude, even insulting, and workers must count backwards from a hundred in an effort to stifle their outrage. Servicing the customer with a smile pleases management because making money depends on keeping the clientele happy, but it can be an exercise in humiliation for teenagers. It is hard for them to refrain from reading this public nastiness as another instance of society's low estimation of their worth. But they soon realize that if they want to hold on to their minimum-wage jobs, they have to tolerate comments that would almost certainly provoke a fistfight outside the workplace.

It is well known among ghetto customers that crew members have to put up with whatever verbal abuse comes across the counter. That knowledge occasionally prompts nasty exchanges designed explicitly to anger the worker, to push him or her to retaliate verbally. Testing those limits is

a favorite pastime of teenage customers in particular, for this may be the
one opportunity they have to put a peer on the defensive in a public setting, knowing that there is little the victim can do in return.

It is bad enough to be on the receiving end of this kind of abuse from
adults, especially white adults, for that has its own significance along race
lines. It is even worse to have to accept it from minority peers, for there is
much more personal honor at stake, more pride to be lost, and an audi-
ence whose opinion matters more. This, no doubt, is why harassment is a
continual problem for fast food workers in Harlem. It burns. Their agemates, with plenty of anger bottled up for all kinds of reasons extraneous
to the restaurant experience, find counterparts working the cash register
convenient targets for venting.

Roberta is a five-year veteran of Burger Barn who has worked her way
up to management. A formidable African-American woman, Roberta has
always prided herself on her ability to make it on her own. Most of her
customers have been perfectly pleasant; many have been longtime repeat
visitors to her restaurant. But Roberta has also encountered many who
radiate disrespect.

> *Could you describe some of the people who came into the store during
> your shift?*
> *The customers? Well, I had alcoholics, derelicts. People that are aggra-
> vated with life. I've had people that don't even have jobs curse me out.
> I've dealt with all kinds. Sometimes it would get to me. If a person yelled
> out [in front of] a lobby full of people . . . "Bitch, that's why you work at
> [Burger Barn]," I would say [to myself], "I'm probably making more
> than you and your mother." It hurts when people don't even know what
> you're making and they say those things. Especially in Harlem, they do
> that to you. They call you all types of names and everything.*

Natasha is younger than Roberta and less practiced at these confronta-
tions. But she has had to contend with them nevertheless, especially from
customers her age who at least claim to be higher up the status hierarchy.
Though she tries, Natasha can't always control her temper and respond
the way the firm wants her to.

> *It's hard dealing with the public. There are good things, like old peo-
> ple. They sweet. But the younger people around my age are always snotty.
> Think they better than you because they not working at [Burger Barn].
> They probably work at something better than you.*

How do you deal with rude or unfriendly customers?
They told us that we just suppose to walk to the back and ignore it,
but when they in your face like that, you get so upset that you have to
say something. . . . I got threatened with a gun one time. 'Cause this cus-
tomer had threw a piece of straw paper in the back and told me to pick it
up like I'm a dog. I said, "No." And he cursed at me. I cursed at him back,
and he was like, "Yeah, next time you won't have nothing to say when I
come back with my gun and shoot your ass." Oh, excuse me.

Ianna, who had just turned sixteen the summer she found her first job
at Burger Barn, has had many of the same kinds of problems Natasha
complains of. The customers who are rude to her are just looking for a
place to vent their anger about things that have nothing to do with buying
lunch. Ianna recognizes that this kind of thing could happen in any
restaurant, but believes it is a special problem in Harlem, for ghetto residents have more to be angry about and fewer accessible targets. So
cashiers in fast food shops become prime victims.

What I hate about [Burger Barn] is the customers, well, some of them
that I can't stand. . . . I don't want to stereotype Harlem . . . but since I
only worked in Harlem that's all I can speak for. Some people have a chip
on their shoulders. . . . Most of the people that come into the restaurant
are black. Most of them have a lot of kids. It's in the ghetto. Maybe, you
know, they are depressed about their lifestyles or whatever else that is
going on in their lives and they just . . . I don't know. They just are like,
urff! And no matter what you do you cannot please them. I'm not sup-
posed to say anything to the customer, but that's not like me. I have a
mouth and I don't take no short from nobody. I don't care who it is, don't
take anybody's crap.

Despite this bravado, Ianna knows well that to use her mouth is to risk
her job. She has had to work hard to find ways to cope with this frustration that don't get her in trouble with management.

I don't say stuff to people most of the time. Mostly I just look at them like
they stupid. Because my mother always told me that as long as you don't
say nothin' to nobody, you can't never get in trouble. If you look at them
stupid, what are they going to do? If you roll your eyes at somebody like
that, I mean, that's really nothing [compared to] . . . cursing at them.
Most of the time I try to walk away.

As Ianna observes, there is enough free-floating fury in Harlem to keep a steady supply of customer antagonism coming the way of service employees every day of their work lives. The problem is constant enough to warrant official company policies on how crew members should respond to insults, on what managers should do to help, on the evasive tactics that will work best to quell an ugly situation without losing the business. Management tries to minimize the likelihood of incidents by placing girls on the registers rather than boys, in the apparent belief that young women attract less abuse and find it easier to quash their anger than young men.

Burger Barn does what it can to contend with these problems in the workplace. But the neighborhood is beyond their reach, and there, too, fast food workers are often met with ridicule from the people they grew up with. They have to learn to defend themselves against criticism that they have lowered themselves by taking these jobs, criticism from people they have known all their lives. As Stephanie explains, here too she leans on the divide between the worker and the do-nothing:

> People I hang out with, they know me since I was little. We all grew up together. When they see me comin', they laugh and say, "Here come Calvin, here come Calvin sister." I just laugh and keep on going. I say, "You're crazy. But that's okay 'cause I got a job and you all standing out here on the corner." Or I say, "This is my job, it's legal." Something like that. That Calvin commercial show you that even though his friends tease him he just brushed them off, then he got a higher position. Then you see how they change toward him.

Tiffany, also a teen worker in a central Harlem Burger Barn, thinks she knows why kids in her community who don't work give her such a hard time. They don't want her to succeed because if no one is "making it," then no one needs to feel bad about failing. But if someone claws her way up and it looks as if she has a chance to escape the syndrome of failure, it implies that everyone could, in theory, do so as well. The teasing, a thinly veiled attempt to enforce conformity, is designed to drag would-be success stories back into the fold.

> What you will find in any situation, more so in the black community, is that if you are in the community and you try to excel, you will get ridicule from your own peers. It's like the "crab down" syndrome. . . . If

> *you put a bunch of crabs in a big bucket and one crab tries to get out, what do you think the other crabs would do now? According to my thinking, they should pull 'em up or push 'em or help 'em get out. But the crabs pull him back in the barrel. That's just an analogy for what happens in the community a lot.*

Keeping everyone down protects against that creeping sense of despair which comes from believing things could be otherwise for oneself.

Swallowing ridicule would be a hardship for almost anyone in this culture, but it is particularly hard on minority youth in the inner city. They have already logged four or five years' worth of interracial and cross-class friction by the time they get behind a Burger Barn cash register. More likely than not, they have also learned from peers that self-respecting people don't allow themselves to be "dissed" without striking back. Yet this is precisely what they must do if they are going to survive in the workplace.

This is one of the main reasons why these jobs carry such a powerful stigma in American popular culture: they fly in the face of a national attraction to autonomy, independence, and the individual's "right" to respond in kind when dignity is threatened. In ghetto communities, this stigma is even more powerful because—ironically—it is in these enclaves that this mainstream value of independence is most vigorously elaborated and embellished. Film characters, rap stars, and local idols base their claim to notoriety on standing above the crowd, going their own way, being free of the ties that bind ordinary mortals. There are white parallels, to be sure, but this is a powerful genre of icons in the black community, not because it is a disconnected subculture but because it is an intensified version of a perfectly recognizable American middle-class and working-class fixation.

It is therefore noteworthy that thousands upon thousands of minority teens, young adults, and even middle-aged adults line up for jobs that will subject them, at least potentially, to a kind of character assassination. They do so not because they start the job-seeking process with a different set of values, one that can withstand society's contempt for fast food workers. They take these jobs because in so many inner-city communities, there is nothing better in the offing. In general, they have already tried to get better jobs and have failed, landing at the door of Burger Barn as a last resort.

Social stigma has other sources besides the constraints of enforced deference. Money and mobility matter as well. Fast food jobs are invariably minimum-wage positions.[4] Salaries rise very little over time, even for first-line management. In ghetto areas, where jobs are scarce and the supply of would-be workers chasing them is relatively large, downward pressure on wages keeps these jobs right down at the bottom of the wage scale.[5]

The public perception (fueled by knowledge of wage conditions) is that there is very little potential for improvement in status or responsibility either. Even though there are Horatio Algers in this industry, there are no myths to prop up a more glorified image. As a result, the epithet "McJob" develops out of the perception that fast food workers are not likely to end up in a prestigious job as a general manager or restaurant owner; they are going to spend their whole lives flipping burgers.

As it happens, this is only half true. The fast food industry is actually very good about internal promotion. Workplace management is nearly always recruited from the ranks of entry-level workers. Carefully planned training programs make it possible for employees to move up, to acquire transferable skills, and to at least take a shot at entrepreneurial ownership. McDonald's, for example, is proud of the fact that half of its board of directors started out as crew members. One couldn't say as much for the rest of the nation's Fortune 500 firms.

However, the vast majority never even get close to management. The typical entry-level worker passes through his or her job in short order, with an industry-average job tenure of less than six months. Since this is an average, it suggests that a large number of employees are there and gone in a matter of weeks. It is this pattern, a planned operation built around low skills and high turnover, that has given fast food jobs such a bad name. In order for the industry to keep functioning with such an unstable labor force, the jobs themselves must be broken down so that each step can be learned, at least at a rudimentary level, in a very short time. A vicious circle develops in which low wages are attached to low skills, encouraging high departure rates. Hence, although it is quite possible to rise above the fray and make a very respectable living as a general manager overseeing a restaurant, most crew members remain at the entry level and leave too soon to see much upward movement. Observing this pattern on such a large scale—in practically every town and city in the country—Americans naturally conclude that one can't get anywhere in a job like this, that there is no real future in it, and that anyone with more "on the ball" wouldn't be caught dead working behind the counter. As I explain in Chapter 6, mobility isn't necessarily that limited, but since that is not widely known, the negative impression sticks.

The stigma also stems from the low social status of the people who hold these jobs: minorities, teenagers, immigrants who often speak halting English, those with little education, and (increasingly in affluent communities afflicted with labor shortages) the elderly. To the extent that the prestige of a job refracts the social characteristics of its average incumbents, fast food jobs are hobbled by the perception that people with better choices would never purposely opt for a "McJob." Succeeding chapters will show that entry-level jobs of this kind are undeserving of this scorn: more skill, discretion, and responsibility are locked up in a fast food job than is apparent to the public. But this truth hardly matters where public perception is concerned. There is no quicker way to indicate that a person is barely deserving of notice than to point out he or she holds a "chump change" job at Kentucky Fried Chicken or Burger King. We "know" this is the case just by looking at the age, skin color, or educational credentials of the people already on the job: the tautology has a staying power that even the smartest public relations campaign cannot shake.

Ghetto youth are particularly sensitive to the status degradation entailed in stigmatized employment. As Elijah Anderson (in *Streetwise*, University of Chicago Press, 1990) and others have pointed out, a high premium is placed on independence, autonomy, and respect among minority youth in inner-city communities—particularly by young men. No small amount of mayhem is committed every year in the name of injured pride. Hence jobs that routinely demand displays of deference force those who hold them to violate "macho" behavior codes that are central to the definition of teen culture. There are, therefore, considerable social risks involved in seeking a fast food job in the first place, one that the employees and job-seekers are keenly aware of from the very beginning of their search for employment.

It is hard to know the extent to which this stigma discourages young people in places like central Harlem from knocking on the door of a fast food restaurant. It is clear that the other choices aren't much better and that necessity drives thousands, if not millions, of teens and older job-seekers to ignore the stigma or learn to live with it. But no one enters the central Harlem job market without having to face this gauntlet.

Tiffany started working in the underground economy bagging groceries when she was little more than ten years old because her mother was having trouble supporting the family, "checks weren't coming in," and there was "really a need for food." She graduated to summer youth by the time she was fourteen, but two years later she needed a "real" job that would last beyond the summer, so she set about looking—everywhere. As a young black teenager, she quickly discovered there wasn't a great deal open to her. Tiffany ended up at Burger Barn in the Bronx, a restaurant two blocks from her house and close enough to her high school to make after-school hours feasible.

> *The first Burger Barn I worked at was because nobody else would take me. It was a last resort. I didn't want to go to [Burger Barn]. You flip burgers. People would laugh at you. In high school, I didn't wanna be in that kind of environment. But lo and behold, after everything else failed, Martin Paints, other jobs, [Burger Barn] was welcoming me with open arms. So I started working there.*

Tiffany moved to Harlem when she finished high school, and found she couldn't commute back to the Bronx. Still sensitive to the stigma attaching to her old job, she tried her luck at moving up, out of the fast food business and into a service job with more of a "white-collar" flavor; she looked everywhere for a position in stores where the jobs are free of hamburger grease and hot oil for french fries, stores where clerks don't wear aprons or hairnets. Despite her best efforts, nothing panned out.

> *I'm looking at Lerners and Plymouth [clothing stores] and going to all these stores, but nothing is coming through. But [Burger Barn] was waitin' for me because I had two years of experience by then.*

The new Burger Barn franchise was right in the middle of Harlem, not far from the room she rents over a storefront church, and it had the additional appeal of being "a black-owned business," something that mattered to Tiffany in terms of the "more cultural reasons why [she] decided to work there." She was glad to land a job, but worried that her high school diploma couldn't take her any farther than this entry-level position. It didn't augur well for the future.

William followed a similar pathway to Burger Barn, graduating from summer youth jobs in the middle of high school and looking for something that would help pay for his books and carfare. The Department of Labor gave him a referral to Burger Barn, but he was reluctant at first to pursue it.

To go there and work for [Burger Barn], that was one of those real cloak-and-dagger kinds of things. You'll be coming out [and your friends say], "Yo, where you going?" You be, "I'm going, don't worry about where I'm going." And you see your friends coming [to the restaurant] and see you working there and now you be, "No, the whole [housing] project gonna know I work in [Burger Barn]." It's not something I personally proclaim with pride and stuff. . . . If you are a crew member, you really aren't shit there. . . . You got nothing there, no benefits, nothing. It was like that [when I was younger] and it's like that now.

William tried every subterfuge he could think of to conceal his job from the kids he knew. He kept his uniform in a bag and put it on in the back of the restaurant so that it would never be visible on the street. He made up fake jobs to explain to his friends where his spending money was coming from. He took circuitous routes to the Barn and hid back by the gigantic freezer when he spotted a friend coming in. The last thing William wanted was to be publicly identified as a shift worker at Burger Barn.

In this he was much like the other teen and young adult workers we encountered. They are very sensitive to stigma, to challenges to their status, and by taking low-wage jobs of this kind they have made themselves vulnerable to exactly the kind of insults they most fear. But the fact is that they do take these risks and, in time, latch on to other "narratives" that undergird their legitimacy.

Breaking the Stigma

One of the chief challenges facing an organization like Burger Barn involves taking people who have come to it on the defensive and turn them into workers who appear at least on the surface to enjoy their work. Customers have choices; they can vote with their feet. If ordering french fries at Burger Barn requires them to put up with rudeness or indifference from the person who takes their order, they can easily cross the street to a competitor the next time. It is clearly in the company's interest to find ways to turn the situation around. Ideally, from the industry's viewpoint, it would be best if the whole reputation of these jobs could be reversed. This is what McDonald's had in mind when it launched the Calvin series. But for all the reasons outlined earlier in this chapter, this probably won't come to pass, since the conditions that give rise to the stigma in the first place—low wages, high turnover, enforced deference—

are not likely to change. Beyond publicizing the opportunities that are within reach, much of which falls on deaf ears, there is little the industry can do to rehabilitate its workers in the eyes of the public and thereby reduce the tension across the counter.

Yet behind the scenes, managers and workers and peers working together in restaurant crews do build a moral defense of their work. They call upon timeless American values to undergird their respectability. Pointing to the essential virtues of the gainfully employed, Burger Barn workers align themselves with the great mass of men and women who work for a living. "We are like them," they declare, and in so doing they separate themselves from the people in their midst who are not employed. And they have plenty of experience of individuals who don't work, often including members of their own families. They see beggars come around the restaurants looking for handouts every day; fast-talkers who walk into Burger Barn hoping for free food; agemates who prefer to deal drugs. In general, these low-wage workers are far less forgiving, far less tolerant, of these "losers" than are many liberal writers. Since they hold hard, poorly paid jobs, people like Kyesha or Jamal see little reason why anyone else ought to get a free ride. What the indigent should do is to follow their example: get a job, any job.

Ianna is an articulate case in point. She has had to confront the social degradation that comes from holding a "low job" and has developed a tough hide in response. Her dignity is underwritten by the critique she has absorbed about the "welfare-dependent":

I'm not ashamed because I have a job. Most people don't, and I'm proud of myself that I decided to get up and do something at an early age. So as I look at it, I'm not on welfare. I'm doing something.

I'm not knocking welfare, but I know people that are on it that can get up and work. There's nothing wrong with them. And they just choose not to. . . . They don't really need to be on [welfare]. They just want it because they can get away with it. I don't think it's right, because that's my tax dollars going for somebody who is lazy, who don't wanna get up. I can see if a woman had three children, her husband left her, and she don't have no job 'cause she was a housewife. Okay. But after a while, you know, welfare will send you to school. Be a nurse assistant, a home attendant, something!

Even if you were on welfare, it should be like, you see all these dirty streets we have? Why can't they go out and sweep the streets, clean up the parks? I mean, there is so much stuff that needs to be done in this city.

They can do that and give them their money. Not just sit home and not do anything.

Patricia, a mother of five children in her late thirties, has worked at Burger Barn for five years. She moved up to New York from Tennessee after her husband walked out on her, hoping to find more job opportunities than were available in the rural South. It took a long time for Patty to get on her feet; during the time she was really desperate, she turned to the welfare system to put food on the table. Eventually she broke free of her heavy-handed caseworker and landed her Burger Barn job. Given this background, one imagines Patty would be tolerant of AFDC recipients. After all, she has been there. Not so. Having finally taken the hard road to a real job, she sees no reason why anyone else should have an easier ride.

There's so much in this city; it's always hiring. It may not be what you want. It may not be the pay you want. But you will always get a job. If I can work at Burger Barn all week and come home tired and then have to deal with the kids and all of that, and be happy with one twenty-five a week, so can you. Why would I give quarters [to bums on the street]? My quarter is tax-free money for you! No way.

Or, in a variation on the same theme, Larry reminds us that any job is better than no job. The kids who dare to hard-time Larry get nothing but a cold shoulder in return, because he knows deep down that he has something they don't have: work for which he gets paid.

I don't care what other people think. You know, I just do not care. I have a job, you know. It's my job. You ain't puttin' no food on my table; you ain't puttin' no clothes on my back. I will walk tall with my Burger Barn uniform on. Be proud of it, you know.

Danielle is a little less confident, and allows that she doesn't advertise the nature of her job by wearing her uniform on the street. But she agrees with Larry that what is most important is that you work at all. What a person does for a living is less critical than willingness and ability to find and keep a job of any kind.

Regardless of what kind of work you do, you still can be respected. Ain't saying I'm ashamed of my job, but I wouldn't walk down the street wearing the uniform. . . . Guys know you work there will say, "Hi, Burger Barn." I ain't gonna lie and say I'm not ashamed, period. But I'm proud that I'm working. You know, my daughter's father . . . used to grab pigs and clean pigs all day. But he was respected for his job. I respected him because he worked, regardless of what kind of work it was. He got laid off a better job, and that was the only job he could find at the time. So he took it, and I respect him for that. Anybody who could work any kind of job should be respected. Because they was getting that money honestly. They don't have to go out there and get it illegal.

These conservative views trade on a sentiment shared by the working poor and the working class: work equals dignity and no one deserves a free ride. Of course, this means more coming from people who have stood on their feet for eight or nine hours at a stretch for the minimum wage. Virtually all they have to show for their trouble is the self-respect that comes from being on the right side of the chasm that separates the deserving (read "working") and the undeserving (read "nonworking") poor.

Other retorts to status insults are possible as well. Flaunting financial independence often provides a way of lashing back at acquaintances who deride young workers for taking jobs at Burger Barn. Brian, born in Jamaica but raised in some of Harlem's tougher neighborhoods, knows that his peers don't think much of his job. "They would just make fun," he says. " 'Ah, you flipping burgers. You gettin' paid four twenty-five.' They'd go snickering down the street." But it wasn't long after Brian started working that he piled up some serious money, and everyone around him knew it.

What I did was make Sam [the general manager] save my money for me. Then I got the best of clothes and the best sneakers with my own money. Then I added two chains. Then [my friends] were like, "Where you selling drugs at?" and I'm like, "The same place you said making fun of me, flipping burgers. That's where I'm getting my money from. Now, where are you getting yours from?" They couldn't answer.

Media attention given to the glamour of the drug trade suggests that it is an attractive magnet for kids who need money. But the young adults we met in Harlem are frightened of the drug lords and want to stay as far away from their business as possible. They know too many people who are dead, in jail, or permanently disabled from the ravages of drugs. Kyesha explained:

> *People like to down me, like this job wasn't anything, like it was a low job. Like selling drugs was better than working at fast foods. But I was like, "Nah." I never went that way, toward drugs, so I'm just gonna stick to what I do. Now they locked up, and I don't think I'm gonna get locked up for selling hamburgers and french fries!*

If you aren't willing to join the underground economy, where are you going to get the money to dress yourself, go out on the town, and do the other things teens throughout the middle class do on Mom and Dad's sufferance? Harlem families cannot provide it. That leaves the youth themselves to earn the cash to support their lifestyle, a primary force pushing them to find jobs. A young man like Brian can remain a player in the local social scene by supporting his consumer needs with a job. He takes no small amount of pleasure outdoing his friends on style grounds they value as much as he does.

It might be comforting to believe that these hardworking, low-wage workers were, from the very beginning, different from their non-working counterparts, equipped somehow to withstand the gauntlet of criticism that comes their way when they start out on the bottom of the labor market. It would be comforting because we would then be able to sort the admirable poor (who recognize the fundamental value of work and are willing to ignore stigma) from the rest (who collapse in the face of peer pressure and therefore prefer to go on the dole). This is simplistic. Burger Barn workers of all ages and colors have been the butt of jokes and the target of ridicule. Some, like Jamal, claim they don't care what other people think, but when you get to know them personally, they will admit that it took a long time, a lot of swallowed pride, to build up this confidence. The sting of public criticism did get to them.

How, then, did they manage to develop the backbone it takes to stay the course in a stigmatized job? How do ghetto residents develop the rejoinders that make it possible to recapture their dignity in the face of social disapproval? To some degree, they can call on widely accepted American values that honor working people, values that "float" in the culture at large.[6] But this is not enough to construct a positive identity when the reminders of low status—coming from customers, friends, and the media—are relentless. Something stronger is required: a workplace culture that actively functions to overcome the negatives by reinforcing the value of the work ethic. Managers and veteran employees play a critical role in the reinforcement process. Together they create a cocoonlike atmosphere in the back of the restaurant where they counsel new workers distressed by bad-mouthing.

Kimberly, a twenty-year-old African-American woman, began working at Burger Barn when she was sixteen and discovered firsthand how her "friends" would turn on her for taking a low-wage job. Fortunately, she found a good friend at work who steadied her with a piece of advice:

> Say it's a job. You are making money. Right? Don't care what nobody say. You know? If they don't like it, too bad. They sitting on the corner doing what they are doing. You got to work making money. You know? Don't bother with what anybody has to say about it.

Kim's friend and adviser, a Burger Barn veteran who had long since come to terms with the insults of his peers, called upon a general status hierarchy that places the working above the nonworking as a bulwark against the slights. The advice Kim gleaned from her friend and her manager made a big difference in helping her to see that she deserves her dignity.

> Kids come in here . . . they don't have enough money. I'll be like, "You don't have enough money; you can't get [the food you ordered]." One night this little boy came in there and cursed me out. He [said], "That's why you are working at [Burger Barn]. You can't get a better job. . . ." I was upset and everything. I started crying. [My manager] was like, "Kim, don't bother with him. I'm saying, <u>you got a job</u>. You know. It is a <u>job</u>."

Immigrants who have taken jobs in central Harlem are particularly in need of a defense against character assassination, because they are targets for the ire of African-Americans who resent their presence in a community with an insufficient number of jobs to go around. Ana, a native of Ecuador, had a very difficult time when she first began working as a hostess at Burger Barn. A pretty, petite nineteen-year-old, she was selected for the job because she has a sparkle and vivaciousness that any restaurant manager would want customers to see. But some of her more antagonistic black customers seemed to see her as an archetype: the immigrant who barely speaks a word of English and snaps up a job they may have tried to get themselves. Without the support of her bilingual Latino manager, she would not have been able to pull herself together and get on with the work.

> *I wasn't sent to the grill or the fries [where you don't need to communicate with customers]. I was sent to the cash register, even though the managers knew I couldn't speak English. That was only one week after my arrival in the U.S.! So I wasn't feeling very well at all. Black people were cursing me out, saying I shouldn't have that job. Thank God, three weeks later I met a manager who was Puerto Rican. He was my salvation. He told me, "Ana, it's not that bad." He'd speak to me in English, even though he knows Spanish. He'd tell me, "Don't cry. Dry off those tears. You'll be all right, you'll make it." So he encouraged me like no other person in that Burger Barn, especially when the customers would curse at me for not knowing English. He gave me courage, and after that it went much better.*

Among the things this manager taught Ana was that she should never listen to people who give her a hard time about holding a job at Burger Barn. Having been a white-collar clerical worker in her native country, Ana was unhappy that she had slipped down the status hierarchy—and she still is. She was grateful to have a way to earn money, and her family was desperate for her contribution. But when customers insulted her, insinuating that someone who spoke limited English was barely worthy of notice, she turned to management for help. And she found it in the form of fellow Latino bosses who told her to hold her head up because she was, after all, working, while her critics, on the whole, were not.

With this moral armor in hand, Burger Barn workers often take the process of carving an honored identity one step further: they argue their jobs have hidden virtues that make them more valuable than most people credit. Tiffany decided in the end that there was more substance to her job than she initially believed:

> *When I got in there, I realized it's not what people think. It's a lot more to it than flipping burgers. It's a real system of business. That's when I really got to see a big corporation at play. I mean, one part of it, the foundation of it. Cashiers. The store, how it's run. Production of food, crew workers, service. Things of that nature. That's when I really got into it and understood a lot more.*

Americans tend to think of values as embedded in individuals, trans-mitted through families, and occasionally reinforced by media images or role models. We tend not to focus on the powerful contribution that institutions and organizations make to the creation and sustenance of beliefs. Yet it is clear that the workplace itself is a major force in the cre-ation of a "rebuttal culture" among these workers. Without this haven of the fellow-stigmatized, it would be very hard for Burger Barn employees to retain their dignity. With this support, however, they are able to hold their heads up, not by defining themselves as separate from society, but by calling upon their commonality with the rest of the working world.

This is but one of the reasons why exclusion from the society of the employed is such a devastating source of social isolation. We could hand people money, as various guaranteed-income plans of the past thirty years have suggested. But we can't hand out honor. Honor comes from participation in this central setting in our culture and from the positive identity it confers.

Roosevelt understood this during the Great Depression and responded with the creation of thousands of publicly funded jobs designed to put people to work building the national parks, the railway stations, the great highways that crisscross the country, and the murals that decorate pub-lic walls from San Francisco to New York. Social scientists studying the unemployed in the 1930s showed that people who held WPA jobs were far happier and healthier than those who were on the dole, even when their incomes did not differ significantly.[7] WPA workers had their dignity in the midst of poverty; those on the dole were vilified and could not justify their existence or find an effective cultural rationale for the support they received.

This historical example has its powerful parallels in the present. Join-ing the workforce is a fundamental, transformative experience that moves people across barriers of subculture, race, gender, and class. It never com-pletely eradicates these differences, and in some divisive settings it may even reinforce consciousness of them—through glass ceilings, discrimi-natory promotion policies, and the like. But even in places where perni-cious distinctions are maintained, there is another, overarching identity competing with forms that stress difference: a common bond within the organization and across the nation of fellow workers. This is what makes getting a job so much more than a means to a financial end.

NEVER ENOUGH TIME

The acquisition of a mainstream identity as a working stiff is only one of the important changes that befall an inner-city youth who gets a job. He is also likely to experience a sudden shortage of time. Hours that might once have been spent hanging out with friends, relaxing at home, doing schoolwork, or just doing nothing at all suddenly evaporate. Now he has to establish priorities, decide what's important, and face the fact that many pleasurable pastimes have to be sacrificed in favor of earning a living. This is part of the process of joining the adult world that may appear unremarkable to readers who long ago left behind the glories of long summer vacations, lazy weekends, and after-school sports. But for young people first joining the workforce, time binds of this magnitude are a new experience.

For older workers, especially those with families, the bind is even more extreme. They too find they can no longer afford the time to hang out with friends and family who aren't working. Whatever time and energy they have left after the workday is over has to go into taking care of their own children and getting as much rest as they can steal (which is never enough).

Latoya, the twenty-four-year-old first-line manager at Burger Barn, and one of Kyesha's closest friends, worked her way up over a three-year period. The mother of three kids, she has a sister and a cousin who work alongside her at the Barn. All three were known to be heavy partygoers before they started these jobs. These days, the parties are history. The work is too tiring.

My boyfriend thought I was joking. He was like, "[Burger Barn]—how could you be tired? They don't do nothing. All you do is flip burgers!" I'm like, "It's hard. It's really hard work." He sees that some days I come home from work, all I wanna do is just take my shoes off and get in the tub. I wind up sleeping in the tub and have to be woken up, and he be like, "Get to bed!"

So I don't hang out no more. I mean, before I was working I was like, "A party? I'm in there. We goin' to a club? I'm goin'." Now they be like, "A party?" I go to bed at eight o'clock. So [my friends] see that I'm really trying to get into work. So they be like, "Don't mention a party to Latoya. She don't wanna go. She's the working girl."

This is a common refrain among Burger Barn workers. They can no longer keep up with their friends who aren't on such tight schedules.

They are too tired to stay up until two in the morning. It doesn't take long before everyone in the neighborhood knows it, and they find themselves outside the party circles they used to run in. Whatever time they have left outside of their work hours is given over to school, to family obligations, or to blessed sleep.

There is a hidden benefit to these time conflicts. The more workers withdraw from nonworking friends and neighbors, the more the influence of the workplace—its mores, customs, networks, and expectations—shapes them. More and more of their waking hours are spent in structured activities that have real rewards, goals to work toward. Of course, no young person in his or her right mind wants to be a school-and-work robot. The young have to find ways to have fun on the job, to gossip, steal a few minutes to look at a clothes catalog, tease the manager, joke about the rude customers, and chat with the nicer ones. When the workday is done, they have to find a way to sustain a social life, since the intrinsic value of these jobs is not high enough to justify the sacrifice of all pleasure. But given the time these jobs take up, where is that social life to come from?

The twin pressures of holding down a stigmatized job and having to spend a lot of time on it conspire to squeeze a worker's friendship circles, wringing out people in the neighborhood or passing acquaintances from school in favor of fellow workers, especially people from the same workplace. No one likes to be constantly ragged and teased about his or her job and over time will move away from the source of the oppression. The time demands of the job push the same person into the arms of the organizational culture, or at least into the presence of fellow workers. And the similarity of workers' schedules and daily experiences creates a new, natural circle of friends. Over time, then, employees begin to spend many of their leisure hours with one another. When they do go to the clubs, or to movies, or to someone's house for dinner, they are more likely to do so with someone they've come to know from Burger Barn. The more they run with a crowd of fellow workers, the more they think of themselves as belonging to the work world first. Their neighbors, friends from the projects, and acquaintances who don't work begin to take a backseat to work friends.

This is exactly what happened to Kyesha Smith. The more time she put in at work, the less time she had for her old buddies from the projects. At first they badgered her, asking when she was going to spend time with them. She tried to keep them in her daily orbit, but eventually gave up: between school and work she had no time for them. But Kyesha is gregarious and fun-loving, and when she wanted to go out and have a good time, it was her friends Latoya and Natasha from Burger Barn who became her companions. They hang out together, go to the movies, go shopping on payday, and corral their kids together for the occasional afternoon. Kyesha no longer really has any friends who are not part of the Burger Barn world. That, no doubt, is why she voluntarily turns up at the restaurant on her days off: who else is she going to spend time with?

Rosa is a Dominican student who works in a restaurant in the middle of a Latino neighborhood on Manhattan's far Upper West Side. She lives with her mother and some of her siblings; her father and the rest of the family are still in Santo Domingo, hoping to emigrate in the next few years. Her very first job was at Burger Barn in midtown, a job she held for nine months while she was a junior in high school. She went to school and then commuted down to the business district, worked from 4:00 p.m. until 10:30 at night, and then collapsed. It was hard to fit her homework in, but Rosa soldiered on until she got so tired she quit work. But the pressure to earn money was still there, so she took a job at a children's store in the Bronx and thereafter at a supermarket in the Dominican neighborhood near where she lived.

When that job petered out, Rosa fell back on the experience she had already compiled and found a job at a new Burger Barn that opened in her neighborhood, thus eliminating the commute and putting her in the middle of a business where most of the other workers were Dominicans as well. Rosa found this a fine trolling ground for new friends, but it gradually put some distance between her and the kids she had been hanging out with before.

> *I like working at Burger Barn because I work with people of my own race. . . . You know, working there we always hang out, we go out together. . . . There is a sense of unity. When we go out, we go out together, the managers, the assistant manager, all of them.*

> **Do you think your circle of friends has changed since you started working at Burger Barn?**
> *Yes, because I have three different kinds of friends. The friends in Santo Domingo. My friends of four years, since I arrived here. And since I started working at Burger Barn, I'm almost always with people from the restaurant. With the guys and the girls. I've neglected my other friends a little; they've gotten jealous.*

They said something to you?
Yes. They've told me, "Oh, because you're working there you've forgotten about us."

Tiffany does not like her job. It is a dull routine for her, more of a means to a financial end than anything else. But precisely because the job is no picnic, Tiffany looks to pass the time by having as much fun as she can with friends in the workplace. Over time these joking relations have developed into friendships that transcend the job.

When you get away from the hard, cold business ethos, that "Oh, we have to make money," we can just go with the flow and enjoy what we are doing. Then the job is fun, and you still make money. You make it fun for yourself. Most employees get together pretty often—we get along pretty good. People always have their cliques and remain in them. We do things for entertainment outside the restaurant. I've gone out shopping with some of the girls from the job. We spend time together, maybe a movie, clubs.

For Antonia, who came to New York from Santo Domingo, the possibility of making a social circle out of people from work was a godsend. As a non-English-speaker and a new immigrant, she suffered from an isolation reinforced by her role as a housewife. Few of her friends from the Dominican Republic had moved to the neighborhood where she lived. She knew almost no one and spent the whole day looking after her kids. But her sister and brother, both younger, finally landed jobs at Burger Barn and helped her get one as well. She found plenty of Dominican friends on the shop floor.

I've been working at Burger Barn for a little more than a year now. The best thing that's happened there is that almost all my friends—no, all my friends—are from work. Other than work, I don't have any more friends. I've met everyone I know there.

As time spent in the workplace increases, and the mix of one's social acquaintances shifts toward other employees, work culture comes to dominate the rest of life. The rhythm of the workday, the structure it imposes, the regularity of obligations and expectations, become second nature. Other people depend upon you; an organization requires you, and being on time matters. What recedes from view is the more irregular, episodic culture of the neighborhood and the streets. Working people gradually leave those less ordered worlds for the more predictable, more demanding, and, in the long run, more rewarding life of a wage earner. This is as true for the long-term fast food worker as it is for the claims processor at an insurance company or a nurse's assistant. There are, of course, more skills, greater future prospects, and certainly more money wrapped up in those other careers. But what all three jobs share is a regular structure, a structure that comes to set the parameters for most other aspects of life—including leisure, family, and time alone.

The dominance of work culture reinforces the division between the working man and woman and those among their acquaintances who do not work. It causes them to pull away from people who don't share their schedules, their problems, and, in time, their way of looking at the world. Indeed, as I have shown earlier, this separation can proceed to the point where workers in some of the most stigmatized occupations (like food service) identify more powerfully with other wage-earners than they do with people they've known for years who are not part of the labor force. And while most of those "nonworking" people are also working in a sense, taking care of little children or elderly people who need them, most fast food workers also know a fair number of people who are embedded in the underground economy as dealers or runners. The further Burger Barn workers sink into their jobs, the more they pull away from the negative elements in their environment and distinguish themselves in every respect from the friends and acquaintances who have taken a wrong turn in life.

Tamara provides a good example of the way in which working youth pull away from the bad apples in their environment as the grip of work culture tightens around them. Tammy grew up in a tough part of Harlem, surrounded by boarded-up row houses and broken glass on the sidewalk. Most of the folks in her neighborhood were looking for work, but relatively few had steady jobs. To have regular employment was to be an object of envy on Tamara's block.

> *Everybody there, on the block, did not have a job. It was a big thing to have a job, you understand. People would look at me [when I started working at Burger Barn], "Oh! She's goin' out to work!" 'Cause everybody just sat and gossiped about everybody else.*

Tammy was one of the lucky ones who did find work, mostly thanks to the intervention of her mother's best friend, who was the manager of a

Burger Barn. Most people in Tamara's neighborhood didn't have these connections and didn't find it so simple to get a job.

Kids on her block looked up to those with money, cars, and nice clothes, people with visible means. Some of them happened to be drug dealers, while others came by their solvency legitimately. Everyone on the block had to choose which means to glory was worthy of admiration. Tamara's own hard work tipped her in the direction of the working man.

Malcolm was one of the people in the neighborhood who had a good job. He owned a game room, owned the building it was in. He drove a nice car and he was building a laundromat next to the game room. That's where I used to sell newspapers. Malcolm always gave to the block. We would come in there sometime, the kids didn't have money, and he'd put quarters in for them. Or one day he'd say, "Giving out free cheeseburgers today." Yes! And you'd come in and get your cheeseburger. He always gave. All of us who grew up, all the girls around my age, he made sure nobody bothered us.

There was also another guy on the block, [Harry], but he was selling drugs. He'd sell a lot of drugs, but he gave to the block too. I mean he gave free bus trips to Great Adventure and everything. He'd come into the game room and put quarters into the machine for everybody.

Malcolm and Harry couldn't stand each other, 'cause one made his way of living selling drugs, but always gave to others and was never stingy with his money. Malcolm was making it legally and he just gave, gave, gave. . . . They would try to outdo each other. People liked both of them, but Harry could do so much more.

Most kids look up to you and wanna be all under [your wing] when you have a lot of money. I tried to get under Malcolm because he was helping me out. Harry, I never tried to be up under him 'cause I knew, I . . . knew something was wrong. 'Cause it's not legal and you can get arrested for it. And I knew at that age. I always looked at him and I'd be like, "What's it like to have that much money." But Malcolm would say, "He may have more money than me, but I make mine legally."

Juan, Kyesha's ex, has had to make the same kinds of choices. Once he secured his Burger Barn job, he had to decide what to do about his friends and acquaintances who operate on the wrong side of the law. Two of his best friends are in jail. Another is dealing drugs and probably isn't far from a jail term himself. What Juan does is try to maintain a cordial relationship with these guys, but put as much distance between himself and them as he can without giving offense.

> *This friend of mine is selling and stuff like that, but he's my friend. We used to go to school back then. He was like, "Damn, you still doin' that Burger Barn shit? I can get you a real job!" I think he respects me—at least he don't criticize me behind my back. But I try to avoid him, you know.*

Drug dealers are not the only problem cases Harlem workers must contend with. At least until welfare reform began to force women on AFDC into workfare jobs, many young mothers working low-wage jobs were faced with the choice that leads either to a job at a place like Burger Barn or to public assistance. For many, there was no real choice: no matter how much they had internalized the work ethic, the costs of child care and transportation, plus the loss of Medicaid, foreclosed the low-wage job option. Until welfare reform was implemented, AFDC offered greater financial benefits—health coverage, food stamps, and subsidized housing are part of the package[8]—than these jobs provide. Nonetheless, many a young woman opts for the work world instead and sacrifices some of her standard of living in order to live by the mainstream credo.[9]

Patty has been on both sides of the fence. Her experience on the job convinced her that the honor gained has been worth the costs. But she has had to make the conscious choice to pull back from welfare:

> *I tell the managers, "I'm here 'cause I wanna be." I tell them, "This is no hobby—I'm your best employee." And I felt that way when I told them. I depend on this job. But a year ago, this was a hobby. I mean, I could've easily gone back to public assistance and got two hundred dollars more a month than working in Burger Barn. So I really wanted to be here.*

Young people in Harlem are constantly faced with choices, presented with drastically different models of adulthood and asked to decide between them. What getting a job has done for the lucky ones like Tammy or Patty is to reinforce the "right choice." For on the job, young workers are provided moral armor to be used in going "against the flow," opting for the legal, honorable, though poorly paid path in life. They join the fraternity of the minimum-wage worker, who sits at the very bottom of one pyramid—the status system that places professionals, white-collar workers, and even salespeople in Gap stores above them—and the very top of another—the world of people around them who may be dealing drugs, hanging on the street corner, or suffering the indignities and intrusions of the welfare bureaucracy. The more they adhere to the community of the workplace, the more they separate themselves from the irregular, the excluded, the despised, and cleave to the regular, the accepted, yet stigmatized.

They inhabit this strange "sandwich" world that denies them the prestige which more affluent and educated workers possess, while according them the respect that working people give one another. They can look up at those who have so much more than they do and hope that by dint of their hard work, whatever education they can put together in the future, and the prospect of advancement at Burger Barn, they might someday climb up that ladder. But most end up just staring up that tunnel, because the deck is stacked against upward mobility. And they know that people located above them in the prestige order look down on them as losers, drones who lack the brains to do any better.

Ianna finds these attitudes difficult to endure. Even within Burger Barn, where she expects some regard, she often feels that she is deemed below notice.

> It's not that I'm conceited or anything. But I don't use my brain to the capacity I know it can hold, which is dumb. But I'm very smart and they ain't just gonna pay me enough money to do what I know needs to be done. They just couldn't do it. 'Cause, I mean, I'm a loyal worker. If you need me, I'll stay. I'll do anything. It's not so much the money; management just doesn't show the appreciation. . . . As soon as you display some kind of intelligence they look down upon you like, she doesn't know what she's talking about.

Ianna has had enough of being on the bottom of the deck and hopes to get a job as a clerk with a city agency so that her occupation will come closer to the kind of status she thinks she deserves.

William knows what it is to be accorded respect, because he used to have a white-collar job in a brokerage firm downtown. He manned the copy room, doing the photocopying for the lawyers and accountants. He was making good money, he wore a tie to work, and he could hold his head up on his way down the street in Harlem. William moved from there to a big insurance firm, where he worked as a filing clerk, handling the microfiche, supporting the investigative claims division. Both white-collar jobs paid well, but, more than that, they were jobs with potential for a future. But he made a lot of mistakes, goofed off once too often, flirted with the women on the job, and lost what was then his best chance for a solid future in a decent job. "I was young and didn't realize what I had," he admits. "I had no plan, no sense of responsibility. I never looked at the job and asked where this job can honestly take me."

Moving down to Burger Barn has been a humbling experience. It has taught William about starting anew.

Working at Burger Barn is like, "Yo, you gotta relearn all that stuff all over again." You gotta learn the value of a dollar, learn what it is to be responsible. Learn to appreciate what you got, not just look at it at face value.

But it doesn't make William feel like cheering to know that he has tumbled down to the bottom of the employment system. Nobody hard-times him to his face, but he knows he doesn't carry much weight as a burger flipper. And he feels that he blew it out of his own foolishness, pushed himself down a ladder that society has constructed, a ladder whose validity he fully believes in.

Although scraping the bottom of the employment barrel is no pleasure, Burger Barn workers can look down at all the people who aren't even in the barrel and feel superior to them. Drug dealers, welfare recipients, the hustlers, the jailed and forgotten—these are the people whom the working poor see as occupying the lower rungs of ghetto social organization. Working men and women, no matter how lowly their jobs, can hold their heads up in this company and know that American culture "validates" their claim to social rank above them.

Indeed, some take on an activist or missionary role in an effort to become role models for people in their community who have fallen by the wayside. Rather than leave these acquaintances in the dust, they try to exert some positive influence over them by showing that there is another, more socially acceptable, way of living. Frank, an eighteen-year-old Dominican worker, selects his friends carefully, weeding out those people who are "goin' nowhere." But as Frank sees it, many of the young people around him seem destined for a life of hanging out. Because he can't completely isolate himself from them, he tries to use himself as an example of better values.

Today, a friend of mine told me, "Yeah, I know you busted out on the report card," because they know that I be gettin' good grades and stuff. I told him, "Yeah, I got so-so grades." But I failed one. It was like, "Oh?" Like they'd be shocked. They'd be, "Wow, you didn't do good." And they'd be concerned with why. Because I usually show them [my report card]. I try to be a role model, let them know I'm trying, let them know I'd help them out. I'll say, "Look at my report card . . . where's yours? Why didn't you pass?" I don't say, "Yo, you should do this, you should do that." Because I don't wanna seem like I'm their mother or father.

Like my friend. He used to be real good at school, when we was little, and stuff like that. He used to get awards. Not now, so I'll say, "What happened? You failed three classes. You dropping off. Not doing too good in school." He was, "Naw, it got harder." I was, "You better study, you know. Do what you got to do just to get out." And I see him going now. He is going to summer school and stuff like that.

Larry plays a similar role in his friends' lives. He is struggling to work and finish high school, a combination that is never easy to manage. "Some of my friends think I should just go get my GED," Larry allows. "They think I should take the easy way out." But that is not what he has in mind. "I want to stick in there," Larry says with determination, "and go the whole nine yards." His example has had its effect, though. His friends have started to look at him as the model to follow.

Since they've been around me, they tend to look my way. They look for my advice, they look for my decisions. They look for what I want to go through so they can follow me.

Larry's determination to finish school and continue working has made an impression on his friends and boosted his currency in a neighborhood where many young people do neither. They can sense his resolve, and this they honor.

While taking a fast food job subjects inner-city dwellers to stigma and social rejection, sticking with that job can, in the end, return to them some of the respect that has been lost. For friends, neighbors, and family members understand that it takes real strength of character to stay with something—a job, school, a relationship, almost anything. Sheer duration, coupled with the willingness to buck the tide of local public opinion, conveys a kind of individualistic resolve that is valued. Sean endured months of ragging by friends who, like him, were in their early twenties but, unlike him, were unwilling to "stoop" to a job like the one he holds at Burger Barn. Eventually they could see he was not about to succumb to the pressure to conform by giving up his job. They began to come around to the view that Sean was something of a real man for sticking to his guns.

> *I see the people relating to me better. Acknowledging what I've done. Acknowledging how I am doing and how I'm gonna be doing. So this job means a lot to me. . . . My friends say it's good. You are doing something. You're working still. You could be out there in the streets.*

Many young workers told similar stories. Their friends admit, almost sheepishly, that it takes guts to carry on in the face of so much criticism, that it is important to be persistent and hold a job, almost any job, for a long time. No small number end up asking for help in finding the very same job that they ridiculed a few months earlier.

Here too the power of mainstream ideals is clear. Americans value individualism, running against the tide, the square-jawed hero who stands against the crowd. This is not without ambiguity, for clearly we also place a value on conformity, on membership in communities of the similar. But there is a cultural subtext to which people can refer with pride when they stand alone and fight the base morals of the group. Young adults who accept stigmatized jobs experience the pressures of conformity through the workings of teasing and ostracism. If there are alternative venues to attach themselves to, like a welcoming workplace full of similar outcasts, they may respond by detaching themselves from the problematic crowd and attaching to this more hospitable group. But over the long run, they may find that they can achieve a modicum of acceptance among peers, if not reintegration, by claiming a whole new status: the individualist who stood against local pressure to conform in pursuit of widely respected purposes like working for a living.

Still, the ambiguous social position of the low-wage service worker does not completely satisfy anyone who has it. Claiming a mainstream identity as gainfully employed certainly helps to ward off the stigma that customers, neighbors, agemates, and society at large heap on people who earn very little and are under orders to be subservient. By linking his claim to an honored status as a working person, the low-wage employee pushes back. But he can only push so far, for he soon hits the wall, knowing full well that people who wear white collars to work, who don't come home covered with grease, who hang diplomas on their walls, and who can count more zeros on their paychecks than any Burger Barn workers will ever see barely rate them as in the same category. As Ron, a particularly perceptive young black man at Burger Barn, put the matter:

> You accept the fact that you're not gonna get rich. You're working, man, but you're still struggling. You're not laid back. You're still humble. . . . What makes it difficult is when you're smart. [Burger Barn] is not for anybody that has any type of brains. . . . You're being overworked and underpaid. You're making somebody else rich. So . . . you really got to brainwash yourself to say, "Well, okay, I'm going to make this guy rich and I'm just happy to be making this little five dollars an hour."

No one navigates this contradiction-filled cultural maze alone, though. Low-wage workers can do so only in the company of others who are similarly positioned "betwixt and between." They learn the cultural defenses against the scorn heaped upon them in the workplace, from concerned managers and veteran workers who have already "been there." The more they participate in this rebuttal culture, the more they are drawn into a social world that revolves around the work ethic, the company of fellow workers, and friendships that reinforce the cocoonlike quality of the low-wage workplace. Ultimately, being a member of this fraternity shifts their identities from kid in the neighborhood to worker, albeit a worker with a complex identity: part admired, part scorned.

INTIMATE TIES

Drawing closer to workmates leads some employees to develop romantic links. There is nothing surprising about this, for beyond one's school years, there are few other sources of new acquaintances than the workplace (or friends of friends). During the two years we spent working around various Burger Barns in Harlem, we saw the birth (and, sadly, the demise) of many romances and a number of marriages.

Although there is nothing remarkable about these ties in and of themselves, they do signal something else quite crucial about the importance of work opportunities for young people. When time binds restrict one's friendship circles to fellow workers, the choice of mates tends to narrow down as well to men and women who are gainfully employed. This has important implications for family formation patterns and for the support of dependent children, in or out of wedlock.

Kyesha Smith and her former partner, Juan, are good examples. Though their relationship did not work out over the long run, the fact that they are both gainfully employed makes a big difference in their capacity to be contributors to their mothers' households and responsible parents of the son they have in common. Because Juan lives with his mother, he does what he can to support her.

> *Right now I'm living in my mother's place. . . . When I started working, [my family] would be like, "Juan's making his money, so he can start helping out." My mother began asking me for money. "I could use forty dollars" [she'd say]. Whether I was spending money or not, like it was big money. So every week I help my mother out. Fifty dollars a week. She needs help with her bills. She can't be paying all the bills by herself, so she'll ask me for money.*

Kyesha is under the same constraint.

Juan contributes regularly to his son's care, bears him in mind in making decisions about his work life, and takes a strong—often controlling—role in determining how he is to be raised in Kyesha's household. Most of all, his having a child means that his Burger Barn job has taken on a whole new meaning. It is now less a stain on his reputation and more a means toward responsible parenthood.

> *I did the sneakers thing [with my money] for about a year, but right now what's keeping me at [Burger Barn] is that I have a responsibility. I have a son and he needs things too. Now I got to stay there and just take what I got. That's keeping me there. 'Cause there's been times when I've said that I want to leave. There's been times when I don't come in. . . . But then you go to look at the larger part. I got a son. He needs and I need too. You got to stay there until something better comes along.*

This is a father speaking, even though he is a father who doesn't live with his son or his son's mother.

What keeps a young man like Juan feeling this degree of responsibility for his child? Since he long ago broke up with Kyesha, it is clearly not his affection for his former girlfriend. What Juan has that so many young men in the ghetto lack is a regular job. It isn't a great job, but it is a steady one that makes it possible for him to "do the right thing." His son's mother also has a real job.

Wrapped inside this one local example is a wealth of cautionary tales and some hopeful signs for anyone interested in poverty, out-of-wedlock birth, and the support of children at the bottom of our social system. The first lesson is that young people who have the opportunity to work are more likely to choose partners out of their stable of work friends. Partnerships nurtured in this soil have a greater chance of producing support streams for children than do unemployed parents. Even though wage levels at the bottom of the occupational pyramid are too low to permit most of these partners to establish independent households and regular marriages of the kind familiar to higher-earning families, they are enough to shunt critical earnings toward the support of young children.

Second, it is important to recognize that although Kyesha and Juan had a child out of wedlock, it was their first and last, not their third.[10] Kyesha was twenty years old by the time Anthony was born, a working girl with five years of experience behind her. Juan was twenty-one, also a veteran low-wage worker. Both of them have acquaintances who are now on their second or third child, locked into what is left of the welfare system. By contrast, these two have only one child, neither is on welfare, and they are not teenagers.[11]

The bad news, though, is that although Kyesha and Juan are both working adults, their *combined* incomes—$9 an hour—would not underwrite a decent standard of living if they were living in an autonomous household. Were it not for Dana's access to AFDC and her willingness to assist with child care,[12] either Kyesha or Juan would have to drop out of the labor force. The advent of welfare reform may well unravel this arrangement, but during the time we spent together it was holding fast. Many of the immigrants in the low-wage system manage in the same fashion: their oldest relatives receive SSI, and "work" for the family by taking responsibility for the babies.[13]

One can imagine, of course, a completely different arrangement: higher wages for both, or some form of child care allowance, that would permit young people like Juan and Kyesha some independence from their kin. But such is not the case, hence the structural forces that impinge upon them (coupled with their personal dispositions, of course) lead them into separate households, distributed responsibility for child care, and joint financial contributions buttressed by state support for the care of their child.[14]

Above all, however, this case illustrates the critical importance of work opportunities for inner-city youth. Employment brought these two young people together, generated a sense of responsibility that keeps them involved in the care of their child, provided the wherewithal for them to act as reasonably responsible parents, and gave them something else to focus on besides serial pregnancies. Kyesha has no intention of having more children until she marries, and Juan wants no other responsibilities of this kind, as he has his hands full doing what he can for his son.

Cultivating a sense of responsibility is a cornerstone of American morality vis-à-vis childbearing. If it is impossible to eliminate out-of-wedlock births altogether, we would at least like to encourage, even mandate, responsible parenting. Yet much of the time, our efforts to foster it are limited to moralistic exhortations about sex outside marriage, or punitive efforts to withdraw state support from those who make the mistake of having children they cannot fully support. We rarely read about the importance of work opportunities as a means of cutting down on teenage pregnancy. Young people who work are less likely to have kids before they are ready and are better able to support the ones they do have. They are more inclined to develop precisely the values politicians and frustrated taxpayers want them to have: family values, responsibility, prudence.

They will not do so perfectly, and the expression of these values may take the shape of irregular families (no doubt as long as their jobs are so poorly paid and their benefits nonexistent). But working for a living leads to a closer approximation of these "good" behaviors than does a life on the dole, or a life spent searching for jobs that do not exist in communities where people want to work precisely so they can be the responsible parents everyone else urges them to become.

The Importance of Going to Work

Although having a meaningful, respected career is prized above all else in the United States, our culture confers honor on those who hold down jobs of any kind over those who are outside of the labor force. Independence and self-sufficiency—these are virtues that have no equal in this society. But there are other reasons why we value workers besides the fact that their earnings keep them above water and therefore less in need of help from government, communities, or charities. We also value workers because they share certain common views, experiences, and expectations. The work ethic is more than an attitude toward earning money—it is a disciplined existence, a social life woven around the workplace.

For all the talk of "family values," we know that in the contemporary period, family takes a backseat to the requirements of the job, even when the job involves flipping burgers. We are supposed to orient primarily toward the workplace and its demands. This point could not have been made more forcefully than it was in the context of the welfare reform bills of 1996. Where once Americans expected women to stay home to raise children and were critical of those who didn't, public policy in the late 1990s makes clear that women are now supposed to be employed even if they have young children. With the vast majority of women with children—even children under a year of age—in the labor force, we are not prepared to "cut much slack" for those who have been on welfare. They can and should work "like the rest of us," or so the policy mantra goes. This represents no small change in the space of a few decades in our views of what honorable women and mothers should do.[15] But it also reflects the growing dominance of work in our understanding of adult priorities.

We could attribute this increasingly work-centered view of life as a reflection of America's uneven economic history in the late twentieth century, a pragmatic response to wage stagnation, downsizing, and international competition: we must work harder. It is also part of a secular transformation that has been going on for decades as the United States has moved away from a home-centered agrarian economy to employment-centered lives outside the domestic sphere altogether. The more work departs from home, the more it becomes a social system of its own, a primary form of integration that rivals the family as a source of identity, belonging, and friendship.[16] Women like Kyesha no longer feel content to take care of children at home, bereft of adult friends. They want a life that is adult-centered, where they have peers they can talk to. Where they might once have found that company in the neighborhood, now they are more likely to find it in the workplace. Those primary social ties are grounded in workplace relations, hence to be a worker is also to be integrated into a meaningful community of fellow workers, the community that increasingly becomes the source of personal friends, intimate relations, and the worldview that comes with them.

Work is therefore much more than a means to a financial end. This is particularly the case when the job holds little intrinsic satisfaction. Those who get paid for boiling french fries in hot oil do not think they are performing a world-shattering role. They know their jobs are poorly valued; they can see that in their paychecks and in the tone of voice of the people whom they serve across the counter. But what they have that their non-working counterparts lack is both the dignity of being employed and the opportunity to participate in social activities that increasingly define their adult lives. This community gives their lives structure and purpose, humor and pleasure, support and understanding in hard times, and a backstop that extends beyond the instrumental purposes of a fast food restaurant.

CHAPTER FIVE

School and Skill in the Low-Wage World

THE JULY 1993 EDITION of *Life* magazine opened up to glossy pictures of Veronica Vega, a San Antonio teenager sound asleep over her books, exhausted from having spent a full day in school and then a six-and-a-half-hour shift scanning groceries at a local supermarket. The magazine laments her decision to work rather than do her homework; her mother complains that she is no longer performing well in school. National concerns are rising that young people like Veronica are abandoning a solid educational future in favor of short-term jobs that leave them too tired to pay attention in class, too sleepy to do well on exams.

Sociologists and psychologists who have studied the impact of employment on school performance also worry. Examining national surveys of high school students, they conclude that teenagers who work more than fifteen or twenty hours per week get lower grades, fight with their peers, have problems with their parents and teachers, and, most important, tend to disengage their energies from educational performance (and its long-term payoffs) in favor of job performance.[1] When young people are faced with competition for their time, so the argument goes, those who opt for the short-term strategy may get more sneakers and gold chains, but over the long run they will be stuck in low-wage jobs. They will be "scarred" for life by the lack of credentials they need to advance in a labor market that increasingly rewards the well-educated and punishes the low-skilled.[2] And, as the advantages reaped from higher education pile up in study after study of the labor market,[3] it is hard to argue with the view that schooling is of the greatest value for career development.[4]

Yet national studies tend to cover over the vast differences that constrain young people from different backgrounds. A middle-class student who is college-bound may well find that spending time working at Wendy's will lower her grades and compromise her future. But students in central Harlem face a far different climate and much starker choices.[5] For millions of inner city youths, getting a job can make the difference between staying in school at all and dropping out (clearly the most catastrophic of all outcomes). The income earned on the job can make the cost of going to school feasible for young people in poor families in which all the available dollars are overcommitted, dedicated to the most basic needs of housing and food. There is often nothing left over to pay for the cost of books, transportation, clothing, and the like.

But more than this, a young person in a poor community often finds that the workplace provides a strong backbone of structure that can be infused into school. As Ron, a young black high school student, explains, jobs help pay the bills, but they do even more to organize the day:

> *I go to school, I need carfare and money to get around. But the job helps because sometimes in the morning it motivates you. It motivates me because I go to work before I go to school. My head is already moving. Everything is circulating.*

The discipline that workers must cultivate—to get to work by the appointed hour, to put in the time, to show some initiative—goes a long way toward the kind of dedication that it takes to push through high school,[6] especially the dilapidated, overcrowded urban high schools in New York City. Moreover, success in one realm—the workplace—builds confidence that success is possible in another—the schoolroom. As Tamara explains, when you excel in one domain, you want to repeat your successes:

> *Having a job pushed me to go to school. And going to school has pushed me to be . . . Okay, like in my job, I feel that I'm very good. So I wanted to be excellent in school too, you know. 'Cuz you wanna be good at both of them.*

It may well be that the best thing we could do to encourage school performance among those who are at the highest risk for dropping out is to saturate their neighborhoods with part-time jobs and permit the structured environment of the workplace to work its magic on the other, often less orderly, parts of the day.

RECOGNIZING THE VALUE OF EDUCATION

Scholars writing about America's urban underclass are dismayed by the educational aspirations of young people from poor neighborhoods. They argue that the walls of despair which surround youth are so high that few can see over them to the opportunities that lie beyond. Inside those walls, the poor are said to have become so concentrated, so isolated in their misery, and so bereft of examples of success that they no longer understand the connection between school and work, between educational credentials and labor market prospects.[7] With few examples before them of people who have ridden higher education to better jobs, so the literature tells us, poor youths disengage from school and throw away whatever chance they might have had to escape poverty.

Burger Barn workers come from exactly the kind of backgrounds that worry scholars writing in the underclass tradition. They live in high-poverty neighborhoods; welfare is an important mainstay in 25 percent of their households; most grew up in single-parent homes or are presently single parents themselves; their parents are poorly educated;[8] and their own experience with education has been confined to ghetto schools that are often little more than warehouses.[9] If ever there was a recipe for disinvestment in education, this would be it.[10]

Contrary to these negative expectations, however, Burger Barn workers in central Harlem do invest in education. As we saw in Chapter 2, about half of them already had high school diplomas, and among these graduates, half again were combining school and work in search of post-high-school credentials of some kind. The half who had not finished high school were almost all enrolled in school in pursuit of that diploma or a GED degree. Among the working poor, at least, the message about education seems to have gotten through.

Danielle has five children to take care of on her minimum-wage job. Her husband abandoned the family several years ago and has contributed nothing to his children's support since. Danielle turned to welfare for a time, but she never wanted AFDC to be a way of life, and she put her energies behind that aspiration when she took a job at Burger Barn and persuaded her cousins (some of whom also work for the Barn) to help her out with after-school child care. It is a struggle for her to make ends meet by the end of the month; she still needs partial support from public assistance to supplement her salary, since she could not even pay the rent on her apartment on what she earns.

This is not the kind of background one normally associates with placing high value on education. Yet Danielle knows all too well that this is all the future holds for her if she cannot go back to school. Without further schooling, Danielle is almost certainly going to spend her working years in jobs that provide nothing more for her family than the meager income she brings home from Burger Barn.[11]

> *I'm going back to school if it's the last thing I do. My kids are gonna have something of worth. They happy and everything, but I wanna see them have some security. And I need a bank account. They need everything that makes a home. They don't have a father living there. But they need the rest of it. . . . Getting an education is very important. . . . That's the only way you can survive today. You don't have your education, you don't have anything.*

Danielle has always wanted to be a nurse or a teacher. Both ambitions would require years more schooling than she has now. Her life circumstances, primarily the need to support her children, make it unlikely that she will be able to realize these dreams. But the fact is that she has them—she knows what would make a difference in her life. And if she can't achieve her goals, she is going to do her level best to make sure her children follow a different path in life by getting an education. Her cousin and fellow Burger Barn worker Latoya agrees that you have to drum that message into the kids' heads so that they don't leave school too early (as their mothers did).

> *I try to get this into my daughters' heads. . . . Sheila, she's eight, she's like, "Well, [I don't wanna go]." I be like, "Sheila, do you know how important it is to have a education?" I wanna inflict that into her head. You know, when my mother told me [this message], I was like, "Yeah, whatever." [I didn't pay attention.] It is very, very important. That's why I want all of my children to go to college.*

Like Latoya, Patty is desperate to get back to school, but can't afford it. She displaces all her desires onto her children, whom she is absolutely determined to see eclipse her own record. She has spent hundreds of dollars on materials she thinks will make a difference in an effort to give them the skills they need.

> I got the encyclopedia, the dictionary, the "hooked on phonics" factory, language charts, math, reading and comprehension, and all that stuff. And we play school every day. And if they don't have homework [from their school], they have homework [from me]. 'Cause we read like five stories and then they take the words from the five stories and they define them. 'Cause I'm gonna have some college students. And they have to get scholarships, don't they. So don't I have to have A-plus students to get scholarships?

Patty's investments amount to a huge sacrifice. She barely clears $150 a week from Burger Barn and cannot afford to quit this job to go back to school for credentials that might benefit her. But she has knocked herself out to give her children the materials that she believes will put them ahead in school, the next best prospect for her family after the long shot of improving her own human capital.

Larry goes to Martin Luther King High School, a short walk from Lincoln Center, the heart of Manhattan's high-culture world of opera and ballet. He works part-time at a Burger Barn in Harlem in order to earn enough money to help out his family with the cost of sending him through high school. For Larry, flipping burgers is not a particularly meaningful job. He likes the people he works with and thinks of them as a "third or fourth family," a group of friends with whom he can share his problems and triumphs. But he has no illusions about what he has to do if he is going to get a good job when he gets older.

> To get a good job you need a good education, patience, and skills. You need to be able to read and write. The only way you'll be able to survive life is to get a good education. You'll get where you want to go with it. If you strive for it, you know, don't let no one put you down. If you don't have an education, people ain't gonna pay that much attention to you. 'Cause they'll think you wasted your life away. Why would they waste they time on you?

Once he finishes high school, Larry hopes to go on to college to study to be a paralegal or a court stenographer, an ambition he developed during the course of a job giving out flyers for a small personal injury law firm. To get that far, he has to discipline himself to define school as a form of work and his job as a means of supporting his schooling goals. But Larry knows full well why it is worth it to him to be this "nose to the grindstone": he wants to show that he has "done something" with himself so that employers will have a reason to choose him in the years to come.

Not everyone shares these virtuous attitudes. Burger Barn employs people like Jamal, who barely got through his GED and whose vague thoughts about college are, by his own admission, mainly fantasy. Kyesha Smith was never a good student, did not particularly like school, and often expresses amazement that she finished high school at all. Even though she recognizes the advantage higher education confers, she is not moved to crack the books in hopes of a higher degree. Burger Barn also has its share, though in declining proportions, of people who did not finish high school at all. They tend to be immigrants who signal to employers in other ways that they are worthy workers. However, increasingly the Barn turns away native-born dropouts and favors people who see these entry-level jobs as a temporary pit stop on the way to something better, a path to upward mobility more likely to be opened by schooling than by work experience of this kind. Hence one of the reasons we see such high levels of attachment to schooling within this workforce is that those who don't share it are not getting these jobs to begin with. In social science parlance, they are not in our sample.

Work Begets Attachment to School

There are a number of reasons why getting a job can have a very positive influence on school involvement. As I noted in the last chapter, the time crunch that accompanies the combination of school and employment inclines working students away from their unemployed peers. Readers might wonder why these young workers don't solve the time crunch in a different fashion, by subtracting school from the equation in favor of wages and friends. Some do exactly that. But there are aspects of workplace culture that militate in favor of making school a high priority. The most important of these is the role of managers in overseeing the educational performance of their younger charges. Harlem's fast food business owners are civic-minded—they define their jobs more broadly than many of their counterparts in the business world. They have learned that one of the most effective ways to counter the negative image of their industry (as exploitive of young people) is to visibly support school-related programs.[12] The message is not lost on their young workers. Frank, an eighteen-year-old part-time worker at Burger Barn, knows that there is an image problem afoot.

If you have students working, you have to keep them interested in school. Not have them work, work, work. And not worry about school. If [a manager] asks them, "Can you stay late [at work]?" they have to say, "Is it a problem? Is it going to affect your school? Do you need to leave early because you have homework to catch up on?" You know, managers are interested in you doing good in school. They see school comes first before the job and they want you to work, of course. But if it is going to hurt school they don't want to have a part of saying, "Well, it was [Burger Barn's] fault for you messing up in school." They want you to say, "Well, [Burger Barn] helped me out through school. They gave me time to study, plus I was working and getting paid." That's how they see it.

Minority business owners in Harlem often possess a missionary impulse. They are not saints; profit is a critical motive, they are as concerned about making money as the next entrepreneur. But if this were their sole ambition they could find other, easier places to get ahead. Instead, they choose to locate in the heart of the ghetto because it is important to them to bring job opportunities to depressed neighborhoods, to lift their own people up though the most mainstream of mechanisms: a steady job. They are true believers in the virtues of hard work and live the example themselves, yet see themselves as responsible for the well-being of others (as long as they are willing to play by the traditional rules). The provision of employment opportunities, then, is central to their mission. Encouraging school performance is a close cousin.

The business owners I came to know put serious time into these civic obligations (and indeed were expected to do so under the terms of their franchise agreements with Burger Barn's corporate headquarters). They could be found visiting local schools, where they are often featured as successful entrepreneurs who stand as models in the black and Latino communities. Squads of schoolchildren were shepherded through the restaurants on regular field trips designed to show them how the business world works. And they make it known that they consider the academic performance of their younger employees to be, at least partially, their responsibility to oversee.

It hardly matters that this civic spirit was born with an eye toward its public relations payoff. The fact is, it works. Harlem restaurateurs monitor the report cards of their charges, pay for books, and sponsor tutoring programs for their workers to help them boost their proficiency in writing. They threaten to cut back on a young worker's hours if his grades fall. They make sure that paychecks are held until after the school day is over so that kids don't succumb to the temptation to spend their cash rather than finish their classes. And some simply pay their workers a bonus if they have a good semester or get accepted to a college.

For Tawana, who has worked at Burger Barn off and on since she was fourteen, this surveillance motivated her toward greater involvement in school.

> *I don't think I could have made it* [in school] *without a job, because that was my inspiration. If I hadn't had a job I don't think I would have went to school or nothing like that.* [The restaurant] *really helped me out, because you know if you have one thing going for you, you want another thing going for you. And it's . . . like a chain reaction.*
>
> *See, when I first started* [working], *I didn't like to go to school at all. But see, my manager told me, "I wanna see your report card. If you're not doing this or you're not doing that, we don't want you here." They told me just like that. My first-period class, I was failing it because I was late. My manager told me, "Why are you failing this class?" I told her that I didn't get there on time. She said, "Well, I think I should cut your hours* [at work], *'cause maybe you're not getting enough sleep."*
>
> *They just pushed me. If I wanted to keep this job, I had to go* [to that class]. *You know, they really tried hard, 'cause they say, "We don't want you to work here forever. We want you to move on."*

Ebony found the same kind of support, or oversight, at the Barn where she worked on the other side of Harlem. Her bosses took more interest in her schoolwork than did the other adults in her life.

> *They tell you if you need time off to go get your grades together, then you stop working. Or they'll tell you to quit. And if you get yourself back together you come back and we'll see if we have an opening for you. It's not a* [blow-off]. *When you finish your grade, you come back and you can start whenever you finish.*

This purposive intervention of Burger Barn managers makes a difference, for the combination of managerial interest and time pressure works to glue inner-city students more firmly to their schools than their non-working counterparts (who sport some of the highest dropout rates in the country). The flexibility of these largely part-time jobs makes it possible for owners to shape schedules to accommodate school careers, while providing enough structure to organize their student workers into more efficient and motivated performers in both realms.

Roberta, now in her late twenties, was never particularly motivated in school. The atmosphere was a drag, the school was crowded, and teachers took no particular interest in a slightly portly black girl who often seemed disengaged and distracted. Getting a job at Burger Barn when she was sixteen did not turn Roberta into a star student. The more complicated the curriculum became, the more she thought about packing it in. But the restaurant manager kept a close watch on her report card and made a difference that could last a lifetime.

> My manager was very supportive. If I scored a high grade in a certain subject, he would give me an incentive. He would give me money. So I tried to make good grades. And I took more interest in business studies in school. I took business all four years. The administrative work that they taught me in school, the basics helped me once I got into Burger Barn. I did a lot of administrative work [on the job]. And I graduated!

The fact that Roberta completed high school puts her far ahead of the many Harlem residents who have not gotten that far and whose prospects in the labor market will be seriously compromised as a consequence. It is hard to believe she would have done as well without the structured support that the workplace provided, support that spilled back into her school performance.[13]

Still, even though fast food managers are doing what they can to underpin school performance, there is no getting around the fact that finding the perfect balance between education and work is hard. Workers eliminate a great deal of their social life, cut back on sleep, and still find themselves struggling to fit everything into a day that won't stretch beyond twenty-four hours. The balancing act takes a major toll, leaving many exhausted or doing a less-than-sterling job on one end or the other of the school-to-work continuum. For William, the happy medium has been hard to achieve:

> Sometimes I'd be so tired coming home from closing [the restaurant after midnight]. By the time you get home and realize that you gotta stay up for another two hours or three hours to study, you just don't have it in you. And then, you know, you have midterms coming up and you still

*don't have it in you, you are in trouble. So that has happened a few times
and I have to make some serious corrections about that.*

*You gotta have some type of equilibrium between the two [school and
work]. You can't really take so much for granted. Sometimes one super-
sedes the other. But in the long run you are still gonna be counting both of
them until you finish one or the other.*

Tawana experienced the same tug-of-war and found she had to scramble
to prevent her work commitment from wreaking havoc with her grades
in high school.

*I like working. I mean, you work in school, but you don't get money for it.
You just get a paper that says you completed your courses in high school.
You work and you get money for it, so I like that. But working at Burger
Barn did interfere with school a little bit. My grades went down some.
My mom was, "If you don't bring your grades up you have to quit." Then
I brought my grades back up real quick. Work do interfere if you don't
know how to level with it. But some people don't know how to level with
it. I try to put equal amount of time into both.*

Others, like Kimberly, find they can maintain some kind of balance,
but only by sacrificing much of what counts as fun among teenagers. Even
though the owner of the Burger Barn where she was working tried to help
her get to her homework, she found that the only real "solution" lay in
giving up things that matter a lot to teens:

*[My boss] took an interest. He was like, "Kim, we can give you all the
breaks. You can get the homework out [during your breaks]." I was, "I
won't be able to study in a place like this!" It's always busy. People pulling
back and forth, yelling. Beepers [timing mechanisms for the microwave
ovens] going off. Buttons going off. And it don't make no sense to try to
get out of work early, because they can't do that—they need me.*

*So I had to stop hanging out and stuff 'cuz I had no time to. I had to
drop my track, because I was on the track team. And I had to drop cheerleading, 'cuz I was on the cheerleading squad. And like tutoring after
school, like exams coming up, SATs and all that. They had tutoring for
the test I couldn't attend.*

As I pointed out in Chapter 4, there is an upside to this dilemma. "Hanging out" can be a negative influence on kids in ghetto neighborhoods, and

a reduction in loose time spent doing nothing may be a good idea. Constructive activities like track or cheerleading and, even more critically, tutoring for college entrance examinations are another matter. These are real losses that may diminish Kim's human capital.

Balancing the two demanding regimes of school and work is clearly not a simple matter. It was no easy task for poor people in past generations who had no choice but to juggle education and the pressure to earn a living. In many respects it would be easier if Harlem's young adults had the luxury that middle-class kids in the suburbs take for granted—the freedom to go to school and have a life on the side. We may as well be dreaming. Poor kids from minority families face a much starker obstacle course if they are going to finish school. While working may not be the ideal choice for them, it is probably the best choice under real-world circumstances, one that provides structure, sources of discipline, caring adults who watch over them, and a better shot at a future than is available to their nonworking friends, many of whom are destined to drop out altogether.

Getting a job can do more than kindle a desire to finish high school. A stint at Burger Barn teaches many workers the concrete importance of higher education or a certificate in a skilled trade that could lead to a job making serious money. Because the job market is so bad in Harlem, young people who may start out with little interest in school find themselves working alongside college students, college-bound seniors, and high school grads enrolled in trade courses. In a better labor market, these folks probably wouldn't be caught dead working at Burger Barn. They would have migrated to the downtown law firm or into a more lucrative apprenticeship in a local auto body shop. But in slack labor markets, these overqualified, better-educated youth are pushed down into minimum-wage jobs where they mix with agemates who haven't gone that far in school. The exposure makes a difference, for it shows younger workers a potential pathway, one that might—in time—lead beyond Burger Barn to the world of better jobs. In short, the workplace is one of the few institutions where young people without high educational ambitions work alongside (and in the same capacity as) people who are locked into post-high-school training of some kind.

You Don't Want to Be Here When You're Thirty

On the downside, working at Burger Barn, at least as an entry-level burger flipper, is no one's idea of a success story. Getting a job of this kind teaches many a young woman in her early twenties precisely what she does *not* want to be doing when she hits thirty. Most Burger Barn workers are of the opinion that these jobs are "okay for kids" and might even be acceptable for people in their early twenties. But no one, not even management, wants to see crew workers there into their late twenties—even though this is happening at an ever-increasing rate in Harlem's slack labor market. There is nothing quite like slaving over a hot, greasy deep fryer for eight hours to teach people that they need to put some effort into making sure they have the credentials to qualify for something better in the future. The fact that there are so many people who are indeed in their thirties and still working for low wages at Burger Barn means this is no abstract worry. Nearly half of our working sample were over twenty-five, and although their ranks included a sprinkling of managers who were earning a better living, this older group was composed mainly of people who were doing no better than the minimum wage.

When Tawana was sixteen she had the good fortune to get a summer job in a midtown law firm, working in its library. She answered phones, picked up mail, put books back on the shelf, learned to use a computer—a general clerical job. But this was Tawana's first experience in a high-powered professional setting—her first glimpse of what life is like for well-educated, polished men and women who work in those glass towers. The summer job kindled a desire to follow in their footsteps and made Tawana realize that to do so was going to take many years of working hard in school. The job she has at Burger Barn, which helps pay the bills during the school year, has taught her the exact opposite: what she doesn't want to do for the rest of her life.

> *If you don't get an education you can't be what you wanna be. I wanna be a corporate lawyer, so I have to get my education. All my degrees that I need to get. All the tests that I need to pass, I'm gonna pass them to be a corporate lawyer. Yeah. If you don't have a degree, you don't have an education, you don't have nothin'. You can't do nothin'. You don't have a job. Well, you may have a job in Burger Barn. But I mean you can't get a good job, good-paying money. You can work in Burger Barn all your life. What I want is a job that's gonna bring me six or seven hundred dollars, maybe even a thousand [a week].*

Tawana hopes to make it to John Jay College or perhaps to Howard University, both potential stepping-stones to that corporate law job. If she has to work at Burger Barn to make that happen, then so be it. What she doesn't want is to find herself flipping burgers when she grows up.

Tawana can look around the fast food counter and see plenty of people who have already met that fate: they are in their mid- and late twenties and still earn the minimum wage. This is the future she is running from. But she knows just what she has to do to avoid it: complete her education.

This lesson is just as clear to Harlem's immigrant workers as it is to the native-born. In fact, it may be even more critical for low-wage workers who have emigrated from countries where schools are inadequate or inaccessible to the poor. Sean came to New York from Jamaica in the early 1990s. He had grown up with his grandmother on the island and had little experience of school. During his early teenage years, he took small construction jobs, pulling down walls, carrying cement blocks, anything he could pick up to help his grandmother support him and his eight siblings. Sean's parents had immigrated to New York years before, but when they finally had enough money to send for him (and he had enough earning potential to make it worth bringing him to the Big Apple), he joined them and immediately began looking for a job. Sean's family was depending upon him to bring in money to a household that, over a five-year period, expanded to include all of his brothers and sisters.

Sean was handicapped by the fact that he spoke a deep Jamaican dialect, often unintelligible to native speakers of American English. He was also limited in his employment prospects because he could not read. He began taking courses at a local community center in Harlem to attack his literacy problem. The experience made him realize not only that he needed a lot more education, but how deficient his whole educational experience in Jamaica had been.

> When I was in Jamaica, I never went to school every day. I don't go to school. I miss all the school back home, a lot. Almost fifteen years of school. So I couldn't read. As soon as I be in New York, I start going to James Baldwin Center. That's when I started reading ABC. I been going there two years and a couple of months. It's free. They got two teaching one class, a tutor and teacher, three times a week.

Had Sean attended school in Jamaica, he might have been in a competitive position in New York. But for a poor boy with seven siblings to help support, school was a secondary consideration. He recognizes that his opportunities are greater in the United States, that he would probably have never learned to read if he hadn't left Jamaica. Sean also knows, however, that if he had been born and raised in New York, his prospects in life would certainly have been more promising. "I'll talk different," he notes. "And maybe I'd be in college now, if I was [born] here." He appreciates the fact that in New York he can improve his education, but he also knows he is paying for the accident of his birth to a poor family in a poor country.

Brad, a fellow Jamaican, moved to New York when he was older than Sean. Now twenty-four, he has found it hard to advance beyond his entry-level job at Burger Barn, for many of the same reasons. He quit school as a teenager in Jamaica and took a job in construction, working iron and steel. That kind of work didn't require a high school diploma, but in Jamaica it paid poorly. Once Brad married and started a family of his own, the pressure to earn a better living grew, prompting him to come to the United States, leaving his wife behind. His mother and eight siblings followed suit, supported on the strength of her income and eventually the earnings of all her working children. Brad pays his own way in her home and sends money back to Jamaica twice a month to support his family. But his lack of education means that he has little prospect of moving up the ladder to better jobs. He knows he is going to have to work with his hands all his life. Clearly, if he had gone further in school he would have an easier time.

> *When you have a good education you don't have to work that hard. A guy who don't have a good education, he have to work real hard. Even though the guy with an education, he work hard too with his brain and stuff. But the guy without an education, he gotta go live for a wage. . . . And without an education, you always in trouble to get a job. I'd rather be in school [than work at Burger Barn] because I need an education. After I graduated from school, I wouldn't gotta be worried about jobs.*

Brad has tried to combine school and work by taking a night job on top of his day classes, but he found the combination too difficult, especially because he was so far behind his American counterparts in school. His experience typifies that of many immigrants who landed in the United States with adult obligations in place. Younger arrivals, or those who have not yet established families, can take advantage of English classes, GED diplomas, literacy centers, and other means of improving their qualifications. It is possible, but much harder, for established adults to do so. They are often locked inside the low-wage economy and can advance only so far as their good fortune inside the immigrant enclave economy will take them.

Fast Food as Financial Aid

Low-wage jobs are crucial sources of financial aid for young people looking to stay in school, whether high school or college. Once their parents cover the rent and food, little remains in many of these households for books or transportation to a community college. Discretionary expenses have to be kept to a minimum, including school expenses that most middle-class parents would expect to provide as a matter of course for their children. Financial aid, a staple of well-informed and relatively well-off college students, is not available for high school kids (who face expenses like lab fees, field trips, subway fares, clothing, and the like) and cannot cover full living expenses for older students enrolled in junior college.

Hence the pressure falls on the backs of young people to fund their own educational endeavors. And that is precisely what Burger Barn workers who are enrolled in school are doing with their earnings: they are paying their own way. Karen lives in the South Bronx, one of New York's notoriously run-down communities. Her mother is on welfare and they live in public housing. Karen has been working since she was fourteen years old. She had been picking up a few dollars as a baby-sitter for the wife of a Burger Barn manager and was able to parlay this contact into a real job before she was really "legal."

Once Karen began at the Barn, she could then relieve her mother of at least the marginal expenses of her presence in the household, and on occasion she could go one step further and contribute to the household pot for the basic family budget. By the time we met, Karen had logged almost six years at various Burger Barns, ending up in one on Harlem's western edge, a thirty-minute bus ride from her home. She was now enrolled in college on a scholarship, coming back to the Barn during her vacations to earn money to use in school for the next term.

> Burger Barn is flexible. You get paid every week. And since I'm going to college now, when I come home for the week-and-a-half vacation, two weeks, that's when the flexibility really matters. I can ask the owner to write out a personal check in case I'm going back to school; he'll give me my pay a few days earlier.

There is no way that Karen's mother could afford to give her the money to pursue her educational dreams. But between Karen's earnings, her scholarship, and loans, she is moving out of the ghetto and into an entirely different set of possibilities.

Ianna has been working at Burger Barn for two years, throughout the time she has been attending a technical college in Brooklyn, where she is in a management course. If Ianna had her way, she would be in school full-time without the burden of working. Instead, she has to balance her time between school and work, because that is the only way school is going to happen at all.

> *I don't want to work—I fear that if I work I might be setting myself up to fail [in school]. But then again, I don't have any other money. I mean, I'm gonna get financial aid. But I need clothes, I need to buy books and supplies. And transportation is a killer, that alone. And I need to eat, you know, lunch money, stuff like that. So it's rough . . . but I've gotta work and study.*

Ianna's biography has put her in the position of having no choice but to look after herself and seek the best foundation for an adult life.

> *My mother died when I was young. Me and my father, we get along, but only every now and then. . . . He doesn't support me now. And I know that going to school is the only way that is going to secure my future. So that's why I work and go to school at the same time.*

Were it not for her Burger Barn job, it is unlikely that Ianna would be in school at all.

Tomas was born in the Dominican Republic, lived for a time in Puerto Rico, and came to New York as a young teenager. His parents were both well educated and worked as professionals in agricultural engineering and nursing before they arrived in the United States. Immigration cost them their professional status; they were unable to continue working in their chosen fields once they made the decision to stay in New York. Tomas started in a Puerto Rican iron foundry when he was just twelve, and thereafter put his time in packing broken watches into boxes in a Seiko factory when he was in high school. These were good jobs by local standards, but the promise of higher wages and a better standard of living sent him to the mainland, and he joined his aunt and uncle in the Bronx. He was under immediate pressure to find a job in New York, and so at seventeen took himself down to the shopping district in midtown

Manhattan and landed a job at Burger Barn. His limited English handicapped him from the start; in the three months he worked in that store he learned almost nothing.

Fortunately, he was able to use local contacts in the Dominican neighborhood where his relatives lived to get a new job at a Burger Barn owned by Dominicans on the far Upper West Side. There language was less of a barrier and Tomas quickly climbed up to the first rank of management. At nineteen, he has set his sights on a college degree to be financed by his earnings at Burger Barn.

This job is important to me, because it means I make my own money. But for now what is really important to me is college. So Burger Barn is really at a secondary level. First is college. What I really want, while I'm studying, is to continue to work at the Barn. Because I like my job and it's not very demanding. So while it's there and I can do it . . . I'll keep doing it.

Tomas's family cannot afford to pay for his college education. But with his assistant manager's job, he can fund it himself. Burger Barn has become a way station for him, not a career goal—just a place to make some money that will further his real ambitions.

School is not a guaranteed salvation. As the rates of high school completion have grown in many of the nation's urban areas (partly in response to declining job opportunities), the payoff to a diploma has declined.[14] While being a high school dropout is clearly a one-way ticket to occupational oblivion, having the sheepskin provides only a minimally better chance at a decent job. Burger Barn's younger workers are all too aware that pursuing an education is, at best, a hedge. They know too many people who have diligently applied themselves in school, earning degrees, only to find themselves stranded in the labor market anyway. Ianna's cousin got a bachelor's degree in economics and has had trouble landing a job. Juan has his high school diploma and discovered it wasn't enough.

Sometimes not even a diploma helps. 'Cause I got my diploma, but I don't got no experience [other than Burger Barn]. [Companies] hire you for the experience, not just because you got that diploma. I know people who have good jobs. They come to me and say, "Damn, you at Burger Barn and you have a diploma. Why are you still here?" I say that it's not like that. . . . A diploma is just a piece of paper. So basically the trick is getting that experience and having that diploma.

It is a sad fact that for many young workers, the more education they have, the more they come to understand the limits of their prospects. In a world arrayed in layers of privilege, Harlem's workers usually find themselves at the bottom of the heap. They look with envy downtown, toward the gleaming buildings of Stuyvesant High School, a highly selective public academy for the city's most gifted students, built for $30 million, with a view of the Statue of Liberty. In their own neighborhoods, they see schools ringed by metal detectors, with slits of windows covered with wrought iron so that virtually no natural light penetrates. In these schools, the ceilings are rotting through, police cars are posted outside when the last bell rings, and classes are packed so tight that invariably four or five students have no desks.

When they soldier on and graduate from high school, the wise ones among them begin to realize just how long is the line that stretches ahead of them, how crowded the job market is, and how students who went to Stuyvesant are likely to ace them out in the competition. Adults like William recognize that the diplomas they have struggled hard to achieve may confer very little advantage.

Nowadays a basic education is almost obsolete. When I was growing up in the seventies all you needed was basically a high school diploma and you would do just fine. If you had a bachelor's degree, you were the man. A master's, you were the epitome. Nowadays you need a Ph.D. just to break even. And a master's just says you tried extra hard. That's about it.

William is not arguing that education is a waste of time. He realizes that anyone who stops short of high school has no chance of a decent work life, but high school graduates should understand that they are unlikely to escape the clutches of the low-wage labor system. "You have a high school diploma," he nods sagely, "you may as well stay at Burger Barn, 'cause that's as far as you gonna go unless you get lucky and know somebody."

Accruing Human Capital on the Job

While schooling separates those destined for good jobs from those likely to spend their lives in the low-wage world, entry-level positions in industries like fast food do provide opportunities for learning, for developing skills that should make a difference in occupational mobility. This, of course, is hardly what "McJobs" are known for. Indeed, when journalists want to call upon an image that connotes a deadening, routinized, almost "skill-free" job, they routinely invoke the fast food burger flipper as the iconic example.

Writers interested in championing the cause of the de-skilled worker have also contributed to this image problem. Barbara Garson, writing about McDonald's in *The Electronic Sweatshop*,[15] lambastes the nation's largest fast food employer for dumbing down the jobs to the point where, she argues, a mindless idiot could do the work. Garson interviewed a handful of crew members in a Massachusetts McDonald's and concluded that there is no skill left in the job; human judgment has been entirely replaced by a deadening regime of preset oven timers and blinking lights, the kind of monotonous routine that would send any worker with half a brain running for the door. Indeed, that appears to be exactly how Jason Pratt, a former McDonald's employee Garson interviewed, saw his predicament:

> *You don't have to understand. You follow the beepers, you follow the buzzers, and you turn your meat as fast as you can. It's like I told you, to work at McDonald's you don't need a face, you don't need a brain. You need to have two hands and two legs and move 'em as fast as you can. That's the whole system. I wouldn't go back there again for anything.*

Garson recounts the history of the McDonald's french fry machine, one of the first computerized pieces of cooking equipment. McDonald's brass were searching for a way to guarantee uniformity in the production of fries by reducing the human judgment (of color and texture as a measure of the finished product). They installed computers in the fry vats and automated the decision-making right out of the whole process. This tells Garson that a monkey could be taught to run the fry machine and that the whole future of the American workplace is in danger of becoming a brave new world of skillfree computerized assembly lines where no one needs to think because mean-spirited management finds it more convenient, and cheaper, to employ brain-dead workers.

No one can dispute the fact that computers have become important production tools, even in service industries like fast foods. They do indeed routinize much of the cooking process. But if one pays attention to what goes on behind the scenes at Burger Barn, one can see that there is a lot more to the job than Garson suggests. A close observer on the shop floor, as orders delivered across a bustling counter space turn into stacks of hot food in the space of three minutes, finds that it's not that easy.

Contrast Garson's account of working at McDonald's with one of the many episodes recorded by my graduate student Eric Clemons, who valiantly essayed the job of a crew member in order to learn firsthand what kind of demands the work poses:[16]

> *Déjà vu; it was chaos once again at work today. Several no-shows: Anthony was not there, the manager was off for the day, Harry clocked out, Fernando snuck away, and it became evident very quickly that there was no way I was to be formally trained. So . . . I began to help Candace make burgers. She assumed the role of "super worker" that Juan had handled three days before. The orders were flying and Candy and I went to work. We were the only two working all stations [except the fries] during my entire time there. Michelle came back occasionally to help us, though she had her hands full up front.*

After just two hours of this regimen, Eric collapsed in a frazzled heap. A regular crew member may have to work at this pace for an eight-hour shift and forgo breaks if replacement help does not arrive. The only way a worker can function in such a setting is to master the entire repertoire of tasks that are normally divided up: cooking five different kinds of burgers, fish, and chicken sandwiches and a variety of new entrants to the fast food menu (breakfasts, burritos, salads, etc.). Each procedure is somewhat tailored, requiring different temperature settings, different assembly processes, different storage rules, and the like. While it might be possible for an automaton to perform any one of these tasks, it takes a more flexible creature to handle them all simultaneously, with half the number of people who ought to be there to handle the flow, and do so without making mistakes that violate state laws on food preparation. Management makes quality-control checks at random throughout the day, and workers who flunk them get into trouble, as Eric found out.

> *The manager noticed that I was preparing the fish sandwiches incorrectly. He criticized my trainer for not monitoring my work. I was not putting enough tartar sauce on the sandwiches, too much cheese, and the bun order in the warmer was incorrect. So he got on Juan and Reynaldo for not keeping me in check. Turns out that the half slice of cheese was broken and not cut as it should be. Juan told me later that though the cheese was required to be cut with a knife, it was routinely broken by hand instead because there was no knife and the spatula was usually being used to make burgers.*

Understanding the rules, and then understanding the "work-arounds" that crew members devise to get out from under the rules, is a big part of what it takes to fit into the work routine. New workers have to learn the difference between the canonical preparation process and the informal practices that most people resort to in order to get the job done.

They must do so in the midst of a confusing atmosphere that only occasionally slows to a dull roar. At rush hour, information is being passed along from the order-taker to the people who fill orders; people are moving at rapid speed in coordination with one another; those timers and buzzers have to be set so that they come out in a coordinated fashion; the machinery breaks down and workers have to improvise to get the orders out; six or seven different production processes must fit together so that the elements of an order are ready at the same time; the room for error is minimal, and the customers are tapping their feet and expect to wait no more than a minute or two. William conveys the harried life of the "grill man" at a Burger Barn in New York's midtown retail district:

> *They had a sale . . . buy one burger and get another for twenty-five cents. It was in a midtown store, so you got all those businesses, and they was on the jump. You come in and you see nothing but burgers from the floor to the ceiling. They put me on the grill by myself, a grill they designated just for the sale business. And I tore it up. Now to help you appreciate it, it's kind of like . . . you are laying out meat, and you are trying to dress buns. You putting sauce and lettuce and onions and pickles and all that good stuff that the burger goes with. And all that is speed. The meat takes about two minutes and thirty seconds to cook. So you had [that time] not only to take the meat out and put it on the grill. You gotta sear it, turn it over, season it. You also got to go to the table. You gotta take the buns out. You gotta separate them. You gotta dress the buns. You gotta run over before the timer goes off. And if you are turning late, that means that you have more, two to four sets of meat on the grill. Sets of twelve. And you doing all this all at the same time.*

William was exhausted by the sale, but elated as well. Everything worked. Everyone worked together. They met a challenge.

> *As far as us working together, it was a team. It was cool. It was fact, actually. Everybody understood what everybody was doing. Everyone backed up everyone. So it wasn't no thing where you do what you [are assigned] to do.*

Supply and demand have to be carefully calibrated in these restaurants: there must be enough food ready to go into the microwave or the deep fryer so that orders can be filled quickly, but not so much as to generate excess. Strict regulations govern the length of time a burger can sit on the shelf, and miscalculations produce wastage. These businesses operate under tight margins, so waste is frowned upon: food thrown away is potential profit deducted from the owner's pocket. The only way to keep overproduction under control is to accurately forecast demand through the hours of the day and night, information that has to be formulated and monitored by the workers.

A good crew member knows that crowds of people will begin showing up at about 11:15 a.m. and will keep flowing through the door until about 2:00, when the lunch hour rush is over. During those peak periods, more patties have to be ready to go, more fries have to hit the vats of oil, and people have to be on their toes ready to man the grills. The rush subsides until about 4:30, when the dinner traffic begins to dribble in, sparking another crush that may last as late as 8:00 during the week, and 9:30 or 10:00 on a Saturday night. On Friday afternoons, when the schools let out, a minor rush will crop up as kids make their way toward home and stop into Burger Barn for a snack. In neighborhoods near parochial schools, a goodly portion of the Friday demand will be for fish sandwiches, reflecting the culinary tradition of a meatless Friday in New York's Catholic neighborhoods. A mini-anthropology of local food customs is essential to running a tight restaurant, for these practices shape the demand, a demand that has to be fairly well understood if burgers are to be ready fast, without too many left sitting on the shelf.

When business is booming and the burgers are practically flying off the grill, the workers have to be able to move quickly to back one another up, to meet unexpected demand that may require more people to man the grill, more to work the cash registers. It helps a great deal if the crew members can read one another's mind, move in to help out in dressing the buns and setting the timers without being told that their attention is needed. And the personal style of each individual is sufficiently distinct that new pairings of workers (who happen to show up on the same shift) require a certain amount of adjustment on the part of both. Without this kind of choreography, a smooth operation is impossible to maintain in peak hours. Anything less irritates customers, who can vote with their feet; hence management and the workforce develop a craft ethic, a pride in their ability to meet the challenge of a heavy workload without skipping a beat.

Elise has worked the "drive-through" window at Burger Barn for the better part of three years. She is a virtuoso in a role that totally defeated one of my brightest doctoral students, who tried to work alongside her for a week or two. Her job pays only 25 cents above the minimum wage (after five years), but it requires that she listen to orders coming in through a speaker, send out a stream of instructions to coworkers who are preparing the food, pick up and check orders for customers already at the window, and receive money and make change, all more or less simultaneously. She has to make sure she keeps the sequence of orders straight so that the Big Burger goes to the man in the blue Mustang and not the woman right behind him in the red Camaro who has now revised her order for the third time. The memory and information-processing skills required to perform this job at a minimally acceptable level are considerable. Elise makes the operation look easy, but it clearly is a skilled job, as demanding as any of the dozen better-paid positions in the Post Office or the Gap stores where she has tried in vain to find higher-status employment.

This is not to suggest that working at Burger Barn is as complex as brain surgery. It is true that the component parts of the ballet, the multiple stations behind the counter, have been broken down into the simplest operations. Yet to make them work together under time pressure while minimizing wastage requires higher-order skills. We can think of these jobs as lowly, repetitive, routinized, and demeaning, or we can recognize that doing them right requires their incumbents to process information, coordinate with others, and track inventory. These valuable competencies are tucked away inside jobs that are popularly characterized as utterly lacking in skill.

If coordination were the only task required of these employees, then experience would probably eliminate the difficulty after a while. But there are many unpredictable events in the course of a workday that require some finesse to manage. Chief among them are abrasive encounters with customers, who, as we saw in the last chapter, often have nothing better to do than rake a poor working stiff over the coals for a missing catsup packet or a batch of french fries that aren't quite hot enough. One afternoon at a Burger Barn cash register is enough to send most sane people into psychological counseling. It takes patience, forbearance, and an eye for the long-range goal (of holding on to your job, of impressing management with your fortitude) to get through some of these encounters. If ever there was an illustration of "people skills," this would be it.

Coping with rude customers and coordinating the many components of the production process are made all the more complex by the fact that in most Harlem Burger Barns, the workers hail from a multitude of countries and speak in a variety of languages. Monolingual Spanish speakers fresh from the Dominican Republic have to figure out orders spoken in Jamaican English. Puerto Ricans, who are generally bilingual, at least in the second generation, have to cope with the English dialects of African-Americans. All of these people have to figure out how to serve customers who may be fresh off the boat from Guyana, West Africa, Honduras. The workplace melting pot bubbles along because people from these divergent groups are able to come together and learn bits and snatches of each other's languages—"workplace Spanish" or street English. They can communicate at a very rudimentary level in several dialects, and they know enough about each other's cultural traditions to be able to interpret actions, practices, dress styles, and gender norms in ways that smooth over what can become major conflicts on the street.

In a world where residential segregation is sharp and racial antagonism no laughing matter, it is striking how well workers get along with one another. Friendships develop across lines that have hardened in the streets. Romances are born between African-Americans and Puerto Ricans, legendary antagonists in the neighborhoods beyond the workplace. This is even more remarkable when one considers the competition that these groups are locked into in a declining labor market. They know very well that employers are using race- and class-based preferences to decide who gets a job, and that their ability to foster the employment chances of friends and family members may well be compromised by a manager's racial biases. One can hear in their conversations behind the counter complaints about how they cannot get their friends jobs because—they believe—the manager wants to pick immigrants first and leave the native-born jobless.[17] In this context, resentment builds against unfair barriers. Even so, workers of different ethnic backgrounds are able to reach across the walls of competition and cultural difference.

We are often admonished to remember that the United States is a multicultural society and that the workforce of the future will be increasingly composed of minorities and foreigners. Consultants make thousands of dollars advising companies on "diversity training" in order to manage the process of amalgamation. Burger Barn is a living laboratory of diversity, the ultimate melting pot for the working poor. They live in segregated spaces, but they work side by side with people whom they would rarely encounter on the block. If we regard the ability to work in a multiethnic, multilingual environment as a skill, as the consulting industry argues we should, then there is much to recommend the cultural capital acquired in the low-wage workplaces of the inner city.

Restaurant owners are loath to cut their profits by calling in expensive repair services when their equipment breaks down, the plumbing goes out, or the electrical wiring blows. Indeed, general managers are required to spend time in training centers maintained by Burger Barn's corporate headquarters learning how to disassemble the machinery and rebuild it from scratch. The philosophers in the training centers say this is done to teach managers a "ground-up" appreciation for the equipment they are working with. Any store owner will confess, however, that this knowledge is mainly good for holding labor costs down by making it unnecessary to call a repairman every time a milk shake machine malfunctions. What this means in practice is that managers must teach entry-level workers, especially the men (but women as well), the art of mechanical repair and press them into service when the need strikes. Indeed, in one Harlem restaurant, workers had learned how to replace floor-to-ceiling windows (needed because of some bullet holes), a task they performed for well below the prevailing rates of a skilled glazier.

Then, of course, there is the matter of money. Burger Barn cash registers have been reengineered to make it possible for people with limited math abilities to operate them. Buttons on the face of the machine display the names of the items on the menu, and an internal program belts out the prices, adds them up, and figures out how much change is due a customer, all with no more than the push of a finger on the right "pad." Still, the workers who man the registers have to be careful to account for all the money that is in the till. Anything amiss and they are in deep trouble: they must replace any missing cash out of their wages. If money goes missing more than once, they are routinely fired. And money can disappear for a variety of reasons: someone makes a mistake in making change, an unexpected interloper uses the machine when the main register worker has gone into the back for some extra mustard packets, a customer changes her mind and wants to return an item (a transaction that isn't programmed into the machine). Even though much of the calculation involved in handling funds is done by computer chips, modest management skills are still required to keep everything in order.

While this is not computer programming, the demands of the job are nonetheless quite real. This becomes all too clear, even to managers who are of the opinion that these are "no-skill" jobs, when key people are missing. Workers who know the secrets of the trade—how to cut corners with the official procedures mandated by the company on food preparation, how to "trick" the cash register into giving the right amount of change when a mistake has been made, how to keep the orders straight when there are twenty people backed up in the drive-through line, how to teach new employees the real methods of food production (as opposed to the official script), and what to do when a customer throws a screaming fit and disrupts the whole restaurant—keep the complicated ballet of a fast food operation moving smoothly. When "experts" disappear from the shift, nothing works the way it should. When they quit, the whole crew is thrown into a state of near-chaos, a situation that can take weeks to remedy as new people come "on line." If these jobs were truly as denuded of skill as they are popularly believed to be, none of this would matter. In fact, however, they are richer in cognitive complexity and individual responsibility than we acknowledge.

This is particularly evident when one watches closely and over time how new people are trained. Burger Barn, like most of its competitors, has prepared training tapes designed to show new workers with limited literacy skills how to operate the equipment, assemble the raw materials, and serve customers courteously. Managers are told to use these tapes to instruct all new crew members. In the real world, though, the tapes go missing, the VCR machine doesn't work, and new workers come on board in the middle of the hamburger rush hour when no one has time to sit them down in front of a TV set for a lesson. They have to be taught the old-fashioned way—person to person—with the more experienced and capable workers serving as teachers.

One of my graduate students learned this lesson the hard way. A native of Puerto Rico, Ana Ramos-Zayas made her way to a restaurant in the Dominican neighborhood of upper Harlem and put on an apron in the middle of the peak midday demand. Nobody could find the tapes, so she made do by trying to mimic the workers around her. People were screaming at her that she was doing it all wrong, but they were also moving like greased lightning in the kitchen. Ana couldn't figure out how to place the cheese on the hamburger patty so that it fit properly. She tried it one way and then another—nothing came out right. The experienced workers around her, who were all Spanish-speakers, were not initially inclined to help her out, in part because they mistook her for a white girl—something they had not seen behind the counter before. But when they discovered, quite by accident, that Ana was a Latina (she muttered a Spanish curse upon dropping the fifth bun in a row), they embraced her as a fellow migrant and quickly set about making sure she understood the right way to position the cheese.

From that day forward, these workers taught Ana all there was to know about the french fry machine, about how to get a milk shake to come out right, about the difference between cooking a fish sandwich and a chicken sandwich, and about how to forecast demand for each so that the bins do not overfill and force wastage. Without their help, provided entirely along informal lines, Ana would have been at sea. Her experience is typical in the way it reveals the hidden knowledge locked up inside what appears to surface observers (and to many employees themselves) as a job that requires no thinking, no planning, and no skill.

As entry-level employment, fast food jobs provide the worker with experience and knowledge that ought to be useful as a platform for advancement in the work world. After all, many white-collar positions require similar talents: memory skills, inventory management, the ability to work with a diverse crowd of employees, and versatility in covering for fellow workers when the demand increases. Most jobs require "soft skills" in people management, and those that involve customer contact almost always require the ability to placate angry clients.[18] With experience of this kind, Burger Barn workers ought to be able to parlay their "human capital" into jobs that will boost their incomes and advance them up the status ladder.

The fact that this happens so rarely is only partially a function of the diplomas they lack or the mediocre test scores they have to offer employers who use these screening devices. They are equally limited by the popular impression that the jobs they hold now are devoid of value. The fast food industry's reputation for de-skilling its work combines with the low social standing of these inner-city employees to make their skills invisible. Employers with better jobs to offer do recognize that Burger Barn veterans are disciplined: they show up for work on time, they know how to serve the public. Yet if the jobs they are trying to fill require more advanced skills (inventory, the ability to learn new technologies, communication skills), Burger Barn is just about the last place that comes to mind as an appropriate proving ground. A week behind the counter of the average fast food restaurant might convince them otherwise, but employers are not anthropologists out looking for a fresh view of entry-level employment. They operate on the basis of assumptions that are widely shared and have neither the time nor the inclination to seek out the hidden skills that Barn employees have developed.

Perhaps fast food veterans would do better in the search for good jobs if they could reveal that hidden reservoir of human capital. But they are as much the victims of the poor reputation of their jobs as the employers they now seek to impress. When we asked them to explain the skills involved in their work, they invariably looked at us in surprise: "Any fool could do this job. Are you kidding?" They saw themselves as sitting at the bottom of the job chain and the negative valence of their jobs as more or less justified. A lot of energy goes into living with that "truth" and retaining some sense of dignity, but that effort does not involve rethinking the reputation of their work as skillfree. Hence they are the last people to try to overturn a stereotype and sell themselves to other employers as workers who qualify for better jobs.

I have suggested here that neither the employers nor the job-seekers have got it right. There are competencies involved in these jobs that should be more widely known and more easily built upon as the basis for advancement in the labor market. Yet even if we could work some magic along these lines, the limitations built into the social networks of most low-wage workers in the inner city could make it hard to parlay that new reputation into success.

CHAPTER SIX

Getting Stuck, Moving Up

THE SUMMER OF my freshman year of college, I was living in a small tourist town on the coast of central California, desperate for a job to keep body and soul together, with enough extra to help my parents with the care of my three younger brothers. Since my father was basically unemployed and my mother was working as a cashier making the minimum wage herself, it was incumbent upon me to take care of myself and do what I could to help out my family. Being a newcomer in the Morro Bay area, I had no friends or family to turn to for help in finding a job, so I hit the want ads and scoured the community for any kind of employment. After a false start in a fish market on the pier, I finally landed a full-time job in one of the many motels that line the coastal highway near San Simeon, that monument to conspicuous consumption built by William Randolph Hearst in his heyday as the newspaper baron of America. The tourist trade generated by Hearst's castle and the dazzling California seacoast kept the hotel business hopping in the summer and produced seasonal employment possibilities.

This was by far the worst job I have ever had. Eight hours a day, I stripped beds, lifted heavy mattresses, bent over bathtubs and toilets, lugged a heavy vacuum cleaner up and down the stairs, and endured the unbearably officious manager of the cleaning crew, who inspected every room, denouncing the motel maids for every minute mistake. By the end of the day, I was totally exhausted. My feet ached, my back hurt, and my eyes glazed over with boredom. There were days I would be broiling with anger at the supervisor, who seemed to delight in making us do everything over again. The meager paycheck I brought home barely covered my own expenses, and only by forgoing all extras was I able to give my mother money for my brothers' clothes.

A small army of veteran motel maids worked alongside me, women who had been doing this backbreaking work for years. They endured the surveillance, the reprimands, and the low wages with a sullen acquiescence, never letting the boss hear the blasphemous language they used behind her back. They were hardly happy with their work, but they had adjusted to the atmosphere and did not invest themselves in the job any more than was necessary to get by.

For me, however, the job was a dramatic encounter with life at the end of a real dead end. I worried about whether I would find myself trapped in this limbo, unable to afford to go back to school, prisoner of my family's need for my earnings. On the days when the future seemed to recede from my grasp, the full weight of the manager's heavy-handed treatment of the workers, the terror of a slim bank balance, and the worry about what would happen if, God forbid, I had to go to the doctor or I couldn't pay the utility bill would sit in the pit of my stomach. Yet as the daughter of a once prosperous middle-class family now fallen on hard times, I was fortunate to have many personal resources to draw on, particularly the availability of scholarships and student loans that ultimately pulled me through.

The women who worked alongside me, whose husbands were in and out of the canning factories, whose children took on summer jobs in California's agricultural fields, had no such luck. Absent a winning lottery ticket, they would spend their lives lifting mattresses, cleaning toilets, and muttering under their breath when the supervisor came around with her stopwatch to time them as they polished the mirrors. They were stuck.

For a young person to enter the labor force at such a low level is no great tragedy. What *is* tragic is to see that same person stuck in a job that will never pay a living wage. For all too many Burger Barn workers, the future ends up looking just like the present. They do not graduate; they remain in jobs designed for teenagers and try to manage adult responsibilities on hopelessly inadequate wages.

This is hardly for lack of trying. Fast food workers, particularly the adults among them who are no longer in school, devote a great deal of time to looking for better jobs. If effort plus experience as a steady worker were all it took to move ahead in the labor market, these people would be sitting pretty. Some do succeed, either because they are selected out for promotion inside Burger Barn or because they get a lucky break and find a new job outside the fast food domain altogether, but during the years I followed them, the majority churned from one low-wage job to another.* To appreciate the Sisyphean character of their struggle to better themselves, we must look closely at what happens to these workers when they leave the confines of Burger Barn to look for better jobs.

GOOD JOBS

The people in my neighborhood who are really making it? Well, my friend Ellie, her husband works for the Post Office. You know, he's been there a lot of years. I live fairly comfortably because, you know, my baby's father is a correction officer. He still takes care of us even though he's not there [doesn't live with us].

Roberta, a mother of two young children, graduated from high school before she had her kids. She had an entry-level clerical job with United Parcel Service and had hoped to move up the managerial ladder in that firm. Her lack of white-collar work experience and limited skills made that unlikely, so she left UPS and found a job at Burger Barn, where she was soon advanced to the position of a salaried manager. Roberta earned almost $400 a week as a manager, a yearly gross income of about $19,000.

She could make ends meet on that salary as long as nothing went wrong. Roberta's retired parents were able to take care of her youngest child during her work hours and ferried her older son to and from school, which relieved her of the need to pay for child care. She was living in a public housing project near her parents' home, and was fortunate to have a two-bedroom apartment for a modest rent. As long as everyone in her family was in good health, Roberta was okay. Unexpected illness presented major problems, even for someone with earnings well above the poverty line.

You have no medical benefits [in my job]. If my kids get chicken pox, I have to take them to the hospital. I have to pay out of my pocket. [Burger Barn] is not paying me that great, you know.

---

* To be fair, we were able to follow these workers for only eighteen months, which is not a sufficient period to judge their long-term mobility prospects. My convictions about their immobility are based on many observations of failed attempts to get better jobs, plus the age distribution (and prior work profile) of the workforce in Harlem's Burger Barns, where more than half of the entry-level employees were over twenty-five. However, in 1997 we began collecting data on 120 people who participated in this original study. Over the next five years, we will learn more about their long-term career patterns.

Roberta has other worries that are longer-term. At thirty-three, with parents who are retired, she wonders whether she will ever have the luxury of retiring herself. None of the jobs she has held offered pension plans, and her income has not been high enough to leave room for savings.

> *Look how many years I put into Burger Barn. When I came here, no benefits, no pension. I mean, when I get old . . . I'm thirty-three now. When I get old, what do I have to collect on?*

Roberta's checking account is always dry by the end of the month, so she cannot expect to accumulate much, if anything, in personal savings. Social Security will be meager even if current benefit levels are maintained. Her work history is confined to low-wage jobs for the most part, and even those jobs have been more sporadic than they should have been if she is going to lay claim to much in the way of retirement benefits at sixty-five. Unless something dramatic happens to change her work world, Roberta is always going to have to struggle and will have little left over to give her children a better life.

What would make a difference, in her opinion, would be finding the kind of job her father had before he retired: a government position. "A city job," she says with conviction, "that's what I need. That's where the benefits are. Everything is right there: the pension, everything." Her best friend, Ellie, nods in agreement. "Everything. City or federal job, you get every benefit that you can."

James, a sixteen-year-old black kid who worked at Burger Barn for a summer before going back to high school, knows just what Roberta is talking about. Jim's father had a good job working for Con Edison, but he lost it because of absenteeism. The family lost their health insurance, the retirement benefits that would have protected Jim's parents in old age, and a steady income well beyond anything that his father has been able to secure since he lost the Con Edison job. What Jim learned out of this experience is the value of employment in a public utility. When he compares what he earns at Burger Barn to what his father made in the good old days, he recognizes the difference. Hence Jim, like Roberta, has set his sights on landing a "union job."

Among the employed parents of the Burger Barn workers we surveyed, by far the largest proportion were working for the public hospitals in New York City. They are unionized workers, and although most are at the bottom of the occupational ladder in the hospitals, they benefit from being part of organized labor. Union contracts protect them from the most irregular aspects of the low-wage, unorganized sector of the labor market, especially unpredictable hours (and therefore unreliable income). While the public unions in cities like New York now face new challenges—downsizing, governments pressing them to accept "workfare" recipients into their ranks, and downward wage pressure—collective bargaining ensures at least some important features of good jobs. It is hardly surprising, then, that far less privileged workers like Roberta and Jim, who are without health insurance, retirement benefits, disability insurance, life insurance, or any other tangible protection for their families, would hope against hope for an opportunity to join the legions of city workers in unionized public sector jobs.

Burger Barn workers do more than just dream about the day such a job might come their way. They take the civil service tests whenever they are offered and then wait for city and state positions to open up. In theory, decent test scores put them on a list that the agencies are required to move down in a methodical fashion. In practice, most sit and wait for nothing.

Roberta has followed this recipe many times over, but success eludes her. She has a hard time figuring out why her efforts have not paid off; the whole experience has a magical quality to it, since it is impossible to figure out why some people get called off the civil service lists while others languish for years.

> I have eight list numbers and I'm just waiting. People I know already in the city three, four years and took just one test. I done took eight tests. When is somebody gonna call me? I don't know. This old man in my neighborhood was telling me, "You know, you're trying too hard. The people that try too hard usually don't get it." People that just sit back after taking the test. Boom. [They get called.] Some people just have all the luck.

It takes guts for workers with little education to sit for examinations that require levels of literacy and fluency in mathematics that they may not command. In other respects, however, looking for jobs off the civil service lists is a passive strategy. It does not involve pumping networks for information about employment opportunities, trudging from one firm to another, or an embarrassing encounter with personal rejection.

Burger Barn workers do not shy away from more aggressive methods of job-seeking either. They do put in applications with other firms, particularly those that are in their neighborhoods and those they can reach by subway. Small groups of workers from the restaurant get together and make a social occasion out of job-seeking, walking from one potential employer to another. Their primary targets are Gap clothing stores, drugstores, and grocery stores. Jobs of this kind are perceived as better than those at Burger Barn because they do not involve grease, heat, or quite as much deference as the fast food industry requires. "Clean" service jobs do not necessarily pay better at the entry level than restaurants. Their appeal lies in the superior status accorded sales clerks compared to food service workers, a status that inclines the former toward the white-collar side of the occupational divide.

The cachet of these retail service jobs reflects the polish of those who hold them, and therein lies an often difficult hurdle for inner-city workers to surmount. To employers looking to hire clerks who will interface with upscale customers, these would-be workers do not look the part. Native-born African-Americans often speak in a nonstandard dialect, as do their immigrant counterparts (who often have only a partial command of any form of English). Moreover, dress and hair styles born of the inner-city fashion scene don't look quite so appealing in midtown Manhattan. Job-seekers who know this and try to adjust accordingly often lack the money to dress the part, even when they understand what employers are looking for. Their current income does not permit them to dress in a fashion that appeals to boutique managers.

And then there are the thorny questions of race and class. As I explain in greater detail in Chapter 8, race plays a role at the gateway to the low-wage labor market. Latino applicants searching for work in central Harlem are less likely to be rejected than their African-American counterparts. When we move up to jobs that are outside the ghetto, jobs that are more highly valued, race and class combine to create more formidable barriers.

African-Americans are aware that they face higher hurdles and more scrutiny because of their skin color, the assumptions employers make about the neighborhoods they live in or the schools they graduated from, the dialect of English they speak, and the earrings they wear. Seeking a good job is an object lesson in frustration as these workers discover that the track records they have built up working for years at Burger Barn do not actually speak for themselves. What employers seem to see coming in the front door is a black face, and they fill in the negative assumptions accordingly. Ron had a lot to say on the subject:

> *I went for a lot of jobs. I got a little certificate in maintenance. You notice that you see mostly white people. They've sewed up all the maintenance jobs. All the jobs making ten, twelve dollars an hour just starting.*

[Whites] hook up their own people that ain't really doin' nothin', so they can have something. I got the skills and they hire other white guys, and he doesn't have the skills. They're gonna train him, but I'm already trained.

Dana, a sixteen-year-old black student, has seen a similar pattern:

I went into the Gap store downtown. Me and my friend went to get an application. We came in and this girl came in who was Caucasian. She asked for an application and they gave her one. She walked out with it. That's when we went in and asked for one and they said, "We don't have any more." So we say, "Didn't she just have one?" "We don't have any more right now," they told us. So it was like, "Okay. . . ."

Karen has done quite well in the world, in part because her earnings at Burger Barn helped her get through high school and into the college where she is studying for her bachelor's degree. She has a good track record, and her old employer lets her come back to work part-time whenever she is home from college. But she believes that blacks have to be careful to avoid attracting negative attention.

If I was working in a small business, more would be expected of me than someone who's white. Say, okay, a young lady, you know, same age as myself who happens to be white. She could probably slip up a couple of times and go unnoticed. Whereas for me, I would have that feeling of being watched. Little mistakes I might do, I'm confronted and you have to "watch out with what you're doing." . . . Whereas the next person, who happens to be white, well, that girl, it's different.

Basically I feel that by me being black I have to go out of my way, do exceptionally well.

Several studies conducted in Chicago have shown that employers carry around a set of beliefs about job applicants from the inner city that are deeply ingrained and fundamentally prejudicial.[1] African-Americans meet a wall of suspicion from employers and managers who believe they are more trouble than they are worth. Chicago employers are prone to seeing the men as belligerent, the women as saddled with children that they cannot take care of, and both men and women as illiterate. The employers I interviewed in Harlem were less likely to lean on the color line, since they were themselves African-Americans. However, they had their own stereotypes about *lower-class* minorities, their poor educational preparation, motivation, dependability, and dress style, that made it harder for some people to pass through the employment barrier than others. Jamal, the worker we met in Chapter 1, who stands six feet tall and weighs about 220 pounds, can feel their nervousness.

> *I'm a bigger black person and I have a certain intimidating, harsh look all the time. When I'm applying for jobs, people say I look kind of intimidating and sometimes evil. And sometimes I do feel that way, so . . . impressions sometimes are hard to keep off my face.*

Jamal has grown up in ghettos so tough that he long ago adopted a hardened appearance, a "don't mess with me" demeanor. This "act" has gone on for such a long time now that he has a hard time shedding it even when he knows it works against him. Behind that tough facade he is good-natured, but it is the facade that employers see and it confirms what they already believe about black men: they are too dangerous to have around in large numbers.

African-Americans are not the only minority group to face barriers. Dominicans and Puerto Ricans are not notably better off when it comes to upward mobility. Outside of the enclave economy, in which fellow ethnics hire within close circles of friends and relatives from the islands, the labor market is dotted with hurdles for them as well. Managers who run restaurants in the Dominican and Puerto Rican neighborhoods will happily hire co-ethnics for jobs at all levels of the business, including the managerial ranks (especially if the applicants have reasonable educational credentials). But outside these urban villages, the English-language barrier is a significant roadblock. Even very experienced employees who are regarded as hard workers find it tough to progress from low-wage jobs to jobs that pay well and offer benefits.

Rosa emigrated from the Dominican Republic in her teens. Her mother, disabled and separated from Rosa's father, remained in the islands, sending Rosa to live with an aunt and uncle who had arrived in New York a decade earlier. Her troubled introduction to New York's schools did not ease her way in learning English.

> *When I came to this country, they left me back a grade. All the classes in the grade I was supposed to enter were filled. And there weren't any bilingual classes. They put me in an [English-based] program and I failed. You see, without knowing any English, I failed. Then they put me in another grade and I passed there. They sent me to a really bad school in*

the Bronx, a school that had a very bad reputation, and I didn't want to
go. But they sent me and I was there for eight months.²

Racial tensions in Rosa's new school were so extreme that she had to leave.
Black and Latino students were at each other's throats. Rosa was jumped
several times, and eventually the tension got to her and she left the school.
Having been bounced from one grade to another, and then from school
to school, Rosa was falling far behind her agemates. By the end of ninth
grade she was fed up and asked her mother's permission to drop out in
favor of a GED program. Her mother insisted that she finish high school,
so Rosa dutifully enrolled in yet another school and finally finished at the
age of twenty. This irregular path through urban high schools did little to
improve her English.

Ironically, whatever facility Rosa now has in English came to her as
a result of her experience at Burger Barn. When she hit sixteen, her
mother's needs for remittances began to grow back in the Dominican
Republic, and her aunt gently hinted that it would make life easier if Rosa
could pay more of her own way. With her limited English skills, Rosa
was confined to job-seeking in the Spanish-speaking neighborhoods of
upper Manhattan. The Burger Barn restaurant in the heart of Washington Heights' Dominican neighborhood—where Carmen found work as
well—looked like a good bet. Although most of the other workers in the
restaurant were also native Spanish-speakers, Rosa picked up much of the
English she knows on the job. But, as she would be the first to admit, her
English is still quite halting and hardly good enough to make her eligible
for well-paying jobs. Her friends who have managed to learn the language
have had much greater success.

> *I don't know that much English. I write it and read it. I know how to*
> *speak it, a long time. My friends work in offices. They speak English bet-*
> *ter than me and that makes it easier for them. Because you have to know*
> *English. A friend of mine found me a job. It was the only one that [was*
> *really good]. But I quit because I couldn't, it was too much paper. I had to*
> *write. And it paid as much as five-fifty an hour!*

Rosa's friends have banked more years of education in the United States
than she has and they are therefore able to extend their job searches well
beyond the Spanish-speaking enclaves to which she is limited. "The only
one missing [from the good life] is me," Rosa says quietly.

Hence where race and weaker skills limit African-Americans to the low-wage labor market, language barriers have much the same impact on Latinos. The experience that both groups of workers accumulate inside the fast food world does not translate into upward mobility.

Realizing Educational Ambitions

If *values* alone were all that mattered in pushing people through American schools, we would have little cause for concern among Harlem's working poor. The recognition that school matters, that educational credentials separate those with a real shot at a decent career from those who will spend the rest of their lives at the bottom of the job ladder, could not be clearer. Indeed, more than a handful of the workers I met at Burger Barn were in a state of anxiety because they could not see how they were going to pay for their return to school. As Lara, a Dominican immigrant working full-time on the far Upper West Side of Manhattan, put it:

> Going back to school? Yes, I think about going back all the time. Sometimes I have thought I didn't have a chance. And I thought, Well, if the time comes when I don't have the chance, I don't know what I'm going to do. Because I really know that I'm not going to have a future without going to school. In other words, a good future. And sometimes it worries me. But now I know I can go back in September, God willing.

Few of Lara's friends behind the counter would disagree with her assessment of a future without a degree. But values are only part of the story. Social structure tells the rest. Some people are positioned to act on their ambitions and others are trapped by choices they have made in the past.

David is one of the lucky people, because he was in a position to use his earnings to further his training. Twenty-two years old, a native of Haiti, he came to New York with his father, after his parents divorced; his mother was left behind. David's father, who works sporadically as a mechanic, could not afford a desirable neighborhood, and so lives among characters with a penchant for drugs and guns. David stayed with his father until he finished school, but then decamped for an immigrant enclave on Long Island where his aunt and uncle run a livery agency, a poor man's taxi service, mostly for fellow Haitians. His relatives were willing to let him live with them and did not need to ask him for room and board. He could be in a safe space and it didn't cost him a dime.

With this basic support in hand—a roof over his head and food on the table—David could use the earnings he accumulated working at Burger Barn to pay for an expensive trade school course in refrigeration and air-conditioning installation and repair. Four days a week for nearly two years, David worked a full eight-hour shift at the Barn, then boarded the subway for an hour-long commute to the trade school, where he would put in another two or three hours' worth of classroom instruction and hands-on training. He paid dearly for this privilege: tuition for the trade course eventually came to about $4,000, a sum completely beyond the means of David's father or anyone else in the family. The only way David was going to get through air-conditioning school was to pay for it himself. But since his relatives were willing to supply his basic living expenses, he was able to do so.

The minute he received his certificate, David hit the job market. He went to job fairs sponsored by the trade school and made the rounds of Long Island employers looking for installation technicians. He called the older brothers of some Burger Barn friends who had jobs at the Metropolitan Transportation Agency to see whether there were any openings for men with his skills. It took almost six months to land a "good" job, but these days David takes home about $13 an hour, about three times what he made at Burger Barn. He has marketable skills, a steady income, a real future. He does not expect to have to work for the minimum wage again.

Ana also has aspirations for better things. But her immigrant family needs her earnings and cannot afford to let her go back to school. She is now in her twenties and getting edgy about this dilemma, for what benefits her natal family may well destroy her chances as an individual. She knows that a Burger Barn job is probably not going to take her anywhere unless she can advance up the management ranks—a feat that would require a better command of English than she has at this early stage in her career as a U.S. resident. She also realizes that without more education or vocational training, she may never break out of the low-wage ghetto. It is hard not to turn the resentment back on her parents, who are, she admits, doing the best they can for the family as a whole.

What David had that Ana lacks was the ability to use the money he earned to "purchase" credentials that benefited him over the long run.[3] Many of his friends on the shop floor—including Ana—would like to follow his example. For without special skills or a college degree, they will most likely be consigned to jobs like low-wage positions they hold now.[4] That is not what any of them want for the future, but their options are few.

Latoya—like the other parents working in Burger Barn—is trapped by obligations she cannot abandon, commitments that absorb all of her time, not to mention her earnings. She has three kids, all under the age of ten. Latoya does not lack the desire to go to school, just the life circumstances that would make more education feasible.

> I do *wanna go back to school, but given their hours and working hours, I can't do it. I can't go to school and then have to be to work at eleven o'clock at night and then have to get up. No I can't. For me to do it I would have to go to work, come home, spend some time with my kids, then go to school. I can't do that. But I do want to go back to school. I gotta find me a job where I can just work, you know, a certain amount of hours, then spend some time with the kids, and then take my days off and go to school. That's what I'm looking for.*

It is hard to imagine that Latoya will ever find this dream job.

MAKING CONNECTIONS

Everyone knows that connections matter for upward mobility. But if you live in a community whose adult members are largely employed in low-wage jobs or are unemployed, whom do you know who can help you get "hooked up" to a good job? The conventional wisdom holds that the poor stay poor in part because they have impoverished social networks. Most of the people in William Julius Wilson's high-poverty neighborhoods in Chicago report high levels of unemployment among their friends and relatives.

Burger Barn workers *do* have networks that make a difference in the scramble for jobs. What these connections don't do very well is produce opportunity for upward mobility. There is a difference, however, between networks that promote employment and those that facilitate mobility, though both are important to a poor person's survival.

Harlem's working poor travel in two kinds of social circles. The first is a network of like-situated friends working in the same kinds of jobs that Burger Barn workers already possess. The second involves a set of acquaintances and relatives who have or once had better jobs, sometimes significantly better, and who often live outside of the ghetto in suburbs, or working-class enclaves that are largely composed of minorities. To understand why neither of these sets of connections provides much help for Burger Barn workers who are trying to move out of the minimum-wage world, we need to look closely at what these two networks do to provide the working poor with information about job openings and personal references that increase the chances of landing a better job.

Kyesha Smith is blessed with both kinds of networks. She has been working in the same restaurant since she was fourteen years old and has seen many other employees come and go. Some of them moved from the restaurant where Kyesha works to other Burger Barn franchises in different boroughs of New York. While Kyesha does not keep in active contact with all of them, she knows a handful fairly well and could call on them for help if she needed to. Her closest friends, Natasha and Latoya, are fellow employees in the same restaurant where she works, and through them, Kyesha has come to know another social network composed of their family members. All of them have jobs just like the one Kyesha already occupies.

Jamal has his acquaintances. Some of them are local no-goods who live on his block, guys who deal drugs or guns for a living. But the others, the ones he depends upon when he needs to find work, have jobs in other fast food firms, small grocery stores in Queens, convalescent hospitals in the Bronx. Most of these acquaintances have come into his social universe on the job, and Jamal has managed to stay in touch with them as they shifted to other positions. When he has a blowup with his manager and needs to move on, he calls up one of his buddies who he knows has a job in some distant neighborhood and asks him to put in a good word. Since entry-level positions turn over relatively quickly and Jamal has some experience, at least the kind Burger Barn needs, he "scores" about half of the time.

The benefits of maintaining a constellation of friends who work at minimum-wage jobs are not trivial. For people who face the need to move on—because they have been let go from the jobs they now hold or because the hours their managers are willing to give them just don't add up to a living wage or because their families have been evicted and they have to relocate to a distant neighborhood—these lateral "partners" are critical resources. They facilitate movement from one position to the next and shorten spells of unemployment. Jamal has had to move from Florida to Brooklyn and then to Manhattan, and in all of these stops he has found work at Burger Barn, thanks in part to the skills he picked up the first time around and to the networks he has kept alive as he goes from one restaurant to the next.

In a population that tends to be residentially unstable,[5] this is particularly helpful, because frequent relocation puts a strain on commute patterns and makes it necessary for workers to find jobs in communities that are new to them. High-turnover jobs, like the ones at Burger Barn, are constantly spitting people out into the job market. Having a dispersed set of "associates" makes mobility easier. What a lateral network doesn't do, however, is promote upward job movement. Kyesha's friends, those who are roughly her own age, those whom she's encountered in the workplace and around her housing project, are not doing any better in terms of income or occupational prestige than she is. They cannot help her move up because the only jobs they know about and can recommend her for are ones that are roughly comparable to the one she already holds. Jamal's friends are a more motley crew, since many are out of the labor force altogether. But those who are gainfully employed are also working at low-wage jobs and can, at best, only help him find new positions just like the ones he has abandoned.

In characterizing the youth labor market for the 1970s, Paul Osterman argued that youth workers typically "churn" in a number of low-wage jobs during their early years in the labor market, but usually establish themselves in a single good position by their early twenties.[6] More recent studies concur that milling around in short-term jobs is not a big problem for the typical youth worker.[7] It should not be cause for concern, it is said, because ultimately these young people either return to school or settle down into something that looks more like an adult-pattern of stable employment. In fact, it is probably productive for youths to churn, because movement from one job to the next provides them with a variety of experiences in the workplace, a sense of the possibilities, and therefore a better vantage point from which to choose a real career. A closer examination of ghetto-dwelling minority workers, however, suggests that they may not have the same opportunities to settle down, much less to move up into higher-wage jobs. In stagnating labor markets, like Harlem, there is very little to move up to, and even entry-level jobs have become hard for young people and high school dropouts to access. Over half of the workers in these Harlem restaurants are over the age of twenty-five, yet they are still stuck in low-wage jobs through which they cycle with considerable frequency, even if at a lower rate than one might find in healthier, suburban labor markets.[8]

Nonetheless, lateral movement in the low-wage labor market certainly beats being unemployed. Neither Kyesha nor Jamal would trade places with the many people they know on the streets and in the housing projects who are out of work altogether. Hence, we should not dismiss the benefits of having an active collection of homogeneous acquaintances who can assist in furthering the churning process. These "weak ties," as Mark Granovetter termed them, can mean the difference between having any kind of job and real desperation.

- All of Dana's sisters and her mother, Evie, live in the same town on Long Island, but they all grew up in the project where Dana now lives. Dana, Cara, Mary, and Nell were born in Virginia.
- Evie and Harry formerly owned a home on Long Island. They sold it to Beth for $100,000 and moved to an apartment complex. Evie kicked out all of her children but Therese, her youngest daughter, because they were too much to handle. Nell and her family have since moved in.
- Harry was like a father to most of Evie's kids.

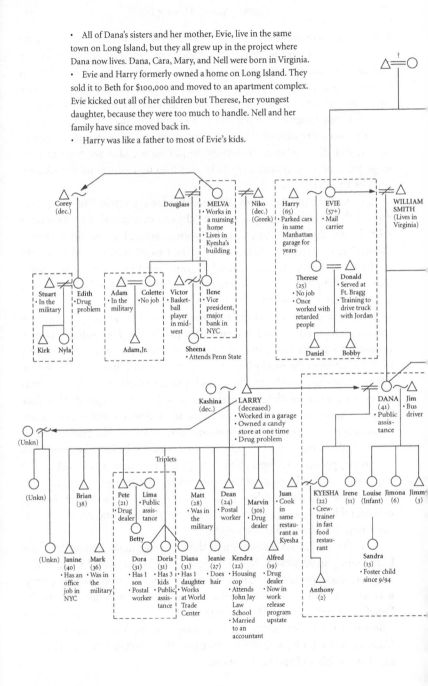

Figure 1. Kyesha's Family Tree, 1995

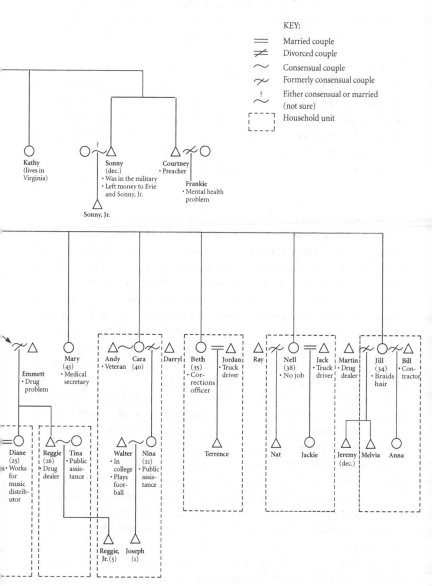

KEY:
═ Married couple
≠ Divorced couple
~ Consensual couple
⌇ Formerly consensual couple
? Either consensual or married (not sure)
⌐ ¬ Household unit

Kyesha is an active participant in another kind of network, one we might term "vertical" because of the way it "hooks her up" with people who have or once had much better jobs than the one she holds at Burger Barn.

Scanning Figure 1, a representation of Kyesha's extended family tree, one need only look to the ascendant generations, to her grandmother's contemporaries, to see that jobs in the public sector were critical to the family's well-being. Evie was a mail carrier; her son-in-law was in the military; her brother was in the military. Among Evie's children, Dana (Kyesha's mother) is a longtime welfare recipient and others of her children work in the underground economy as, for example, a hair braider. But the most successful of them, Beth, is a corrections officer. This, no doubt, is where Kyesha (and most of her fellow workers at Burger Barn) get the idea that a city job is the path to heaven.

Besides telling us that the public sector has played an important role in the prosperity of some parts of Kyesha's family, this family tree also shows that within her social purview are a fair number of people who have jobs that are far superior to the one Kyesha holds. These are not abstract connections: Kyesha regularly visits her grandmother and her aunt on Long Island; she knows her cousins, many of whom grew up in the suburbs, where they benefited from better schools and a much calmer environment. In theory, these relatives should serve as an effective network for Kyesha, a set of connections that could exercise some clout on her behalf and help her exit the minimum-wage domain.

Yet the dominance of public-sector employment among the more fortunate of her relatives makes this quite unlikely in an era when virtually every government agency in New York is shedding workers. Evie is not in a position to influence hiring at the post office; besides, ranks there are shrinking, not growing. The corrections department is expanding in upstate New York, where prisons have become a growth industry, but it is a hard nut to crack in the city, hence sister Beth counts herself lucky just to have held on to her job. Military cutbacks have truncated yet another avenue of mobility for young black men and women. Some of these opportunities have been bestowed on Kyesha's half siblings, who number among them two postal workers (Dean and Dora) and a housing cop (Kendra). Her brother-in-law (Alex) found a job cleaning cars for the Long Island Railroad. But most of the family members in Kyesha's generation have fared poorly: her older brother is a drug dealer (quite a wealthy one in fact), and she has several half brothers who have also been involved in the illicit drug economy.[9]

The vertical links Kyesha has are not paying off in upward mobility because they are lodged in declining industries, but their presence means that low-wage workers like Kyesha do not lack for role models. Sterling examples only go so far, however: Kyesha's grandmother cannot get her a job in the post office, and her aunt can't slot her into the corrections department. What they can do, by example, is to inspire Kyesha with the idea that she might someday get lucky and follow in their footsteps.

Survey researchers are not likely to spot the complex and variegated nature of a family tree like Kyesha's. One has to dig deep into the intergenerational history of the working poor to see these networks, to understand the full range of people, employed and unemployed, legitimate and underground, who populate her social universe. Yet when we explore that history we come away with a more nuanced understanding of what her "people resources" look like, of the folks she really knows and what they might be able to do to help her.

We also develop a better grasp of who Kyesha really is in a sociological sense. If we look at her immediate household, we might describe her as the daughter of a long-term welfare mother.[10] Once we look up the generations to her grandparents, her great-aunts and great-uncles, or sideways to her half siblings and cousins, she appears in a different light. Kyesha is a product of downward mobility, the erosion of job opportunities that has progressively disadvantaged every succeeding generation in her family. Where the jobs her relatives once held were public-sector positions that paid enough to make suburban home ownership possible, those available to Kyesha's generation are more likely to be of the minimum-wage variety. A twenty-year period of postwar prosperity coupled with a federal commitment to equal opportunity opened up avenues of mobility for African-Americans in Evie's generation. Those conditions began to change in the mid-seventies and have been worsening ever since; the historical record is well known. In the example of Kyesha's family we glimpse what that history means for many black families: inequality between generations that leads to tensions as those experiencing declining opportunity try to lean on those who benefited from the good years.

Of course, the erosion of job opportunities does not explain the whole picture, for there are people in Kyesha's own generation who have done far better than she has: half sisters who have jobs as transit cops or housing cops, for example. Education matters; skills matter. Both translate into greater opportunities for people who bring more to employment than Kyesha, who is just a high school graduate. We should not minimize the role of skills in exploring the limits to mobility among low-wage workers. If they had more to offer in the way of credentials, they might be able to compete for positions in more desirable parts of the labor market.

The willingness of one's connections to intervene and help out when they have the power to do so is important as well. That kind of assistance is not always forthcoming. Gaps tend to open up in a family whose members have experienced divergent fates. Those who have escaped the ghetto are not particularly proud of those among their children or grandchildren who have been on welfare for years, living in trashy neighborhoods. Kyesha has often felt that her older relatives look down on her because her mother has been on AFDC for twenty-five years. Dana is not exactly the pride of her daughter's life either, but Kyesha doesn't feel it's fair to damn her for her mother's mistakes, and she believes her more affluent relatives could be more helpful if they really wanted to.

This is hardly a new story. Established German Jews who had gained success in America by the end of the nineteenth century were embarrassed by their poor brethren from the shtetls of Eastern Europe who were then landing in boatloads. The middle-class reformers among them who established well-financed and effective social service agencies to take care of their poor "Russian" kinsmen were motivated in no small measure by the desire to conceal these mortifying cases from the watchful eyes of the mainstream society.[11] Economic prosperity is not necessarily a spur to selfless action, though immigrants (and internal migrants from, for example, the rural South) are justly famous for their efforts to sponsor, recruit, and advance their relatives in the pursuit of employment. Nonetheless, the generous impulse is not universal, and in the case of African-Americans in the inner city, it is complicated by a powerful discourse of condemnation that attributes to people like Dana the capacity to do more for themselves if only the will were there. Middle-class minorities are just as likely to subscribe to this critical perspective as whites in the suburbs, in fact perhaps more likely, and to want to cut themselves off from any contaminating links with the "underclass."

There is a perverse incentive for them to turn a blind eye to their relatives in need. Because African-Americans are overrepresented among the poor, those who have "made it" are far more likely to have family members in economic distress than is the case for any other ethnic or racial group in the United States. The success stories often fear that the floodgates will open, and an avalanche of demands from their inner-city relations cascade down upon them. Many, in fact, have family trees so loaded down with poor people that the help they could offer would quickly be exhausted, their resources drained, and their own standard of living imperiled. One look at Kyesha's family tree illustrates the dimensions of the problem. Grandmother Evie has had to take in various of her adult children and their kids as they have fallen on hard times. But the number of children and grandchildren in Evie's family who are struggling is so large relative to her resources that she would be totally overwhelmed if she responded to all their needs. Indeed, Evie sold her house and moved to the apartment where she lives now in part because she had a constant parade of family members coming back to live with her, and reasoned that a smaller space would make it easier to hold such requests at bay.

These tensions often boil over into feelings of rejection by the poorer members of a family, who come to feel that their more prosperous relatives have labeled them "no good." Ron, an African-American in his midtwenties, knows these sentiments all too well. Ron's older sister, fifteen years his senior, is a major in the Army who lives in Texas. She is by far the most successful of Ron's siblings. Under her influence, Ron went to military school in Texas from the age of twelve to fourteen, part of his mother's plan to distance him from the streets of New York where he lived for most of his childhood. He hated the experience, and as soon as he could talk his mother into it, he fled back to the city.

Those two years in Texas were enough to teach Ron exactly how his sister, revered in the family for her achievements, thought about the folks she had left behind.

> *My sister was braggin' about how she was the only one that went to college and that the rest of us ain't S-H-I-T. She'd say, "You ain't shit." Stuff like that, you know. And I loved the rest of my brothers and sisters; I didn't want to be a part of that type of attitude, that hate toward my own family.*
>
> *She said of the whole family, "I'm the best." Praising herself so greatly. You know . . . it made me cry, man. She was like, "You should be appreciatin' what I do. You lucky that you here with me [in Texas]." So I'm sitting there listening to my sister talking about my family like a dog. And I would be like, "I got to go back to New York."*

Nadine didn't go to military school, but she appreciates Ron's experience because there are class divisions in her family as well, and they cause quarrels.[12] Nadine has worked at Burger Barn since she was fourteen years old, because her family was desperately poor. Her father died in a car crash when she was a child, but had never really worked. Her mother has been on AFDC for the best part of the past twenty-two years and is now disabled by illness. One of her brothers has been hospitalized for depression, leaving Nadine and her twin sisters (one is a butcher in a meat-packing plant and the other works in a paint store in lower Manhattan) to support the family. But not all of her relatives are struggling this hard. Her uncle is a businessman who has done quite well for himself. The two families do not get along.

> We didn't finish school, so he's looking down on us. And he throws his kids in our faces. "They gonna be better than you." One of my sisters has a kid, a girl. The other's got a boy and she is pregnant now. So he's like, "Ya'll ain't really no good [for anything] but to have kids and ya'll ain't finished school." Then [my uncle's] sayin' I'm next [to have kids], but I'm not next. I know what I want out of life.

Neither of Nadine's sisters finished high school, though they both went back to get their GED degrees. Her brother was too disturbed to make it very far in school. Yet three of the four of them are working full-time, pulling their weight, supporting the children in the extended family. Her grandmother and grandfather are still working full-time, albeit in low-wage jobs. In short, her clan is full of people who are holding down jobs, a fact which ought to qualify them for some respect. But it cuts no ice with Nadine's uncle, who sees himself and his own children as superior to this branch of the family.

Indeed, pointing to her uncle and thinking of other success stories she knows has convinced Nadine that people who have "made it" beat it out of their neighborhoods and the lives of their poorer family members about as fast as their new cars will carry them. "All those people moved," she notes. "That's how well they were doing. They were doing very well and just left." Nadine doesn't really blame them, since she would move out of her run-down neighborhood too if she could afford to.

> They probably moved out because of the block. If you lived on that block for a month, you would want to go too. You would definitely want to leave. The streets are bad. . . . They had a body over there a few days ago, shot like eight or nine times. Our building is a hundred years old—it's disgusting, roach-infested. The neighbors are loud, very loud. Always cursing at their kids, playing their music loud, fighting.

It is no mystery to Nadine, then, why people who have good jobs and a lot of money don't want to stick around.[13]

Both Ron and Nadine could, in a pinch, ask these more advantaged relatives for help if they were desperate, and indeed (as Ron's Texas stint shows) there have been times when the luckier ones have lent a hand. But it is an open question whether these folks could or would bother to serve as a useful node in their social networks, actively looking to hook up either Ron or Nadine to a better job. Nadine has not finished high school and has had no choice but to work at a low-wage job for years now. She is hardly prime material in the business world where her uncle has contacts. This alone may incline him to ignore her even when job openings do come to his attention.

The cultural rift between the prosperous parts of an extended family and those down on their luck can open up such a huge gulf that the former are too ashamed of the latter to have much to do with them at all. This is a particularly painful problem for poor African-Americans who see race as a common bond and an inescapable barrier that makes self-help and the support of fellow blacks essential to any real upward mobility. When class divides them, the prospects look even dimmer for overcoming the problems race poses in the labor market. As Sean put it:

> *If [black people] spend more time trying to help one another, [it would be better]. But every time we get some money, we put somebody down, saying, "Oh look at him. He ain't makin' no money. He don't wanna do [work]." . . . That's the biggest problem we have. Every time we get money, you wanna move away, three million miles away. You don't wanna know nobody no more. All you wanna do is ride [with] other people who's in your class. Which is understandable; you are your own individual. But still, don't forget where you came from. Help people to know [they] can do something for themselves. You can uplift yourself.*

Social distance sets up tensions among millions of families who have never set foot in the ghetto. Comfortable middle-class Americans of blue-collar origins often pull away from their struggling siblings who work in factories or car repair shops.[14] But for the urban poor, those gaps have consequences beyond hurt feelings and a defensive rejection of relatives who are "stuck up" or "think they're too good for us." They erode efficacy of job linkages that might otherwise help a young worker move up and out of the Burger Barn circuit.

It is important, however, to distinguish between the failure of vertical networks to produce upward mobility and the absolute absence of "connections." Much of the social science literature on the urban poor argues that the flight of the middle class out of the inner city has destroyed these social relations completely, leaving ghetto residents in high-poverty neighborhoods with no friends or relatives who are working, much less in decent jobs. But survey research is a particularly weak method for picking up on the nuances of social relations, especially those that are as carefully calibrated as the connections between Kyesha and her grandmother, or Nadine and her uncle.[15] It is likely to underestimate the diversity of ties that ghetto dwellers have to the outside world, and cannot offer a very subtle account of the attitudes that might incline a more privileged relative or friend to help a young job-seeker or turn a deaf ear.

Harlem's low-wage workers have spun a web of social ties that include many people who are out of the labor force, but just as many who are working hard. Many of them are positioned in secure employment, the kind that makes the average Burger Barn worker sigh with envy. Others are sitting in jobs that are no better than the ones our Barn workers already have. Both kinds of networks pay off, though the latter are more "productive" of new jobs than the former because so many of the richer contacts in the pool are employed in a shrinking public sector, or because the jobs they know about require more education than most low-wage workers have. These networks do enhance the chances of being employed, but they have their limits where upward mobility is concerned.

This is no small problem for the working poor. They do derive dignity from the mere fact of their employment, but a minimum-wage job is nothing to crow about. Depression sets in as it begins to dawn on Burger Barn workers in their mid- and late twenties that the future will probably look a lot like the present. Tiffany, daughter of a troubled welfare mother, has been working since she was thirteen years old. Without her income, Tiffany and her mother would have been in dire straits. But she wants more in life than a job at Burger Barn.

> *I tried to stay away from [getting stuck], but you can get locked in [to Burger Barn]. And I feel bad because . . . I'm nineteen, I have three years of experience in fast foods and I want jobs in child care. The only thing I have going for me is that I made a conscious effort to stay in high school to go through a nursing program the last two years. I have experience and a certification, but the board of education certificate is not a license [for child care]. Every time I try to get a [child care] job, they want a license. People say, "Go get a license," but there's a whole lot you gotta go through.*

Courses and stuff. I'm stuck on this Burger Barn treadmill and wanna get off.

The only way out of this dilemma, as Tiffany knows all to well, would be to pursue that license. But because she has to provide for her own support and contribute to her mother's, she lacks the time and money to do it. The more she talked about the roadblocks, the more upset she would get. "I can't seem to be able to get another type of job," she said, crying. "Burger Barn is the only corporation that wants me, and I hate it." Tiffany has begun to wonder whether working in fast food has actually damaged her prospects for moving into day care.

I wonder if employers like this Burger Barn stuff. Back in high school when teachers say, "Don't be ashamed of getting a job at Burger Barn, 'cause when you go for other jobs they are gonna see that, and they are gonna say, 'This woman worked hard.'" Yeah, that's a cute devil. Why can't I get another job now? The employers just see Burger Barn and they are like, "That's all she knows?"

In some respects Tiffany's fears are unfounded. A track record of steady employment speaks volumes about a job-seeker. But this alone is not sufficient to break into higher-skilled employment; for that she needs the credentials that she could get only if she could afford to quit work for school or find a scholarship generous enough to replace her earnings and pay her tuition. Neither scenario is plausible, and she knows it.

Jamal was another portrait of frustration. He knew that he had almost no chance of getting a better job and that he lacked the money to go back to school, the only meaningful avenue toward changing his prospects. Jamal had big dreams, but he realized all too well that they would never be more than fantasies.

I think about the future, but I don't know what the outcome's gonna be. I have fantasies about what I want to do. I'd like to be a pilot or a cop, one of the two. But it is hard just to get through the day-to-day stuff: paying rent, going to work. It's a mental frustration, being that I want so much but don't have the power to grasp it, or the willpower anymore that I used to [have]. The future is more like a wish than a plan.

To make it real I would have to have support, you know. Housing support, a definite place. If I had a year somewhere I could stay without paying and had a nice little job and could go to school, I would say that by the next year, I would be prepared. But I can't get there because it's like my money's all messed up. It's all crazy.

Years of struggle, of fending for himself and his wife without any real help from anyone else, have taken a huge toll on Jamal. They are indeed making him crazy.

THE INSIDE TRACK

Some people do succeed in moving up the ladder. We have already seen that those favored workers tend to be the ones who have the "luxury" to spend their hard-earned cash on furthering their education or training. David put in three hard years working at Burger Barn while earning his certificate in refrigeration and air-conditioning repair. Karen used her earnings to save money for college. These success stories suggest not only that it is possible to push toward the top, but that for those fortunate to have few other obligations pulling them down, working while young makes progress more likely.

Where does that leave the others? The most ambitious focus their hopes on rising within the firm. Fortunately, the fast food industry looks favorably on internal promotion. At the highest reaches of Burger Barn's corporate leadership one finds a surprising number of executives who got their start cooking french fries and setting the timers on micro-wave ovens. The chain of command that reaches from those fry vats, to first-line management, to general manager positions, and on up into the regional and national hierarchy is populated almost entirely by employees who have served their time behind the counter. In its heyday, when Burger Barn was growing incredibly fast and had little competition, the demand for managerial labor was increasing too rapidly to be met just by moving people up the line. These days, market share is on the wane, and much of the fastest growth is developing overseas as the Barn expands its reach into Asia, Eastern Europe, and other parts of the world that are just beginning to develop a taste for burgers and Cokes. Still, the market is healthy enough to open up many managerial jobs in the United States, and the industry is committed enough to its workforce (and unpopular enough among outsiders) to open those opportunities to promising internal candidates.

Many years ago, in the wake of the Watts riots in Los Angeles, the firm realized that it would be wise to promote more minorities into its managerial ranks, especially in communities where the population is largely

African-American, Latino, or Asian. Corporate leaders saw this policy as more than an expression of goodwill: it shields them from the destructive anger of ghetto populations during riots. When the Watts disturbances spread across Los Angeles in the 1960s, Burger Barn franchises were destroyed in significant number. With the new policy of "ethnic management" and minority ownership in place, where riots following the Rodney King verdict broke out in 1992, black-owned Burger Barns were largely spared. Civic-mindedness turned out to be good business.

The policy has opened up management opportunities for minority workers and has required franchise owners and senior managers to turn their attention toward grooming men and women in their employ for the promotion track. A whole curriculum, complete with books and quizzes, was developed for would-be managers, a course of study they must complete under the tutelage of their supervisors. Success in this training track leads to regional courses given periodically in area hotels, where those who have "matriculated" in local restaurants go for more sophisticated training in the company of other management trainees. Harlem workers looking for promotion spend their regional training period in a comfortable hotel on Long Island, the first hotel most have ever visited.

The training is intended to introduce them to the elements of human relations, supervision of workers, the management of money, the repair of equipment, and inventory control. But it is also meant to make them feel part of a larger organization, to instill some pride in their attachment to Burger Barn itself—no small accomplishment, since the whole industry carries the McJob stigma. Workers are supposed to come away with the understanding that they now have a different status, one they can feel good about.

They also gain some valuable contacts, an unintended consequence of bringing management material from all over the New York City region together in one place. Although franchise owners subscribe to an informal prohibition against stealing managers from one another, they actually do so all the time. Regional conclaves provide them with an opportunity to see "who is out there" and to take advantage of the investment other owners have already made in their trainees. By pulling managerial trainees within a large geographical area together, Burger Barn builds an internal labor market in managers, some of whom end up moving to new jobs as a result of the contacts they make (and bringing some of their crew members along). The value of promotion, then, lies almost as much in the entry it provides to this internal market as in its local rewards.

Who, then, gets to make this leap, and how does the selection process work? In a typical Burger Barn restaurant, perhaps as many as forty people are on the payroll in entry-level slots, while another ten fill managerial roles of varying degrees of authority. Because turnover is high, more than twice as many workers pass under the watchful eye of management in any given year. Of them, four to six will be selected for promotion to first-line management, either in the restaurant where they began or in another "shop" under the same ownership. How are these people selected?

Fernando, a first-line manager and a native of the Dominican Republic, gives a great deal of thought to the grooming of his successors. What he is looking for, in a nutshell, is someone willing to go the extra mile.

> When you ask them to have something done, they don't give you the "but" or the runaround, you know. He will say, "Okay, I will take care of it." That's how you know. Now, a person that you tell him to do something and they always [say], "Well, why don't you send this one [instead]?"—giving you excuses—you will know he won't be a good manager.

Fernando is looking for the person who shows initiative, who accepts responsibility, and who does not default or shirk when asked to take charge of a task that is in his or her job description. Such a person can be a big help to the more senior managers, who cannot run a smooth operation if they have to micromanage every detail of the organization's operation. As Fernando knows only too well, choosing the right person to work under him means cutting his own workload.

> If they develop [properly], it's not like less work for you, but the thing you cannot do they will see. You forget something, they will try to work on it. They will let you know. . . . "Why don't you do it this way? Because I think it is better." So you will always get input from them.

Fernando wants people who can act as his eyes and ears, who can be instructed in the general goal—customer satisfaction—and let loose to achieve it.

He was declared just such a worker himself several years ago when his African-American supervisor, a matronly woman who is universally respected in his restaurant, took him aside and began to groom him for a leadership role. Ms. Porter, the only person in the whole shop who is called by her last name, could see that Fernando was an eager worker, standing out from the crowd of young people who were just passing through and clearly had no intention of doing more than was necessary to get by. Fernando sought out new responsibilities, carried out the tasks she asked him to assume, and displayed the appropriate respect for her, even though they come from different racial backgrounds.

Fernando was able to attract Ms. Porter's attention because he came into the workforce with good credentials to begin with. He started his career as the youngest member of an extended family of Dominicans who all work for Burger Barn in central Harlem. Fernando's sister, aunt, cousin, and brother-in-law were all hired, one after another, and eventually were able to sponsor him in the system. Even though the older members of the family are monolingual Spanish-speakers—which limits their mobility prospects—the whole clan is known for its hardworking, no-nonsense, orderly behavior. Fernando clearly benefited from the connections, not only because they landed him the job in the first place, but because they "cast a halo" around him. Fernando emigrated when he was eleven and completed high school in New York, so his command of English surpasses that of his older relations. The combination of his language skills and his connections to a family with a good reputation in the firm positioned him to catch Ms. Porter's eye as she looked around for new crew chiefs.

Fernando was also ahead of the game because he has managerial blood in the family. Both of his parents were born in the Dominican countryside to poor families, but his father went to school and then worked his way up in a medical laboratory to a managerial position. When the firm relocated to Virginia, Fernando's father took the leap that so many immigrants aspire to: he opened his own bodega in a community with a large Latino population. Fernando's mother, long since divorced, lives in East Harlem, where she has retired from her sewing job in a clothing factory. Though his mother never had any managerial opportunities, his father was quite accustomed to exercising authority on the job. Working for a living is the center of his existence, as it is for the other adults in Fernando's family. Even Fernando's wife, a former Burger Barn worker now at home with their first child, is planning to go back to work in the near future. With this background, it is hardly surprising that Fernando understood how to "signal" his potential.

Yet he believes that the battle to work his way out of the pack was not an easy one. When he came into the Burger Barn labor force it was predominantly African-American, as it still is to a large extent. He felt the sting of disapproval from his black coworkers, who, in turn, worried about the competition growing across ethnic lines for the few managerial

opportunities there are in Harlem. As a minority in the land of another
minority, Fernando was unsure he was welcome, much less defined as
management material.

> *For a Spanish person, there was not much of an opportunity. Out of eight
> stores [the owner] had, there was only one Spanish manager, general
> manager. The rest were black, so we were stuck on the bottom. It wasn't
> just because we spoke Spanish. You know, we were the minority and they
> were the majority.*

As it happened, though, his race turned out to be less of a barrier than
Fernando expected. The neighborhood where his Barn is located is
undergoing transition, with an increasing "Spanish" immigrant presence
growing to the north. Burger Barn owners know that the racial composition of their workforce acts as a signal of welcome and deliberately set
about altering the ethnic mix behind the counter and among the managers in order to attract a new customer base. As Fernando explained:

> *Before [the current owner] took over this store, ninety percent of the
> store's staff and ninety percent of the managers were black. And since he
> took over, now it's fifty-fifty [Latino and Black]. Spanish customers are
> coming in because they know that we got Spanish-speaking people work-
> ing here. So . . . you have to change the store over from what it was 'cuz
> the community is about fifty–twenty-five–twenty-five, Puerto Ricans
> and Dominicans.*

The same owner had done essentially the same thing in a Burger Barn in
Chinatown, which had, prior to his coming, been staffed largely with
Latinos and a few African-Americans. He slowly shifted the workforce to
Asians and watched his profits rise.

The transition is hardly an easy one, though. Those in the ethnic group
on the losing end are aware that they are being displaced in the name
of marketing and feel the squeeze as an assault on the livelihood of
friends and family members who might otherwise be "networked" into a
job. Managers like Fernando, one of the first nonblacks to be promoted,
know that they are a vanguard and that they may attract resentment for
what they symbolize: the encroachment of the "Spanish" into African-
American territory.

Despite his worry about "being on the bottom," Fernando benefited,
and not only from management's desire to diversify the supervisory staff

and its preexisting view that Latino immigrants are harder workers than many of the African-Americans. Ms. Porter reached across the divide and picked him out because what she needed was someone she could rely on, and that was her highest priority. From the day she got permission from the general manager to take Fernando under her wing, Ms. Porter schooled him in the arts of scheduling, worker training, cash control, human relations and conflict resolution, and inventory and the ordering of supplies. And she encouraged him to stay in school so that he could continue to move up the ladder, something he has done at a local junior college.

With Ms. Porter as his sponsor, Fernando has become a capable supervisor who has worked hard to gather the respect of the workers who report to him. He could not afford to let any ripple of racial hostility control the mood, nor could he cope with the conflict by becoming a hardhead, an authoritarian.

> *Respect is necessary. If they don't respect you, they will do anything they want to. You know, like you tell them to sweep and mop, they won't sweep and mop. You ain't nobody!*

Ninety percent of Fernando's job involves coaxing his workforce to abide by the dozens of rules the firm imposes over the preparation of food. There are regulations covering virtually every move a worker makes in the production process. While he has the authority to discipline workers who fail to cooperate, he has discovered what most managers come to know in time: a willing workforce is much easier to supervise. And as Fernando points out, you cannot keep a constant watch on everybody.

It was no simple matter in the beginning for him to generate respect, partly because of the racial tension and partly because he was perceived as just another crew member: who was Fernando to exercise authority over people who had been his equals only the day before? In time these concerns faded, because nothing functions unless someone takes control, and most workers understand that. They would rather work efficiently than suffer the headaches of disorganization. This is an important reason why interethnic cooperation flourishes in these workplaces, even when there is competitive tension under the surface. Workers have to get along or they cannot deliver the goods; those who are recalcitrant are ultimately squeezed out. But no manager, certainly not Fernando, wants those tensions to dominate the workplace, and they all try hard to smooth them over while getting the hamburgers flipped.

Bob, the African-American general manager of Fernando's restaurant, is the ranking supervisor of the whole enterprise, the man who reports directly to the owner. He has been working at one Burger Barn or another since he left high school nearly fifteen years ago. The imperative to work came early in Bob's life, for he lived with his grandmother after a long stint in a group home for youth abused or abandoned by their parents. Bob's grandmother, who died when he was in his early twenties, was a sickly woman. Periodically she would tell him he had to go find work because she was running out of money and wasn't well enough to maintain her social service job.[16] In his last years of high school, Bob worked two jobs—one part-time after school and another on the weekends—just to help make ends meet. By the time he managed to get into college, his grandmother was in very bad health and urged him to earn more. He turned to his manager at Burger Barn and began to court a promotion into the managerial ranks.

Bob was unlikely material in some respects. Always smart, quick to absorb production procedures, and adept at figuring out more efficient ways to accomplish the basic task of a crew member, he was also quick to anger. His long years of exposure to pecking orders enforced by personal slights and violence as a means of solving disputes, left him with some bad habits.

> I used to be a street kid—I was wild. I had a hot temper—I still have a hot temper. I can control it now, but when I was younger I used to fight. Every five minutes—I mean, you'd say, "Damn, he's fightin' again, he's fightin' again." That started in high school. After that, if you ticked me off—bap! I didn't like people running over me.

Had Bob not held down a steady job, he would almost certainly have ended up in deep trouble with the law. But Bob had a job, and he had Sam, a boss who corraled him and broke him of those bad habits, taught him how to manage frustration in the face of abusive customers, just the kind of situation that would have provoked the young Bob to explode.

> I remember one time I got arrested in Burger Barn. This guy threw coffee on me, and then he called me a nigger and like hit me in the face. That was it, I lost it. I beat the shit out of him! I was arrested. Sam, my manager, had to come down and get me [from the police station]. Sam told me, "You can't act like that. You have to ignore people." He looked out for me and helped me move up the ranks after that.

Sam, who had been something of a street kid himself, recognized a kindred spirit in Bob and shepherded him through the hurdles to the position of general manager he occupies now. Without Sam's guidance, Bob almost certainly would have derailed. But thanks to his native intelligence, his drive, and Sam's steadying influence, Bob was able to prosper. At the age of twenty-three, his grandmother now gone, he was earning $25,000 a year—a great deal of money for a young black man raised in a group home.

It falls to Bob now to spot new talent, to move people up the ranks from crew trainers to swing managers and on into the most coveted spots: general managers and their assistants, positions that represent "real money" because they are salaried rather than hourly. Having been the beneficiary of the recruiting process, Bob knows well what he is looking for: a hint of leadership. He wants to see a flicker of authority, or at least the potential for it, so that he can build upon the latent talent. Jessica, a young black woman working under his direction, was selected for managerial training because she has this special spark.

> *People listen to Jessica. I don't know if it's a tone of voice, or the way she talks, but if Jessy tells someone something, she can get it done, without a hassle. So I took that [quality] and built the rest around her, like showing her how to, you know, delegate, counsel, make decisions, all of that. We're still working with her. But that's why I picked Jessy, because of her mouth. She can get things done. She'll speak up and people will move.*

Bob observed Jessica for several months before he reached this conclusion. He listened as she took responsibility before it was built into her job description, realized that her "bossiness" could be converted into managerial control, and made a pitch to the restaurant's owner that they single Jessica out for training.

The same quality attracted Bob to Latoya, Kyesha's good friend. The logistical skills required to balance the needs of her three kids against the demands of the workplace have left Latoya with the same kind of authoritative air that Jessica has acquired. Her kids listen to her, and so do the employees who work around her. It took many months for this to be clear to Bob, but ultimately he picked her out for these leadership characteristics too.

> *If the workers didn't know what they were doing, they would ask Latoya. Or Latoya would see something [out of order] and she would fix it.*

Latoya did not leap at the idea of a managerial track initially because she lacked confidence in herself. Thinking back on it, Bob remembered, "She thought people wouldn't listen to her." Marshaling his own observations of her take-charge personality, Bob convinced her she was selling herself short. "I just told her what I saw in her," he noted, and then prevailed on the restaurant owner to do the same. In the end, Latoya accepted their challenge and began the training program that leads to a salaried job.

Given this leadership requirement, it is easy to see how certain kinds of people are overlooked. Quiet characters, the kind who come to work just to get the job done and get out of there, are not selected for promotion. Juan, the father of Kyesha's son, is on these grounds not managerial material. As Bob sees it, "Juan is quiet; he has no ambition. He's just there, just content to do what he's doing right now. He wouldn't even give me an answer if I asked him if he wanted to manage—that's how quiet he is."

Young people whose main ambition, apart from earning some money, involves having a good time on the job (and therefore looking for opportunities to goof off), do not advance either. Bob would place the majority of teenagers who work for him in this category and would not think of them for future supervisory roles.

Individuals who seem, or are assumed, to have a chip on their shoulders are rarely candidates for promotion. Here especially there is room for considerable discretion and judgment. When Bob sees an "attitude case" coming, he can't conceive of that person as managerial material. Ron is a case in point. Ron comes from a tough background and has brothers who have been in jail off and on most of their adolescent lives. He alternates between jobs like Burger Barn and selling T-shirts in the Harlem street markets. Ron is an articulate character with a sharper sense of racial injustice and a stronger commitment to black nationalism than any other fast food employee we met. He chafes at the deference demanded of him in the chain of command, and this, more than anything else, rubs Bob the wrong way. But Ron is smart and efficient. He has mastered the grill and can run the operation almost by himself. These skills might make him managerial material. But Bob's view is that Ron is trouble.

He is lookin' for handouts. I look at him every day and say, "What is he doin' to make himself better?" He's not doin' anything. . . . He's working, but he's barely holding on. The reason why I don't want to fire him is because I don't want another knucklehead out on the street. But if he got me upset, I would get rid of him today. He thinks we supposed to give him something; he's not supposed to work for it. That's how he thinks. He wants to be a manager, but he has no qualities.

Ron, not realizing that he is one step away from losing his job altogether, has asked whether he could be considered for management. The response he got was unequivocally negative. Bob told him that he would have to do something about "his mouth on the floor, his leadership, his appearance, hygiene, you name it . . . attitude." Not much chance of promotion for Ron.

Bob's disgust comes not only from the frustration he experiences in supervising Ron, a less deferential or "obedient" employee than what he is looking for, but the discouragement he and his fellow managers feel when workers who are clearly smart enough to advance disappoint them with behavior that marks them as lower-class. Managers and business owners in ghetto settings like Harlem are attracted to their own positions for more than the money they can earn. They are also on something of a personal mission to lift their own people up through conventional means: working for a living. They believe that the able-bodied do not deserve handouts, that employment is the only meaningful source of dignity, and that at least in a place like Burger Barn, one need only show a modicum of ambition and leadership to reap the rewards of upward movement.

Managers invest a great deal of time and no small amount of their sense of personal reward in the cultivation of their employees. They arrange for glasses for those who have trouble with their eyesight, help young people open bank accounts when they have no one else to cosign for them, give advice on housing, make sure that people who have never had identification get driver's licenses or ID cards, counsel young women worried about pregnancy, provide literacy training for adults who have not learned to read, and perform countless other tasks more like social work than fast food management. But this involvement is willingly provided—without any particular corporate support—because these inner-city managers are committed to change in the quality of life for people living in the ghetto.

This mixture of traditional expectations and missionary zeal fuses with the mobility experiences and class backgrounds of managers to produce frustration when they encounter young adults who share neither their expectations nor their confidence in the likelihood of success. Managers like Bob, who have come up the hard way, give no quarter to young black men like Ron, who appears to be arrogant and unwilling to embrace the hierarchy that structures most work organizations. His supervisory counterparts in other Harlem restaurants, some of whom have military backgrounds, are equally intolerant when workers flout the rules of etiquette (or food production). They are searching for workers who come from depressed communities, but have emerged with something approximating middle-class values and behaviors—people who embrace the same conservative view of getting ahead that the managers themselves do.

This does not mean they expect or require potential managers to be conventional in their family structures, religious beliefs, attitudes toward education, or child-rearing practices. Theirs is not a blanket traditionalism. Bob has one child born out of wedlock himself, and he is not unusual. The conduct they are concerned with is decoupled from these extra-occupational domains and focuses instead on how people comport themselves at work. That is precisely what they find in a goodly number of Burger Barn workers, which is why competition for promotion is hot. But they also see a fair amount of the opposite: people who have the brains to prosper, but who lack the disposition to show deference to authority, or who display behavioral characteristics that are emblems of resistance (hairstyles, gold jewelry, linguistic styles, or eye contact patterns)—whether or not resistance is what they mean to communicate.

HUMAN CAPITAL IN THE PROMOTION PROCESS

The three success stories Bob has fostered—Fernando, Jessica, and Latoya—are not people who brought sparkling academic records to the table. Latoya, in particular, struggled to finish a GED degree. Formal schooling is of limited importance for advancement in the lower ranks of Burger Barn.[17] Once their personal qualities attract the general manager's attention, however, academic skills do matter. Managerial trainees have to master a thick textbook that covers running shifts, delegating tasks, monitoring inventory, repairing equipment, accounting for cash, and a whole series of other chores that are essential management responsibilities. Bob had to issue pop quizzes on this material not unlike the ones these trainees once faced in high school algebra.

With that course work under their belts, the managers-to-be were sent to a regional training program, where they faced a series of formal examinations, followed by the design of "action plans," a series of goals and objectives each person has promised to master, plans their supervisors must certify as complete. Only when these steps are done can these workers graduate to swing managers, a move that provides only a modest increase in salary. The three swing managers described here were never star students in high school, but they were able to perform well enough in these school-like training exercises to be promoted. General managers do not select for promotion individuals who cannot master this book learning. Hardworking immigrant employees whose English-language skills don't cut it will not be promoted, even if they are virtuous in all other respects. Indeed, we met many native-born employees who were valued for their industriousness but were functionally illiterate and were therefore passed over.[18]

It is a long way from first-line management to the point where that "real money" comes their way. And at any point in time, eight to ten swing managers will be competing for the two salaried positions that lie above them in the hierarchy. Only in a business that is expanding rapidly can a large number of crew members expect to move up into this ever-narrowing pyramid by being absorbed into the managerial ranks of newly opened restaurants. This does in fact happen, and because the inner city is actually an expanding market for Burger Barn, demand for management is steady. But the expansion is not great enough to absorb all those who would like to reach the salaried ranks, hence competition for those precious openings is stiff.

With upward mobility circumscribed and wages held low by the desire to contain costs, the typical Burger Barn worker can expect to come and go from the firm without seeing much advancement at all. The jobs are built for churning, a pattern that is acceptable for teenagers looking for summer jobs, but distressingly limited for adults who are trying to make a real go of it in the private labor market.

CHAPTER SEVEN

Family Values

Rosa Lee Cunningham, the subject of Leon Dash's Pulitzer Prize–winning series in the *Washington Post*, is an epitome of poverty for the end of the twentieth century.[1] Born the eldest girl in a Washington, D.C., family that had been liberated from the privations of southern sharecropping only in the 1930s, Rosa Lee quickly spiraled down into oblivion. Rosa Lee's first child was born when she was a mere fourteen years old. By the time she was twenty-four, Rosa Lee's children numbered eight and their six fathers were nowhere to be seen. She raised her kids on her own by waitressing in nightclubs, selling drugs, and shoplifting. In the wake of her own disillusionment and the overwhelming burden of taking care of her children, Rosa Lee was drawn to heroin. When stealing to support her family and her habit proved unreliable, she sold herself on the street and then turned her own daughter into a hooker to maintain the needed cash flow.

Responses to Dash's series, and the book that followed, have taken a predictable path: reviewers have been as worried as they have been disgusted by the cultural disintegration Rosa Lee and her ilk represent. Rosa Lee, who could not stay away from men of questionable character, and then did disastrously poorly by the children that resulted, takes center stage as the prototypical underclass mother, the prime mover in her own despair. And the crime and degradation that follow are depicted as the inevitable result of a culture of poverty so deep that it defies remedy. No jobs program, no drug program, no heavenly social worker, can rescue someone like Rosa Lee Cunningham. She is a lost soul, with children condemned to repeat her mistakes,[2] while the rest of society suffers the consequences of predatory criminals in its midst.

Powerful portraits of this kind have shaped public impressions of inner-city families. They present implicit explanations for how poor people fall to the bottom of society's heap: by failing to control their impulses. American culture is predisposed to find such an explanation appealing, since it rests upon the view that people are masters of their own destinies, that they can, by dint of individual effort, control the circumstances of their lives. Those that fail fall to the ground where they belong, not because they have been denied opportunity, or are victims of forces larger than anyone could control, but because they have succumbed to temptation or lack the brains to do any better—the story told by Herrnstein and Murray's book *The Bell Curve.* It is a story as old as the Puritans and as resonant today as it was in the seventeenth century.

The inner city does indeed have more than its share of families like the Cunninghams. Their problems reflect the crushing personal costs of living in parts of our country where good jobs have gone the way of the dinosaurs, where schools can be hard to distinguish from penitentiaries, and where holding families together has become women's work, while the means to do so have become the object of a fierce competition. More than a few in central Harlem have found themselves in Rosa Lee's situation.

But they are a minority, and a despised one at that. They are so far from the accepted, approved personification of motherhood and family life that they do not even belong in the same world with the families of Latoya or Carmen. Journalists and scholars who write about the Rosa Lees of this world have focused their energies on those inner-city residents who are the most troubled and who inflict the greatest damage on their neighbors. Their passions are understandable, for in keeping with the spirit that animated the original War on Poverty, they want to reawaken America's conscience and persuade us that we have a cancer growing in the midst of our prosperity. That message worked effectively in the 1960s, when the country was bursting with economic growth, the middle class was secure in its comforts, and faith in the capacity of government to eradicate social ills had not yet been eviscerated.

The same message delivered in the 1990s has had the opposite impact. Focusing on the deviant cases, on the whoring mothers, the criminal fathers, the wilding teenagers, and the abandoned toddlers, merely confirms a knowing hopelessness or worse: a Darwinian conviction that perhaps we should just "let it burn," sacrificing the present generation in the hope of rehabilitating future ghetto dwellers. Attitudes have hardened in part as the litany of broken lives dominates the only "news" in print from the inner city.

It would be absurd to suggest that the downbeat reports are untrue. The "underclass" story is a persistent, intractable, and most of all depressing reality for those who cannot escape it. But there is a war for the soul of the ghetto, and it has two sides. On the other side of deviance lie the families who embrace mainstream values, even if they don't look like Ozzie and Harriet, who push their children to do better, even when they have not progressed far in life themselves. Indeed, these families—the working poor and many a "welfare family" as well—are the first to condemn the Rosa Lees of their own neighborhood, to point to them as examples of what they don't want to be.

Who is winning this culture war? What are the *dominant* values of inner-city residents? The sociological emphasis on separated subcultures in the inner city has ignored the power of mainstream models and institutions like schools, the influence of the media, the convictions of poor parents, and the power of negative examples to shape the moral world of the ghetto poor. We must not confuse the irregular social structures of families—which do indeed depart from the canonical forms of middle-class society—with a separate set of values. Structure and culture can diverge in ghetto society as they do elsewhere in this country.

FAMILY VALUES

Latoya has a complicated family tree. Her mother, Ilene, who is on disability because of her diabetes, lives in the Bronx, far enough away to be in another world. Latoya's father, Alvin, has had many jobs in the course of his adult life—working mainly as a truck driver—and has only recently, in his later years, become once again a constant presence in Latoya's life. His problems with alcohol have made him a nuisance at times, but he has been welcomed back into the extended family fold because "he's blood" and has, for now at least, made a sincere effort to leave the booze behind.

Many years ago, Latoya's father began living with Elizabeth, then a recent migrant from rural Georgia, from a sleepy little town where there was nothing much to do and nowhere to go. First chance she got, Lizzie had boarded a bus for New York and begun her lifelong career cleaning houses for wealthy whites on New York's Upper East Side. She has been doing domestic work now for about twenty-five years, during which she gave birth to two daughters, Natasha and Stephanie, Latoya's half sisters through the father they share.

Though Alvin has been only sporadically in the picture, Latoya, Natasha, and Stephanie became a devoted band of sisters who look to Lizzie as the spiritual and practical head of the family. Together they form an extended family of long standing. They live within a few blocks of one another; they attend church together, especially on the important holidays.

Latoya was the first of the sisters to land a job at Burger Barn, but she was able to get Natasha on the crew not long thereafter. The two half sisters have worked together, covering for one another, blowing off the steam generated by confrontational customers, and supporting one another in the face of problem-seeking managers for nearly five years now. Little sister Stephanie, a junior in high school who has also had a summer stint at the Barn, makes it possible for Latoya to maintain a steady presence at work. It falls to Stephanie to retrieve Latoya's children from their city-funded day care center and after-school programs on those days when Latoya has to work late. Stephanie is often the one who stays with her nieces and nephews when Latoya has to work the night shift. Natasha used to do the same for Latoya.

Without the support that Natasha and Stephanie provide, Latoya would have a very hard time holding on to her job. But if we reduced the role these sisters play in Latoya's life to the instrumental need for emergency child care, we would miss the true depth of their interdependence. This is really one family, spread over several physical households in a pattern that will be familiar to readers of Carol Stack's classic book *All Our Kin*. Stack describes the complex exchange relations that characterize the families of the "Flats," a poor community in southern Illinois where goods and people circulate in a never-ending swap system. Reciprocal relations provide mothers with an insurance system against scarcity, unpredictable landlords, jobs that come and go, AFDC checks that get cut off without warning, and men who give what they can but much of the time find they have little to contribute.

FAMILY CIRCLES — SUPPORT STRUCTURES AMONG THE WORKING POOR

No one in Latoya's extended family network is on welfare; the adults are all working, even Alvin, drinking problem and all. The children are in school. Yet because they are poor as well, these folk live in clusters of households that are perpetually intertwined. Although Latoya and Lizzie are separate "heads of households" as the Census Bureau might define them, in a very real sense they are one social system with moving parts that cannot stand alone. The older sisters, Natasha and Latoya, go out to clubs together when they can get Stephanie to baby-sit; together they hatch surprise birthday celebrations for Lizzie. Joining forces with their

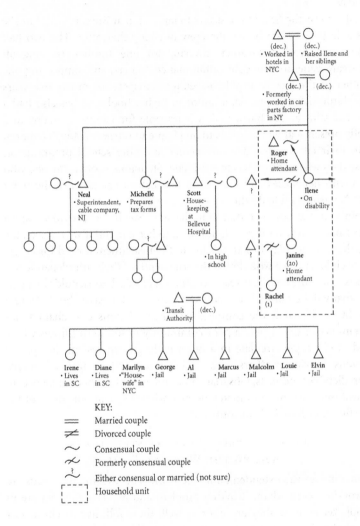

KEY:

=	Married couple
≠	Divorced couple
~	Consensual couple
≁	Formerly consensual couple
?~	Either consensual or married (not sure)
⌐ ⌐	Household unit

Figure 2. Latoya's Family Tree—1995

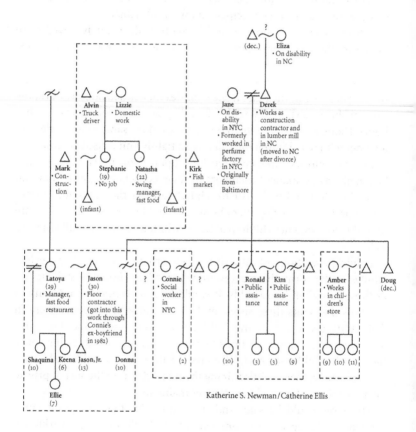

Katherine S. Newman / Catherine Ellis

cousins, aunts, and uncles, they haul turkeys and cranberries up the stairs to whichever apartment can hold the largest number of people when it is time to host the Thanksgiving feast. And when Christmas comes, Latoya's children, sisters, and cousins and Lizzie and Alvin dress up in their Sunday best and lay claim to nearly a whole pew in the Baptist church several blocks away. Lizzie complains that her children don't attend church in the regular way she does, a habit born of her southern origins. But like many American families, Latoya and her sisters honor their mother's attachment to the church and participate in this family ritual.

Latoya, Natasha, Stephanie, and Lizzie have deliberately stayed close to one another not only because they need one another for practical support but because they value family above all else. "Family are your best friends," Natasha explains. Latoya is Natasha's closest friend, the person she socializes with, the person she confides in, her defender at work, the woman she goes shopping with when they want to look their best after hours. Danielle, cousin to them both, is part of the same inner circle, and together with her children they all form a tightly knit extended family.

Indeed, Latoya's three children look upon their aunts, Natasha and Stephanie, as permanent members of their household, people they can depend on to braid their hair for church, answer the occasional homework question, and bring them home an illicit burger or two. It was rare to find Latoya and her children at home without one of her half sisters as well.

Public perceptions of America center around middle-class nuclear families as the norm, the goal toward which others should be striving. Yet in those suburban households, it would be rare to find the intensity of relations that knits these sisters and cousins together, keeping them in daily contact with one another. Middle-class Americans value autonomy, including autonomous relations between generations and siblings once they reach adulthood. And, of course, if they have a stable hold on a decent income, there is little forcing them together into the sort of private safety net that Latoya and her relatives maintain.

The same could be said, and then some, for the immigrant families who make up a significant part of Harlem's low-wage workforce. Dominicans, Haitians, Jamaicans, West Africans, and South Americans from various countries have settled in Harlem's outer pockets. Immigrant workers in the low-wage economy depend upon extensive family networks—composed of seasoned migrants who have lived in New York for some time and those newly arrived—to organize their housing, child care, and a pool of income that they can tap when the need arises.

Streaming into New York in an age-old pattern of chain migration, immigrants are often faced with the need to support family members back home while they attempt to meet the far higher costs of living they encounter in their adopted city. Families that are ineligible for government benefits routinely provided to the native-born must work long hours, pack a large number of people into small apartments, and recruit as many wage earners into the network as possible.

Immigrants cluster into apartment buildings in much the same fashion as the African-American poor do, both because relatives have been instrumental in helping their family members find housing and because proximity makes it that much easier to organize collective child-minding or communal meals. In Carmen's building there are five households linked together by kinship connections. Their members move freely between them, opening the refrigerator door in one to see whether there's anything good to eat, watching television in another because it has a cable hookup, using the one phone that hasn't been cut off for nonpayment. Carmen's grandmother watches her grandchildren, a half-dozen in all now, so that their parents can go to work.

Yet to really understand the meaning of family in Carmen's life, one has to look back to the Dominican Republic, where her mother and one of her sisters still live. Carmen had to leave her mother behind to join her father and his kin, a transition necessitated both by her ambitions and by the declining purchasing power of her mother's paycheck. Carmen sends back money whenever she can, usually once a month, and that remittance spells the difference between a decent standard of living in *La Republica* and a slide into poverty.[3] For Carmen, though, this is a poor substitute for the intimacy she longs for, the daily love and affection of her mother. What she really wants, more than anything in this world, is to obtain a green card so that she can sponsor her mother and younger sister in New York. Now that she is a young parent herself, she wants her own mother close by so that she does not have to depend exclusively on her paternal relatives. That prospect is far off, though, and Carmen has to be content with the occasional trip back to her homeland, something she manages once every two or three years.

For immigrants, then, the meaning of family stretches over the seas and persists through long absences. It is organized into daisy chains of people who have followed each other, one by one, and then settled into pockets that turn into ethnic enclaves dense with interlocking ties. Families that lived next door to one another in Haiti land on adjacent blocks in Harlem. The same pattern organizes the native migrants from America's rural South, who also put down roots in Harlem neighborhoods. One can still find blocks dominated by people from particular towns in Georgia or the Carolinas and their descendants. In this respect, the native-born and the international migrant share common settlement patterns, which, in turn, provide the social structure that is so vital to the survival of the working poor.

Well-heeled families can buy the services they need to manage the demands of work and family. They can purchase child care, borrow from banks when they need to, pay their bills out of their salaries, and lean on health insurance when a doctor is needed. Affluence loosens the ties that remain tight, even oppressive at times, in poor communities. Yet there is an enduring uneasiness in our culture about the degree of independence generations and members of nuclear families maintain from one another, a sense that something has been lost. We look back with nostalgia at the close-knit family ties that were characteristic of the "immigrant generations" of the past and that still bind together newcomers to our shores, for the same reasons immigrants clung together at the turn of the century.[4]

What we fail to recognize is that many inner-city families, especially the majority who work to support themselves, maintain these close links with one another, preserving a form of social capital that has all but disappeared in many an American suburb.[5] These strong ties are the center of social life for the likes of Latoya and Natasha. It is true that these family values compete with other ambitions: the desire for a nice house and a picket fence in a suburb where graffiti doesn't mar the scenery and mothers needn't worry constantly about street violence. They dream about the prospect of owning a home and garden somewhere far away from Harlem. Yet if that miracle day arrived, they would be faced with a serious dilemma: unless they could afford to take everyone near and dear to them along on the adventure, they would find it very hard to live with the distance such a move would put between them and their relatives.

Why do we assume that family values of this kind are a thing of the past in the ghetto? While the answer lies in part on the emphasis that writers have given to people like Rosa Lee, it is just as much an artifact of the way we confuse kinship structures with the moral culture of family life in the inner city. Very few of the people who work for Burger Barn live in households that resemble the Bill Cosby model. Most are adult children in single-parent households, and some are single parents themselves. Latoya, for example, divorced her first husband when he turned to drugs, and has for a number of years now had a common-law relationship with Jason, the father of her son, the youngest child (at age two) in her household.

Jason has lived with Latoya's family most of this time, taking on much of the financial responsibility for Latoya's children, since his earnings as a skilled craftsman are much higher than her Burger Barn wages. Still, their relationship has had its ups and downs; they have broken up and reconciled more than once.

Family patterns of this kind certainly do not sound like suburban America, or at least not the middle-class culture we would like to believe defines mainstream life.[6] The instability of family organization in America's ghettos has been the source of much hand-wringing. There can be little doubt that children born out of wedlock face an uphill battle, as they are more likely to be raised in poverty,[7] and that children of divorce, no matter what segment of society they come from, are similarly disadvantaged.[8]

However, we should not assume that "irregular" household structures suggest a diminished regard for the importance of family life, for the closeness of kin. Even though Latoya anguishes over Jason during their rough spots, she is no less attached to or attentive to her children. She draws the rest of her kin, especially her female kin, closer to her and builds a nest of loving relatives who sustain the familial bond and help her create a stable environment for her children. Latoya's values place family, particularly the well-being of her children, at the top of her priorities. Were we to look at the structure of her household and focus only on the ways it deviates from the nuclear family norm, we would miss what is most important about it: the quality of the relationships inside and the links between them and the web of kin who live in nearby apartments. Without them, it is true, Latoya would have a difficult time sustaining order or protecting her children in the dicey neighborhood where they live. But her story is a success in part because it is a story of a family that has pulled together against considerable adversity.

Patty began her career ten years ago at Burger Barn. She worked full-time for the entire nine months of her first pregnancy and didn't leave work until the baby was born. She continued working and finished high school even though her second child was on the way. Her attachment to the job, through the thick-and-thin of a failed marriage and a stint on welfare, reflects the values her mother instilled. Patty's mother has worked all her life as a home attendant, first with mothers recently home from the hospital with their new babies in tow and then with homebound elderly. Working as a home aide was something of an upward step in the family, for Patty's maternal grandmother spent her whole life as a housekeeper.

My grandmother, who just passed [away], was my idol all during the
time I was growing up. She bought a house in Queens off scrubbing
floors. She bought that house and mortgaged it two or three times, so she
had to start all over paying it off. But she did it.

Hence Patty and her sister, who also is in home health care, taking care of
AIDS patients, have come from a long line of women who have shoul-
dered the burdens of earning a living and raising their children. None of
them would have been able to manage these responsibilities were it not
for the fact that each in turn has made the extended family the core of her
life. Patty's mother lives on the sixth floor of her building and still has her
son, Patty's brother, under her wing. Patty's sister lives just a few blocks
away. Their proximity has made a big difference in Patty's life, for with
their collective help, she has been able to go to work knowing that there
are other adults in her family who can help watch her children.

This web of kinship does not supersede the individual household or
substitute collective child-rearing for that of the mother-in-charge. Patty
remains the main figure around whom her kids' lives revolve. She is the
one who feeds and clothes them, watches over their homework, and puts
the Band-Aids on when they skin their knees. She keeps them safe from
the pitfalls of the streets that surround her apartment in a Harlem public
housing complex. She has gone without things she needs for herself so
she could afford air-conditioning and a Nintendo machine, items that
sound like luxuries but turn out to be the key—or at least one key—to
keeping her kids indoors and safe through the hot summer months. They
must have something to play with and somewhere to cool off if she is
to leave the teenagers to their own devices while she is working. At
least equally important, however, is Patty's reliance upon her siblings and
her mother as substitute supervisors of her kids, her adjunct eyes and
ears, when she is at work. Without them, she would be faced with some
unhappy choices.

While family support is critical for working parents, it is no less important in the lives of working youth. Teenagers at Burger Barn are often on
the receiving end of the same kind of care from older relatives or "friends
of the family" who are so close they constitute what anthropologists call
"fictive kin," honorary aunts and uncles. Shaquena, who began working
in a gym for little kids sponsored by a local church when she was just
eleven, has had a difficult life. Her mother has been in and out of jail on
drug convictions; one of her brothers was convicted of murder. Had her

grandmother not been willing to take her in, Shaquena might have joined the thousands of New York City children shuffled into foster care.

As it is, she lives with her grandmother, who has raised her since she was ten years old. And Shaquena isn't the only one in the family who has sheltered under Grandma's wing. The household includes Shaquena's aunt, her aunt's two children, a cousin, two unmarried uncles, and an aunt and uncle who have a child as well. The grandmother has taken in her adult children and grandchildren, so that the household is a three-generation affair, albeit with several missing links (like Shaquena's own mother). Together the generations share the burden of supporting this extended household, relying on a combination of earned income and state aid: SSI for the grandmother, unemployment insurance for one of the aunts, the wages brought in by one of the uncles who works in a police station, the underground earnings of another who washes cars, and Shaquena's Burger Barn salary.

The Harlem neighborhood Shaquena calls home is jam-packed with people—kin and friends—who visit one another, eat together, and borrow from one another when the need arises.

> *My aunt . . . lives right across the street from us. She, like last night, my grandmother ran out of sugar. My grandmother called my aunt and my aunt bought her the sugar. The guy down the hall, he real cool with us, he give us stuff, and my grandmother's cool with a lot of elderly on our floor. She will ask her daughter, my aunt, for things before she asks a friend, but she's got friends [to ask]. If I need something, I go right upstairs, because my best friend lives right upstairs. Her grandmother and my grandmother are friends and they keep a kitchen full of food.*

Shaquena can depend upon this circle of friends and relatives to take care of her basic needs, so she can reserve her own earnings for the necessities of teenage life. But she is conscious of the dry periods when funds are tight and often uses her savings to buy toothpaste, soap, and little things for the baby in the house or for her godson who lives across the street with her aunt. It is important to her to pull her own weight and to contribute to the collective well-being of her family whenever she knows it's needed.

The practical side of this arrangement is important. Yet so too is the emotional value of having a big family, especially since Shaquena has had such a rocky relationship with her mother. With her grandmother, aunts, uncles, and cousins, she has a secure place in a situation that is as real and important to her as any nuclear family, suburban-style.

"Absent" Men

Popular accounts of the ghetto world often lament the declining presence of men—especially fathers—in the life of the family. Men are in jail in record numbers; they have no interest in marrying the mothers of their children; they "hit" and run. That men cause grief to the women and children who need them is hardly news. As the divorce statistics remind us, this is a sad story repeated in every class. All over America there are children who need fathers but don't have them. We have developed a culture, both in the ghetto and outside it, that assigns to women the responsibility for raising children, leaving men peripheral to the task.

This is not to minimize the difference between a jailed father and a divorced father, a poor father who has never married the mother of his children and a more affluent father who fails to pay child support. There are differences, and they have consequences. Survey research tells us, for example, that single-parent children of never-married mothers are more likely than those of divorced parents to drop out of high school, and that daughters of never-married mothers are more likely than those of divorced parents to become teen mothers—though, it should be added, the differences are not as large as some pundits might claim.[9]

Yet it would be drawing too broad a brush stroke to suggest that men have absented themselves wholesale from the inner city. Uncles, fathers, brothers, sons, boyfriends—and husbands—are very much in evidence in the daily comings-and-goings of working poor families in Harlem. They help to support the households they live in and often provide regular infusions of cash, food, and time to the mothers of their children with whom they do not live.[10] The Bureau of the Census or a sociologist looking at a survey could easily miss the presence of men in Harlem households where they do not officially live, but to which they are nonetheless important as providers. Juan, father of Kyesha's son, is a case in point. He regularly gives part of his paycheck to his mother, who has several younger children and has been on AFDC for as long as he can remember. Juan also gives money to Kyesha to help take care of their son. Little of this check is left by the time he takes care of everyone who depends on him.

It is a struggle to make ends meet. Like if I plan on buying something that week, then I got to hold back on that. 'Cause we got cable and you got to

*help out, you know. Or say the lights got to be paid. So I give a hundred
dollars this week, fifty the next week. My mother has a bad habit sometimes. She doesn't think reasonably. So sometimes a lot of money has to
come out of my pocket—I pay whole bills so I can get that off my back.*

When the welfare authorities discovered that Juan was giving his mother
money, they moved to take away some of her grant. He countered by finding a couch to sleep on in a friend's apartment so that his mother could
report that he no longer lives in her home.

Reynaldo, whose mother is Puerto Rican and father from Ecuador, is a
jack-of-all-trades who worked for a brief time at Burger Barn in between
various hustles as a nonunion electrician, car repairman, carpenter, and
cellular phone dealer for fellow Latinos in his Dominican neighborhood.
A tall, stocky young man with a love of baggy pants and gold chains, Rey
is a classic entrepreneur. He mixes and matches his job opportunities,
picking up anything he can get on the side. For a time he had a job stocking shelves in a drugstore, but during his off-hours he made money fixing
up broken-down cars for neighbors and rewiring a vacant apartment for
his landlord. Rey works all the hours that are not consumed by school, his
girlfriend, and hanging out with his younger brother.

No doubt he is influenced in his own brand of workaholism by the
example of his father, Ernie, who taught him much of what he knows
about electrical and machine repair. Ernie has never met a mechanical
device he couldn't tear down to the foundation and rebuild just like new.
Outside on the street curb sit the broken-down Fords, Dodges, and GM
cars that await his attention. His auto repair shop is just the sidewalk in
front of their apartment building, but everyone in the neighborhood
knows that this is a business venue. Ernie is forever walking around with
a cloth in his hands, wiping away the grease and oil from an old car he
has torn apart and made whole again. The shelves of the family's back
room are crammed with blowtorches, pliers, hammers, wrenches, reels of
plastic-coated wiring—all the equipment needed to fix the long line of
radios and TV sets that friends and friends of friends have left behind for
repair.

As if he weren't busy enough, Ernie has a lively sideline as an off-the-
books contractor, renovating apartments destined for immigrant families
just like his own. Old apartment buildings in the Dominican neighborhoods have bad plumbing, plaster weeping off the walls, tiles missing,
caulking cracked and flaking, windows shattered and taped. Landlords
claim to have little money for keeping apartments up to code and in any

case prefer to use local workers and avoid union labor. Their preferences keep Ernie in work as the apartments turn over. In turn, Ernie has kept Rey at his side and taught him everything he knows so he can turn over some of the work he has no time for, maintaining the opportunity "in the family."

Rey's mother is a student, working toward an Associate in Arts degree that will, she hopes, make it possible for her to work in computer administration someday. Most of her days are spent going to a community college that is a long subway ride from home. Until Mayor Giuliani canceled the policy, her education was subsidized by the city welfare system (in an effort to further the long-term career prospects of women on AFDC). After many years of working in a bra factory, she has come to understand the importance of credentials and is determined to accumulate them so that she can get a good job with decent pay.

Rey's younger brother, now sixteen, has staked his future on the prospect of going to college, for he seems to have the academic gifts. Where Rey coasts through school and sees little purpose in it, his brother would visit me at Columbia University and look eagerly at the college as heaven. He works during the summers and on the weekends for a print shop that is owned by a friend of the family.

In contrast to the households discussed earlier, whose earnings come mainly from the hard work of women, Rey's family relies largely on the income of the menfolk. While his mother has worked odd factory jobs now and again and hopes to find a real job when she finishes her studies, it is the entrepreneurial spirit of the men in the household that keeps the family going. Between them, father and sons earn enough in the (non-taxed) underground economy and the formal (wage-labor) system to keep the family at a lower-working-class standard of living. They have nothing to spare, they cannot do without any of these sources of income, but they are not starving. They can even hope that the youngest child will be able to get through high school and make it into a public college, something that will require heavy doses of financial aid, but is not an unthinkable goal.

It is tempting to look at Rey's family as an inner-city exception, an icon of middle-class virtue. The two-parent family, the loving brothers, and the entrepreneurial energy all add up to an admirable portrait of a stable, supportive circle of kin pulling together. And there is much truth to the view. Yet, Rey's parents are actually divorced. They broke up years ago in order to qualify the household for welfare. Rey's father maintains an official address elsewhere.

If we were to look at an official government census of Rey's household, we would find that the adults within it are classified as out of the labor force. Indeed, it would be deemed a single-parent household supported by the welfare system. Harlem is populated by thousands of families whose official profiles look just like this. Yet there is a steady income stream coming into Rey's home, because most of the adults are indeed working, often in the mostly unregulated economy of small-scale services and self-employment, including home-based seamstresses, food vendors, gypsy cab drivers, and carpenters.[11] Most of this income never sees the tax man.

Much of what has been written about this underground system focuses on the drug world. But for thousands of poor people in New York who cannot afford a unionized plumber or electrician, unlicensed craftsmen and informal service workers (who provide child care or personal services) are more important exemplars of the shadow economy. Men like Rey and his father provide reasonably priced services and products, making it possible for people who would otherwise have to do without to get their cars fixed, their leaking roofs patched, or their children looked after. Immigrants who lack legal papers find employment in this shadow world, and those who are legal take second jobs in the underground economy.

It has proved extremely hard to estimate the size of this alternative system,[12] but it is so widespread in poor communities that it often rivals the formal economy. The multipurpose shop Rey's father runs from the living room and the street corner is the mainstay of the family's income, and in this they are hardly alone. The thoroughfares of Harlem have, for many years, had an active sidewalk market trade that is largely invisible to the Internal Revenue Service.[13]

Whether we look at employment or "family structure," Rey's household departs from the normative model of the nuclear family. The statistical observer or census-taker might lump this family together with others as dissolved, or as one whose adult members have been out of the labor force for many years. But anyone who is paying closer attention will see that this makes no sense. These people do make up an actively functioning family, and in fact kinship means everything to them. Their values place work and family at the center of their own culture in a form that would be embraced even by conservative forces in American society. And the men of the family are at least as committed to these norms as the women.

Jamal is the only income-earner in his tiny household. His common-law wife, Kathy, once received SSA, a government support provided to her because her father died when she was just a child. But once she ran away to live with Jamal, these funds were appropriated by her mother. Nowadays Jamal spends hours on the bus to reach his job sweeping floors and cleaning toilets in a Burger Barn in another borough. In Jamal's opinion, a real man earns a living and supports his family, and he puts his dictum into practice daily in a job that most Americans wouldn't waste their time on. In this, he follows a path, a cultural definition of manhood, that continues to emphasize responsibility to family, responsibility that is sometimes expressed from a distance (as in Juan's case), while other times defined by coresidence (as is true for Ernie or Jamal).

Black men have been blanketed with negative publicity, excoriated as no good, irresponsible, swaggering in their masculinity, trapped in a swamp of "ghetto-related behavior."[14] Is this simply the force of stereotypes at work on a national psyche predisposed to believe the worst? Of course not. There are men in Harlem who have turned their backs on their mothers, wives, girlfriends, and children. Yet while we deplore the damage these males cause, we may overlook people like Jamal or Juan, or fifteen-year-old James, who brings his paycheck home to his parents to help with the rent, or Salvador, who works two jobs so that his wife, Carmen, and daughter will have a roof over their heads. We will not see the contributions that Latoya's common-law husband has made to the support of her children. And if we are to truly understand the role that men play in sustaining family values, we have to credit the existence of these honorable examples, while recognizing that many of their brethren have failed to follow through.

Some of those "failures" are young blacks who have irregular connections to family, who have no real place to live, whose seasonal labor is so poorly paid that there isn't much they can do to provide for their girlfriends even when they are so inclined.[15] Ron's mother died when he was a teenager. He now lives somewhat uneasily on the sufferance of his girlfriend while working at Burger Barn off and on. Since this relationship also is off and on, his living arrangements are precarious.

> *You could say I work and pay my rent. I pay for where I stay at with my girl. My girl is my landlord, but nobody knows that. She does want money. I don't like to say this is my own bread, 'cause I don't like to be caught up in that "I'm gonna kick you out." So I always stay in contact with my family. That way, if something happens between me and her, my sister lives in Brooklyn and she always has the door open for me until I make me another power move. My sister's household is secure, but me,*

I'm on the edge when it comes to financial things. 'Cause if Burger Barn falls off, then I'm off.

Ron is so close to the edge that he cannot do anything more than contribute some of his wages to whatever household he lands in for the time being. People in his situation have nothing left over for anyone else, which is one of the reasons they don't behave like people with commitments. This is no excuse for siring children they can't support, but it does point to the importance of steady, reasonably paid employment in encouraging responsibility, a point William Julius Wilson has brought to national attention in *When Work Disappears*. Men who lack the wherewithal to be good fathers, often aren't.

FAMILY FLAWS

In pointing to the continuous importance of family as a set of values expressed in practice, I do not mean to paint the households of the working poor as indistinguishable from the "mainstream model." Seen through middle-class eyes, there is much to worry about. Parents who work at the bottom of the income pyramid are stressed, tired, and stretched to the limit of their ability to cope. The irregularity of the income they receive, whether from low-wage jobs, undependable partners, or both, subjects families like Latoya's to unpredictable shortages, gnawing insecurities. Welfare reform is blowing like an ill wind through many of these kin networks, and because the working poor and the AFDC recipients are interleaved, policy directives aimed at the latter are derailing many of the former. Lacking vacations, having little left over to pamper themselves with after a long day flipping burgers, and seeing so little advancement ahead of them, Burger Barn workers are often short-tempered at home. Economic pressures cannot descend upon families without showing their effects, especially on young kids.

Kyesha's two-year-old son, Anthony, spends much of his day in front of a television set tuned perpetually to soap operas and game shows. Sesame Street crosses the screen on occasion, but the purpose of the tube is not to educate little Anthony but to entertain his grandmother, stuck at home with him and several children of her own. Grandma Dana is not particularly attentive to Anthony's emotional needs, even though she keeps him fed and safe. He is never left alone, he does not run into the street, and his clothes are clean. But the focus stops there, and Anthony's behavior reflects the absence of sustained adult attention.

When Kyesha comes home, she wants to flop down on her bed and skim through movie star magazines. She lacks the energy to play with an active child.[16] She spends a lot of time figuring out how she is going to get to see her boyfriend and works on Dana in the hope that she will baby-sit Anthony for yet another evening so she can go out. The little boy is given to wandering into the tiny room they share and sounding off in an attempt to get Kyesha's attention. More often than not, she shoos him away so she can relax. If, like any normal two-year-old, he fails to obey, he is likely to be swatted.

Anthony will not start kindergarten knowing his colors and numbers, or the daily drill of communal "circle time" that is thoroughly familiar to any child who has spent time in a quality day care center. He will head down the road with a lack of basic experience that will weigh heavily when his teachers begin to assess his reading readiness or language fluency. There are consequences to growing up poor in a household of people who are pedaling hard just to stay afloat and have no time or reserve capacity left to provide the kind of enrichment that middle-class families can offer in abundance.

Shaquena has a rich array of people to turn to when she needs help. She has a web of kin and family friends living all around her, people who feed her and give her a place to hang out when all is not well at home. Yet her mother is a drug addict and her family broke up long ago under the strain. Had it not been for her grandmother, she would have found herself in foster care, her mother declared unfit. Hanging out with her girl-friends in the public housing project near her apartment in her younger years, she was known for getting into trouble. Fights, retaliation for insults, conflicts over boys—all have escalated to the point of serious violence. Shaquena's attachment to the work world is impressive because of this unlikely background, but the traces of her upbringing are visible enough in her temper, in the difficulty she has getting along with people at work from time to time. Her family cares about her, but to say that they are just as loving and stable in their irregular configuration as any Bill Cosby family in the suburbs would be pure romanticism.

Latoya and her common-law husband have had an on-again-off-again relationship that has caused her no end of grief. He messes up and she kicks him out. Left behind is his ten-year-old daughter by a previous relationship, not to mention the son they have in common. Latoya dreams of having a house in the suburbs, something she could afford if she could get her man to settle down, for he has a well-paid job as a carpenter, a union-ized position that gives him benefits and upward of $15 an hour. Together they could make a break for it, but the instability of their relationship renders this fantasy almost unattainable. Latoya's heart bears the scars of his irresponsibility, and her children miss their dad when he is not around. Latoya's salary from Burger Barn barely stretches to meet the mounting expenses of a family of five, even with Jason's contributions. When they are together, though, their joint income puts them well above the poverty line, straight into the blue-collar working class. Hence family stability and standard of living go hand in hand in Latoya's household: when the family is together, everything looks rosy, and when things fall apart, the struggle is monumental.

Middle-class families have their ups and downs too, of course. Television is a baby-sitter in many families. Suburban marriages break up, leaving children in serious economic straits, with divorced mothers facing a job market that will not allow them to keep a secure hold on the lives their children are accustomed to.[17] The poor have no lock on the pitfalls of modern family life. Yet the consequences of family instability in poor neighborhoods are clearly more devastating because the whole institutional structure that surrounds folks at the bottom—the schools, the low-wage workplace, the overcrowded labor market, the potholed streets, the unsavory crack dealers on the front stoop—creates more vulnerability in families that have to deal with internal troubles. Support is more problematic, more likely to depend upon the resources of relatives and friends who are, in turn, also poor and troubled.

HEALTH AND POVERTY

Familes at the bottom are also more likely to experience chronic health problems, leading to lower life expectancy than for those blessed with more resources.[18] They live in crowded spaces and are exposed to high levels of noise, pollution, stress, and violence.[19] Jobs held by the working poor often subject them to physical danger, and their elevated rates of on-the-job injury reflect the risk.[20] Low-wage workers are much more likely to sustain a serious injury than are employees with better jobs. Poor dietary practices and cigarette smoking do not help matters: the poor are more likely to engage in behaviors that are linked to chronic disease.[21]

Regular doctors are a luxury in most poor communities,[22] where the emergency room at the nearest hospital is the closest one comes to medical care. Harlem's hospitals have been downsizing as the city seeks to consolidate its costs. Columbia Presbyterian Hospital and Harlem Hospital serve the community as best they can, but the wait can be long and the care is seldom continuous.

When we read about these trends in medical journals, they sound like so many abstract statistics. When we see health problems woven into the daily lives of Harlem workers, they become immediate, threatening, and destabilizing for families that are always poised on the precipice, barely able to manage without any catastrophes to interfere. Yet medical disasters do visit the poor in far greater proportion than the nonpoor and leave a trail of frustration, missed opportunities, and family strain in their wake.

Hilda was called home from Burger Barn to assist her mother, who had just lost a finger in a factory accident. She had to take three days off to get the proper medical attention and help her mother recover from the shock. Charley's mother died of a drug overdose when he was just three years old. His aunt and uncle took him in and raised him as one of their own, a responsibility that forced the aunt to drop out of the labor force for two years. Kyesha has diabetes, and try as she might, she occasionally indulges in a candy binge, which sends her sugar level up. Sitting in the waiting area of the local hospital emergency room for eight hours waiting for Kyesha to get an insulin injection, one cannot help but wonder whether someday that shot won't come too late.

Patty's grandmother, who worked as a housekeeper through her early years in Harlem, put her daughter through nursing school by scrubbing the floors of wealthy families on the East Side of Manhattan. Thereafter, mother and daughter joined forces to take care of foster children. When diabetes confined Patty's grandmother to bed, the impact spread to the whole family and forced them to move.

> I was nine at the time. I'll never forget it. My mother had to leave all her furniture and pick up and move to Queens to take care of Grandma until she got better. She was bedridden for two years. We lived in Queens and went to school there. Mommy had to take over all Grandma's bills. We didn't come back to Harlem until I was finished with junior high.

Health problems elsewhere in Patty's family filtered down to succeeding generations and once again disrupted her education. Her younger brother, Sammy, was in and out of the hospital and then sent home for weeks at a time.

> I was an A student. But Sammy was asthmatic. Maybe I could've gotten further in school if I didn't stay so many days home with Sammy. But Mommy had to put bread on the table. These are things that happen. I could be bitter, but that was my life. That's how it was.

Danielle, Latoya's cousin, had one daughter and a steady job in a department store stocking shelves when she discovered she was pregnant with a son. She managed to carry on at work, patching together a child care arrangement that, while not great, was at least reasonably reliable. When her little boy developed asthma, Danielle faced a real crisis. Her regular baby-sitter was not able to handle a child with serious illness, so Danielle left the labor force.

When he was a baby, he caught asthma a lot. He developed pneumonia in the hospital. They gave me pills and [the baby-sitter] didn't know how to give [the medication] to him. And by me not thinking, he was in trouble. I should've stayed home. But I was trying to work. So he got dehydrated because he wasn't eating or drinking. I couldn't find nobody to watch him because he was so sickly. He stayed at the hospital; they kept him two weeks. Back and forth, every two, three weeks he was back in the hospital for one reason or another. He had a seizure. So after that I was like, forget it, stayed at home. I left [the department store]. I just quit. I said, I quit until he get better, till either he get better or just . . . Either way I had to stay home. So when he got two years old, two or three, then I went back to work.

This pattern of debilitating illness is not unusual among Harlem's working poor. Family trees are studded with empty spaces where working adults ought to be and would be in more affluent communities. Long before death or total disability claims lives, family members have to step forward and take care of their loved ones. Medical insurance is hard to come by, especially for the working poor who are not Medicaid-eligible; older workers who have labored outside the formal economy (as Patty's grandmother did during her housekeeping days) receive little in Social Security benefits. Money to pay for home attendants is that much harder to come by. Whom does this leave outside of family members who, given a choice, would rather be in school or at work? No one.

Middle-class families confront similar problems as parents grow old and need help, or serious illness strikes young children who need round-the-clock attention. Even those with resources to pay for home nurses, elder day care, or residence in an assisted living facility find it hard to manage. The "sandwich generation," stretched between responsibilities for teenage children and declining elders, comes under stress that even money cannot resolve. Yet resources surely make a difference. They buy some freedom from the daily burdens.

Harlem families lack this financial backstop. They must shoulder the cross of chronic health problems in elders who are often not so very old—the legacy of poor health throughout their lives—during the prime of their own work lives, when their children are small. When chronic, long-term health problems threaten the independence of a fifty-year-old grandmother, her daughter and grandchildren may be staring a twenty-year problem in the face, one that inevitably threatens their own careers. Workdays are missed, school days are interrupted, savings accounts are drained to pay for doctors and medicine, families double up to provide personal care. No element of life is left unscathed.

Employers become exasperated with the missed days; schools lose patience with students who disappear to take care of their sick relatives. As absence turns into jobs lost or diplomas forgone, the scars deepen. Poverty produces disability, which derails the caregivers, which pushes the extended family farther down the economic ladder. Yet there is also a sense among the poor that family is the center of the universe and that other elements of life should take a backseat to this responsibility, even if damage is done. Harlem's working poor are not saints; frustration and fury follow when these sacrifices are called for. Family members who are so poor or disorganized that they can never reciprocate do fall out of the support system, becoming homeless.

But just as earlier generations of Americans responded to the Great Depression by leaning upon the extended family, so too do these modern survivors of an inner-city depression. In the 1930s, many a career or education path was derailed by the compelling demands of family. So too in our own time are brothers and sisters, children and grandchildren, responding to the needy claims of their kin—and paying the price for their generosity.

The fact that families rally round to help their members tells us something important about the very meaning of family among the working poor. Kin matter enough to sacrifice for. Grandma does not end up in a nursing home with strangers looking after her. She stays in her bed and her children move in with her. Brothers develop asthma and their sisters stay home from school to look after them. Chronic health problems in poor communities create secondary fallout for the siblings, children, and grandchildren on whom the responsibility falls.

WORK ETHICS

National newspapers covering the approach of welfare time limits have featured many an AFDC recipient who proclaims that the last thing he or she wants is to "end up at McDonald's." The image of fast food work as the end of the line, the least desirable outcome in a worker's biography, couldn't be more ubiquitous. Yet even in a community where there is great sensitivity to personal image, young people and many of their elders seek out these jobs and learn to find dignity in them as (perhaps the least respected) members of the great American workforce.

Where does this drive come from, this desire to be a working person? Why do black and brown youth don the apron of the hamburger flipper, smiling courteously at customers who treat them rudely? It is central to family values, to the messages that older relations—parents, aunts and uncles, grandparents—and neighbors convey to them: you cannot be a whole person without getting a job. We typically associate the work ethic with America's middle class. Yet in well-heeled communities, young people are protected from these demands, expected instead to go to school and leave the work role to their elders.

In the inner city, the last place most Americans would look for expressions of the work ethic, the drive to join the labor force is stronger than it is in Westchester. Harlem's Burger Barn labor force is composed of minorities who typically took their first job between thirteen and fifteen years of age. They go to work younger, take the jobs no one else wants, and work much harder as a consequence than their counterparts in the middle-class communities that we think of as emblems of the work ethic.

While many of these working youth have parents who are also employed in lowly jobs, no small number have mothers and fathers who are out of the labor force altogether, often because they are disabled, sometimes because they are on welfare. It is a mistake to assume that the work ethic develops only in those families where parents can or have chosen to teach by example. Young people with parents who have been in and out of the labor force often need nothing more than this problematic example sitting in front of them. They draw their own conclusions about the path to stability, consciously modeling themselves on the opposite of what they have observed. Tiffany is a case in point:

How important has working been in helping your family to get to where they are in life?
Bad question, because my family is in a bad situation. Even though work may have helped, other things happened and life circumstances [interfered]. My mom is in a shelter for battered women in the Village. They are supposed to provide her with an apartment or something within another week. . . . My sister is in a Section 8 house in Queens. She should

be finding a job, which she is not too urgently doing. So, she's still using the services of the system. My brother, he's thirty-something now. He hasn't had a job in years. He's a street performer.

I want a form of security. I wanna work all my life. I mean work in the sense of having to work to provide for myself and make sure I eat. I want to be taken care of [retire] by a certain point.

Shaquena works two jobs to keep afloat but has, as far as she knows, never met her father. Tamara is the only person in her family who has a steady job. Michael's mother spends most of her time smoking weed, and his father is driving a truck in another state and rarely comes around. Michael works full-time at Burger Barn.

While it certainly helps to have families convey the "right message" about the importance of working and being self-sufficient, many ghetto dwellers get the message from elsewhere: from television, the public schools, the church pulpit, and the evidence they absorb while walking in affluent neighborhoods nearby. Our assumptions about the power of the natal family to imprint children with values, coupled with a conception of the inner city as a separate society, blind us to the other, equally powerful sources of moral messages. Just as succeeding generations of immigrants have been absorbed into American culture, so too do ghetto dwellers receive and assimilate the tenets of mainstream culture.

These messages, whether delivered by parents or by the culture as a whole, do not always get through, of course; they influence some children and bypass others in the very same family. Family trees among the working poor display a curious pattern of working siblings and jailed ones, of men and women who have made it to maturity alongside brothers who have died young. Tiffany has worked since she was fourteen, but her older brother has been a drug dealer in and out of jail since his own teen years. She barely completed high school, but has half siblings who finished college and now work as housing cops, as well as sisters who braid hair for a living and collect AFDC on the side.

To my knowledge, we have no compelling explanations of why the same family produces such divergent pathways in life. Undoubtedly we have made simplistic assumptions about family environments over time. The family into which Jamal was born was one with a working mother who had a good job in the Post Office. That "same" family ten years later was one headed up by a mother addicted to crack. Is that the "same" environment? Will the changes leave their mark not only on Jamal but on his little brother, who has never known a stable, working mother firsthand?

We must also recognize that people who do not themselves conform to the lessons of the work ethic can nonetheless transmit society's core values. Working mothers who have been reliant on AFDC in the past call upon these social messages when hammering home to their children the importance of getting a job. They admonish them about the need to do better than they have done, about the strain of having so few choices in life. Often having children pushes a young mother to do better precisely so that her kids will see a better example before them. Tamara, at nineteen a two-year veteran of Burger Barn, had her son when she was just fifteen.

> [*Having*] *my son helped me. He pushed me to go to school and to work for everything. Because when I was home, I had nothing to move forward for, 'cause I was tired of school. I was about to become another dropout. I didn't care one way or the other. I'd say, "Well, money will come from some source." But he pushed me to make myself look better in his eyes. And show him from my experience.*

Arline Geronimus has argued that there are many reasons why poor African-American women are more likely to have children at a young age.[23] Among them is the fear that postponing childbearing to later years is risky since older black women tend to develop health conditions that can impair fertility.[24] Another reason is that early childbearing gives young women a better chance to enlist the aid of their own mothers in primary child care while they, the grandmothers, are still healthy. Given the fact that poor communities, and especially inner-city neighborhoods, have such high rates of debilitating illness and early death, the choice to have children early in life appears quite "rational," especially when establishment in the labor force at a young age is not expected to bring about later affluence.[25]

Having children may provide young women with a powerful motivation to make more of themselves in life than they otherwise might, for now they have something important to live for, to prove themselves for. While bearing a baby in the teen years poses serious obstacles for most young people with respect to education and employment, it also catalyzes a sense of responsibility, of having someone important to provide for. Recent research shows, in fact, that early childbearing does not further disadvantage poor mothers.[26] What can be a formidable obstacle, then, can also become a powerful incentive for participation in the labor market. When working is impossible, the incentive often transmutes into a stream of encouragement directed at boosting the prospects of the children. Whether children do what their parents say, as opposed to imitating what they have done in life, is hard to predict. But if we want to understand what kinds of values are being promoted, discussed, and encouraged, we have to give credit where it is due: plenty of young mothers are working hard to see to it their children make it in this world.

Hence, while we tend to assume that core values like the work ethic are stressed by families that exemplify other central mores (like marriage before childbearing or the preservation of dual-parent households), Harlem's working poor show us this is often not the case. The relationship between family values and family structure is complex.

A Folk Sociology of Deviance

Ghetto culture is often described as lionizing deviant characters: the flash of the drug king, the easy life of the welfare queen. I have argued that these iconic figures compete, generally on the losing side, with a variety of mainstream morals, including the importance of work and the value of family. Positive mores alone are not enough, however. They have to be reinforced by a repertoire of negatives, a litany of messages about who should be despised and what people should strive to leave behind. The working poor, who inhabit jobs that are low on the prestige hierarchy, understand their lot in life in part by comparison with people they see as below themselves.

Sean was born in Alabama and grew up in Chicago. He is a religious man who was "brought up right," to have respect, to work hard, and to blame no one but himself for his problems. These are values Sean and his wife have passed along to their children, precepts he believes must guide the lives of all right-thinking people.

You go out there and you try, I always tell people. They come to me [and say], "I can't find a job. It's hard." I say, "Keep on trying. Don't give up." I know, believe me, I know how it feels to be down. To have to ask somebody for something, I know. You just keep trying, keep praying, have faith, and you'll be all right. Don't go robbing or stealing. I know you're saying, "Oh man, if . . . I'm a good guy, why don't I have a job?" Things happen for a reason. Maybe you need to understand how to maintain a job.

Yet Sean knows that some people in his community either cannot hear this message or willfully reject it. They believe that the world owes them something, that they can get a job even if they dress poorly or behave with disrespect. These are the kids who have another think coming to them, Sean believes.

> *I get upset with these kids. It's ridiculous. [They arrive] with their pants hanging down. You can thank [rap star] Kriss Kross for that. That mentality keeps people from getting jobs. I see kids walking around with guns and everything, forties of malt liquor. Who do you think is gonna hire you? You going inside of a business place, you gonna look for a job, and on the back of your shirt it says, "niggers with attitude." You got a big beer in your hand and you'd like an application. They are gonna hire you? I don't think so. . . . And we quick to buy these [stories]. You think, "We failed at this; we bad." . . . That mentality keeps you down.*

As Sean sees it, people who make excuses for themselves, who torpedo their chances for jobs by dressing as lowlifes, are exhibit A on the list of fools who have no one but themselves, and possibly their parents, to blame for their sorry condition. These are the folks that he distinguishes himself from when he assesses his place in the social pecking order. Sean may be treading water in a bad job, but he is clearly miles ahead of those who shoot themselves in the foot while job-seeking.

Kimberly has much the same critique to offer of women she knows who seem to have given up, or never started, trying to make it in school or on the job. She does not blame the environment, broken families, or any other external pressure. Kim blames the person who has caved in.

> *They's a lot of people who don't try. People get jobs, but they don't try. Like there is this girl in my building, she has four kids, and she don't. . . . She dropped out. She doesn't try to go to school, she don't try to get a job. I mean, I understand it's rough. But you could find a day care center while you go get a GED. She is young. But people just don't try, that's what I think.*

Kim allows that things might be harder for black people, since others "see us as slow, like we can't do anything. Getting into trouble, especially teenagers." Yet from Kim's point of view, "It doesn't matter what color you are. You could get a job whether you are black or white. Everyone is born the same."

What is most notable about conversations on the subject of values is how conservative Burger Barn workers are in their views about what constitutes appropriate behavior, regardless of how unorthodox their own family backgrounds may be. Ianna lost her mother to a drug overdose when she was a young girl. Her father left her with an aunt to raise her, but Ianna has worked steadily since she was fourteen. Lakisha was raised by her grandmother and has had virtually no contact with her parents or her siblings, and has had her share of psychological grief over her abandonment. But she has worked steadily since she was fourteen and plans to work her way right through junior college so she can make something of herself. Sean has never met his father, but this has not stopped him from defining real manhood as the holding of a steady job. Shaquena doesn't know her father and hasn't heard from her mother in years, but works two jobs. James's father lost the best job he ever had, working for the city transit system, as a result of drug abuse. He has an aunt in jail for murder. But at the age of sixteen, James works a steady part-time job on weekends and after school so that he can contribute to the family.

Ebony's past is a case study in troubled families. Her father has a heavy drug habit and "works" as a hit man. His problems spread early on to her mother and brought chaos upon the whole household on many occasions.

> My home was always in an uproar because my mother had me at a young age, when she was seventeen. She was still in school when she had me and trying to take care of me. But she couldn't do both. She was still living with my grandmother at the time, so it wasn't as hard because my grandmother helped take care of me.
>
> When my mother finished high school, she left to go to college. Instead of her staying here in the city, she went away. I stayed with my grandmother. When my mother came back home and got back involved with my father and his bad ways, everything came back. . . . I was maybe four or five years old. She had a bad drug habit. It was something always with her or with him, or somebody in that house. Always some type of drug action in that apartment.

Despite this rocky beginning in life, Ebony believes that it is her responsibility to work, to finish school, to look after her grandmother, and to do what she can to help her mother back onto the straight and narrow path. She holds herself to a high standard and claims no credit from a distressed childhood.

Ebony's story, like the many others recounted in this chapter, is not simply one of overcoming a bad beginning, or becoming a paragon of virtue in a sea of vice. If we merely point to the outstanding diamonds in the rough and chalk up their victories to exceptional personality, we have learned nothing of any practical value. We do not know how to grow exceptional personalities; we can merely stand back and marvel at their existence. What is more important about these biographies is not their exceptional nature but their common appearance. In so many *routine* ways ghetto residents read the negative evidence before them and conclude that only a fool would follow in the footsteps of a loser, even when the loser is your own parent. Many a middle-class child has drawn the same conclusion when examining with a critical eye the mistakes of his or her own parents or siblings. It should not surprise us to learn that poor people do the same.

Theories of human development, which have stressed the power of intergenerational transmission of culture, take it on faith that the examples before us lead us to the same paths, rather than down the other fork in the road. Or, if we make exceptions for individualism, we are more inclined to believe that advantaged youth will make the right choices, while the disadvantaged will be unduly influenced by the circumstances around them. The trajectories of Harlem's working poor tell us that this is untrue in many cases and that the messages of the mainstream world get through.

Those messages do not arrive in an unfiltered fashion, however. They pass through the sieve of personal experience and of observations of the fact that some groups of people arrive in this world with all the luck and others have to engage in uphill battles from day one. While holding their own feet to the fire, Burger Barn workers argue that black men, in particular, have it harder than the rest. The deck is stacked against them, and they come to recognize that truth and are hardened by it. Many of the African-American women at Burger Barn have had boyfriends, husbands, or brothers who have been defeated by relentless refusals, cold shoulders, and suspicion on the part of teachers, landlords, employers, and cops. Minority workers are not blind to the vast difference in life chances that separate them from the mostly well-to-do college students at Columbia College, less than ten blocks away, or the wealthy co-op dwellers on Manhattan's East Side. They do not assume that the distribution of good fortune is merely a reflection of merit, of just deserts. Forces of inequality, racism, and birthright have interfered with pure merit and help to explain why some people are living the good life and others must struggle.

Burger Barn workers know this as an experiential truth. It colors their sense of who deserves to be let down easily from the kind of blanket critique they often make of the bad apples in their own community. They do not back away from the commitment, so familiar to mainstream Americans, that we are, each and every one of us, responsible for our destinies, masters of our own fates. This belief they share with the great American middle class, for whom forces of economic destiny, structural inequalities, and the winds of change brought about by changing government policy pale beside the assumption of individual autonomy, control, and mastery. Poor people in the depths of the ghetto are at one with the rest of American culture in believing that whatever hand you have been dealt, you must make the most of it. They do temper their criticism just a bit when it comes to children they know who have been raised by incompetent parents, or young people who have been exposed relentlessly to the flash of drug money. All in all, however, they offer less of a moral safety net than the average liberal academic, who may be inclined to excuse most signs of deviance in favor of environmental explanations for character flaws. For the working poor, who have struggled against the odds, no one is entitled to a free ride.

The Working Poor in Ghetto Neighborhoods

Not far from some of New York's most crowded housing projects lies one of the wealthiest census tracts in the country, home to the Museum Mile, hospitals that serve the well-to-do, and Fifth Avenue's elegant shopping district. One would have to be blind not to recognize the wide gulf that separates the city's black and brown poor from the affluent whites.[27] The buses that deliver low-wage workers from home to work and back have large windows through which the rider can glimpse the elegant mannequins draped in diamonds and velvet, the antique furniture bathed in soft light, and the gourmet chocolate shops that are strung along Madison Avenue. Abruptly, just above 96th Street, the chic and trendy stores give way to the neon signs of the liquor stores, discount drugstores, check-cashing outlets, and the dingy little grocery stores that serve the Harlem projects. Anyone who has traversed this route, as Harlem's poor do quite often, can measure the vast economic distance that separates these few blocks.

Harlem neighborhoods have seen their share of trouble in the last two decades. The combination—not unrelated—of declining job opportunities and a flourishing drug trade has taken a toll on the stability of neighborhoods and the quality of life for people who lack the resources to move out. The crack cocaine fever that snared Jamal's mother was particularly devastating. A highly addictive drug that was inexpensive compared to heroin, crack spread quickly and drew into its orbit far more women than other epidemics had. The consequences for families were more severe as a result, and the foster care caseload has grown by leaps and bounds.

Families who had the choice fled the neighborhoods where these social cancers spread. The working poor had no exit. They have had to find ways to navigate their surroundings and instruct their children in defensive strategies intended to guard their safety while parents are at work. Family values must stretch to accommodate the special demands that living in a poor neighborhood imposes.

For William, that means developing a public demeanor that signals control.

You gotta have attitude. You gotta have tenacity. In a rough neighborhood, you gotta have balls, simply put. You have a lot of caring people there, as you do in any type of neighborhood that has a bad face to it. But you have to know how to carry yourself.

As a tall and rather imposing black man, William knows that bravado has to be part of his repertoire, lest people think he's an easy target. But William has to be careful not to let the bluster blow too hard, lest some trigger-happy type conclude he is deliberately "downing" him by his very presence. Toughness—a walk, a talk, an attitude—has to be mixed with displays of respect[28] and a dose of vigilance—all elements of a careful calculus William has developed over the years. His street repertoire fits like a second skin; without it, he would be vulnerable.

You have to keep that other eye out looking. If you are talking to someone in the street, you can't always focus on him. You got to focus on what's around you. You never know when someone is gonna get hot and pull out a gun and start shooting, because it has happened. It has happened to me, my mother, and my brother. We were walking up the block, coming through a store. We are talking to a friend, next thing you know, "Paw, paw, paw," guy across the street pointed the gun right at the door, at the guy that's rolling on the floor [of the store]. He didn't get hit, but the guy shooting, just like right out there! The guy on the floor gets up and just as my mother pushes me down behind a car and she gets down, the guy [with the gun] runs right by us. Always be alert. Always keep your eye out. You have to watch your back for yourself and for others too.

Black and Latino youth who work have already made key decisions about whom they must avoid at school and in the neighborhood. They know who the major troublemakers are and make sure to give a wide berth to anyone known to be a problem case. Frank, a Puerto Rican who goes to a tough high school in Harlem, knows that he can't avoid all the shoals, but that his odds for success are increased because he stays away from bad people.

It's who you be with! If you are with the right people, you should be out of trouble. If you are with the wrong people, you know you might be in trouble, and you know that you can't say, "Well, nothing is going to happen." Because you don't know that.

Frank cannot stop his peers from making mistakes, and he risks ostracism by being too insistent about the differences between them and himself. His strategy is to turn a blind eye toward destructive behavior.

I deal with them by treating them the same, but I try to let them know [dealing drugs] is not the move. That's not the thing to be doing. But, it's nothing to do with me. I hope they take what I say into consideration. But other than that, as long as you are not doing it around me or if I don't have anything to do with it . . . I really don't care. If you don't want to listen to me, hey, you do what you want to do. When you mess yourself up, I'm [saying] you know, I told you so.

Most of all, Frank tries to spend as little time as possible in his own neighborhood. He finds other, calmer spaces to hang out in. Here the workplace looms large, for in addition to being an oasis of relative peace, it is also a meeting ground where kids from rough neighborhoods come to know people who have it a little better, fellow workers who may live in more working-class communities.

Knowing that the environment is problematic, inner-city parents keep a close watch on their children. They monitor their whereabouts, veto potential playmates that come from unreliable families, set strict rules for their children's comings and goings, scan the blocks and corners where they live for troublemakers, and position themselves visibly near the playgrounds where their children romp around. The physical presence of these guiding hands is crucial to the safety and well-being of ghetto kids. No parent or older sibling saddled with this responsibility can be as carefree as their suburban counterparts, for whom it is still possible to send children off to the playground on their own with a simple warning about talking to strangers.

It takes time to monitor public space. Mothers on welfare often shoulder the burden for working mothers who simply cannot be around enough to exercise vigilance. They provide an adult presence in the parks and on the sidewalks where it is most needed. Without these stay-at-home moms in the neighborhood, many a working-poor parent would have no choice but to force the kids to stay home alone all day during the summer vacation, where they would at least be safe. Long summer vacations produce stories of kids left to watch TV in sweltering fifth-floor walk-ups because their parents lack the resources—financial and social—to do anything else for them that is safe.

One important navigation strategy involves relying on the goodwill of long-standing acquaintances who may be unsavory characters. Drug dealers and gun-happy toughs are rarely total strangers. Older people in the same communities, particularly the women (who make it their business to know unrelated children), have often watched them grow up. They may have had children who were their playmates at one time.

A code of honor regulates the relationships between denizens of the underground economy and the straight residents of inner-city neighborhoods: you don't deliberately harm people whom you've known a long time, unless they get tangled up in your business affairs. Innocent bystanders who have been neighbors or friends for a period of years are protected by these social ties. Respect for the elderly still holds some sway as a cultural practice, if the seniors are people who know your family and have some personal connection to you. For this reason, the working poor are careful to acknowledge troublemakers, to recognize their existence rather than ignore them or behave with total disdain toward them. Building this social relation, however perfunctory, is a protective act. As Patty explains, dangerous types shield the people they know well from the kind of treatment they might mete out to others:

> *My building is very close-knit. Everybody knows me and my kids. The neighborhood is kind of rough. I can't say I know everybody, but I know most of the people. And I'm even respected by the drug dealers. So it's like a code of honor.*

So you know some of the people who might be considered trouble-makers?
Right.

And you talk to them?
Yeah. "Hi. How y'all doing?" Early in the morning, like when I go to work at six o'clock in the morning, who's out there? "How you doing, Patty?" "How y'all doing?"

So they leave you alone.
They totally protect you. You're kind of glad to see them, because if some-body outside of the neighborhood comes in, it's no way they can bother me. And that goes for my kids too; it's a code of honor.

Strangers are the ultimate threat in a crime-plagued community. The behavior of known characters is at least somewhat predictable. Unknowns are far more dangerous: their actions are hard to anticipate and they have no social investment in the relationships that define the neighborhood. This is one of the principal reasons poor people hate the drug trade: it attracts the unknown into the area. Under these circum-stances, it is best to develop an instinctive mistrust of strangers.

SAFETY NETS AND OLD HEADS

Some of Harlem's neighborhoods have succumbed to the disorganization of the drug trade and the curse of gangs. Others, though, have fought off the worst effects of urban decay by relying on the "old heads," elders who know everybody's business. Brian, a Burger Barn worker now in his early thirties, was born in a rural community in Arkansas and lived there until he was in his early teenage years. Where Brian comes from, adult pillars of the community acted as a surveillance system for parents out working in poultry factories or cotton fields.

When we were little, it was very quiet in my town. Everybody knew each other. You could sit in the porch and talk and carry on. If one of us did something, we could rest assured that by the time I got home, my mom knew it.

Transplanted to Brooklyn's front stoops or the common courtyards of the city's housing projects, old heads impose a degree of order in urban ghettos. In the Harlem housing project where Patty grew up in the early 1970s, you didn't cross Miss Jacobs without your parents finding out:

We all knew each other. All the parents knew each other. And that's basi-cally how you hung out. If Mommy works late, all the kids would be at Miss Jacobs's house. Miss Jacobs was like the foundation. 'Cause she didn't work [outside the projects]. As a matter of fact, she was the super of the building. Her job was right there so she never had to go nowhere.

And everybody was responsible for all the kids. Like if you walk down the street and you saw my kids, you are responsible to make sure they be safe. In spite of the fact that you wasn't the mother. And that was accepted and that was acknowledged.

So you respected older people?
Old people, yeah, 'cause they knew your mom and everybody had to do the right thing. And everywhere you went, somebody knew you.

Before Latoya moved to Harlem, she lived in a predominantly black area of Queens. She remembers very well how certain adults she knew played key roles in the lives of the kids in her neighborhood.

Like Miss Rosie. Everybody went to Miss Rosie's house to talk, you know, and my mother's house. All the teenagers were at my mother's house. You could eat there, you could joke. If you had a problem . . . [you could go to her]. Back then I was too little, so I didn't know what they was talking about. But my mother could tell them about boy problems and all of that stuff. So it was either Miss Rosie's or my mother's.

Latoya has been on the receiving end of advice, stern lectures, and safe havens from old heads like Miss Rosie, and as she has gotten older, she has increasingly moved toward adopting the same kind of responsibility for unrelated youngsters on the block. We saw her act the part one day while walking down one of Harlem's main shopping streets. She passed by a teenage girl, wheeled around, and tapped her on the shoulder. The girl had heavy makeup on and a short skirt; she looked like she was up to no good. Latoya began to lecture her. "Does your mama know what you're doin' out here? You can't dress like that! You gotta stay away from those boys and their drugs. They will leave you flat! I'm gonna have a talk with your mama." The girl walked away, looking a bit sheepish, and Latoya continued down the block, muttering about how this girl was getting into drugs, which would lead to prostitution if she got hooked. How well does she know this family? Not well at all, she says, but you have to look out for these teenagers or they just go wild on you.

Elijah Anderson has written about the disappearance of the "old heads" from ghetto neighborhoods, elderly people who took responsibility for public order by counseling, admonishing, and simply observing the street scene from the porches of their Philadelphia homes.[29] He argues that this is but one more symptom of social disorder in the slums. Harlem's social structure is, at least in places, more organized. Latoya does not have the time to sit on a front stoop and play the role of the stern matriarch all day, but she is something of an old head in the making. The same pattern of collective social control characterizes the building where Patty Hull lives with her children.

> We all know each other. . . . We are co-renters and know each other. If my kids [do something bad], I know it before they know it!

Shaquena, a young black woman who has worked since she was sixteen at Burger Barn, sees the same thing in her neighborhood.

> Everybody [knows] everybody. It's like you lived in one big town. Like if you go to the supermarket, you get in trouble. People in the supermarket tell your parents. Everybody [knows] everybody. That's how everybody is in that block. You can't do nothin' [wrong]. You get a slap coming out of nowhere!

Collective responsibility is expressed in other forms as well. At the urging of public housing authorities, tenant patrols have formed in many Harlem housing projects to offer protection against gangs, to increase the "eyes" of the official police force, and to enforce rules of conduct that might otherwise be ignored. In the high-rise complex where Roberta lives, patrols of all kinds have proliferated in an effort to exert greater control over public space. When Roberta was a kid, she was on a youth patrol that would "go around the project and have certain buildings to watch out for. [You'd] watch certain people coming into the area and we would monitor. People would monitor them in the community center." Now that Roberta works full-time, her father participates in the community center's patrol squad, walking around the area with a walkie-talkie in hand.

Organized efforts to control the conditions of their lives are very much in evidence among the nation's poor. The magnitude of the difficulties they face threatens their ability to make a major difference, but the spirit is there. Neighbors still come together for block parties, engage the local churches and schools in after-school programs that will make a positive difference, and agitate for the attention of the police so that they can clamp down on people who don't share their values.

The working poor play a special role in these communities. They are a stabilizing force with a regular rhythm to their days. However, since the workplace claims much of their time, the neighborhoods where they live would come unhinged were it not for the efforts that their friends and family members on welfare have contributed to neighborhood well-being. Parallels with suburbia are striking. In middle-class communities now dominated by dual-income families who commute out of the area during the day, stay-at-home mothers perform vital roles of class parents, volunteer workers, and casual monitors of tree-lined streets. In central Harlem, it is the welfare mother and the retired workers who are around during the day. As they go about their daily business, they are the eyes and ears of the community, doing what they can to keep watch over children and property, while the working poor are on the job.

RACIAL FLASHPOINTS

In a country where the racial divide grows sharper by the day, the inner city is a crossroads. Race heightens the stresses of poverty, especially when a tightening job market forces minorities of all colors into a scramble for shares of a shrinking pie. When job-seekers come away empty-handed, they are often inclined to blame "the other" for their misfortunes or rail at affirmative action, in an echo of the larger culture's political assault on public policies designed to redress decades of discrimination.

Latinos, particularly those newly arrived in the United States, often come from countries where racial distinctions are differently defined or less pronounced than they are in America.[30] They quickly learn, however, that there is nothing more damning than being black in this country. The linkage between poverty and skin color is made explicit in the media and repeated on the street. Blacks are poor, they are segregated, they are reputed to be trapped on welfare indefinitely, they don't work hard—the entire litany of stereotypes hits immigrants (especially black immigrants)[31] in the face. African-Americans, in turn, are exposed to the prevailing anti-immigrant sentiment and often voice the view that native-born English speakers should come first in the United States.

Polarization of this kind becomes an explicit line of division in the arenas where blacks and Latinos compete: school resources, housing, and employment. But it also has an impact in the street, in daily life, as poor people of all colors go about their business. Rubbing shoulders with members of another ethnic group in a society as racialized as this causes tension. Hilda, a native of the Dominican Republic, lives in a neighborhood that is almost entirely Dominican. One can speak Spanish from dawn to dusk on Hilda's block, buy tropical fruits and vegetables foreign to most Americans, and never be aware of being in the middle of the biggest city in the United States. Yet not six blocks south of Hilda's neighborhood, the signs shift into English, and as the gigantic towers of central Harlem housing projects appear on the horizon more African-American faces appear on the sidewalks.

Living in close proximity to one another, Latinos and blacks have to negotiate the border regions. For most people, this is not a problem. Coming and going to work, school and home, they hurry by, thinking more about what they have to do when they arrive than about who they are passing on the street. But when a problem erupts, as it does more often among the young than anyone else, it can quickly turn from a simple dispute about an open fire hydrant into a racial incident. Hilda has been caught in the middle.

Yesterday I went out. I felt like going out in the street. But I don't feel like going out anymore, because I had a problem with a black woman.

What happened?
A bunch of Hispanics were under the water hydrant [cooling off]. This black woman wanted to close it, so I told her, "No," and why did she want to close it? People from the street started bad-mouthing us. Then I just didn't say anything else.

And what happened in the end?
Ay, it was a [black] man and a woman. They came looking for some people to beat up. They were staring at me. And I'd stare back at them. Because they thought I was scared of them, but I wasn't scared of them.

African-Americans see Spanish-speaking people moving into neighborhoods that were once dominated by Harlem blacks. Whole districts have turned over from one group to the next, in a march of ethnic succession as old as the immigration story itself. But the consequences do not seem benign to them when the transformation coincides with the collapse of the inner-city job market and the wholesale abandonment of entire city blocks by landlords, merchants, and city government. The confluence of these trends has suggested to some that the Latino immigrants are responsible for ruining the neighborhood. James, at sixteen one of the youngest African-Americans working at Burger Barn, knows that most of his Puerto Rican and Dominican neighbors are hard workers whose kids are trying to make it in school. Still, when he looks at the high-crime blocks immediately adjacent to his, he sees a lot of people who look unsavory.

> *The building supers sit outside and do nothing. The buildings inside are disgusting, smelling like piss. You see, a lot of them are Dominican, Spanish. They won't keep up with the building, cleaning, fixing the apartments.*

James also attributes the recent buildup in the drug trade to the influx of Dominicans.

> *There were shootouts every night. The Dominicans on the corner, in one building, there would be a lot of drug raids, like at three o'clock in the morning. Now [that the cops ran them out] it's mostly quiet.*

Ironically, the Latino workers at Burger Barn make the same kind of observations about black neighborhoods: dope-infested, trashy places that decent people should avoid. Indeed, Dominicans often point to themselves as sources of revitalization in black enclaves. "Before we came," they say, "these places were dumps. We made the difference." Low-income workers of all colors have suffered the loss of peace and quiet, stability and safety. Still, when a racial reading of deterioration is available in the culture at large, it surfaces among the poor as well.

CITY LIMITS

City government bears much of the blame for the difficulties that inner-city dwellers face. Lax supervision of landlords, the withdrawal of city services (especially the fire department) from poor neighborhoods, and police corruption all contribute to the unholy atmosphere that working people in the ghetto must put up with.[32] Particularly damaging are the consequences of arson and building abandonment. Landlords who are in the process of defaulting on their property taxes frequently secure the services of arsonists, who burn buildings down and make it possible for owners to secure insurance compensation. Abandoned buildings are magnets for scavengers, who pull out anything that is salvageable (radiators, wiring, copper pipes, anything that can be sold to a junkyard), and for drug dealers, who consider empty apartments a prime location for plying their trade.

Bob, the general manager of one of the Harlem Burger Barns, was looking to escape such headaches when he moved into a better neighborhood farther north in Harlem. It took twelve years to get there, but finally Bob had enough money to buy his own home. With an income of $25,000 a year, Bob couldn't afford grand quarters, not even in Harlem. Rejecting the suburbs as too far away from his job, he finally found a neighborhood of old brownstones up on the far Upper West Side, a community of African-American homeowners who couldn't quite afford the stately neighborhood of Sugar Hill (a very elegant community near City College). There Bob staked his claim to the American dream, buying a "fixer-upper" that had been claimed by the city because of the original owner's failure to pay back taxes. Tall mahogany staircases lead from the ground floor to the upper stories of the brownstone, long ago broken up into separate flats. The original wood is still there, and soaring ceilings give the place an air of majesty, an elegance utterly lacking in the housing projects that surround the neighborhood.

When Bob put his life savings on the line for this house, he thought that the area was about to turn around. The city was encouraging people to invest and redevelop the community and made it relatively easy to do. Teachers, lower-level managers, and other families of modest means arrived like so many urban cowboys, ready to homestead in the ghetto and gentrify it with people of color and local capital. It seemed like a great investment and a statement of personal achievement, for a man like Bob—raised in the projects, never thinking he would have a place of his own. But nothing quite turned out the way he had hoped.

The city said, "Yeah, you can buy this building . . . you renovate the building and then you can move in." But it just so happened, out of my whole block, only two buildings were done [over]. So the rest of the block is still the same. You got your crack houses, your addicts, the girls out there prostituting themselves. . . . They don't mess with my house, and we

> tell 'em, "Don't sit on the porch; don't sell drugs in front of my house;
> don't leave your crack vials around." But we gotta go out and sweep it up.

Harlem residents have all but lost confidence in the willingness or the ability of city government to address these problems. When they see the smoke from a building fire nearby, residents like Patty rest assured that a cascade of problems will follow in short order.

> There's one abandoned building right next door to me. 'Cause it got
> burnt out two years ago. It was owned by the city, so there's no telling
> how long it'll be like that. They have one down the block that has just
> been renovated, a brownstone. But two or three of them are abandoned,
> and that's basically where the drugs are coming from. That makes the
> neighborhood unsafe. It's considered unsafe rightfully, 'cause you could
> hear gunshots. I mean, we have looked out the window and somebody's
> got shot. Somebody's been killed on our block this past summer. Shot.

Dolores is only sixteen, one of the youngest black workers at Burger Barn. She has been working steadily since she was fourteen years old and first landed a job with the city summer youth program. She has lived in Harlem all her life and is completely in her element, walking to high school, getting to work on the weekends and after school, when she puts in a part-time shift. Peace and quiet are not to be found at any hour where Dolores lives.

> It's loud, constantly. Three in the morning, people yelling and fight-
> ing. . . . Neighbors always bothering you, always begging, always making
> noise. Always fighting. There's a lot of unemployed people living around
> here. People who stay up all times of night. Where I live there are shelters
> right there. Kids, their mothers send them outside.

Noise and congestion come with living in most cities. One cannot expect rural peace in a place the size and density of Manhattan. Yet the social disorganization that surrounds Dolores's apartment reflects something more than city life. It is a consequence of the concentration of troubled people whom the city has deposited on her doorstep. One doesn't find many homeless shelters on Park Avenue, but they are in ample supply in Harlem. Families living in overcrowded, dangerous shelters where kids have nowhere to play, men and women with ragged clothes and cups in hand—all of this spills out onto the streets and surrounds Dolores. Even at sixteen, she gets tired from the lack of restful sleep and irritated by the never-ending turmoil on the sidewalks surrounding her high-rise housing project.

The condition of the projects themselves contributes to the depressing quality of life for the working poor. Madison Avenue rarely has potholes, but when they open up on 126th Street, those holes can stay in the ground for years. Living in a place that everyone wants to run from and no one wants to repair makes it harder for residents like Dolores to hold on to their dignity, the sense that they are entitled to something better.

> Bad plumbing, rats galore, scary rats. Everything . . . makes you not wanna do anything. You don't even have to be black, but be poor. To live in an area where everything around is dead, it's dead like you don't wanna live either.

Neighborhoods strewn with trash, broken glass, and graffiti drag the spirit down into a ditch from which even the highly motivated and strong may not be able to emerge. "It's like putting on the same shoes every day," Dolores says. "You just don't wanna try a new pair because you done worn these so much that they are comfortable to you. That's how it is in a way for a lot of people in Harlem."

The drug and danger nexus is exacerbated by the removal of economic resources that used to provide young people with jobs and maintain the local infrastructure at the same time. Jobs are much harder to find, even summer youth jobs, which used to be a real mainstay for young folk in Harlem, a way to make some money cleaning up the area or watching over the little kids who were out of school. Gesturing out the window of the beauty parlor toward the park across the street, Roberta notes:

> There used to be youths out there mowing the lawn and, you know, doing a lot of work so you could see the difference. There was a time when you would see like, ten or fifteen kids out there painting the park, doing things like that. Now you don't see it anymore. So I know times have changed. And not for the better.

Cuts in the Parks and Recreation Department and the summer youth training funds have had a palpable impact on the only open spaces available where Roberta and Dolores live. Places that used to be freely accessible to kids who wanted to shoot baskets or play hopscotch are walled off these days by barbed wire and locked fences. And the government jobs that used to go to young kids, the jobs they used as a foot in the door of the legitimate labor market, are gone too. A double whammy results: services diminish, and so do the prospects of the kids who used to do the cleanup work. Everyone loses.[33]

THE WORKING POOR live a series of contradictions in the urban landscape. In many respects their daily concerns mirror those of their suburban counterparts. They worry about job security and the quality of their children's schools. They put in a full day at tiring, boring jobs and slog their way through crowded buses and subways in time to get dinner on the table and manage the homework routine.

Beyond this, the similarities end, for the working poor face a far more difficult environment within which they must manage these universal tasks. Whatever energy is left over from the daily grind must be poured into surveillance of their children, participation in tenant patrols, and the task of training their kids to be wary of dicey people who may live just down the hallway. As their children move toward adolescence, mothers and fathers must step up their efforts to train them in navigational skills that will make it possible for them to move around the city. This is particularly taxing for parents who work full-time and cannot be around as much as they would like to be. Indeed, the working poor often depend on welfare mothers to be an adult presence in the neighborhood during the daytime.

Despite considerable effort to bring order and stability to urban communities, the working poor often fail to make a major difference. Their family values cannot turn back the damage done by arsonists, the failures of the city to invest in the schools in their neighborhoods, the disappearing job base, and the infection of drugs. Nonetheless, they persevere in their attempts to make a modest difference because they lack the resources to run from the problems that surround them.

CHAPTER EIGHT

Who's In, Who's Out?

1996 SAW THE CULMINATION of a national debate over welfare reform that had been going on, in various forms, ever since Aid to Families with Dependent Children was born. With President Clinton's announcement that he would eliminate "welfare as we know it," a debate erupted pitting conservatives bent on eliminating assistance to the poor against liberals who, for different reasons, also wanted to transform the system, but with more protections for the jobless poor. One by-product of this argument was the spreading assumption that "anyone can get a job," that jobs are going begging, and that welfare recipients cut off aid would simply go out and get them. Pointing to the success of unschooled immigrants in America's low-wage labor market, conservatives have suggested that this trend proves that the native-born have lost the thirst for work.[1] Ronald Reagan was famous for holding up the want-ads section of the *Washington Post* when he wanted to make the same point. Since labor markets tightened to an unprecedented degree in the late 1990s, his assumption appears on the surface to be all the more reasonable.

This book is not about AFDC recipients per se. Yet many of the controversies born of the Washington fracas over welfare reform apply to the employment problems of the working poor. Just how easy is it to get a job in a place like Harlem, where so many have been reduced to taking welfare? If it proves harder than we imagine, who is succeeding and who is failing to leap this entry hurdle? What are the characteristics that make a difference, that help some people and hurt others in the scramble to find work? If it is true that low-skilled, non-English-speaking immigrants trump the native-born, especially African-Americans, why is that?

These questions cannot be answered by interviewing the success stories, the people like Jamal, Carmen, Kyesha, and others who managed to crash through the barriers and get jobs. They can only be addressed by comparing these fortunate workers—the ones lucky enough to get minimum-wage jobs that still keep them well below the poverty line—with the less fortunate who have not been able to get this far.

In 1994–95, my research team and I set out to do just that. We tracked down a random sample of about one hundred people who had tried to get jobs at Burger Barn in central Harlem.[2] It took us almost a year to find them, and the journey took us far and wide, for these would-be workers had come into Harlem from all over New York City—especially from the Bronx and Brooklyn. We talked to dozens of immigrants—from Africa, South Asia, and the Caribbean. We met people in their homes and in the subway stations nearby when there was no other private place to talk. Because many of these job-seekers were in their twenties, we had the chance to talk with their parents, who helped us make contact with a population that is often in transition to adulthood.

The experience was sobering. *Seventy-three percent of these job-seekers were unemployed again a year after they had applied for minimum-wage positions at Burger Barn.*[3] And this was not for lack of trying: they had been looking for work all over the city. They had applied at Macy's downtown, at the Gap stores that dot the city, at a raft of other fast food establishments, at drugstores and grocery stores. In some cases, we had to add extra pages to our questionnaires just to list the places these job-seekers had turned to in their search for employment. It was the rare interviewee who did not ask me or a member of my research team if there was anything we could do to help him or her find a job, whether we knew of any openings at the university. We were, in essence, total strangers to these job-seekers. Still, we looked like the kind of people who could be useful contacts, and they were not about to waste an opportunity to network.

Evaporating Youth Labor Markets

My attraction to the study of low-wage jobs was originally premised on the idea that I would be studying teenagers entering the labor market at the bottom of the service sector. One glance at the shop floor of these Harlem restaurants told me I would have a hard time finding my intended target: younger workers, especially those eighteen and under, were more the exception than the rule. Older workers had been "pushed down" into a labor market niche that was, not long ago, a youth job. Over half of the new hires were more than twenty-three years old.[4] This stands in contrast to the age breakdown of the applicants. Well over half of the people applying for Burger Barn jobs are under twenty-two, but these young applicants are disproportionately rejected.

Forty percent of the people rejected for these fast food jobs were eighteen years old or younger, while only 20 percent of those hired in the same year were in this age group. This is not what we would expect to see in suburbia, where the same jobs are almost stereotypically youth employment slots. Ghetto employers have choices that suburban managers in tighter labor markets rarely encounter: they can select adults. It makes sense that managers responsible for the crew prefer older workers who are more stable and more likely to stick with the job than quit at the end of the summer or when school gets too taxing.

This preference has not gone unnoticed by young people who have found it hard to find entry to the work world. Even those who were fortunate enough to beat the odds understand just how high those odds are. Like many other Burger Barn workers, Brian—a first-generation American-born of Jamaican descent—started working when he was fourteen at the supermarket where his mother shopped in a suburb of Queens. Brian bagged groceries and collected stray shopping carts in the parking lot, a job he stuck with for two years on weekends and after school. By the time he turned seventeen, however, Brian's need for spending money had grown and he started looking for something more substantial. He turned to an older friend who was already working in a Burger Barn in the neighboring suburb of Springfield Gardens. Brian landed an entry-level position working alongside his buddy and from that experience has been able to move laterally to other Barns in Harlem (where we found him) and Queens.

By any measure, Brian has been successful at finding and keeping a job, even though he was quite young when he made his first moves. But he is skeptical about whether other young people could follow in his footsteps now. He's seen a flood of older people enter the same market, crowding out the young ones.

Nowadays, everybody is looking for a job in Burger Barn and they can't get it.

Why can't they get it?
They can get it. But a lot of people is coming back that have experience, and, of course, Burger Barn is gonna hire the experienced person first before the not experienced, 'cause they don't have to waste time to train

anybody. A lot of people, twenty-seven years old, twenty-nine, they're coming back applying for a job. Talking about they have experience. They used to work. So, it's hard to find jobs now. Burger Barn is like the first time and place you go [to find work], but they can't get in.

As Brian sees it, not only are these older applicants coming into the fast food job market, they are actually "recycled" workers: people who used to work in restaurants and who are now falling back into these low-wage jobs as other, better opportunities evaporate. The advantages they bring to employers in terms of experience and the stability of age make them by far the more desirable choice, particularly when stacked up against a newcomer who is a teenager.

Brian believes this competition, while regrettable, is fair. Others, like Lakisha, a sixteen-year-old African-American working in the same Barn, think that older people should get out of this end of the labor market and leave it for kids who need a break. In her view, any real grown-up in a Burger Barn is a grown-up in trouble, someone who has failed to leap some hurdle.

Compared to my parents, times have changed. It's harder to get a good job in my generation because the older generation is working at Burger Barn now. And Burger Barn is not really a job for older people. It's for the young.

Why do you say that?
Actually, [the adults] should be able to get a better job than the Barn.

And you think they are not able to?
Yeah. But they can't because they didn't go to school. They are probably dropouts. . . . They didn't want to go to school. . . . The older should try to find better work and the younger should get the fast food restaurants and sneaker stores.

Employer preferences for mature workers are clearly damaging to young people: they are finding it harder to get a foot in the door of the private sector.[5] This is more than a problem of the moment; it has long-range implications that are rarely considered. How will this generation of young people prove to future employers that they are a good bet? Many will not have the track record that earlier generations of job-seekers were able to compile in better times.

RACIAL COMPETITION AND EXCLUSION

The Burger Barn restaurants I focused on are located in the middle of a completely segregated commercial area of Harlem. Yet the workforce—at least at Burger Barn—is much more diverse than the immediate neighborhood, because other groups are clearly deemed desirable by employers. The Dominicans and Puerto Ricans are "commuting in" to Harlem to find work in the middle of this historic black enclave. And they are succeeding in a competitive market.

The numbers tell us that African-Americans are at a disadvantage in the hiring process compared to Latinos and others. Employers (including black employers) reject African-American applicants for jobs at Burger Barn at a greater rate than they reject those of other ethnic groups, primarily Dominicans and other Latinos. This does not mean that blacks are never hired: on the contrary, they represent about 70 percent of the new hires in these entry-level jobs. But they apply for these jobs in far greater numbers than do the ethnic groups with which they are in competition. Those "others" are far more likely to get hired than are their black counterparts, even though they are the smaller proportion of the pool of would-be employees looking to break into Burger Barn.

TABLE 8.1
RECENTLY HIRED* AND REJECTED APPLICANTS BY RACE

	Hired	Rejected	Total
African-American	52 14.4%	309 85.6%	361
Latino and other	20 34.8%	37 65.2%	57
Total	72	346	418

Chi-square significant at p=<.0001

If conversation behind the counter is any guide, the racial groups that are competing against one another for the limited supply of jobs recog-

---

* This table (and all other tables in this chapter) compares workers with less than six months tenure with applicants rejected during the same six-month period, in order to control for time on the job. Hence workers with extensive experience at Burger Barn are excluded from these comparisons.

nize the fault lines that separate them. They are aware that jobs are hard to get and that racial stereotypes and preferences intrude into the decisions that sort the success stories from the failures. Most of all, Latinos and African-Americans, the two principal groups we encountered in Harlem, recognize that whatever internal differences they may perceive among themselves, employers often look at them as representatives of a bloc and impute to them as individuals the qualities ascribed to the groups they belong to.

Danielle, a southern-born woman who came to New York to join her extended family, has worked for Burger Barn for two years now. She found the job through Latoya and Natasha, her Harlem-born cousins, who were able to get hired and then help their female kin. This network has worked well, largely because Latoya—the first success story in the group—impressed the manager as a good worker (and indeed is now a manager herself). This network of African-American women beat the odds and found work, alongside many Puerto Ricans and Dominicans coming down into Harlem from the far Upper West Side. Yet, as Danielle explains, they were fighting something of an uphill battle, for management is interested in immigrant labor:

Employers discriminate in favor of Hispanics in the job I'm on now. You could tell, truthfully, you see more Hispanics. It's hard not to say that [managers] are racist. When it comes to race, I try to listen first before I react and say, "that person's a racist." . . . But I've seen a lot of black people come in there, apply, and they haven't gotten hired. Plenty. Girls, guys, all kinds of people, every day. A lot of Puerto Ricans I see haven't even filled out applications and they're hired the next week. And they only last like a month or two months and then they are out. I'm not saying a black person or a white person wouldn't [quit]. But it's like that's where the scale is tilted, toward a lot of Puerto Ricans. And I think it should be balanced.

Danielle can scan her Barn and count the increasing number of Latinos who are working these days compared to two years ago. The "tipping" has become quite dramatic. Out of twelve workers on the morning shift, there are now only two blacks. The afternoon shift has three, other than the managers, who are African-American themselves. Danielle hedges in labeling the decision-makers racially biased. But the outcome troubles her mightily.

Even though the owner is black, he still may feel that black people is not gonna work. I don't know the reasons and I can't go in to the managers and say why are they doing it. And you can't say because it's racism, because they are black and we are black people. . . . Unless you're racist against your own kind.

Observations of this sort tend to be voiced when restaurants are experiencing a turnover, a racial shift from one group to another. In several of the Burger Barns where we worked, the shift had occurred since new owners had taken over. Slowly, but inexorably, what was once a nearly all-black workforce has become more diverse, with Dominicans edging into territory where they were previously unknown. As long as these "newcomers" remained a small minority, they went largely unnoticed. But when the balance tipped in the other direction—primarily because new owners shifted into Dominican networks for their new hires—the change became the *sotto voce* talk of the workplace among the African-Americans. They began to notice that their recommendations would be passed over in favor of connections maintained by Latinos.

Dominicans, in turn, often encounter hostility from Puerto Ricans, a population with a longer immigration history in New York. The feeling is often mutual, for in Latino enclaves (where African-Americans are less of a presence) competition runs along lines of national origin rather than race. Dominicans are particularly aware of the advantages Puerto Ricans enjoy in their superior command of English, their easy access to work papers, the freedom they have to unite their families without the headaches of visas and the endless years of waiting. All immigrants are keenly aware of the power of enclave-based networks in shaping job opportunities and are jealous of the ability of "others" to invade their turf. Because the pie is limited to begin with, these fractures can heat up into a royal conflict. Yet, both groups confront the task of finding a job knowing full well that there is never a level playing field. In the countries from which they come, there is little pretense of fairness. Whom you know dictates most aspects of where you end up in life.

The Ghetto You Don't Know

Common sense suggests that employers would prefer to hire people who live nearby, especially for jobs that do not pay enough to justify a costly commute. After all, a nearby employee can be called in when an emergency arises, and he or she is not likely to be late to work because of a track fire on the subway in Brooklyn. Efficiency considerations alone, then, ought to predispose employers to favor qualified people who live in the neighborhood. In reality, the opposite seems to hold: *Employers prefer job applicants who are commuting from more distant neighborhoods, and avoid those from the immediate area.*

Among those applicants who lived within two miles, 10 percent were hired, while 38 percent of those who lived over two miles away were hired.[6] But more than 80 percent of the rejected applicants live this close to businesses where they tried to find a job. Hence, the "reject rate" for local applicants is higher than the rate for individuals who live farther away, even when they are virtually identical in most other respects. That is, this finding on preferences for "outsiders" remains even when one looks at "locals" and "nonlocals" of similar racial, gender, educational, and age groups.*

TABLE 8.2
RECENTLY HIRED AND REJECTED APPLICANTS
BY DISTANCE OF RESIDENCE FROM JOB SITE

	Hired	Rejected	Total
<2 miles	33 (10.4%)	284 (89.6%)	317
>2 miles	39 (38.5%)	62 (61.5%)	101
Total	72	346	418

This finding is not exactly news to the fast food employers I came to know. They have an explanation for their preferences: local kids cause problems because their friends are wont to come by and ask for free french fries. Working close to all the "homeboys" makes it more likely that a worker will be tempted to goof off on the job. The disruptions are not worth the risk to employers, who run a tight ship, who have to be sure they can serve customers fast and risk minimal losses to under-the-counter handouts.

Worker preferences also contribute to the prevalence of outsiders in the Harlem Burger Barns. One franchise owner told me:

* For a multivariate model controlling for race, age, and educational background, see Appendix II.

When I first took over this store, we had so many people that traveled for hours on trains and took two, three trains to get to work to make five dollars an hour. That's because they were coming from communities similar to Harlem, and . . . a lot of people did not think that Burger Barn was the greatest place to work in terms of prestige. So people did not want to work in a Barn where they lived. Also, the younger people did not want to be in a position where they could be hurt or intimidated by folks coming in saying, "If you don't give me free food, I'll get you outside," or whatever. So we had people who came to work from four of the five boroughs, everywhere except Staten Island.

Tawana is a sixteen-year-old African-American who spent a summer working at Burger Barn, a job she took to help pay expenses after finishing summer school. The restaurant was right in the middle of Harlem's busiest shopping street and not far from her home turf. Although Tawana had the reputation of being a good worker—and now is employed in a downtown law firm—it was indeed a hassle to be within easy striking distance of friends and family who presumed she was good for a free burger or two.

Everybody was always trying to get free food from me because I worked at [Burger Barn]. "Ooh, you work at [the Barn] girl? Where at? I'm 'a come there." I'd say, "Don't come to my job." But my uncle, every day I worked he would show up. [The managers] started to think he was my father coming in giving me money or something. Every day I went there he came. "Can I have a burger? Can I have some french fries?" . . . I don't know how he knew my schedule, 'cause I never showed him my schedule. Every time he asked where I worked, I'd say, "Oh, I quit. I don't work no more," or "They told me they don't want me coming today." I said stupid little things like that 'cause I didn't want him coming down there.

As this example suggests, the employer's allergy to local applicants makes some sense. It is indeed troublesome to manage a shop if too many people come in to bother the workers.

However, the pattern of employer avoidance of local labor has been reported by other researchers studying totally different industries. Philip Kasinitz and Jan Rosenberg have done extensive research in Red Hook, an inner-city neighborhood in Brooklyn that still has a large number of unskilled blue-collar jobs in the warehouses and manufacturing industries that take advantage of the nearby waterfront.[7] They too found that employers prefer to hire outsiders, though their reasons were somewhat different. Red Hook employers associated local people with crime and unreliable work habits and were reluctant to hire them. Harlem employers occasionally invoke the same rationale, turning away applicants from local housing projects because they believe the projects are dens of criminality, likely to spawn youngsters who are no good. They know the immediate neighborhood well enough to attach differential value to residents of particular projects.

Mercer Sullivan, who has studied patterns of employment and crime in three Brooklyn neighborhoods, also found that in the predominantly Latino and African-American enclaves local labor is eschewed in favor of outsiders.[8] Only in the relatively poor white neighborhoods did Sullivan find that local kids could get jobs—mainly by exercising the networks their working parents could put at their disposal. Sullivan echoes Kasinitz and Rosenberg in seeing employers as wary of young people from the immediate neighborhoods. Sullivan's work points the way toward the unholy mixture of racial segregation—which concentrates particular groups into enclaves—and employer preferences, which favor outsiders. Because segregation operates to sort people into confined spaces, a preference for hiring "outsiders" may add up to a higher rejection rate for locals in African-American neighborhoods. But simple racial preference is not the whole explanation, for Burger Barn employers favor outsiders over locals even within race groups (that is, among African-Americans).

It may well be that "the ghetto you don't know," the one that is far away from the housing projects right around the restaurants, is more attractive to employers. Its residents may be given the benefit of the doubt, a privilege not extended as readily to people who live nearby, whose "culture" can be judged at close range and found wanting. Managers who have had bad experiences with local kids they have hired often generalize from single cases, assuming that "everyone" in the area behaves in the same fashion as the rotten apple who happened to cross their paths. They are well aware, for example, of the sociological differences among nearby housing projects and the reputations of local schools. These snippets of information, often not very reliable, permit managers to jump to conclusions that they feel to be reasoned judgments even if they are not. While employers will argue that one should never judge a book by its cover, they are in the business of making choices when it comes to potential employees, and they use hard information as well as rumors and stereotypes in the process.

Local applicants are hired, of course, but less often and with a higher threshold of qualifications (in terms of demeanor, appearance, and other "soft skills" that are not reflected in measurements of human capital like education, for example).⁹ But the preferences matter; they have consequences for job-seekers trying to find employment in their own backyards. Young people, especially those in high school, tend to confine their job search to the areas where they live. They are aware of other locales, but they favor the places they know best, especially if they have to combine work and school. Among the people rejected for jobs at Burger Barn who were eighteen years old or younger, about 83 percent lived within two miles—the less-preferred origin.¹⁰ The added demands of commuting a long distance are hard to meet in a day that is already loaded with school responsibilities.

Older people search far and wide, but there are geographical constraints for them as well. Transportation is good within the boundaries of New York City, but more difficult and expensive beyond the city's confines. For mothers of young children, long commutes impose burdens because their child care arrangements may leave them little extra time, particularly if they are so poor that they have to depend upon the generosity of family members who are doing them a favor. Low-wage mothers also find commuting costs prohibitive.

For all of these reasons, a drought of nearby accessible jobs poses a problem for ghetto job-seekers. It is even more painful when the jobs exist but are harder to get *because* the applicant happens to live close by. The consequences of this concern about local employment came home to me when I learned that the owner of one of the Burger Barns we studied had acquired a new restaurant in another part of Harlem. What was he going to do about finding new workers?

Locals would be considered for jobs, but they would face an uphill battle. George, the Barn's owner, considered the new neighborhood so dodgy that he *wanted* employees who lived nearby and were familiar with the local residents. He figured the locals would know better than others how to handle difficult customers. But Bob, who does the actual hiring, sees this as a major mistake. "The folks who live around here are irresponsible workers," he told us, "and apt to steal." So when a local applies for a job, Bob gives him or her the third degree. Some have gotten through his gate, but with a vigilant manager who has built other restaurant crews out of commuters, locals may become a minority. The fact that he imported much of the first-line managerial labor from George's other restaurants did not bode well for the locals.

CONNECTIONS

We have already seen that a network of friends and family members who have jobs plays an important role in facilitating the search efforts of a newcomer to the labor market. Networks operating at the bottom of the employment pyramid carry information about openings, provide meaningful linkages and references that managers can trust. They also give the applicant inside information: what day of the week is the best to choose when applying, which manager one should approach with application in hand, even whether it is best to mention the network connection or pretend it doesn't exist.[11]

What becomes of people who, through no particular fault of their own, do not have the right connections? People who may have enough education or experience to qualify them for a job, but simply do not have well-positioned friends? The short answer is that the network-poor job-seeker doesn't stand much of a chance. There is simply no equally effective alternative method for finding a job, even in the minimum-wage, low-skilled sector of the economy. Inner-city job-seekers who rely on the newspaper, on referrals from the Department of Labor, on going door to door filling out applications, will occasionally find success. Most of the time, however, they cannot compete against applicants with an inside track.

TABLE 8.3
RECENTLY HIRED AND REJECTED APPLICANTS BY
"CONTACTS" WITH CURRENT EMPLOYEES

	Hired	Rejected	Total
With personal contact	39 (33.3%)	78 (66.7%)	117
Without personal contact	33 (11.0%)	268 (89.0%)	301
Column totals	72	346	418

Chi-square significant at p = < .0001

As William Julius Wilson has shown, the context of an individual's life exerts tremendous influence over who has contacts to begin with and how effective (or information-rich) those connections are.[12] Obviously, friends and family members who don't work are not likely to help a job-seeker learn about employment opportunities. Living in a segregated neighborhood where the job base has dried up may well shape networks in just this fashion, leaving new entrants to the labor force unable to call upon remote sensors in the world of employment, more dependent upon employment agencies, newspapers, or the age-old route of pounding the pavement. Even knowing well-placed people in good jobs can be of little help if those occupations are shedding workers through downsizing, public-sector budget cuts, and the like. For all of these reasons, it is important to explore the interaction between certain individual characteristics and the quality or range of networks.

The importance of these contacts differs by age. Younger workers need them more than their older counterparts, because they start out at a disadvantage in the hiring preferences of employers. We can see this in the numbers: 70 percent of the employed young workers found their way in via a contact; 50 percent of the older employed workers had contacts. However, while contacts are useful for getting jobs, they are not necessarily decisive. Young people *with* contacts are still less likely to get these jobs than their older counterparts. Connections help, but they do not outweigh entirely the preferences employers have for older workers.

The Longer You've Been Here, the Harder It Gets

Many of the people in our study who identified themselves as African-American were actually born outside of the United States: some are Dominican blacks and some are from other parts of the Caribbean. Now that they have been in the United States for some time, they have adopted American racial identities and define themselves in terms of them. Physically they are not easily distinguished from native-born African-Americans, though they may well be marked linguistically (speaking accented English). These foreign-born African-Americans also seem to enjoy an advantage in the job market: they are more likely to be hired than native-born African-Americans.

It would appear that by being foreign-born, both blacks and Latinos are distinguished in the employer's "queue" as more desirable, even when they do not differ from their native-born counterparts in terms of education, for example. (About half of each group are high school graduates or holders of a GED degree.) We do not speak here of illegal aliens, for Burger Barn is careful not to violate the laws, which require legal status for employment.[13] This is more of a cultural bias that privileges the foreign-born.[14]

As Table 8.4 shows, recent (legal) immigrants have a better chance of being hired than anyone else for fast food jobs in Harlem. This does not mean that the native-born are never hired; on the contrary, they are employed in large numbers. It simply means that the *likelihood* of being hired goes up for immigrants, especially recent immigrants.

TABLE 8.4
RECENTLY HIRED AND REJECTED APPLICANTS BY NATIVITY

	Hired	Rejected	Total
U.S.-born	53 (14.3%)	318 85.7%)	371
Foreign-born	19 (40.8%)	28 (59.2%)	47
Column totals	72	346	418

Chi-square significant at $p = < .00001$

Employers know that the immigrants have come from countries where our minimum wage is their king's ransom. Haitians and Dominicans, in particular, are arriving from two of the most poverty-stricken countries in the western hemisphere, places where people go hungry, where children die young from malnutrition. Until they discover how hard it will be to stretch those earnings to afford city rents and transportation, recent immigrants regard these entry-level jobs as good deals.[15]

Nestor is a Peruvian immigrant, a Burger Barn general manager who came to New York in his childhood and grew up in the Latino enclaves of the Upper West Side. His father found work as a chef and his mother sewed in a factory for many years before she retired. Nestor found his first Burger Barn job in a restaurant about fifteen blocks north of the one he now manages, a store that was less than a block from his home at the time. His sister preceded him at Burger Barn and gradually moved her way up to general manager. Burger Barn has been good to Nestor's entire family and helped him work his way through school, including his college years, so he has never broken his ties to the firm, gradually moving up from summer employment, to part-time work during his high school years, to full-time.

Nestor is responsible for the hiring and firing in a Burger Barn restaurant that is on the edge of Harlem in Washington Heights, a neighborhood almost entirely populated by Dominicans and Puerto Ricans. The dominance of Spanish-speakers is so pronounced that one can easily get by from morning till night without having to speak a word of English. Shopping for groceries, consulting a lawyer, talking to a child's teacher, going to the doctor, reading the newspaper—all these daily activities can be conducted in Spanish without missing a beat. In fact, Nestor regularly hires people who cannot speak English, even though he prefers to take bilinguals into his shop.

Needless to say, this is a community that boasts a large number of immigrants. But it is also a place where immigrants have been arriving for a long enough period of time that many of the job-seekers are no longer foreign-born: they are the U.S.-born children of the immigrants of the 1960s and 1970s. Nestor has no trouble explaining why he prefers to hire the people who are fresh off the boat:

> *Recent immigrants have . . . higher energy levels. I guess it's how they were brought up. They have that extra strive, 'cause I think they come from countries that are poor. Like me . . . well, not me, I came too young. But they come with goals and they wanna strive for them. They give it one hundred and ten percent. Not like people who live here and know the system. They feel like, "Hey, I'm okay. My parents are here [to take care of me]," and all that.*

Nestor expresses a view common to many managers, that the experience of hard times, coupled with an immigrant's awareness that he or she has few better options, makes an applicant born and raised in a Third World country a more desirable prospect.

This aspect of the managerial belief system does not come as news to workers caught in a job market that is highly competitive and racially structured. Sean, born in Alabama but raised mainly in Chicago by a single mother who worked for the telephone company (though her first job was also at a Burger Barn), has been with three different Burger Barns so far; his wife is with the Department of Transportation, an extremely good job by local standards. Sean has a second job as a security guard, for his Barn position does not pay enough, even with his wife's income, for them to take care of their eight-year-old daughter. Sean hopes to make it into management someday—either at Burger Barn or at the security company—but for now is happy just to have the jobs he has, since he knows many black men who are out of work. Part of the reason, as he sees it, is the preference managers have for immigrants from almost anywhere over people who were born in the United States.

My security boss. He'd hire a Pakistani in a minute. Indian guy, because he know they gonna work for four dollars [an hour]. He very rarely hire black or someone like that, 'cause he knows we want money quick. You know, he thinks we want fast money and we do no work. But these [immigrant] guys come in and say, "Yes sir!" And they are willing to do anything. They work for nothing. So they hire them. The management benefits. You get a [security contract] for twelve dollars an hour. You put a [native-born worker] there who wants five, six dollars, you not making so much. But what about the guy you put there for four dollars? All these jobs where they pay you twelve dollars. You making money. So who would hire [the black] employee? It's business. Some of it is not even personal. Some of these people I wouldn't even say was racist. Some of it is. But some of it is business.

Old-Time Job-Seekers

We typically think of entry-level jobs as targets for newcomers to the labor market. After all, that is whom employers with these low-wage jobs normally have in mind when they create the positions in the first place. No one would be surprised to learn that seasoned workers beat out the novices for better jobs that demand skills and experience. If the same thing is happening at the very portals to the labor market, the "no skill" jobs like those at Burger Barn, then we know the entryway is jammed, leaving little opportunity for newcomers.

It turns out that the success stories at Burger Barn are not new to the labor market at all. On the contrary, they have had a considerable amount of experience by the time they reach Burger Barn to fill out an application. Nearly 50 percent of the new hires over the age of eighteen found their very first jobs when they were fifteen years old or younger. Even the people rejected for these minimum-wage positions were quite experienced. About one-third of them also began working before they were sixteen. Only a tiny proportion of the whole sample, 4 percent of the applicants for these jobs, are complete newcomers to the job market— for a position routinely defined as entry-level, the first step into the employment system. The vast majority had already worked, with the most frequently reported previous jobs being at other fast food restaurants,[16] publicly funded summer youth programs, sales jobs, and clerical positions.[17]

Clearly, experienced workers are a boon to an employer: they require no training, they already know the ropes, especially in this business, since the uniformity of Burger Barn's production methods is legendary. The restaurants are built to be interchangeable. Still, just having had the same job is not enough to get through the funnel. Central Harlem has such a large population of people looking for work that even those with specific skills of immediate use on the job cannot be assured of getting a minimum-wage job of this kind.

Employers do not seem to hold this criterion constant for all categories of applicants. Previous experience does not appear to be as crucial for immigrants as it is for the native-born. This is evidence, once again, of a strong employer preference for immigrants.

EDUCATION AND THE LOW-WAGE LABOR MARKET

Burger Barn and most other fast food establishments are commonly thought to be the refuge of high school dropouts who lack the skills and credentials to do any better in the labor market. Indeed, this is one of the reasons hamburger flippers rate so poorly in the prestige game: they are defined as uneducated people with no other options.

In many affluent communities, where would-be workers have better options, this kind of entry-level job may remain a haven for the dropout. In central Harlem, however, this is hardly the case. The same forces that give employers the option to choose older people over young people are making it possible for them to select the more educated for minimum-wage work. This fact seems to have registered on New York City's youth, for graduation rates rose throughout the 1980s and 1990s.[18] Increased attachment to schooling is clear enough among the young people looking for work in central Harlem: of those under the age of eighteen, two-thirds are currently in high school and a few others are in GED programs. Only 30 percent are not in school, but of this group about half already have a degree or a GED diploma. Overall, then, only 15 percent of the applicants are high school dropouts; the rest are still in school or have already earned their diplomas.

Unfortunately, these credentials are not enough to pull young people over the employment threshold, even for the minimum wage. It is not an irrelevant benchmark, for those (relatively few) youth who did get hired were more likely to be enrolled in school. In fact, it may be the case that "present enrollment" is more important to employers than graduation, because enrollment testifies to some level of affiliation with an institution that imposes its own structure, an affiliation that employers may take as symptomatic of the ability to stick to yet another structure, that of the workplace. Graduation, however, may place applicants in an entirely new category: people who have finished their education and are "free-floating" in the labor market, particularly if employers place little value on a high school diploma.

Our findings compare people who had been working at Burger Barn for under a year to those who were applying for work at the same time. In looking at the labor market this way, we are comparing a set of success stories to a group of people who flunked a hurdle at one point. Clearly, however, this is not the only effort the "rejects" made to find work; there were other chances down the road. About 26 percent of these "Burger Barn rejects" had found jobs by the time we interviewed them, one year after they were turned away from the Barn. These were success stories too, and their characteristics are instructive for the way in which they confirm our findings for the first set of workers, the people who got the jobs in the Barn.

Among these "employed rejects," men were more likely to have found jobs than women, and older people did better than younger people.[19] Race had no impact: the probability of finding a job was 25 percent for blacks and nonblacks. Twenty-five percent of the native-born had found work, compared to 40 percent of the foreign-born.[20] Educational credentials mattered for older workers, that is, those twenty-three and over: half of those with high school diplomas had found work, but only 20 percent of those without degrees had gotten jobs. Those who got work were concentrated in the occupations listed in Table 8.5.

TABLE 8.5
OCCUPATIONS OF REJECTED APPLICANTS WHO HAD JOBS ONE YEAR LATER

Job	Percentage
Sales/retail	17.5
Transport	15.8
Other Burger Barn	11.6
Government employment	8.2
Security guard	8.2
Clerical (not government)	8.2
Skilled craft	7.6
Medical/hospital paramedic	4.3
Janitorial	4.3
Public youth program	4.3
White-collar manager	3.8
Education	3.8
Other fast food	2.2

There is an interesting age pattern in the type of employment that applicants denied jobs at Burger Barn achieved later on. The youngest gained success in occupational niches that are known for low wages and high turnover: sales/retail, summer youth programs, and fast food.[21] Older job-seekers (age twenty-three and beyond) from this population found employment in those sectors as well, but they were the only ones able to break into skilled crafts or government employment.

These job-winners confirmed several of our findings on the original applicants to Burger Barn. They had contacts[22] and they were outsiders to the neighborhoods where they were now working.[23] Part of the explanation lies in the age distribution of the job-finders. Most of the younger rejects who got work got local jobs. The older "working rejects" were far more likely to have found employment in another neighborhood. This, in turn, points to the powerful impact of an impoverished job base in ghetto communities: it is the young who sustain the most damage from the evaporation of employment opportunities in high-poverty neighborhoods. They are likely to find it harder to get a foot in the door when there are few *nearby* doors to walk through.

Ironically, the workers rejected from Burger Barn who did finally get jobs did better on average in earnings than the workers who landed the fast food jobs in the first place. They were earning an average of just under $200 per week, while the recently hired Burger Barn workers averaged only $125 per week. The older the worker, the higher the salary, which suggests that for this age group (over twenty-three), those who actually find jobs will do better if they wait for something more lucrative than Burger Barn. This finding may also reflect the problems job-seekers experience when they rely on lateral networks that are composed of people with similar jobs: they may be more likely to find work, but the jobs their contacts know about may be limited to the low-wage variety. Those who are able to find work through some other means may actually do better in terms of wages, but find it harder to get a job in the first place.

While these findings confirm the points made earlier (when comparing the recently hired Barn employees and those rejected for the same jobs), it is important to remember that the vast majority of Burger Barn applicants not only failed to get those jobs, but were not working a year later. Only one-fourth were working; the other three-fourths were out of luck. And among those who were fortunate enough to land a position somewhere, the wage story is not an encouraging one. More than half of the "working rejects" were earning no more than they had earned on their most recent job. Twenty percent were doing worse, ranging from $1 per hour less to more than $5 per hour less. This is evidence of a lot of lateral churning, people moving from one job to the next without any sign of upward mobility. And in about one-fifth of the cases, it is evidence of a slump: workers are moving down into the minimum-wage job market even when they've had better luck in the past. Older workers are especially vulnerable to this kind of slump; young employees have, for the most part, not climbed high enough up the wage ladder to fall very far when they finally land jobs.

THE ANSWER TO THE QUESTION "Who is making it, who is not?" in the fast food labor market in Harlem comes down to this: African-Americans, young people, native-born applicants, and those who live nearby are less likely to be hired than others. People who lack "connections" to a network of friends or family members who are already working in the "target" job are also at a disadvantage. Employers appear to be relying on personal references, which will seriously disadvantage anyone who does not have a network of working friends or family.

To maintain, as many political figures anxious to cut the welfare roles do, that anyone who wants a job can get one is clearly to ignore the facts. In a glutted labor market, which is precisely what prevailed in central Harlem in the mid-1990s, employers find a long line of applicants coming in the door, especially for jobs that require little skill or education. Those lines were long enough to permit employers to be choosy: demanding more education or prior work experience makes sense when faced with a tighter labor market.[24] Labor gluts always have these consequences: this is a story as old as supply and demand. What is, perhaps, noteworthy is the degree of saturation in the inner-city labor market. There is a jobs crisis of major proportions. Indeed, serious employment problems remain even though the metropolitan area has experienced some tightening of the job market in recent years. In any crisis, those who have the characteristics employers are looking for—including things they cannot change, like their immigration status or the part of town they come from—will win over those who don't.

HOW HARD ARE THEY TRYING?

Because so many pundits believe that there are jobs out there for the taking, they often imply or outright claim that the reason unemployment is so high among inner-city minorities is that job-seekers in these ghettos do not try very hard to find work. However, these assumptions usually develop in the absence of much hard information about people who are actively trying to break into the job market. We are particularly handicapped in our attempts to learn about inner-city job-seekers because it is infinitely more difficult to collect accurate information in poor communities—even for the decennial census.[25]

For this book, we spent time trying to determine how hard people who had been turned down for jobs at Burger Barn were actually trying to find work. It turns out that even the youngest people in this market (fifteen-to-eighteen-year-olds) had previously applied for two or three positions before they came looking for these fast food jobs. The oldest applicants (over twenty-three) had applied for an average of seven or eight jobs before they got to this point. This suggests that central Harlem laborers (both the success stories and the "rejects") are looking seriously for work, but are having a hard time securing even low-wage jobs.

It has also been suggested that inner-city job-seekers have inflated expectations (high "reservation wages," as economists would put it) compared to what is available. There is evidence that women on welfare who receive medical and housing assistance would have to be able to find jobs paying $8 or $9 per hour before it would be "rational" for them to exit the welfare system in favor of work.[26] From this, policy-makers have concluded that it's best to cut back on those benefits and give welfare mothers no other option but to seek work, at whatever wage they can find. Such was the basic logic of welfare reform.

Do inner-city job-seekers have unreasonable expectations of what they will find or what they can get in the labor market? We asked job-seekers who were refused entry-level positions what they were hoping for and what wages they would accept. Our findings suggest that expectations were modest indeed. The mean wage they hoped for was $4.62 per hour.[27] They were willing to accept even less: on average, $4.19 per hour, below the then-minimum level legally permitted for adult workers. This was the case even though these job-seekers who had previously found work had actually done much better in the past. The average wage for the best job they had ever held was $6.77 per hour. This suggests that many job-seekers in a community like Harlem are suffering from downward mobility, moving into the minimum-wage market even though they have done better in the past. This too suggests a degree of realism that is not often credited in the popular media.[28]

The numbers presented in this chapter should dispel the notion that jobs are easy to find in a ghetto community like central Harlem. In fact, jobs are in short supply in inner-city neighborhoods. There are many, many more people looking for work than there are jobs to be found. The oversupply of job-seekers is raising the credentials that successful applicants must possess in order to find even a minimum-wage job. Employment that was once widely considered the province of young (sixteen-to-eighteen-year-old) people lacking high school diplomas is now dominated by older workers (in their twenties) who are more likely to be high school graduates. Single mothers in particular are poorly represented in this labor market: less than 10 percent of the workers we studied in the fast food business were single parents.

But of course, numbers do not tell the entire story. Skeptics might ask, are these features of a person's identity (race, residence, education) really what is driving the decisions employers make about who they want to hire? What about the less visible features that matter so much: attitude, demeanor, enthusiasm, knowledge of what is expected of a worker? Is this not what an employment interview really tells a manager?

These are important questions, and not simply because the answers would help us understand the fuzzy barriers that may be operating in the labor market. They are also critical because any complete understanding of the labor force—of all the people in the market, including those who have not found work—must take into account the experience and the cultural perspectives of the "failures."

STOPPED AT THE DOOR

Jervis, a nineteen-year-old African-American, has been looking for a job ever since he left high school in the tenth grade. He has walked all over central Harlem, stopping in at most of the fast food and retail shops he encountered. Thus far he has had little luck. But this has not always been his lot in life, for he has had work in the past, both in the New York City summer youth program and at one of Burger Barn's competitors. Jervis learned some important lessons on that job. "It taught me different routines," he says. "Being accountable for certain things, making sure that you knew when you had a certain amount of money coming for the things you did. . . ."

The fast food job he had three years back was not a great position. "I didn't make a whole lot of money, and they bust your butt!" And there is a cost to one's dignity in accepting a position that friends believe only a fool would countenance. "People will say, you know, you sacrifice a lot of your pride to make money," he notes, "and you often feel like you're working harder than your paycheck shows." Yet Jervis was willing to swallow the indignities because he recognized that everyone new to the job market has to take a first step, in the hope it will lead to something better in time.

> *A decent job that give you experience, like Burger Barn that has a chain or something like that, that you could try to make some type of career where you don't always have to be locked into a position. It's a starting place. The bottom line was the overall benefit [of the job]: I moved ahead in life. That was good enough.*

The work Jervis did in the past gave him some experience that he thought would make a difference, "a skill that I can say I know how to do," as he put it. He learned how to run a cash register and how to handle customers who seemed bent on driving him into a fury.

> *Some of them talk rude and expect you to tolerate it; some of them want faster service than they deserve; some of them want you to tolerate them not cooperating with procedure.*

But Jervis figures this just comes with the territory of a fast food job—these are the things you get paid to cope with. Picking up this kind of "people knowledge" helped him learn things he believes he will be able to put to good use. That is why he rejected all the negative talk his friends handed him when he went out to get that fast food job. "All in all," Jervis says, "I'm more interested in what the job is going to teach me than in limiting myself."

Not everyone he knows sees things this way. Some of Jervis's friends have unrealistic ambitions; they want to skip the hard, undignified first step.

> *Most of my friends want to come in and just automatically be doing great. I'm different in that I will start at a starting place.*

We saw before that having contacts makes a big difference in landing a job. Knowing how much this matters does not translate into having contacts, however. Jervis recognizes that what separates the successes from the failures often reduces to networks, but he doesn't know how to convert that knowledge into a game plan.

> *How do people meet job contacts in the first place?*
> *I'd say luck and destiny. People's spirits and bodies and background and*

communities—they all are governing a certain amount of what happens. And where you at, you have a certain exposure to certain people. And the way that you choose to live and go about your life, you'll come into contact with certain people.

The confusing character of his response tells us that Jervis really does not have much of a clue.

Jervis, his mother, and his seventeen-year-old brother (also unemployed) live as a family in a run-down neighborhood just north of the busiest commercial strip in Harlem. Nobody in Jervis's corner of the world has a fancy job, but most people around him are working. They are secretaries, messengers, they work in restaurants, and they do the hard labor in Harlem Hospital, one of the largest institutional employers in the area. He doesn't know any of these people very well, certainly not well enough to find out whether they might know of job openings he could apply for.

Pockets of middle-class African-Americans live near Jervis's apartment. They live on the nicest streets, where trees shade the sidewalk and old brownstones are being gussied up by new money. Their children wear good clothes and new shoes and they look askance when they see someone like Jervis coming, since he wears baggy pants and his cap on backwards when he is out and about. Jervis sees these well-heeled people coming and going in the morning, dressed in suits, driving nice cars. He doesn't know exactly what they do for a living, but one thing he knows is that these people have good jobs. His observations are instructive, because they suggest that being jobless and living in an area with a lot of unemployed does not necessarily produce social isolation, a culture of joblessness built on ignorance of the work world.[29] Neither does a distant set of role models translate into practical connections for Jervis.

Although Jervis no longer has the confidence he once possessed—that he could find work when he wanted it—he distinguishes himself sharply from the people he knows who are no longer trying to make it. What makes the difference, he allows, is that he knows he is responsible for what befalls him in this world. No one else is going to do for him what he must do for himself. Not everyone sees it this way:

Some people are willing to try hard and therefore they can make it regardless if the deck is stacked against them or not. . . . Other people are really the type that don't like to go through tough things, so when things get tough they just give up.

Jervis has no intention of giving up even though he would be the first to admit he doesn't have much to show for his troubles at the moment. And, he admits, he has given up on some things in the past—like high school— which has undoubtedly limited his options now that he is virtually an adult.

There is a tug-of-war at work in Jervis's community, and he keeps coming back to the power of character, to the dignity that real work bestows upon people.

> What people do about going to work or going on welfare depends on two things: their self-esteem and what's giving them the greatest benefit. Your self-esteem will definitely make you want to work. But at the same time, the welfare's giving you the greater benefit in dealing with your bills.

Jervis knows that if you "hang out" with people who have no drive, no ambition to make themselves better, you are likely to succumb to the downward drag of their ennui. "I stay away from negative people," he says, "people who are mad at racism, people who are mad at stereotypes that they don't understand." As Jervis sees it, these are the kind of individuals who are looking for any excuse other than their own failings to explain their sorry state.

Jervis is one of nearly one hundred job applicants we interviewed over a six-month period in 1994, all of whom had been rejected for entry-level positions in Burger Barn restaurants in central Harlem. By the time my research team caught up with them, these people were one year beyond the point where they had first applied to the Barn. In the intervening year, most had continued their search for employment—the application which led us to them being but one stop on a long pilgrimage.

Scholars know relatively little about people who are looking for work. Most of the national data sources track the experiences of people who are already working or who are collecting unemployment insurance. There is a vast "netherworld" of job-seekers, particularly in inner-city ghettos, about whom we have some numbers (from the *Current Population Survey*) but not much else. What kinds of values do unsuccessful job-seekers profess? Without knowing something about their hopes for the future or their past experiences in trying to find work, we are prone to imagining that the ghetto unemployed have forgotten about the work ethic.

Exploring the world of Harlem's unsuccessful job-seekers does not tell us about the whole universe of people living in the community. In particular, it tells us nothing about those who have never made any effort to find work. Readers of the nation's newspapers may get the impression that there are a large number who fall into this category: people who want nothing to do with the world of work. These individuals would not show up in any research enterprise designed to study workers or job-seekers. But how many are there?

Marta Tienda and Haya Stier studied this question by analyzing survey data from inner-city Chicago, a city that experienced high levels of both concentrated poverty and minority unemployment throughout the 1980s.[30] Tienda and Stier used the Urban Poverty and Family Life Survey of Chicago, which is a sample of black, white, and Latino parents aged eighteen to forty-four who, in 1986, lived in Chicago census tracts where 20 percent or more of families had incomes below the 1980 federal poverty line. They found that two-thirds of respondents were economically active, and 87 percent of these held jobs at the time of the survey.[31] Of the 35 percent of Chicago inner-city parents who were not in the labor force,[32] more than half reported past work experience, and most of these wanted to work. While joblessness was common, Tienda and Stier found that less than 6 percent of parents in these neighborhoods were voluntarily idle in 1986.[33] Only this tiny minority could be described as completely disconnected from the world of work.

This chapter does not provide any evidence, one way or the other, about that minority. What it does is take a close look at what people— men and women, black and Hispanic, teenagers and adults—who have faced persistent rejection, but continue trying to find a foothold in the job market, have to say about why things have been so tough for them, and who is responsible for their fate. Speaking to them at length, one comes away with the conviction that there is no meaningful "value divide" that separates them from their more successful counterparts.

At thirty-five, Clarence was having little luck in his search for employment in central Harlem. In the past he had worked as a mail clerk, an office assistant in a clothing firm, and a telex operator, and at a host of temporary agencies. Altogether, he has a total of about seven years of work experience, though most of these jobs were short-term and did not pay well.

Clarence's history reveals something important about the people who are looking for work but have no jobs. Very few have never worked. Most have job experience, and some have quite a lot of it. What they tend to lack is steady work that lasts long enough to provide any prospects for upward movement out of the minimum-wage pool. For some, the lack of consistent, long-term work is a matter of personal habits: they stop showing up on time, they don't come back when the lunch hour is over. Younger persons, those new to the world of work, often fail to understand how critical reliability is on the shop floor. They are more easily distracted by their social lives or the complications of balancing school and work. Clarence's erratic attachment to the jobs he has had has made it difficult for him to assemble references. He does not look like a stable prospect to the average employer.

Many Harlem workers have spotty job histories because the kinds of positions they manage to get are seasonal or short-term by design. Decades ago Elliot Liebow made this point in *Tally's Corner*.[34] Liebow noted that a stranger to most ghettos would drive through in the middle of the day, see grown men on the streets, and conclude that they must not be working. Most, however, would be employed part-time, in seasonal jobs like construction, or in night jobs. The unemployed were often disabled by hard physical labor, one of the few forms of work available to African-American men in the Washington, D.C., ghetto Liebow studied in the early 1960s. Much the same pattern of episodic employment is still in evidence in many inner-city labor markets.[35]

Clarence has had seasonal jobs of this kind. But he has also been employed in places where he could have kept the job but didn't, and none of his explanations for the pattern quite add up. His experience with depression and drug abuse account for many of the gaps. Clarence managed to pull himself back from the brink several times, but his personal ups and downs have taken a toll on his confidence.

> *There's nothing like being able to do something in society, you know. Having a job, being able to perpetuate whatever you do in a positive mode and be rewarded for it in a monetary fashion . . . [When I couldn't find work] I got caught up in drugs. But I straightened myself out. I ain't going to no drug program. I didn't sell my clothes, my food, or myself. You can't buy me. I do have my self-esteem and my integrity. And virtues, which my mother instilled in me and thank God for that. It helps keep me together.*

Despite his own failures, Clarence subscribes to the beliefs that most gainfully employed express about the importance of self-reliance:

> *You can make it if you try. Because there's always someone that's willing to help you if you're willing to help yourself. Someone who wants some-*

thing for you more than you want it yourself. But if you don't try, it's not going to work, it's not going to work. That's the bottom line.

Everything is hard, anything worth achieving, any goal is hard. It's supposed to be. A friendship or marriage or a job or a home—it all takes time and hard work. You have to put yourself into it . . . you have to be positive and you have to be sincere in what you want to do. You can't bullshit yourself and others, because all you're doing is fooling yourself.

Of course, Clarence realizes that stereotypes can throw walls up between an applicant like himself and an employer who brings his own baggage to the task of deciding who is worthy.

People do judge you by your skin color and people do judge you by where you come from. Both apply. It depends on the level of society in which you happen to want to work or choose to be in. You know, the circles you travel in. It does make a difference. They do judge you. That's very unfortunate. If they don't give you a fair chance as an individual, never mind your skin color. What you're capable of, that's what's important.

But like the vast majority of the nearly one hundred job-seekers we interviewed, Clarence does not believe that racial bias provides any moral shelter for ghetto dwellers. They may just have to struggle against a stacked deck. He certainly has no patience with excuses, no time for people who think the rest of the world owes them something.

Why do people in this neighborhood have such a hard time surviving day to day?
I don't think they have a hard time surviving day to day. They make it hard for themselves because they haven't any positive goals or have no direction. That's all. It's not hard [to do better]. They chose to live the way they are, so if it's bad they made it like that for themselves.

It is tempting to compare Clarence's reality against his values and argue that he doesn't really mean what he says, that he is parroting some version of what he believes we want to hear from him, or that he may believe in these values but fail to act on them. Other writers have indeed argued that we must take these attitudes with a grain of salt, for they reflect either a desire to please the researcher or a radical disjuncture between values and behavior.[36] Yet it is a rare soul—indeed, I cannot conjure up a single example—who has not demonstrated attachment to these values by taking jobs that are low in honor and low in pay. Clarence has had many of them. Moreover, the fact that we found these true believers because they were searching for work at Burger Barn suggests that they subscribe to the idea that almost any kind of job is better than unemployment.

Harlem's unsuccessful job-seekers rarely possess resources that will tide them over until they can secure a job.[37] None of the people we interviewed, for example, was a homeowner. Indeed, most were residents of public housing or rental apartments who, by definition, lack the collateral needed to borrow money from a legitimate agency like a bank or a savings and loan (a strategy often pursued by the suburban unemployed). Moreover, most had histories of low-wage labor, work that paid so poorly they were living close to the edge even when they were employed. Very few had been able to amass savings of any magnitude, and those who had something squirreled away ran through it rapidly. Medicaid was their chief source of health insurance, another indication of their general poverty, but no great surprise since more than half of these rejected job applicants report annual incomes under $5,000. They also come from families with much lower annual incomes than our working sample: about one-half of the nonworking rejects were in households with annual earnings below the poverty line for a family of four.[38]

Given these income findings, it is hardly surprising that a large proportion of these unsuccessful job-seekers come from households where someone—usually a mother or sister—has been an AFDC recipient. Indeed, over 40 percent of them were drawing part of the household's support from welfare. But we should also note, contrary to much of the received wisdom about the separation between workers and welfare recipients, that over 55 percent of the "rejects" are in households supported entirely by wages. Clearly the two conditions—work and welfare—are intertwined in households from which the army of job-seekers is coming.

Karen showed us another face for the rejected job-seeker at Burger Barn. When she applied, Karen was only sixteen years old, one of the many high school students who came looking for jobs in the middle of Harlem during the spring of 1994. She was hoping to find something for the summer that would help pay her own expenses and allow her to put a little away for college, her ambition from "day one" of high school. Her mother, a secretary, and her father, who works in construction, are divorced. Although both earn a reasonable living, neither is affluent and money is always tight (even so, they and their daughter are light-years ahead of the circumstances of either Jervis or Clarence).

Karen lives with her mother, whose annual income is about $25,000, which would just about qualify this family of two as lower-middle-class by national standards.[39] Still, New York City's legendary cost of living—astronomical rents, exorbitant food prices, high transportation costs—makes it hard for this single-parent family to get by even though the mother is steadily employed.

The construction business is a precarious one, and Karen's father has experienced occasional bouts of unemployment himself, especially after he lost his job with the Transit Authority, which paid for the family's medical care and held out the prospect of a comfortable retirement. Construction work is seasonal and doesn't provide much in the way of benefits, even though the hourly wage isn't bad—when the hours are there. Hence his contributions to Karen's well-being are irregular, a problem common to divorced families all over the country.

Karen knows a lot of other divorced families that have "gone under," going on welfare even when the parents boast a long history of steady work. These troubled families have less favorable "demographics."

A lot of people aren't doing well. I think that I'm doing, me and my mother, we're doing okay. I think it's because there are only two of us. Because a lot of people have a lot of kids and that's how you get in trouble, you can't afford all the kids that you have.

This observation has led Karen to develop some very specific goals in life: to finish college, get married, have two kids maximum, and "get the hell out of New York City."

Karen is something of a model teenager, a student in one of New York's selective high schools that require high scores on entrance exams for admission. Unlike her more affluent classmates, who go off to camp during the summer or take enrichment courses on a college campus, Karen has devoted her teenage summers to earning some money. She started looking for work at the age of fourteen, but didn't get anywhere until the following summer, when she landed a federally sponsored job as a camp counselor. She enjoyed working outside, going to the swimming pool with her charges, even though they were a handful to manage. "Those kids never listened to me," she complained. She would fall into bed every evening, exhausted by the effort of trying to keep watch over a group of hyperactive little kids. The whole experience taught Karen that "work is hard. You have to work hard to get paid."

The summer she turned sixteen, she tried her hand in the private sector and began to look around Harlem, a subway ride away from her home in Washington Heights. She applied for a dozen jobs, as a cashier, a clerk, or a burger flipper, but nothing came through. In this respect, Karen is typical of the many teenage job-seekers who could be absorbed into an urban labor market if it were *not* saturated with better-qualified (older, more stable, high school graduates) workers. Youths who look for work have a hard time finding anything—even when, like Karen, they are students in an honors program. There just aren't enough jobs to go around.[40]

The desire to work, however, remains high, even among young people who are increasingly aware of the odds against them. Although Karen lives in a neighborhood she considers crowded and noisy, with music blaring at all hours of the night, she also sees most of her neighbors going to work every day. In her apartment building, she is friendly with a home attendant, a factory worker, and another woman who has a job in the same office where her mother works. Out on the streets, she sees lots of people she doesn't know coming home from work in suits. All of these working people constitute the everyday, normal social structure of the community where Karen lives, a barrio neighborhood of blacks and Latinos. But it also has its share of young men who make a living dealing drugs, and kids Karen's age who seem to be looking for trouble. She avoids them by living a controlled life: going to school and coming straight home when the day is done. She doesn't hang out on the street, even when it's hot inside her apartment. And she separates herself from those who seem to be going nowhere, defining them as losers by choice.

Are there people in your neighborhood who are really not making it at all?

Sure. They're lazy. They want to sleep and eat and just hang outside instead of doing something of importance. They want to hang out and have fun. But there's a time for hanging out and a time for work. You know, you have to do something with your life, get some money, make something of yourself.

"Making it" is the key theme in Karen's life. While she would very much like to have a chance to earn some money, to help her mother out of the tight spots, she realizes that over the long run her best bet lies in doing well in school. She would have liked that job at Burger Barn, but this is not where she plans to end up when she is Clarence's age.

> *For someone like me who has little experience—I've never had a job except for the one at summer youth—a job at Burger Barn or someplace like it would be okay. For me that would be a first or second job. But if you graduate high school and you want a good job, then you have to [go to school to] learn how to do something [special] in order to get a better job. You can't just expect someone to give you a job just because you are older or something like that.*

In short, Karen expects to have to earn her way to a decent job and knows that this goal is a long way off.

Her peers do not necessarily accept the notion that you have to start out at the bottom in order to work your way up. They think Burger Barn jobs are exploitive.

> *My friends told me it would be easy to get a job, that anybody can work at Burger Barn, you know. It doesn't take anything [they said], but you only get paid a little bit. Most of the people I know that have worked there didn't work there for a long time. They said [the managers] didn't treat them right, or they just didn't like working at [Burger Barn], or they had a fight with a customer or something like that.*

Karen wasn't particularly persuaded by their point of view, though, for she does not consider an entry-level job to be a comment on her potential for a more respectable occupation. She understands jobs like this for what they are designed to be: stepping-stones along the way to a real future, a future that is going to be defined more by higher education than a summer job. Karen knows that without that next step, she would face the fate that so many young people in Harlem now confront—a lifetime of working poverty in a job that garners little respect.

> *Getting an education is very important, because without it, you'll be working at [Burger Barn] forever. You'll be like these people who don't want to work there but they don't really have a choice, you know?*

Karen is going to make sure this doesn't happen to her, and with a selective high school diploma under her belt, it is not likely to occur anyway.

Yet, as for many other teenagers in Harlem, including the most promising of them, the inability to secure a job along the way is a major problem. Without the extra income, Karen must "burden" her mother with the cost of her books, her transportation to school (which is many miles from her home), her clothing, and all the little extras so important to young people. As long as her mother is steadily employed, Karen will not starve—she is not among the community's poor. Still, she would like that degree of independence, that "proto-adult" status, that comes with earning your keep. The job market, however, is crawling with people her age and sagging under the weight of older high school graduates who will not leave their employers when the summer is over. The latter look like a better bet to most Burger Barn managers, and so Karen is left without the kind of opportunity earlier generations of high school students in the inner city could rely on: a foot in the door of the labor market.

African-Americans are not the only people looking for work in Harlem. Latinos, especially the Dominicans and Puerto Ricans, have begun to stream into the black enclaves in search of work as well. And they have met with success to a far greater degree than have people like Clarence or Karen. For the reasons discussed earlier, these job-seekers are often favored over the African-Americans who apply. Still, Latinos also face rejection in a labor market that is too crowded to absorb all of those trying to find work.

Jaime has had his share of rejections. Born in Puerto Rico, Jaime came to New York when he was ten and settled in central Harlem, not far from the main commercial strip of 125th Street. He dropped out of high school, but recovered his footing enough to earn a GED diploma. He was due to begin the course work for an AA degree, with an emphasis on computer skills, at the time we met—a year after he had been rejected for a job at Burger Barn. Although he was only seventeen, Jaime was an experienced wage earner who began his work life in a steak house, cleaning the floors, during the summer he turned fourteen. He has also had full-time stints working for another fast food chain, for the Gap, and as a clerical worker doing filing and mail delivery. Altogether Jaime has had one and a half years of work experience, much of it "under the counter" because he was still underage and therefore technically not allowed to work.

At the request of a job placement agency he turned to for help, Jaime put in an application at the Burger Barn located only a few blocks from his home, but was turned down. They were not hiring, turnover having slowed down somewhat since the job market is so clogged up. With few openings, young would-be workers like Jaime and Karen are out of luck, even though in Jaime's case he comes with fast food job experience (usually an advantage).

Although Jaime lives in the middle of Harlem and most of his neighbors are African-American, his family is part of a little cluster of Latino families from Colombia, Panama, and Puerto Rico. He lives with his mother, a thirty-four-year-old clerical worker; his older brother is a salesman and his sister is still in high school. Jaime's family has been doing fairly well lately, largely because of his mother's diligent efforts to finish her own schooling in order to secure a better job than what she had when Jaime was little. He remembers that the years she spent studying were the hardest times for the family, for the earnings he and his brother brought in were all the family had, save the very modest grant his mother received from the city welfare agency[41] that helped support her schooling. Now that she has a regular job and his older brother is working too, Jaime feels pretty secure in their self-sufficiency. No one in their house is on "aid" anymore, two of the three "adults" are working, and with luck he will be too in the future.

Nonetheless, it is worrying to Jaime that he is not working, for by his cultural standards he ought to be taking care of himself, not relying on his mother. By the time Jaime was sixteen, he regarded himself as a responsible adult who was supposed to pay for his own expenses and contribute to the household. He no longer thinks of himself as a child and does not believe his mother should take responsibility for his keep, not even his basic necessities. "In my house," he says emphatically, "I pay. My brother and I, we pay." And that is exactly as it should be, as Jaime sees it, for in Puerto Rico he would be past the age where he would be defined as an adult. His mother, after all, had two children to take care of by the time she was Jaime's age. Puerto Rico's poor have a much shorter childhood than their mainland counterparts, for whom adolescence can now stretch into the mid-twenties without raising too many eyebrows. No such luxury for Jaime.

The fact that others around him do not subscribe to this philosophy does not make it any less honorable. Jaime freely admits that it bothered him to learn that some of his Puerto Rican friends thought he should stay away from Burger Barn.

> *They don't want to get a job [at the Barn]. The girls don't like you when you get a job there because you sweat too much, flipping burgers and stuff. They make fun of you.*

Their attitudes did not stop Jaime from trying to get that job anyhow. For he needed the money in order to cure a deficit that was more important than his reputation with the girls: his inability to take care of himself financially, to be a respectable adult in his household.

He believes that this point of view, this latter-day Protestant ethic, distinguishes him from many who live in his neighborhood, but he recognizes that there is variation on this theme and knows that the people in his community come in many different colors and occupations.

> *The adults in the neighborhood—Latinos and Afro-Americans—[lots of them] live off welfare. Some just selling drugs. And regular jobs, you know, supermarket, around the neighborhood stores. . . . I got a lawyer in the building.*

Jaime subscribes to the same mainstream critique of the poor that Karen and Clarence do: the downtrodden people in their neighborhoods are bringing their troubles upon themselves, by not working harder, by relying on welfare, by giving up on the straight life and letting themselves get involved in the underground. All three share a basic conservatism that underlines the need for personal responsibility, the importance of self-sufficiency. But he is confused about the reality of equal opportunity. On the one hand, he thinks things are tougher for people who are in the minority.

> *If you're a minority, it's hard, hard for you to know, to try to go out there and get a better job. It's harder than, you know, the other, higher, like white people.*

One glance around Jaime's neighborhood helps to explain his skepticism. "Lots of people are on welfare around here." But he is not sure whether this represents some ubiquitous system failure, or a consequence of the racial barriers that plague minorities, or the character flaws of individuals:

> *They taking welfare, they want to live for free. They want to live off of people, so they're not going to make it. Because they ain't got no money, the money they get is for the rent and the food [and nothing else]. And they be having too many children.*

Jaime's brother has an out-of-wedlock child, but this does not seem to complicate his analysis of the welfare problem in his community, for his brother makes regular contributions to the baby's mother. The problem, as he sees it, is all those irresponsible people who go ahead and have babies thinking someone else is going to take care of the cost.

Hence Jaime detects patterns in the fates of individuals that he attributes to racial barriers, but also believes the same patterns are the cumulative consequence of individual decisions or motivations: to be "free riders" on society's back, to have children they cannot afford. His observations about the nonrandom nature of poverty in New York are quite contradictory: it is, at once, the outcome of racial biases that hold minorities down and the consequence of individual failures that cluster among the black and brown poor. One view points the finger up above, at unnamed and unknown powers who pull the strings and deny opportunity to minorities. The other points the finger down in what liberals would term a classic "blame-the-victim" formulation.

For Jaime and Karen, the blame-the-victim view of inequality—or rather the perspective that sees America as a land of opportunity—derives some of its authority from the fact that there are examples of success in their own families. They both have working mothers who have overcome considerable odds to complete their schooling and find respectable jobs. They have aunts, uncles, and grandparents who have worked all their lives. But rather than focusing on the odds these relatives faced (and overcame), they draw from their experience the lesson that we inhabit a golden shore. Jaime, who a minute before had argued that minorities have a harder time getting good jobs than do whites, noted in the same breath that:

> *They don't judge you by your skin color. My mother is dark-skinned, but she works with rich people and stuff. She works with, you know, high people. They don't judge us. They just judge my mother for what she is, by the attitude she has and everything.*

This is the same Jaime who, several moments later, argued that "employers discriminate against us." And this was more than an abstract comment; he had run into the problem in the business district.

> *I wanted to work downtown before; I was going to work in the Empire State Building. And then the owner in the office saw me and he didn't like me because I was dark-skinned.*

Both "conversations," one about equal opportunity and individual virtue and the other about prejudice and structural constraints, inhabit the same mind and derive from the observations that poor people, both in or out of the labor market, make about who has ended up where in America. They can see the unequal distribution of resources—housing, schooling, job opportunities, and sheer wealth—and the ways in which minorities are bypassed when these goods are parceled out. At the same time, they can point to people close to them—and, in a good year, to themselves—as examples of people who have "made it."

Because they are Americans, who partake of a powerful mainstream culture that derives from middle-class experience, they accept the basic principle that opportunities are there, that one need merely grasp them. But because they are black and Puerto Rican Americans, who live in neighborhoods that are run-down, who suffer overcrowded and underfunded schools, roads peppered with potholes, and buildings that are falling down from lack of investment or building code enforcement, they know that they confront life with the deck stacked against them. And because they are trying to find a job but haven't met much success, they have to account for their rejection, to understand why perfectly worthy people have not yet surfaced above the waves—as their mothers have.

As Jennifer Hochschild has pointed out in *Facing Up to the American Dream*,[42] survey research confirms the fact that blacks and whites in the United States accept the claim that it is possible for all Americans to "achieve success as they define it . . . through their own efforts." But she argues that African-Americans are increasingly unsure whether the Dream applies to them, while whites (especially lower-class whites) have grown certain that public policy has given blacks a special (read "unwarranted") claim to a large share of it. Without joining the debate over affirmative action, it is important to note here that the dilemmas of race, intertwined with the power of a common cultural ideology and an economy that has privileged some at the expense of others, has produced a refracted and contradictory set of beliefs in most of us: the powerful pull of meritocracy, with its race-blind vision of equal opportunity, and the recognition that race intervenes to shape lives in the most profoundly unfair fashion.

Harlem job-seekers accept the premise that the state should look after those who cannot provide for themselves. Yet they are adamant that crutches shouldn't be given to those who can do for themselves. As Jaime put it, "Any job is good, as long as you're getting paid. It's always better than city help." People should take care of themselves, no matter what the cost to their pride, for dignity stems from working for a living. This fundamental belief is part of what inclines job-seekers and their working-poor counterparts away from the racial separatism that some leadership figures[43] espouse on behalf of Harlem's dispossessed. In general, the people we interviewed—jobless and working—rejected this political stance.[44] For them, the main chance is the mainstream, not some segregated enclave where minorities can be divorced from the rest of the world. Personal responsibility is not supposed to be a ticket to separation: it is an instrument of moral and cultural inclusion, the chief weapon in the fight to overcome unfairness. They do not want to sit in some ghetto sideline; they want to be in the middle of the action.

CHAPTER NINE

What We Can Do for the Working Poor

THE CONDITIONS THAT BESET the nation's poor are cause for concern among all citizens who believe that in a country so blessed there should not be millions among us who do not share in the bounty. If this is so for the poor in general, it is doubly urgent where the working poor are concerned. They bend their backs to change the linens on the beds we occupy in hospitals, work over vats of grease to make the french fries we eat, bag the groceries we take home from the supermarket, clean the floors and the toilets in the hospitals, and then go home to raise their children on wages so low that they sink beneath the poverty line even when they work full-time.

Is this a problem that will go away if we continue to see the historically low levels of unemployment the U.S. has enjoyed of late? Can we assume the market will solve this problem all by itself? Undoubtedly, sustained tight labor markets are the best medicine for the working poor. They draw discouraged workers back into the work world. They push employers past their prejudices and give them no choice but to hire among people they might not have willingly considered before. Wages go up if tight labor markets last long enough.

But there are good reasons not to rest easy. We presently enjoy the lowest levels of unemployment the nation has seen for nearly thirty years. While European countries sag under the weight of double-digit unemployment, in 1998 the U.S. boasted less than 5 percent on the unemployment lines. However, as William Julius Wilson has noted, we do not count in our rosy numbers the millions of people who are no longer searching for work, the people who are "out of the labor force." Millions of them live in places like central Harlem, hence the unemployment statistics routinely understate the dimensions of the job problem in the nation's ghettos.

A focus on the working poor reminds us as well that employment alone won't solve the poverty problem if the wages are too low. The sustained employment boom has not led to a sharp upswing in wage rates. Indeed, wage improvements have been modest at best, and those we can track owe their existence to the 1996–97 increase in the minimum wage.[1] A booming job market can also bypass the very communities that have been discussed in this book. New York City has not had the kind of employment bounce that cities like Milwaukee or Boston have experienced. It still lumbers under the burden of unemployment rates of 7 percent while the rest of the nation enjoys less than 5 percent. Within the city, indeed even within the cities "suffering" from worker shortages, jobless rates in ghetto neighborhoods remain stubbornly high. Harlem routinely posts unemployment figures twice those of the city as a whole. Segregation and concentrated poverty combine to make the problem of joblessness and working poverty more intractable in inner-city neighborhoods than elsewhere.

Finally, although workers everywhere benefit from tight labor markets, it is unlikely that this boom will last indefinitely. And when the next downturn arrives, we will see just what we have wrought through the imposition of time limits on families reliant on welfare. Already we see that those exiting the system in New York are having trouble finding work. Between 1995 and 1998, the population on AFDC in New York City dropped from approximately 1.2 million to 810,000 (more than half of whom are children). The best available tracking data show that among the adults who came off the welfare rolls between July 1996 and March 1997, only 29 percent found full-time or part-time jobs (defined as earning $100 or more within three months of leaving the rolls).[2] The Brookings Institution has studied declining caseloads and has concluded that nationwide, the cities are having a much harder time shifting people off of welfare than the states where they are located.[3]

That would not surprise the fast food workers we studied in Harlem. Long before welfare reform, they were looking at a labor market that could not absorb the thousands of people looking for employment. While tighter labor markets in the late 1990s have undoubtedly shrunk the lines of job-seekers standing outside Burger Barn's door, it would take a very long time indeed for the surplus to dry up. And while one hopes the good news will go on for decades, we have never seen an employment boom last this long. What goes up usually comes down.

Although much of our intellectual energy has been consumed by debates over the nation's welfare system, some economists, education researchers, and policy experts have recognized that the working poor represent a much larger population and have made valuable suggestions about what we might do to attack its problems. While I will not dwell upon the ideas that others have already outlined, it is worthwhile to turn to them briefly and then move on to some new initiatives suggested by the research contained in this book.

WAGE SUBSIDIES AND TAX BREAKS

Over the years, the federal government has experimented with a variety of employer wage subsidy programs in which participating firms receive tax credits on wages paid to various "hard-to-hire" groups of workers.[4] The largest of these is the Targeted Jobs Tax Credit,[5] recently replaced by the Work Opportunity Tax Credit, which provides private-sector employers with a wage subsidy to underwrite the costs of hiring certain groups of workers—disadvantaged youth, welfare recipients, and veterans, as well as others. Subsidy programs such as these have had a mixed track record[6] and at best seem to have had a very modest impact nationwide— employers find the regulations cumbersome and, beyond this, believe the targeted eligible workers are damaged goods.[7] Evidently they prefer to pay the going rate and get the workers they want rather than to receive the government support for workers they believe will be more trouble than they are worth. Nonetheless, economists like Edmund Phelps at Columbia University have argued that we should implement a system of progressive and quite substantial wage subsidies to firms that employ low-wage workers.[8] Coupled with gradual increases in the minimum wage, these subsidies could almost immediately lift poor workers above the poverty line, and this with a minimal amount of paperwork.

Ironically, in central Harlem, fast food employers did not see subsidies in a negative light. Even though they had many more job-seekers at the door than they could accommodate, and therefore could be quite choosy, they often picked people living in criminal halfway houses because there was a nearly 50 percent wage subsidy attached to hiring them (government's effort to get rehabilitated criminals back into the labor market). As one employer told me:

We are a second-chance employer. If you have a [criminal] record, that doesn't necessarily mean that you would be excluded from getting a job at Burger Barn, especially as part of the work release program. We developed a relationship with the counselors and told them who we want. I'm not hiring anybody who has been involved in a violent crime, but some of the other things are okay, so the counselors kind of guide people to apply.

With the number of applications you get that vastly exceed the number of people you hire, why would you hire anyone on work release anyway?
Because you get a tax break. The Targeted Job Tax Credit which Congressman Rangel from Harlem introduced some years back provides an incentive to employers to hire people they wouldn't necessarily look to hire if they just walked in the door. The discount is about fifty percent.

Even though this employer knew full well these workers would disappear as soon as they were released from their supervised (parolelike) status, the cost of the wage bill was sufficiently hard on the bottom line that she regularly took the chance. Clearly, then, there are some special circumstances where wage subsidies are useful in encouraging hiring.

More important, however, for our purposes is the Earned Income Tax Credit, a subsidy that goes directly to parents. It drastically cuts the tax burden for poor workers with children and lets them take home more of their wages. The inspiration for the EITC—which originated in the Nixon administration and became permanent under Gerald Ford—was the slogan "Make work pay." Labor economists and policy-makers eager to reduce welfare spending argued that until there was a dramatic advantage to being in the labor force (which is more expensive in terms of transportation and child care costs than staying home),[9] we couldn't very well expect people to flock to jobs. The EITC—which has been increased three times since the mid-1980s—provides a supplementary refund to working parents with earnings so low that they owe little or no federal income tax.[10] For families with two or more children working at the minimum wage, the EITC effectively increases hourly earnings by $2 per hour—a huge jump in percentage terms.[11] And it works. The Urban Institute has determined that about 4.5 million Americans are lifted above the poverty line through the tax credit.

Despite its successes and its popularity among some conservatives (who favor work) and most liberals (who favor well-targeted support for the poor), periodic efforts have been made to reduce the EITC.[12] Critics level charges of fraud, complain that it is too costly to the nation's treasury, and worry that the leveling off of the credits as a family's income creeps higher might act as a disincentive to work more hours.[13] As Peter Passell of the *New York Times* has pointed out, "Meeting the Republican goal of balancing the budget within seven years without touching Social Security, eliminating cherished weapons programs or raising taxes would require deep cuts just about everywhere else."[14] The strong economy we have lately enjoyed has created budget surpluses that are now the subject of much political debate as conservatives argue for tax cuts and liberals recommend greater investment in education and training. Full coffers may relieve some of the pressure on EITC, but whatever the political outcome, we should recognize that the cheapest, least bureaucratic method of raising working people above the poverty line is to continue expanding the EITC, even for heads of households without children.[15] No one who works full-time should live below the poverty line.

MOVING PEOPLE TO JOBS

The spatial distribution of America's jobs has changed dramatically since the end of World War II. As suburbanization proceeded apace, employers moved out of the cities into the hinterlands, taking their job opportunities with them.[16] Some researchers argue that over time, we've come to suffer from a "spatial mismatch," with jobs going begging in the suburban ring and poor people going begging in urban communities—never the twain to meet. There is great debate over how much this contributes to inner-city unemployment.[17] After all, it is not clear that employers who fled the cities into the largely white suburban belts would be eager to hire poor people from Harlem, in which case, as David Ellwood has pointed out, it is "race not space" that blocks job-seekers.[18] Yet if labor shortages are severe enough, we know that employers relax some of their prejudices, because they have no alternative.[19]

The thick forest of help-wanted signs one sees on suburban Long Island attests to the difficulty more affluent communities have in finding workers, especially for the least desirable jobs. Burger Barn employees in Harlem earn the minimum wage and get stuck just exactly there. But their counterparts in Great Neck or Port Jefferson are earning $3 an hour above the minimum wage because no one who has a choice (as many suburban kids do) will take that job. How could we move the Jamals of Harlem out to Great Neck? Mark Alan Hughes, now a vice president of Public/Private Ventures (a youth-employment think tank in Philadelphia), has developed a series of demonstration projects aimed at moving people out to job-rich areas through subsidized transportation systems.[20] "Bridges to Work" is now up and running in five cities and showing, at this preliminary stage, some positive outcomes. Low-income workers are offered commuting subsidies, special funding for emergency transportation (in case their kids get sick), and job placement assistance so that they can move out of the ghetto and into a suburban job market.

Begun in 1976, the Gautreaux program, a court-mandated[21] housing desegregation project in Chicago, moved several hundred poor families (a few at a time) from their run-down inner-city projects into mostly suburban private apartments, using Section 8 housing subsidies. While the moves were motivated by evidence of housing discrimination, the consequences for employment have not been trivial. James Rosenbaum and Susan Popkin have shown that while the wages of the Gautreaux "movers" did not increase dramatically as a result, the chances of finding a job at all rose substantially.[22]

Of course, we cannot pick up and move millions of Americans. The costs, the social resistance,[23] and the scale of the effort make such a scenario unlikely. How, then, might we bring more jobs to the inner-city communities where the working poor live? William Julius Wilson has argued (in *When Work Disappears*, 1996) that without creating a Marshall Plan for the nation's ghettos, complete with a substantial public job creation program for those who cannot find private employment, we will see little improvement in the lives of inner-city residents. This, coupled with intensive job training and child care support, Wilson suggests, is essential for any meaningful transformation of the dismal conditions of many isolated urban ghettos. He is surely right. Yet political support for federal job creation is weak, to say the least. Until that tide changes, it would be worthwhile to consider alternatives.

Moves to create "empowerment zones" or "enterprise zones" are among the most recent tools adopted by the federal government. In 1994, Congress appropriated $2.5 billion in tax breaks and $1.3 billion in grants to help attract businesses into six depressed urban centers.[24] The jury is still out on how much of a difference these funds will make. The investment is modest, while the scale of the poverty problem is daunting. However, in central Harlem, which is the heart of one of six urban empowerment zones, there is some evidence of forward motion.[25] Large chain stores that have avoided the area are taking advantage of tax breaks and moving into the neighborhood. High-priced bodegas run by small shopkeepers are facing stiff competition nowadays, with local residents the winners (in terms of the commodities they purchase). New jobs are being created in the Pathmark supermarket—a $15 million commercial development funded by developers associated with the Abyssinian Baptist Church, the first large enterprise of its kind in twenty years—and those new positions appear to be more numerous than those that are disappearing in the bodegas. Using funding from the empowerment legislation, Congressman Charles Rangel brokered a deal between Harlem-based City College and several large insurance firms to create new training schemes and new white-collar jobs for residents. Hence the mix of employment opportunities may be changing under the aegis of the empowerment zone.

These place-based strategies have plenty of detractors who believe they do too little too late or merely reshuffle the deck chairs on the *Titanic*—moving a few jobs across the line from a "nonzone" into a favored tax haven.[26] They also have their true believers, among them Republican Jack Kemp and the current head of HUD, Democrat Andrew Cuomo. They have argued for the expanded use of the tax code to favor investment in urban areas, coupled with vigorous enforcement of anti-redlining legislation aimed at preventing banks from excluding poor neighborhoods from needed loan programs.

There can be no question that bringing more jobs to inner-city neighborhoods would make a world of difference, not only for those presently outside the labor market but for the kinds of people who appear in this book, who work every day at low-wage jobs and hope to find something better. Without an increase in job availability, their chances of moving up diminish. Merely being able to put more workers in each household into the labor market increases the resources available for families as a whole. But without the jobs to absorb them and tighter labor markets to drive their wages up,[27] they are likely to labor in poverty for much of their lives.

UNIONS

Supporters of the rejuvenated labor movement, under the leadership of the AFL-CIO's president John Sweeney, would argue that an important key to moving low-wage workers out of poverty lies in increasing their participation in unions.[28] Nationally, conditions are reasonably good for a revitalization of unions, since tight labor markets make union drives less risky and at the same time increase the bargaining power of workers. However, the low-wage labor market is notoriously difficult to organize, as it is made up of so many part-time workers, not to mention workers in saturated inner-city labor markets where the employers can easily turn to the hundreds of people waiting outside their doors to replace those with pro-union sentiments.[29] The advent of the nationwide strike among United Parcel Service workers in the summer of 1997 focused greater attention on the two-tiered labor market that divides part-time workers from their much richer full-time counterparts. But the failure of union drives in companies like Wal-Mart tells us that unions have a long way to go before they will be able to capture inner-city workers at places like Burger Barn. That said, there is no doubt that collective bargaining would make a difference in the lives of poor workers who, for the moment, lack even the most basic benefits accruing to unionized labor.

CHILD CARE AND HEALTH CARE

If there is a silver lining to welfare reform, it is the increased attention and political support it has provided for investment in child care. It cannot come soon enough, for in most of the nation's big cities, the supply of child care—never mind quality child care—is far too low to meet the needs of poor families. New York City subsidizes day care for approximately 75,000 children, 20,000 of whom have parents participating in the mandatory workfare programs. The 75,000 represent only 14 percent of the children eligible under the income guidelines. Child Care, Inc., the city's leading child care advocacy organization, projects that because of welfare changes the city will have to handle an additional 35,600 children.

Working poor parents cannot stay in the labor market[30] without access to child care and city-funded day care centers, which provide affordable, reliable, and comparatively high-quality child care for families whose only other options include family care (when it is available) or unlicensed operators.[31] Yet the working poor are the least likely of all income groups to receive assistance with child care costs. Thirty-seven percent of non-working poor families and middle-income families receive direct or tax assistance with child care costs, but only 30 percent of working-poor families receive such assistance. Ironically, families coming off of AFDC may receive subsidies with their child care costs while those who have been in the labor force for some time discover that availability is compromised and their (unsubsidized) costs are prohibitive, making it that much harder to stay on the job.

It will not serve the cause of reducing poverty long-term to consign the children of the working poor to inadequate care by caving in to the pressure of numbers and relaxing the quality standards we know protect the well-being of children. We need to increase the funding we provide nationally and locally for child care, and take this opportunity to revisit the whole early childhood education enterprise. If we were to follow the example of the French or the Italians, who provide universal coverage for high-quality child care and think of it as the first stepping-stone into formal schooling, we might reap enormous benefits in the educational performance of succeeding generations. We could do this while simultaneously making it possible for more parents to stay in the labor force.

For working-poor and low-income families, health care is a critical priority, especially when the trend is to decrease the rate of employer coverage for children. Kids in working-poor families go without health insurance at a much higher rate than any other group of American children. In 1994, 27 percent of the kids from working-poor families had neither public nor private medical insurance. In many cases, this exposure comes from the fact that their parents' employment does not carry health benefits, yet they are not eligible for Medicaid. If it were not for recent changes to Medicaid in 1991, health care access for children would be much worse. In 1994, more than two-thirds of the working-poor children who had some form of medical coverage received it through Medicaid.[32] The Clinton administration has done a great deal to expand medical insurance for poor children. We must do the same for their parents.

SOME NEW IDEAS

Our research in Harlem, coupled with my own sense of the political scene, convinces me that apart from the ideas discussed above, our energies should be directed at opening up opportunity in the private sector—albeit with limited, targeted assistance from government agencies. Whatever the merits of public employment—and in my view there are some considerable benefits both for job-holders and for the communities they serve—support for public-sector employment is too weak to make it a reality. These programs are too easily, and unfairly, demonized as "make-work," as wasteful pork-barrel spending. Though I disagree with such critiques most of the time, for the purposes of forward motion I believe that we should be pragmatic and accept political realities for the moment, focusing policy energy on improving access to better-paid jobs in the private sector.

From School to Work

Robert Reich, Secretary of Labor in the first Clinton administration, has argued that the United States is in trouble when it comes to training the labor force.[33] Other nations invest more in schools (providing longer

school days and more days per year, not to mention more advanced training in science and math) and encourage apprenticeship programs that
sandwich school and workplace-based training. These efforts pay off: students transit from school to the world of work in something approximating a seamless web, leaving less room for the floundering, churning
period that is typical among youthful Americans entering the labor market.[34] Germany's apprenticeship system—which moves students back and
forth from the classroom to the shop floor in a sustained training process
that lasts for many years—stands as the premier example of a school-to-
work model that (1) keeps kids in school much longer, thereby enabling
them to garner additional skills; (2) provides opportunity for high-
quality skill development of immediate use to employers (who maintain
up-to-date technologies, rather than obsolete ones as many vocational
programs in the United States do); and (3) relies upon a standardized,
nationally recognized set of skills standards that signal to employers from
one end of Germany to the other that a graduate possesses an extensive
body of work-related knowledge and the ability to apply it on the job.

Japanese models of school-to-work transition are less expensive and,
some experts argue, more likely to encourage high academic performance. As James Rosenbaum, one of the leading experts on school and
work, has noted:

> In Japan, employers maintain long-term hiring relationships with certain
> high schools, conditional on teachers providing dependable evaluations
> of students' academic achievement and on employers offering good jobs
> to the schools' work-bound students. The fear that employers might ter-
> minate a relationship that provides good jobs for their students discour-
> ages teachers from inflating evaluations or departing from expected
> criteria. In turn, employers continue offering positions to their partner
> schools in order to maintain access to the best students.[35]

The long-term relationships that have built up between teachers and
employers are the rock upon which this success story is built. Mutual
trust, dependable information, and up-to-date awareness of employer
needs make it work. Moreover, the fact that students cannot easily find
employment without these critical recommendations forces them to pay
attention to school performance. This turns out to be the case even in
schools that are highly stigmatized, that cater to students who have failed
to make the grade in the competitive exam system that leads to university
education in Japan. Where the United States looks on in frustration at

high dropout rates among poor kids, the Japanese see nearly 98 percent graduation rates from their least-respected vocational and technical high schools—the ones that accept students who have washed out elsewhere.[36] The key difference is not just a general, cultural emphasis on education in Japan or even a powerful "culture of shame" that might be expected to keep kids glued to their schools. The difference lies in the lock that teachers have on entry into the labor market: without their support, it is much tougher to find a job—even a lousy job—in Japan than it would be in the United States.

Our society has relied upon the notion that individuals pile up their credentials in one domain (school) and then carry them over to another, disconnected domain (work), in order to see what they can get. In a sense this is the natural expression of a free-market system, where the German and Japanese models rely upon a more managed transition. In the United States, the idea that the realms of school and work should be systematically linked is quite new and undeveloped.[37]

Yet there is reason to believe that we could imitate, if not the German model, then the Japanese system, and some evidence that at least informally, many vocational teachers in America do just that: they cultivate employers and try to place students who have graduated from their technical drafting or automotive engineering classes.[38] Half of the teachers surveyed in one Northwestern University study of vocational instructors spend time matching students to employers, and a significant fraction of them provide "quasi-warranties" to employers, their own stamp of approval for a student's quality. These Chicago-area teachers have evolved their own personal version of the Japanese school-work transition system. Yet because job placement falls squarely outside American definitions of a teacher's professional responsibilities, there is neither an incentive to reward them for this placement work nor relief from other job duties.

Is there any reason why this informal system could not be institutionalized in American high schools? Could we not expand the definition of a teacher's role to include maintaining contact with employers, placing students on the job, and keeping current with changing demand in the labor market?[39] This would require a reconceptualization of what teachers who serve the non-college-bound are for, and entail the addition of new training modules into colleges that prepare future teachers. But the benefits are potentially enormous: students would have greater incentive to perform well in school, schools would be seen as providing more reliable information on student capabilities to employers, and the community service functions of high schools would be greatly enhanced.

One particular program has already taken these ideas to heart and has formalized close relations between schools and employers: the National Youth Apprenticeship Program, developed by a consortium of employers—McDonald's, the Hyatt hotels, and Walgreen's drugstores. Inaugurated in September 1995, the program was pilot-tested in four Chicago high school sites.

Calumet High School was one of the four, and a tougher test of the program's possibilities would be hard to imagine. Calumet routinely posted dismal test scores and terrible attendance and grade-to-grade promotion records. Less than half of the students who started graduated. Over 80 percent of the families of students at Calumet receive public assistance. This all-black school is situated in a run-down neighborhood with few businesses save the liquor stores that stay open late. If ever there was a place where an effective youth jobs program was needed, this was it.

The three employers joined together and, with a minimal amount of funding from the Federal School-to-Work Transition Opportunities Act of 1994, recruited an onsite coordinator and set to work persuading the principal and the teachers to reorganize the school's curriculum. During the year preceding its inauguration, the teachers worked to bring the "real world" into the curriculum. Chemistry classes incorporated food chemistry units; math teachers developed problems that required forecasting demand for hotel rooms; English teachers emphasized communications skills, especially when dealing with customers. Foreign-language teachers readied themselves to teach conversation skills that restaurant or hotel employees might need to accommodate foreigners or nonnative speakers of English. Field trips to the centers of Chicago's business community— the John Hancock Tower, the Stock Exchange—were designed to take students out of their economically and racially isolated neighborhood and give them the opportunity to interact with the "other half." Mentors, managers and executives from the three firms were brought into the school as regular members of the teaching team, to answer student questions and serve as models of a better future.

Eighth-grade students leaving some of Chicago's worst middle schools were invited, through their principals, to apply to the NYAP. They were told that in exchange for their devotion to this new curriculum— including an additional school period every day for foreign language— they would be guaranteed summer job placements with these private employers at the age of sixteen and full-time, managerial-track employment (and support for community college education) at eighteen. Admission to the program was by lottery—a policy reflected in their entrance tests, which showed average reading level of these rising ninth-graders at third-to-sixth-grade levels and math scores that were even worse.

Students admitted to NYAP were separated from the rest of the school, placed in special classes that stayed together throughout the day. As a result, close bonds developed between kids who had the job guarantees and the expectations for solid performance in common. A gulf developed between these "special" students and the regular Calumet kids, but the benefit for the "treatment" group was clear: their social lives began to revolve around a like-minded set of teens heading somewhere rather than nowhere. Classroom attendance rose to 98 percent; promotion from one grade to the next grew 40 points to 99 percent; test scores in math, English, and social studies all showed dramatic and sustained improvement. The numbers told only part of the story. What one could see on the students' faces and hear in their voices was at least as powerful an indicator of how well NYAP was working: students could answer the questions of a total stranger (myself) articulately, with the kind of poise that one might expect of much older kids.

> This is my first real job. I can still remember my interview . . . all I could think about was "Don't do something stupid." My teacher, Mr. Godfred, told me to shake their hand, look them right in the eye, and tell them why I am the right person for the job. He's teaching us to be manager/ entrepreneurs. When I see a customer who's unhappy, I try to help them solve the situation. It's all about staying calm.
>
> —Andre Smith, 16 years old[40]

Young people who had never ventured outside the neighborhood could now describe what the business loop of downtown Chicago looked like, and what the managers they interviewed in the Hancock building told them about preparing for a career. More than just their geographical horizons had opened up: these kids now had a larger sociological sense of the world and their potential place in it. That vision is at least as important as hard skills in pushing a child from the Calumet neighborhood toward a constructive pathway.

"You have to learn Spanish," one young man at Calumet told me earnestly, "because your customers might not speak any English and you have to be able to communicate with them if your business is going to be successful." Another young woman explained the chemical composition of the food her class had prepared that morning and lingered on the nutritional aspects of the bill of fare. Teachers admitted privately that they had been roundly demoralized in the years before this program came on the scene because the kids didn't care, didn't come to class, acted up constantly, and made the instructors feel more like wardens. With the birth of the program in 1994, teachers found the very same kinds of kids—from poor single-parent families in Chicago's segregated housing projects—engaged, prepared, and hopeful. "These kids aren't saints," one male teacher told me in the hallway, "but compared to what we had to contend with in the past, this was a dream come true." Daya Locke, assistant principal at Calumet, agreed: "This is a rebirth for teachers and their students. It motivates teachers to learn from each other, their students, and their business partners."

Why did this program make such a difference so quickly? The random selection of the students suggests that there were no special qualities among them that would have brought the changes about. The answer lies in the explanations the kids gave themselves: they understood that they had real jobs—not great jobs, but real jobs—waiting for them when they turned sixteen. The opportunities were not abstract ("Improve your skills and we're sure you'll do better"), they were concrete ("There is a wage at the end of this rainbow"). A lot was riding on their teachers' perceptions of their performance. Teachers who witnessed bad behavior or lousy academic work could move to terminate students, and the students knew it. As is true in the Japanese system, teacher opinions were critical in job placement, and the kids understood this too. Skills mastered in the classroom were clearly applicable to real-world situations that students knew they would face on the job. They did not have to imagine how they were going to use the information they were compiling. Compared to the available alternatives in their community, NYAP offered a hands-down winner.

Many an American program designed to improve school-to-work transitions relies on the notion that if kids just do better in developing their skills, and schools do a better job of conveying this mastery, the market will take care of the rest. What NYAP does is remove this assumption and make a real, meaningful, ongoing bridge between teachers, the workplace, and the curriculum they develop jointly. That bridge requires resources, but not many of them. Certainly the governmental role is minimal. What it takes is a pledging of mutual cooperation between parts of our society that ordinarily have little to do with each other: schools and employers.

It is too early to tell what the long-range success of this program will be. Only about two hundred students were enrolled in the pilot program; 145 of them had completed their first round of practice job interviews as of 1997, and half of them had completed their tests and assessments and (at sixteen) were old enough to move into employment. The numbers are too small and the duration of the program too short to evaluate at this point. But the news of the program's potential is spreading, with employers like Giant Foods and Holiday Inns in Baltimore, First of America Bank and D&W Food Centers in Muskegon, and five major hotels in Austin signing up to become business partners in the National Youth Apprenticeship Program.

Even if the employment phase of the program takes time to develop, the secondary consequences of the NYAP are already visible: participants are moving toward graduation from Calumet in far greater numbers than nonparticipating counterparts. They have mastered a tougher curriculum. Even if they never work for McDonald's or Walgreen's, they have already beaten out much of their competition in terms of educational performance and are better positioned to go on to higher education than the vast majority of kids at Calumet have ever been. Their teachers feel better about their own contributions, and the whole school is shining a bit more with pride because kids are going somewhere rather than nowhere.

What are the incentives for employers to commit resources—personnel, jobs, and the like—to such a program? After all, they are in business to do business, not to be educators.[41] Why should they bother, especially if thousands of people are beating down their doors trying to get the jobs they have to offer? First, while inner-city communities are oversubscribed by job hunters, in many parts of the country labor shortages have developed that spell trouble for employers in highly competitive industries whose consumers will not brook price hikes. Second, large employers that worry about their public image understand that whatever they do to enhance employment opportunities for young people will rebound to their reputational advantage.

Without a doubt, though, the most important incentive for employers' involvement in schools is their interest in pushing public education to reclaim the basic training function it is supposed to provide but often fails to deliver. From the employers' perspective, schools have become unreliable as a means of delivering literate, numerate workers among the non-college-bound.[42] The cost of training people in these basic skills,[43] as well as the more refined "soft skills" of communication, taking direction, and even showing up on time, is significant. Productivity lost to this training function cuts against the employer's bottom line. Hence, the notion that schools could, in consort with employers, take these functions back and produce workers ready to hit the front lines courtesy of the taxpayer's investment in public education is appetizing indeed. This is certainly the perspective of Maurice Byrd, district manager of a local Walgreen's drugstore, who had direct experience with NYAP-trained workers:

> I hired three Calumet students [in my store]. What set them apart was that they had definite goals, dreams and realistic plans on how to get there. They were equipped coming into the store—good interviews, punctual, the right attire, a high level of customer service—and after more than two years, they're still there.[44]

For young workers, the benefits are enormous as well. Instead of floundering around trying to find work on their own, handicapped by social networks that may not be able to produce many leads or references employers will listen to, Calumet students know they have an opportunity waiting at the end of their schooling. What's more, if they do well in school, the chance to go on to higher education with a hefty subsidy from NYAP is a powerful incentive. While it is indeed too early to judge the outcome of this kind of program, already certain positive, but largely unintended, consequences were visible. Calumet students in this program said their parents were paying more attention to their performance in school, telling the kids that they had "better not mess up" because a job was on the line. Students' social sets were showing an impact as well: they noticed that they were spending more time with other kids in the program and less hanging out with others who were more likely to be going nowhere.

This sorting process will likely have an impact on poverty-related problems like out-of-wedlock childbearing. NYAP kids are selected for the program when they are twelve and thirteen years old, early enough so that they have yet to fall prey to behaviors that can spell long-term labor market handicaps (like teen pregnancy). They have something to hope for, something to work toward, and with each passing day, their social networks solidify around other kids who have these opportunities and commitments in common, since the classes are segregated from the rest of the high school population. While this program was never designed to attack the problem of teen pregnancy, I believe it will make an important difference because it recognizes something that moralistic, "just say no" sex education programs overlook: the need for real, concrete, meaningful jobs that provide for a future. If this proves to be the case, far more might be accomplished by a nationwide imitation of the NYAP program: we might see a bigger dent in the family formation patterns that often lead to poverty.

Programs like NYAP may represent that rarest of policy prospects: the win-win situation. But it is not a government program. It is a private-industry consortium, training for private-sector jobs, using a curriculum developed jointly by industry specialists and schoolteachers. With minimal funding and even less involvement of government agencies, it has made a promising start on a training environment that will undoubtedly change the lives of Calumet students and their families for the better.

Making Connections

Earlier in this book, we saw that one of the main handicaps facing poor workers both at the entry portal and in the long-term mobility phases of their careers is their lack of the right kinds of connections. Job-seekers who do not know the right people—those located in information-poor environments—cannot get advance news about job openings and don't have references; they are handicapped in the search for work even if they have the human capital (the education and experience) employers are looking for. For workers already in the labor market but hoping to move up and out of the low-wage sector, the presence or absence of networks is crucial. Like-situated friends already in the fast food industry help them find low-wage jobs, but generally cannot guide them to better jobs. Relatives and friends who have good jobs in industries that are shedding workers (the post office, the transportation industry, the hospitals, etc.) cannot do much more than act as role models of a positive career path of the past.

The realities of racial and class-based segregation in housing and schooling patterns provide a discouraging backdrop for thinking about how to engineer social networks to aid job-seekers from poor communities. Even in poor neighborhoods with a lot of working residents, like central Harlem, the number of people one could hope to meet who can act as switching stations in the search for high-wage jobs is minimal. Those people have left the community as soon as their higher wages made it possible for them to move to better neighborhoods. While we could vest our hopes in residential or school desegregation, that is at best a long-term strategy, and recent research suggests we are very far from such a goal.[45] What, then, are our alternatives?

Connecting Through Summer Youth

Once upon a time, the federal government's war on poverty invested heavily in summer work opportunities for young people. "Summer youth"[46] was largely an anticrime program, designed to keep youngsters off the streets and out of trouble during the hot season. While summer youth jobs provide some experience in the work world and some valuable skills, these programs are not organized with the explicit purpose of building résumés. They are, in the eyes of their own participants, often "make-work" jobs. No effort is made to use these positions as gateways into the private labor market. We have given only modest attention to the developmental experience or skill training that these jobs might provide and that could, at least potentially, be used to build human capital.[47] As long as summer youth is defined as an anticrime initiative, the resources devoted to it will be underexploited for their potential as avenues for labor market preparation.

Federal monies available for summer youth work have declined dramatically in many cities.[48] I favor restoring these funds as an antipoverty strategy. But even if that never happens, we should make better use of the dollars we are spending. We should consider ways to make summer youth employment connect more directly to private-sector employment. How might this be done? In a number of American cities, "business improvement districts"—BIDs—have been formed to enhance the physical surroundings of commercial neighborhoods. In New York City, there are thirty-seven BIDs, which were first authorized by the city council in the early 1980s. One of the largest and best-known is the 42nd Street BID, which has played a large part in the revitalization of what was for many years the city's premier red-light slum, now reborn as a major tourist destination. The 125th Street BID, which runs from Fifth Avenue to Morningside Avenue,[49] has been responsible for freshening the streets with colorful banners, sponsoring musical events that bring people out into the community (where they spend their dollars), and pressuring the city into repairing streets and sidewalks, which improves the appearance of the area.

Business improvement districts are self-taxing organizations that bind proprietors together in small, geographically contiguous areas. In New York City, BID annual budgets range from $100,000 to more than $1 million and are typically used to hire security officers, maintain garbage pickup, and provide other sidewalk services within a BID's boundaries. Employer networks form as a by-product of the BIDs, though they may be loose. Still, the skeleton of an organization is there and could be used for more purposes than those to which BIDs are presently put. Would it not be possible to deploy some summer youth funds in the direction of private employers through the BIDs? Federal and city funds could be applied to support apprenticeships, temporary job placements, and other opportunities that private employers in these localized networks might design. What would come out the other end of such a program would be not just a summer's earnings but useful connections, ties into the private labor market that might mean something the next time a young person from a poor neighborhood went to look for work.

The Employer Consortium

What might be done to give Burger Barn workers, people who are already experienced employees, a better shot at good jobs? Having followed them around for eighteen months, we saw that very few were able to parlay their experience on the job into a career that was more promising. To the extent that connections were at fault here as well (as opposed to educational deficits, which require other policy strategies), there is not a great deal we can do to influence their prospects. We cannot easily reengineer the friendship networks of Burger Barn employees.

We might, however, be able to bring employers together into cooperating consortia that would facilitate the movement of low-wage workers into better jobs.[50] How would this work? Imagine that it were possible, with a modicum of support from already-existing agencies in the mayor's economic development office, to bring together inner-city employers of the working poor and downtown businesses or nonprofit institutions with higher-paid employees. Employers in the inner-city neighborhoods would periodically select employees they consider reliable, punctual, hardworking, and motivated for entry into a special "pool" deemed eligible for referral to employers with better jobs on offer. Admission into the pool would be conditional on one year's steady performance at the entry-level job and the formal evaluations of managers and business owners. Workers placed in the pool would be put forward as candidates for the jobs that consortium partners in the "primary sector" are looking to fill. Entry-level employers would, in essence, be putting their own good name behind successful workers as they pass them on to their partners for greater opportunities.

Primary-sector employers, for their part, would agree to hire from the pool and meet periodically with their partners in the low-wage industries to review applications and follow up on the performance of those hired through the consortium. Employers "up the line" would have to agree to provide training or educational opportunities to these new employees to keep them moving up the ladder, clearing the bottom rungs for succeeding groups of consortium employees and others.

The success of each new group would, I believe, reinforce the reputation of the employers who recommended them for the pool in the first place. Moreover, their achievements on the job might begin to eat away at the negative stereotypes and fear that many employers express when speaking of the inner-city labor force.[51] Over time, employers might become more willing to hire minorities, especially black men, who face formidable barriers at the moment. By the same token, low-wage jobs like those at Burger Barn might become more attractive to workers, since they would now be something more like a gateway to a job ladder than a dead end.

Given the American penchant for free markets and our allergy to economic management, why would employers find a consortium arrangement such as this attractive? The advantages for employers in areas of low unemployment are obvious enough: they have trouble holding on to their employees without bidding up wages, and this they are afraid of doing because of consumer resistance to higher prices.[52] If they were able to trade wage increases for access to long-term job mobility (through the consortium), these employers might find the turnover problem to be somewhat reduced.

Harlem, unfortunately, does not suffer from this particular disease. Even when national unemployment rates hit historic lows, as they were in 1997, ghetto communities sustain high rates of unemployment, which are even worse than they seem in the statistics. Thousands of Harlem residents are too discouraged to look and have dropped out of the labor force altogether, and our statistical system subtracts their existence, no longer counting them as unemployed.

How would an employer consortium model work in communities with high unemployment? Fast food employers run businesses in highly competitive markets. Constant pressure on prices and profit discourage them from paying wages high enough to keep a steady workforce.[53] In fact, most such employers regard the jobs they fill as temporary placements: they expect successful employees to leave. Even though turnover rates at Burger Barn are half the national average for the industry (because the alternatives aren't very appealing or plentiful), the most a savvy employer can expect is to retain a worker for an average of eight to nine months. Turnover is a fact of life.

That does not make a shifting workforce easy to live with. Sudden departures of knowledgeable workers still disrupts business, increasing wastage, dampening productivity, and giving swing managers a colossal headache as they scramble to replace experienced people at a moment's notice. An employer consortium gives business owners a way to compete for workers who will stay with them longer than usual. In lieu of higher pay, they can offer access to the consortium hiring pool and the prospect, ultimately, of a better-paying job upon graduation from this civilian "boot camp."

The consortium might also provide inner-city business owners with avenues of commerce and interaction with firms elsewhere in the city that might make possible new business ventures. For inner-city businessmen and women are often isolated from rich contacts as well, their own opportunity base restricted by the same forms of segregation that bedevil their workers. A Burger Barn employer who participates in a consortium with a local hospital or university, for example, might seek opportunities to open up additional franchises on that turf, a chance that might otherwise go to someone with no ties to the ghetto.[54]

The practical advantages for primary-sector managers are also considerable. They would be hiring people out of the consortium who are vetted, tested, proven employees who have worked hard to gain access to this opportunity. Skills have been assessed and certified in the most real-world of settings. The ongoing nature of the ties between employers would reinforce the value of recommendations, a cost-effective strategy for managers in firms that have to make significant training investments in their workers, but are often flying by the seat of their pants when they make hiring decisions, having very little reliable information about the people they are choosing. With much more at stake in terms of their time, training investment, and the productivity of their organizations, it would be helpful for these employers to receive new workers who had already proved themselves to a known organization, a consortium partner.

Despite the evident advantages for entry-level and more "advanced" employers, modest incentives to encourage participation might be needed. Harlem business owners might be deterred by the need to give up some of their best employees, for example. Guaranteeing these employers a lump sum or a tax break for every worker they promote into their own management structure or successfully place with a consortium partner might help to break down their reluctance. Primary-sector employers, who would have to provide training and schooling for their new employees, might also require some kind of tax break to subsidize their efforts to upscale their workforce.[55] Still, this would represent a modest public investment in a reinvigorated escalator leading out of the low-wage labor domain and into a world of greater opportunity. Most of all, the employer consortium model addresses problems that private-sector business owners already face and attempts to fix them without the creation of new government agencies and with very modest subsidies.

Promoting Internal Mobility

Moving between firms and industries in search of upward mobility is the key goal of the employer consortium. Yet it should also be possible to do more for the working poor inside the establishments where they work now, especially where the development of new job ladders is concerned. Sometimes the barrier to promotion lies with a worker's lack of education or specialized training. Many a Burger Barn employee was a capable person, for example, but lacked fluency in math, which was needed to manage the complex inventory system. Progressive unions, concerned about the need to upscale their low-wage members, have joined with management to develop innovative programs for on-the-job training and release time for workers bent on seeking new, more lucrative careers.

The Cape Cod Hospital and Hospital Workers Union developed the Career Ladder Program in order to address this need.[56] Working together, the union and hospital management organized positions into a structured series of increasingly skilled (and well-rewarded) jobs in "departments" that had clear job grades. Each grade requires some explicit qualifications. Workers have the option of training for jobs that are contained in their own department (e.g., moving from a sewing room aide to a lead sewing room aide, or an operating room housekeeper to an OR nursing assistant) or preparing themselves for a career change and moving into another department altogether.

On-the-job training leading to certification for the next job up the line is formalized. Traineeships prepare candidates for jobs that require more specialized preparation (e.g., CAT scan technicians or tumor registrars). In-house courses in typing, keyboarding, and medical terminology and a host of basic courses in chemistry and math are offered that would qualify workers for better-paying positions. All openings are formally announced and made available to candidates with the appropriate qualifications in order of seniority.

The Career Ladder Program opens opportunities for people who enter the hospital industry at the very bottom—in jobs that pay no better than Burger Barn—to move up over time by providing accessible training (as opposed to school-based programs that may be expensive and inconvenient) and by making skill requirements transparent. In this respect, the program comes closer to a meritocracy (albeit one based on seniority) than an "open" market in which the premium on personal contacts is so high.

The San Francisco Hotels Partnership Project is another innovative example of union/management cooperation that creates opportunities for upward mobility for a largely low-skilled labor force.[57] Started in 1994, the partnership was embedded in a collective bargaining agreement between twelve downtown hotels and their two major unions.[58] More than sixteen hundred hotel employees were brought together into joint labor/management problem-solving teams that also developed training programs. The goals of the partnership range from increasing the market share of their member hotels to retaining and improving jobs and job security. For our purposes, though, the most important feature of the partnership is its effort to develop new programs of employee training and career development.

The hotel industry is enormously elastic. Peaks and valleys of hotel vacancies create an incentive for employers to maintain a large, low-wage labor force in part-time slots that can be expanded and contracted at will. Workers are vulnerable to layoffs without much warning. Hence these jobs, which require some degree of training, and of necessity emphasize high standards of uniformity, are at the same time quite unstable. The partnership has developed mechanisms for uniform training standards that make movement between employers more practical and open up the prospects for a system of referrals of part-time employees between the hotels with joint, common training as a baseline. The same collective approach is resulting in transfer and promotional opportunities for employees within the industry, rather than just the hotel where they work.

The partnerships training curriculum is translated simultaneously into Chinese and Spanish so that the large number of immigrant workers with limited English proficiency can participate. It introduces new workers not only to their own jobs, but to the entire industry of which they are a part, and to the role of the unions. Courses in "Vocational English as a Second Language," "Kitchen Support, Front Desk, and Engineering Management," and many other on-the-job training courses are mounted by the partnership and made available in all of the participating hotels. All courses explicitly focus on core skills, including communications, critical thinking, problem-solving, and teamwork, reflecting the "high-performance" model of workplace organization that was the inspiration for this design.

For a worker starting out cleaning toilets and making beds, these programs offer the chance for skill development unhampered by language differences, and the opportunity to mix with management and workers in more skilled jobs. The person who begins at the bottom has a chance through these mixed programs to shine in the eyes of someone who might later make a hiring decision. Moreover, because the partnership is a multi-employer organization, it creates opportunities for workers and managers from different hotels to mix with one another, share war stories, learn new techniques, and build up "best practices" in ways that benefit the industry as a whole.

The Center on Wisconsin Strategy has pioneered an innovative approach to worker training that, as a side benefit, enhances opportunities for internal mobility. Sensing a growing demand for skilled workers in the metal trades, the center established the Wisconsin Regional Training Partnership, an organization composed of over forty firms that employ about sixty thousand workers.[59] When each new firm joins the partnership, it promises to adhere to a set of common standards and practices. As Laura Dresser and Joel Rogers, directors of the Center on Wisconsin Strategy, explain, member firms must:

- assign a growing percentage of payroll to training front-line workers;
- train according to standards set on a supra-firm basis;
- gear their hiring and internal labor market promotions to workers' achievement of those standards;
- and administer the enhanced training budgets . . . through joint labor-management committees.[60]

The main purpose of this program is to increase firm investment in training and to cut the costs of technical training by creating facilities for teaching new skills and technologies. That alone promises to raise workers' wages and improve firm productivity. Even more important, however, is the way in which these goals are combined with an explicit emphasis on providing more opportunities for upward mobility within and between firms for workers who have acquired the necessary skills. Because the workers have a common set of skills that employers know can be used in any of their firms, the prospects for movement are high. More-over, the partnership itself has become a network, a source of information about employment opportunities, which makes it easier for workers at the bottom of the ladder to move up into better jobs.

What all of these ideas (the employer consortium) and programs (the hospital ladders, the hotel partnership, and the Wisconsin partnership) have in common is a concern with the long-term mobility of workers, many of whom start out in exactly the kinds of low-wage jobs this book has explored in the context of Burger Barn. There is no shame in start-ing out at the bottom of an occupational structure as long as that is not where a hardworking employee ends up. Different industries and cities will require different models of "engineered" or facilitated mobility. But everyone gains when hard work pays off, when the investment a worker and an employer make at the front end ends up in a career that actually goes somewhere. The best recipe for ending a lifetime of working poverty lies not in government subsidies, but in imaginative reconfigurations of the matching and promotion process that harvests those who have proven themselves and thereby provides everyone else a meaningful incentive for performance.

Place-Based Initiatives

In some areas of the country, job losses have been so devastating and the resulting decay in community life so thoroughgoing that only a full-scale, comprehensive approach to neighborhood economic development and social services will make a meaningful difference. Programs that target particular industries or that address the exigencies of one group (minority teens, pregnant mothers, welfare recipients) will not be suffi-cient, because what needs to be "treated" is the whole community and what needs to be provided is a broad range of services, from employment to child care to health care to crime control.

Welfare reform heightened interest in "place-based" strategies, since the prospect of flooding depressed urban labor markets with thousands of additional job-seekers has created a sense of urgency (or desperation) about what will happen to these neighborhoods as time limits approach. Since this is not a book about welfare per se, my interest here is in con-sidering what these programs have to offer the working poor, above and beyond what they might do for mothers coming off AFDC.

The Rockefeller Foundation, in partnership with the Department of Housing and Urban Development, a handful of state and local governments, and community development organizations, is engaged in testing other strategies for "connecting inner-city residents with the world of work." They have selected five demonstration sites where they aim to saturate bounded areas containing public housing projects with job placement agencies rewarded only for their performance in placement; training programs leading to jobs renovating and maintaining public housing; city-based efforts to attract private employers into these target communities; community service job creation; and various support structures for working families (day care, health care, transportation).[61]

What these policy-makers hope to prove is that a saturation strategy will work better than the more dispersed models typically employed by federal and local governments (which make funds available, for example, for wage subsidies). But an underlying feature of this project is to give inner-city residents a whole new set of readily accessible and supportive contacts that lead not only to jobs but to child care, housing, and other essential services. This comprehensive approach, the foundations and government leaders believe, will encourage those who have been left out of the labor force and those who need more income than they presently earn.

New Hope

Milwaukee's New Hope Project represents a pilot version of this saturation approach and has, thus far, shown some promise. New Hope offers unemployed adults transitional community service jobs, financial help for health insurance, and child care for those with low-income jobs, assistance in obtaining the EITC, and its own earnings supplement to bring workers up above the poverty line. New Hope guarantees its participants that if "you work full-time, year-round, your paycheck plus your earnings supplement will give you a final income that is above the poverty line."

These opportunities were offered to six hundred people in two central-city Milwaukee neighborhoods. Two years later, 56 percent of the participants were working full-time: 83 percent of them were employed in the private sector, while the rest were in community service jobs. Twelve percent were actively looking for work. Only 28 percent of the participants were "inactive." Professional evaluations of the New Hope initiative have suggested that the project is making a modest difference for the better, not only in moving people off welfare, but in curing many of the ills of the working poor, for whom child care and medical insurance are major headaches. The supports provided by New Hope are more generous than those most states are contemplating in the wake of welfare reform. Long-term evaluations will show us whether these supports make a big enough difference to entice more states to "do the right thing."[62]

Project Quest

San Antonio, Texas, is home to one of the most widely respected, successful community-based employment initiatives, one which (like New Hope) relies on the cooperation of employers, local governments, and nonprofit foundations. Project Quest was organized in the wake of profound change in the local economy of San Antonio. Two ends of the spectrum were growing: high-skilled, well-paid jobs and low-skilled, working-poor jobs. The gulf between them was growing too, into a kind of labor market apartheid. Gone were the jobs that used to be in the middle, the reasonably well-paid, low-skilled positions at Kelly Air Force Base or the meat-packing plant and the Levi's Jeans factory. As Paul Osterman and Brenda Lautsch of MIT's Sloan School of Management explained, the situation was worrying local leaders:

> Father Al Jost, a Roman Catholic priest, and Father Will Waters, an Episcopal priest, started to notice the effect [plant closings] had had on the community. They noted an increase in family disruption as a result of the economic pressures, including drug use, divorce and domestic violence. Also evident was a decline in the expectations and aspirations that the children of poorer San Antonio communities expressed.[63]

Project Quest formed out of the partnership of these religious leaders, but grew to encompass local employers, who committed 650 jobs paying above $7.50 an hour; community colleges, which became the exclusive sites for training and further education; and churches and community centers, which were the venues for outreach and screening of potential participants. The aim of the project was to train unemployed high school graduates for jobs with high demand and then place them in real positions at good wages, all the while providing them with social supports (day care, counseling, medical assistance, etc.) so they could stay on the job. Where most federal and state programs are both partial and short-term in their scope, Project Quest was the most comprehensive program of its kind. Participants remained in the program for nearly two years (compared to only four months for those in the typical federal government jobs program).

Between 1993 and 1995, the project enrolled over eight hundred people.

The majority (447) ended up entering a good job or the armed forces, began a registered apprenticeship, completed a major level of education, or passed a critical skills test. Almost two hundred were still in the program in 1995; 182 had left because of "negative termination." This is an admirable track record considering that only people with major barriers to employment (e.g., an arrest record, a single parent) were accepted in the first place. The positive consequences of Quest for participants and their families were significant:

> The average participant's hourly earnings rose by between $1.36 and $2.42 per hour. Average hours worked per week increased by between 3.2 and 6.9 hours. The probability of holding a job increased from .49 to .74. Annual earnings increased by between $4,923 and $7,457 per year.[64]

This project was aimed at San Antonians who were unemployed, rather than those who were working but poor. Still, the project is worthy of note here because these are often one and the same group of people caught at different moments in time. Carmen was working when we first met, but six months later would have been a candidate for Project Quest. For the working poor and the unemployed, a job paying $7.50 an hour represents a leg up the income ladder, hence the value of considering this model program and its potential for helping the working poor.

Most striking about Quest are its duration, the comprehensive nature of the services it provides (education, job training, child care, etc.), and the benefits it conferred to participants. Its success suggests that real change, real improvement, is not likely to come about by quick fix. None of the welfare-to-work programs I am aware of (from Riverside County's GAIN program onward) can match the numbers Quest delivered. Indeed, most show modest, if any, effects and many show serious welfare recidivism. What Quest demonstrates is that with proper training and real opportunity, a living wage can be within reach, even for those with many strikes against them. One imagines that a Project Quest for the working poor, something along the lines of the Wisconsin Partnership program, which would make community-based training and employment services available, would be of great value for those already in the labor market, but stuck at the bottom end.

In the end, place-based strategies are important because the working poor do not live alone. Their communities, indeed their households, are intertwined with the nonworking poor and suffer from the problems that all poor neighborhoods have to contend with. The well-being of working families in the ghetto therefore goes hand in hand with the fortunes of the welfare recipient, for they share a common space. This is why employment training and opportunities need to go hand in hand with expanded programs of community policing[65] to return safe streets to communities that are the primary victims of crime, low-income homeownership programs to ensure greater residential stability and personal investment in local stabilization, increased usage of schools as community centers open late in the evening, and even midnight basketball for teenagers. Working families cannot maintain their sense of hope, their investment in the well-being of their children, and their dignity if at the end of a day what they come home to is an uninterrupted sense of physical devastation, decay, and danger in the neighborhood. Work needs to pay, but that pay has to buy a modicum of decency in one's standard of living for the effort to be worth it. Place-based strategies recognize the comprehensive nature of what needs to be done.

Fortunately, private foundations like Rockefeller, Ford, Annie E. Casey, Carnegie, W. T. Grant, and the Foundation for Child Development and organizations like the NAACP, the Urban League, and the Campaign for Human Development have long recognized this and have been the backbone of support for community development corporations, many of which are looking more seriously at employment training as their next frontier. Even more encouraging, union pension funds and investment banking houses have begun to recognize that inner-city communities represent overlooked opportunities for money-making. As Michael Porter has pointed out,[66] ghettos are often centrally located near far more expensive urban real estate, are accessible to transportation, and are full of consumers looking to spend their money without many local outlets to spend it in. The federal government's empowerment zone program has encouraged private investors to think again about putting their funds into housing rehabilitation, commercial and retail expansion, and even manufacturing development in areas long since written off as domestic war zones. Therein lie the seeds of hope for the rejuvenation of employment in communities like central Harlem, where a willing labor force is hunting for jobs and open doors are sorely needed. For as Porter has argued eloquently, the key to long-term improvement in the quality of inner-city life lies in the economic revitalization of these neighborhoods through private investment, job creation in private industry, and the facilitation of entrepreneurial activity. I would merely add to his list the effective, targeted support of government, which also has an important role to play in addressing the problems of the working poor.

·   ·   ·

AMERICA'S WORKING POOR, particularly those who live in communities like central Harlem, have not claimed a very large piece of the policy stage. Apart from the few weeks Congress spends debating the expansion or elimination of the Earned Income Tax Credit, the level of the minimum wage, and (recently) health and child care coverage for poor children, we hear very little about them. Scholars who focus their attention on poor people who live outside of the labor market and who (some would say) have fallen victim to an underclass culture have done little to shift our national lenses.

Yet there are millions more working-poor families in the United States than there are people on welfare or workfare. And long after the federal welfare system has become a thing of the past, we will still have a substantial population of workers who live below the poverty line even when they are employed year-round and full-time. Indeed, we may well have more working poor than ever, since for many low-skilled and inexperienced welfare recipients this is the most likely destination.

The nation's working poor do not need their values reengineered. They do not need lessons about the dignity of work.[67] Their everyday lives are proof enough that they share the values of their mainstream, middle-class counterparts. Indeed, it would be fair to say that they hold these values dearer because the intrinsic rewards of their employment are so much less than what the rest of us enjoy. They work because they have to, but also because being a worker, a member of the vast community of gainfully employed Americans, is an identity that means something to them. For those of us lucky enough to have jobs we enjoy, jobs that confer prestige and respect, jobs that pay well and allow us to do so much for our children, this value comes easily. Of course we think work is dignity.

For Kyesha, Jamal, and Carmen, working at Burger Barn is both a blessing and a curse. Having a job of this kind keeps them afloat and gives them a modicum of freedom. But it also subjects them to the withering criticism of a society that defines low-wage service jobs as something akin to the untouchable status of the Indian low castes. This is true, in part, because low-wage jobs so often end up as the beginning and the end of the "career" story for inner-city workers. Were they nothing more than way stations toward a better career, then there would be little lasting damage to the stigma. But the stigma sticks now because dead-end jobs signify dead-end lives, or so we believe. The fact that millions of people— including the African-Americans, Dominicans, and Puerto Ricans of central Harlem—slog it out every day in jobs like these and continue to believe that the future will hold something better is a tribute to their own tenacity. But it is also evidence for the way in which our mainstream work culture has penetrated every nook and cranny of American life—including the inner-city ghettos.

That penetration is good news. It means that we need to concentrate on opening up opportunity, not reorganizing the culture. For there is little we can do to solve the conundrums of the inner city unless we fix the labor market problems of the working poor. No amount of moralizing, proselytizing, or punishment will shore up declining families if they do not have jobs, especially jobs that pay a living wage. At the same time, there is little that cannot be fixed if this problem is addressed. Healthy families, motivated children, safe communities stand on a bedrock of gainful employment—and that is as true for central Harlem as it is for the wealthy neighborhoods of Manhattan. Our common need and desire for good jobs is our greatest cultural asset, and the one commitment that transcends the boundaries between us.

Epilogue

Twenty-four years old, Kyesha Smith is now a nine-year veteran of Burger Barn, and after much urging on the part of her boss and some resistance on Kyesha's part, she has become a swing manager. This entitles her to $6 an hour, a modest improvement over the $5 she was earning when we first met her four years ago. Her fears of additional responsibility have declined as she has taken the first step up the ladder of internal promotion, but Kyesha shows no great hunger for advancement on the job, and has yet to be officially certified as a manager (which requires the completion of an off-site training course). Instead, as was true when I saw her more regularly, Kyesha works two jobs. From the morning until the middle of the afternoon, she cleans the outside areas of the project where she lives with her mother. In the afternoon and evenings, she continues to work at Burger Barn. The two jobs exhaust her, but the extra income is welcome indeed.

Kyesha's son, Anthony, now nearly five years old, is fortunate to have a space in a city-sponsored day care program, although Kyesha worries that the child of a welfare recipient will claim his space someday soon. If this happens, Kyesha will be in a real bind, because her mother, the only alternative for reliable baby-sitting in the past, can no longer pick up the slack. Indeed, Dana is having trouble figuring out how to take care of her own young children since she was diagnosed with cancer. It is almost surely a death sentence, but Kyesha hopes it will be a long time before she must face this grim outcome. In between, though, Kyesha has missed work fairly often as her mother takes sick and needs her help.

About a year ago, Kyesha's "number came up" to the top of the public housing wait lists and she was offered her own apartment, something she has been dreaming about for years now. The new place is in a project development just a block from her mother's home. Kyesha took the offer, but rarely stays there because her mother needs her support. Most of the time Dana feels all right, but she has noticed some worrisome symptoms that may prove to be serious. Kyesha hopes for the best but has no idea what will happen when her mother can no longer take care of her own children, not to mention Anthony, in the hours not covered by day care.

Fortunately, Kyesha's supervisors at Burger Barn have been compassionate and flexible, giving her time off when she needs to attend to her mother. The many years she has responded to their requests by filling in for absent workers and taking over supervisory responsibilities have built up a reservoir of trust and affection that makes a difference now. It is testimony to the kinds of bonds that can exist between workers and management, even in industries built on low-wage labor. Yet whatever drive Kyesha may have for advancement is likely to be curtailed by the additional obligations she now faces on the home front.

One source of support in Kyesha's life comes from her close friends Natasha and Latoya. Natasha is now a single parent, living with her mother and stepfather and her sister Stephanie (who is a single mother too). Like Natasha, Stephanie is now employed by Burger Barn. Collectively, the family has a stable child care system in place, which allows all of them to work and pool their earnings in a common household coffer. Stephanie and her mother (Lizzie) leave early in the morning for work, so Natasha watches the two babies during the day. Lizzie returns home from her housekeeping jobs in the early afternoon and watches the little ones until Stephanie finishes at Burger Barn. Lizzie and Stephanie take care of the two boys while Natasha works the evening shift at Burger Barn.

Alvin—father of Natasha, Stephanie, and Latoya—is working once again as a truck driver and after many years of sporadic appearances is now living permanently with his family. The father of Stephanie's child is still a part of the picture, although he does not live with the family; Natasha's former partner comes by once a week to take his son out to play, but cannot offer much more support than this because he has not been able to find steady work.

Kyesha has not been blessed with this kind of family network. Her siblings are either much older (and have long been gone from the family orbit), quite a bit younger (and therefore not able to be of much help), or involved in the drug trade (which means they are not welcome in the house). Lacking the extended support system that Latoya and Natasha have at their disposal, Kyesha has more limited options, and this puts a crimp on her ability to get ahead. It is all she can do to tread water.

Latoya, however, is now the second assistant manager of the Burger Barn restaurant where we met—earning a respectable $15,000 a year after taxes—and has been promised a general manager's position when the current owner opens his next restaurant. That would be a significant step up, with earnings closer to $30,000 a year. But even now, Latoya is ahead of where she was when our research began, and she looks forward to a better future, especially because she will shortly be married to Jason, the father of her son, who makes good money as a skilled craftsman. She is one of the fortunate few who have graduated right out of the purview of this book: she is no longer among the working poor.

Natasha has become a swing manager, but has been told that a salaried managerial job will be hers as soon as she can arrange her child care so she can work more hours. That may not happen anytime soon, as the hand-off pattern for the kids in her household is about as complex as anyone there can handle. Natasha isn't bothered, because she believes she can reorganize in the future, when her son gets a little older and Lizzie finally gives up her physically demanding job as a house cleaner. In any case, for both Latoya and Natasha, keeping up with the requirements of children and the workplace takes just about all their mental reserves. But their heads are well above water, they do not feel threatened by an unpredictable future, and they can hope for better things.

Kyesha, on the other hand, has an uncertain future. To her credit, she keeps plugging away, working twelve-hour days at two jobs so she can afford to take care of her son, her mother, and her siblings and still splurge once in a while on clothes for herself. She has managed to save some money, thanks largely to the Earned Income Tax Credit, which provides her with a windfall once a year. It's not much of a buffer, but it's something, and something is better than the nothing that she had four years before. Kyesha does not expect the future to be much different from the present, except in negative ways (like the loss of her mother). Her hopes, such as they are, tend to rest as they did before on the thought of getting married. No likely suitors have appeared on the scene, however, so Kyesha's dreams are no closer to reality than they were when she broke up with the boyfriends of the past. Nonetheless, she is managing, without much help from anyone else.

Carmen's World

When we left Carmen in the summer of 1994, she had dropped out of school and left work, on the brink of giving birth at the end of a difficult pregnancy. Her husband, Salvador, was working two jobs to make ends meet, but the ends weren't really meeting at all. Carmen and Salvador could not stretch their food budget to the end of the month and ended up eating separately at their families' homes, right down the hallway of the apartment building where they lived. Carmen had gone on welfare in order to secure medical benefits, since she required constant visits to the doctor's office to monitor her pregnancy. She was happy about the baby, but frustrated over her financial dependence on Salvador, who wasn't being very cooperative about money matters. Fortunately, Carmen was literally surrounded by her father's kin, organized into four or five related households, all living on adjacent floors of the same building in Washington Heights. She did not have to worry about starving, and when her phone was cut off because Salvador wouldn't give her the money to pay the bills, she could use her aunt's phone (as did all the other members of the family). Ditto for the cable television that sat in the middle of her grandmother's apartment, child care central for the families (including, Carmen hoped, her own someday).

By the fall of 1996, everything had changed, mostly for the better. Carmen's baby girl is healthy, happy, and chubby as a baby should be. The whole family was doing well economically, though they were now dispersed across the country. In 1995, an aunt living in Michigan called to say that the factory where her husband worked was hiring and encouraged everyone in Carmen's clan to trek west so that they too could earn $14 an hour packaging frozen potatoes for sale to restaurants and supermarkets. Carmen's aunts in Washington Heights decided to take advantage of the opportunity. One had been unemployed before she moved; now she works at the same beauty salon as her sister in Michigan. The other found a job at the local Holiday Inn, making a phenomenal $17 an hour as the concierge. Carmen's grandmother moved too, so she could be nearer to her favorite daughter, the one who had called with the job news. The last of her daughters will be moving to the Midwest shortly.

Carmen's father joined the same migration stream for a while, leaving unemployment in New York behind for a job as a bookkeeper in the same beauty salons where his sisters work and another part-time job at an agency that helps people complete their tax returns. But he wasn't happy in Michigan and has returned to New York, where for a time he worked as a security guard in a downtown office building. He wasn't happy there either and is now unemployed, living in his mother's old apartment in Washington Heights, and, as Carmen puts it, "lazing around."

Salvador has now been promoted from stocking shelves to night manager at a Love's pharmacy on Manhattan's Upper West Side. He works the late shift, from 6:00 p.m. to 2:00 a.m. Carmen, now back at work, is a manager at Burger Barn, working the morning shift. They take turns caring for their daughter, especially now that the extended family has moved to Michigan. Their support system is more limited as a result, but both Salvador and Carmen are earning more money than they once did and have been able to afford a slightly larger apartment. They are encouraged enough about the future to remain in New York, forgoing the high wages their relatives are earning in Michigan. Carmen has returned to school and has completed three semesters at Bronx Community College, where she is focusing on computer skills (data processing). She continues to hope her mother will be able to emigrate from the Dominican Republic someday and has applied for citizenship in the hope of speeding up the process of family reunification.

Carmen has a lot going for her. As the daughter of a schoolteacher, she came to the United States with a fund of cultural capital, albeit one that must now be translated into American credentials. She knows that education is the key and has carefully and deliberately plotted her way to school to get the skills she will need to move ahead. Her father's family has been able to step in and provide critical resources—child care, food, a roof over her head—when she could not do so for herself. These valuable resources have made a difference, a difference that is showing up in the path Carmen is taking in her life as a married mother and future business manager.

JAMAL'S WORLD

Of all the people I came to know in the course of this research project, the one I was most anxious to find when we went back to see how our key "informants" were doing several years later was Jamal. I suppose every researcher develops a favorite or two, and Jamal was certainly mine. Coming as he did from such a hard, unforgiving background as the son of a drug addict, he seemed to me something of a hero. His love for Kathy, his common-law wife, was so touching, his desire to be reunited with his daughter so strong, and his prospects for the future so very depressing, that I could not help but hope that somehow he would find his way out of his minimum-wage job and the slum they lived in.

We tried every avenue we could think of to find Jamal, to no avail. The apartment he and Kathy moved to on the advice of the family court (which had the power to grant or block the return of their child) was empty. None of the employers who had hired him had any idea what had become of him. The foster care agency that had once had custody of his daughter claimed it had no idea where the family had disappeared to. His mother, so strung out on heroin when last we saw her, had vanished from the housing project where we last had contact with her. Like so many other black men in the inner city, Jamal has slipped through the cracks. It is my hope, of course, that he and Kathy have found their way out of the city, back to Tallahassee, where they wanted to relocate in order to escape the problems of a poor life in a bad neighborhood. But I have no idea what has happened to them.

What I do know is that Jamal had great potential and an enormous uphill struggle to make something of those gifts. He proved that to us when he shook himself out of bed during those bitter winter days to board the bus to work. If we can find a way to open up the opportunity structure to people with this kind of drive, we will surely reap the benefits of an inner-city culture that remains focused on the dignity of work, even when the rewards are meager.

Appendixes

TABLE 1
NEIGHBORHOOD POVERTY CONCENTRATION BY WORKING STATUS: CHICAGO URBAN AND FAMILY LIFE SURVEY

Working Status	0–19% Poverty	20–30% Poverty	31–40% Poverty	41+% Poverty
Working	63.6%	54.2%	48.8%	32.5%
Has job, not at work	1.7%	1.7%	1.8%	2.2%
Looking for work	4.7%	6.6%	6.4%	7.8%
Keeping house	18.9%	24.4%	28.3%	37.6%
Going to school	1.3%	4.9%	5.8%	9.7%
Unable to work	2.4%	1.6%	2.1%	2.4%
Other	7.4%	6.6%	6.7%	7.8%

TABLE 2
POVERTY AMONG WORKING AMERICANS, 1996
% OF YEAR-ROUND FULL-TIME WORKERS IN POVERTY

	Black	Hispanic	White	All
Both sexes	4.3	8.5	2.3	2.5
18 to 24	8.2	11.9	5.4	5.6
25 to 34	5.2	9.1	2.9	3.1
Men	3.6	9.9	2.5	2.6
18 to 24	5.0	12.9	5.3	5.3
25 to 34	4.3	11.0	3.4	3.5
Women	5.0	6.1	1.9	2.3
18 to 24	10.5	9.4	5.5	6.1
25 to 34	6.0	5.1	2.0	2.6

% OF PART-TIME OR PART-YEAR WORKERS IN POVERTY

	Black	Hispanic	White	All
Both sexes	27.9	28.3	12.2	14.1
18 to 24	28.5	29.0	15.8	17.4
25 to 34	32.6	29.6	16.8	19.1
Men	20.9	29.4	12.8	13.9
18 to 24	21.6	28.7	13.6	14.4
25 to 34	21.7	28.7	17.3	17.9
Women	33.4	27.2	11.8	14.2
18 to 24	34.5	29.4	18.0	20.3
25 to 34	40.6	30.4	16.6	19.9

Source: Poverty in the United States: 1996, Current Population Reports, pp. 60–198 (Bureau of the Census), Table 3.

TABLE 3

EDUCATIONAL STATUS OF CENTRAL HARLEM BURGER BARN WORKERS

Education	% Completed	% Currently Enrolled	Plans to Enroll/Get Degree
High school	58*	26**	5
Technical/vocational	3	5	19
2-year college	0	4	0
4-year college	10	5	38

* Includes all high school graduates, GED recipients, and second-semester high school seniors age 18 and older.
** Includes all regular high school students below age 18, all enrolled as GED students, or in alternative high schools.

TABLE 4

EDUCATIONAL ATTAINMENT OF FAST FOOD LABOR FORCE, NATIONWIDE

Education/Training Activity	% Having Attained or Almost	% Expecting to Attain
Complete high school	66	29
Attend tech or voc school after HS	14	19
2-yr college: attend	15	50
2-yr college: graduate	4	31
4-yr college: attend	21	30
4-year college: graduate	3	45
Attend grad or prof. school after college	2	31

Source: Ivan Charner and Bryna Shore Fraser, *Fast Food Jobs* (National Institute for Work and Learning, 1984) p. 9, Table 1.3.

TABLE 5

LIVING SITUATION AND FAMILY STATUS OF BURGER BARN WORKERS

Employee's Living Situation		African-American	Dominican	Other Latino	Other	Row Total
				Race Group		
Living alone	*Count*	12	0	1	3	16
	Row Percent	75.0%	0%	6.3%	18.8%	8.7%
	Column Percent	12.2%	0%	3.4%	21.4%	
A single mother living with her child(ren)		11	1	4	0	16
		68.8%	6.3%	25.0%	0%	8.7%
		11.2%	2.3%	13.8%	0%	
A child living in a single-parent household		22	17	12	3	54
		40.7%	31.5%	22.2%	5.6%	29.3%
		22.4%	39.5%	41.4%	21.4%	
A child living in a dual-parent family		7	12	3	2	24
		29.2%	50.0%	12.5%	8.3%	13.0%
		7.1%	27.9%	10.3%	14.3%	
A child living with other relatives		15	4	5	1	25
		60.0%	16.0%	20.0%	4.0%	13.6%
		15.3%	9.3%	17.2%	7.1%	
An adult living with spouse and offspring		13	4	1	3	21
		61.9%	19.0%	4.8%	14.3%	11.4%
		13.3%	9.3%	3.4%	21.4%	
An adult living with roommates or others		17	4	1	0	22
		77.3%	18.2%	4.5%	0%	12.0%
		17.3%	9.3%	3.4%	0%	
Other		1	1	2	2	6
		16.7%	16.7%	33.3%	33.3%	3.3%
		1.0%	2.3%	6.9%	14.3%	
Column total		98	43	29	14	184
		53.3%	23.4%	15.8%	7.6%	100%

TABLE 6
RECENTLY HIRED AND REJECTED APPLICANTS BY AGE

Age	Hired	Rejected	Total
15–18	13 (18.1%)	137 (39.5%)	150
19–22	19 (26.4%)	97 (27.6%)	115
23–32	31 (43.1%)	85 (24.6%)	116
33+	4 (12.5%)	28 (8.2%)	37
Total	72	346	418

Chi square significant at $\rho = .001$

TABLE 7
PREVIOUS JOBS OF ALL APPLICANTS

Previous Job	% of Applicants
Public youth program	31%
Sales/retail	26.9%
Other Burger Barn	24.5%
Clerical, nongovernment	24.3%
Other fast food	19.0%
Other food service	15.8%
Personal service	12.0%
Transport	11.4%
Factory	11.1%
Security	10.4%
Skilled craft	9.8%
Other	7.2%
Medical/hospital	6.7%
Education	5.7%
Janitorial	4.7%
White collar/managerial/professional	2.8%
Telecommunications	2.2%
Family business	2.2%
Own business	1.3%

Appendix II

Log-Linear Regressions
Dependent Variable: HIRED
Variables in the Equation:

Variable	β	Standard Error	Wald	Degrees of Freedom	Signif.	R	Exp(β)
BLACK	−.9033	.4060	4.9487	1	.0261	−.0876	.4052
LOCAL	−1.4152	.3082	21.0888	1	.0000	−.2229	.2429
AGE	.0710	.0221	10.3537	1	.0013	.1475	1.0735
USBORN	−.9382	.4021	5.4434	1	.0196	−.0947	.3913
HSGRAD	.8129	.3098	6.8839	1	.0087	.1128	2.2543
MALE	−.0900	.3098	.0844	1	.7714	.0000	.9139
CONTACT	1.1584	.3097	13.9935	1	.0002	.1767	3.1849
Constant	−1.5101	.7033	4.6113	1	.0318		

	Chi-Square	df	Significance
−2 Log Likelihood	293.993	410	1.000
Model Chi-Square	90.093	7	.0000

Classification table for HIRED

			Predicted		Percent Correct
			0	1	
Observed		0	338	8	97.69%
		1	49	23	31.94%

Overall=86.36%

Notes

PREFACE

1. These congregations are modest in comparison to the enormous, established congregations of the Abyssinian Baptist Church, Riverside Cathedral, and the other institutions favored by many working and middle-class African-Americans who live in the more affluent parts of Harlem or who return to the city from their suburban homes on Sundays.

2. Calculated from the 1990 Census of Population and Housing: Public Use Microdata Sample A (PUMS 5% sample). The variable "how many workers in the family" shows that in the households that the PUMS defines as family households, 31% had zero workers, 35% had one worker, 22% had two workers, and 12% had three or more workers. Hence a total of 69% of the family households had at least one worker in them in 1989. Some clarification of the term "family household" is in order. A family consists of a householder (the person in whose name the home is owned or rented) and one or more other persons living in the same household and related to him or her by birth, marriage, or adoption. All persons in a household who are related to the householder are regarded as members of the family. A household can contain only one family for the purposes of census tabulations. However, not all households contain families, since a household may comprise a group of unrelated persons or a person living alone. In the central Harlem PUMS, 23% of all households were "non-family" households and hence have been excluded from these calculations on workers per household. The Census defines a worker as anyone "16 years and older who worked one or more weeks" in the year.

3. Or, for that matter, with the majority of the population in even the poorest neighborhoods of south Chicago who are working, looking for work, or in school? The Urban Family Life Survey, the main source of data for William Julius Wilson's recent book, *When Work Disappears* (Knopf, 1996), examines labor force participation by neighborhood poverty levels. Wilson shows clearly that as neighborhood poverty increases, engagement in the labor force declines. Nonetheless, even in the poorest neighborhoods Wilson surveyed, where poverty exceeds 40% (a recognized definition of "concentrated poverty"), over half of the respondents are working, looking for work, or in school. See Appendix I, Table 1.

4. Corporate profit rates are now at their highest levels since data on profits were first collected in 1959. According to the Bureau of Economic Analysis, the 1996 before-tax corporate profit rate was 11.4% and the after-tax profit rate was 7.6%. These figures represent a hike of more than 50% in both rates since 1988, the peak of the last business cycle, when the respective rates were 7.3% and 5.0%. Dean Baker, "Corporate Profit Rates Hit New Peak" (news release, Economic Policy Institute, March 28, 1997). See also Dean Baker and Lawrence Mishel, "Profits Up, Wages Down: Worker Losses Yield Big Gains for Business" (Economic Policy Institute, 1995).

5. Little wonder that our counterparts in Europe, straining under the burden of double-digit unemployment rates for the better part of the last fifteen years or so, are beginning to reconsider the wisdom of their generosity toward workers, working families, the poor, the elderly, the out-of-work, and the youth. Americans can only dream about the kinds of benefits that are routinely available in Scandinavia or France, as they have never been available in the United States. Statutory regulations governing worker benefits among the Common Market countries of Western Europe typically allow for twelve public holidays, four weeks annual vacation, one year maximum sick leave with 60% of earnings paid, a maximum of eighteen weeks maternity leave with 90% of earnings paid, a severance package, and sixteen months of unemployment insurance coverage with 50% of earnings paid. In the United States, there are eight to ten public holidays, no statute on vacation, no statute on sick leave, a maximum of thirteen weeks maternity leave with no earnings paid, no statute on severance pay, and six months of unemployment insurance coverage with 50% of earnings paid. See Richard B. Freeman, "How Labor Fares in Advanced Economies," in Richard B. Freeman, ed., *Working Under Different Rules* (Russell Sage Foundation, 1994), table 1.3. In Western Europe, male workers in the bottom 10% of the earnings distribution earn 68% of the median worker's income; in Japan, they earn 61% of the median; in the United States, they earn 38%. Workers in the bottom 10% of the earnings distribution in Germany earn twice as much as their low-wage counterparts in the United States. See Richard B. Freeman, "An Apartheid Economy," *Harvard Business Review* (September–October 1996), pp. 114–21.

6. Lower-skilled workers, however, have experienced sharp declines in real wages, causing increased disparity in our nation's income distribution. See Frank Levy and Richard J. Murnane, "U.S. Earnings Levels and Earnings Inequality: A Review of Recent Trends and Proposed Explanations," *Journal of Economic Literature* 30, no. 3 (1992), pp. 1333–81; Henry S. Farber, "The Incidence and Costs of Job Loss: 1982–91," *Brookings Papers on Economic Activity: Microeconomics* (1993), pp. 73–132; U.S. Department of Labor, "Worker Displacement During the Mid-1990s" (News Release 96-44 6, October 25, 1996); Sheldon Danziger and Peter Gottschalk, *America Unequal* (Russell Sage Foundation, 1995). While there was an abundance of college graduates in the labor market at the end of the 1970s, demands for college-educated workers grew dramatically, and across industries, during the 1980s. These demands were rewarded with employment gains and wage increases for the highly skilled (between 1979 and 1989, wages at the top 90th percentile of the earnings distribution increased by 5%). Between 1979 and 1989, the average hourly wages of male and female earners with five or more years of college rose by about 11% and 19% respectively. Hourly wages of male and female earners with four years of college rose by about 6% and 19%

respectively. Hourly wages of male earners with four years of high school fell by about 5%, while hourly wages of female earners with four years of high school rose by about 3%. Hourly wages of male and female earners with one to three years of high school fell by 13% and 1% respectively. Highly educated earners work more weeks per year and more hours per week than lesser-educated workers, and this trend, too, increased during the 1980s. The wages of workers at the bottom 10th percentile of the earnings distribution fell by 16% between 1979 and 1989, after which time they leveled off. The median worker's real wage, which had fallen by 2% between 1979 and 1989, continues to fall, and has lost another 5% of value between years 1989 and 1997. See Frank Levy, "Incomes and Income Inequality," and James R. Wetzel, "Labor Force, Unemployment, and Earnings," table 2.6, both in Reynolds Farley, ed., *State of the Union: America in the 1990s,* vol. 1 (Russell Sage Foundation, 1995); Alan B. Krueger, "The Truth About Falling Wages," *New York Times,* July 31, 1997, p. A23.

7.   Peter T. Kilborn, "Illness Is Turning Into Financial Catastrophe for More of the Uninsured," *New York Times,* August 1, 1997, p. A10.

8.   It is important to note, however, that the dramatic increase in wage inequality during the 1980s occurred *within* the manufacturing sector as well—the number of semiskilled workers such as assemblers and machine operators declined more than 25%, while the number of precision workers climbed 17%. Elis Berman, John Bound, and Zvi Griliches, 1994, "Changes in the Demand for Skilled Labor within U.S. Manufacturing: Evidence from the Annual Survey of Manufacturers," *Quarterly Journal of Economics* 109 (May 1995), pp. 367–97; Levy, "Incomes and Income Inequality," table 1.3.

9.   Economist Bennett Harrison, in *Lean and Mean: The Changing Landscape of Corporate Power in the Age of Flexibility* (Basic Books, 1994), writes that the now-enduring trend among corporate management across most industries is to take the "low road" to profitability—to compete mainly on the basis of cheapening labor costs rather than the broad-based upgrading of technology and worker talents. Those in lower-tier jobs have met the consequences of this strategy. While the most severe reductions in wages have occurred in entry-level jobs, the three-fourths of the workforce with less than a college degree, the bottom 80% of men, low-wage women workers, and younger workers (the worst hit of these groupings) all lost ground from 1979 to 1993. See Lawrence Mishel and Jared Bernstein, *The State of Working America 1994–1995* (Economic Policy Institute, 1994), pp. 109–57.

10.   Of those aged 16 to 24 who were not enrolled in school in October 1996, about 80% were in the labor force either working or actively looking for work. Of those in the labor force, men and women who graduated from college had unemployment rates of 5% and 3% respectively; men and women with less than a high school diploma had unemployment rates of 22% and 29% respectively. U.S. Department of Labor, "College Enrollment and Work Activity of 1996 High School Graduates" (News Release 97-240, July 23, 1997).

11.   In 1979, high school dropouts made up 20% of the labor force, earning about $10 per hour in 1993 dollars. By 1989, they made up 14% of the labor force, and their wages dropped by 16% to $8.45 per hour. By 1993, dropouts' wages dropped another 7% to $7.85 per hour. Mishel and Bernstein, *State of Working America 1994–1995,* table 3.18.

12.   Earnings of college graduates were about 2% higher in 1995 than they were in 1979, while those of high school graduates were about 15% lower. Growing wage disparities are seen when workers are categorized in other ways. The real earnings of workers in the top decile of earnings distribution increased slightly between 1979 and 1993, but the earnings of the bottom decile decreased by about 15%. The real earnings of workers aged 45 to 54 remained about the same in 1979 and 1994, but earnings of workers aged 16 to 24 dropped by more than 15%. The earnings of professionals increased by about 7% between 1983 and 1995, but the earnings of clerical workers, machine operators, and laborers all fell precipitously. The average weekly earnings of nonsupervisory, nonfarm, private-sector workers fell 12% from 1979 through the mid-1990s. The median weekly earnings of full-time male workers have dropped by 13% in the same time period. See Freeman, "Apartheid Economy," pp. 114–21.

13.   *Kids Count* (Annie Casey Foundation, 1996).

14.   Of the 10,680 babies born in the United States every day, 2,556 are born into poverty. Children's Defense Fund, "Every Day in America" (July 1997). According to one study, (L. Rainwater and T. M. Smeeding, "Doing Poorly: The Real Income of American Children in a Comparative Perspective" (Working Paper no. 127, Luxembourg Income Study, Maxwell School of Citizenship and Public Affairs, Syracuse University, 1995), among seventeen developed countries, the child poverty rate of the United States is 50% higher than the next highest rate. *Kids Count Data Book* (Annie E. Casey Foundation, 1997), p. 17.

15.   Frank Levy and Richard Murnane, *Teaching the New Basic Skills* (Free Press, 1996).

16.   Paul Jargowsky, *Poverty and Place* (Russell Sage Foundation, 1997).

17.   In their study of poor single mothers, *Making Ends Meet: How Single Mothers Survive Welfare And Low-Wage Work* (Russell Sage Foundation, 1997), Kathryn Edin and Laura Lein found that while low-wage mothers brought home more money than what similarly skilled welfare-reliant mothers received in benefits, virtually all of the difference was used up in work-related expenses such as clothing, child care, and transportation. What is more, while all the mothers receiving welfare qualified for Medicaid, almost half the working mothers lacked health insurance.

CHAPTER 1: WORKING LIVES

1.   Andrew Hacker, *Money: Who Has How Much and Why* (Scribner's, 1997); Katherine Newman, *Declining Fortunes: The Withering of the American Dream* (Basic Books, 1993).

CHAPTER 2: THE INVISIBLE POOR

1.   Herbert Gans, *The War Against the Poor* (Basic Books, 1995), pp. 6–7.

2.   The same racializing language was used to denigrate Irish immigrants in the U.S. throughout the antebellum period. For a recent and provocative discussion of this issue, see Noel Ignatiev, *How the Irish Became White* (Routledge, 1995).

3.   In 1992, the nonmetropolitan poverty rate, 16.8%, exceeded the metropolitan

poverty rate, 13.9% (Census figures). Diane McLaughlin and Lauri Perman, "Returns vs. Endowments in the Earnings Attainment Process for Metropolitan and Non-metropolitan Men and Women," *Rural Sociology* 56 (1991), pp. 339–65, reports that most of the difference in average earnings for metropolitan and nonmetropolitan workers resulted from lower earnings returns to human capital (such as skills and educational backgrounds). Economic restructuring and slow employment growth in rural America, where agriculture and nondurable goods manufacturing predomi-nate, have lowered the earnings of already marginal workers. See Daniel Lichter, Gail Johnston, and Diane McLaughlin, "Changing Linkages Between Work and Poverty in Rural America," *Rural Sociology* 59, no. 3 (1994), pp. 395–415.

4. Resentment and discrimination endured as key features of the African-American urban experience. See Marcus E. Jones, *Black Migration in the United States with Emphasis on Selected Central Cities* (Century Twenty One, 1980); and Kenneth L. Kusmer, "African Americans in the City Since World War II: From the Industrial to the Post-Industrial Era," *Journal of Urban History* 21, no. 4 (May 1995).

5. Nicholas Lemann, *The Promised Land* (Knopf, 1991).

6. John E. Schwarz and Thomas J. Volgy, *The Forgotten Americans* (Norton, 1992), p. 64. Schwarz and Volgy define the working poor as workers who hold full-time jobs and earn less than 155% of the official poverty line (in 1989, six million workers) or work part-time or part of the year, would like to work full-time, and earn less than 155% of the official poverty line (in 1989, 5.5 million workers). They add in the number of people in these families (for a total of about 29 million). The authors use 155% of the official poverty line as a level of self-sufficiency. By investigating family budgets of low-income Americans, they show that this income barely covers costs for necessities in today's economy. The official poverty line was defined in the 1960s as three times the cost of a minimal food budget for a household of a given size. This definition was reasonable at that time, since the cost of food accounted for about one-third of an average family's budget. But the same formula, adjusted yearly for infla-tion, is used today, even though the cost of food accounts for a much smaller proportion (about one-sixth) of a family's budget and other costs for basic necessities, such as housing and medical care, have risen. By interviewing working-poor families on their consumption patterns, the authors illustrate that the lifestyle afforded by an income 155% of the official poverty line is one of self-sufficiency and little more. Economists and sociologists have applied a variety of definitions to measure the num-bers of working poor, most often relying upon the official poverty line rather than an adjusted level that estimates true self-sufficiency. Even this task is difficult, because of the crude nature of survey data and the myriad ways one can define a worker. Using a definition of the working poor as "those persons age 16 and older who have worked for at least 27 weeks the previous year, usually for at least 20 hours a week, and who lived in families with incomes below the official poverty threshold," John D. Kasarda, "America's Working Poor: 1980–1990," in Thomas R. Swartz and Kathleen Maas Weigert, eds., *America's Working Poor* (University of Notre Dame Press, 1995), calcu-lates (using Census data) 3.75 million "poor" workers in 1990, a figure that had risen by 400,000 since 1980. In order to find a measure that might have more meaning as a labor force concept—that is, one that sheds some light on how low earnings actually produce poverty conditions—Kasarda also calculated numbers of "poverty-wage workers," defined as "those persons 16 and over who work full-time (50 or more weeks

per year, including paid vacation, usually for 35 hours or more per week) and who do not earn enough to lift a family of four out of poverty." Kasarda calculated just over twelve million "poverty wage workers" in 1990 (16% of all workers), a figure that had risen by nearly three million since 1980. By this definition, the number of poor workers is even higher than that offered by Schwarz and Volgy.

7.   This point was central to the thinking of the National Research Council's Panel on Poverty and Family Assistance, which recommended that a new measurement system for assessing poverty be established that would take benefits into account. Constance Citro and Robert Michael, eds., *Measuring Poverty* (National Academy Press, 1995).

8.   While the eligibility requirements of the Section 8 Housing Assistance program, established in 1975 by HUD, do not exclude labor force participants (and, in fact, eligibility is not even based on poverty level but on a percentage of the median income for a particular local area), the administration of the program and its underfunding effectively restrict access. Housing assistance is not provided as an entitlement to households that "officially" qualify for various kinds of aid, including vouchers that offset monthly rent bills. Providing assistance to all households that qualify—normally those that earn less than 80% of the median income in a particular area—would double the federal outlays required for the program. Local administrators are often forced to lower eligibility income requirements so as not to exceed their appropriated funds. Hence, most federal housing aid is targeted to "very low income" renters. Currently in New York City, no applications are being accepted for leased housing vouchers. Anyone with an income less than $39,200 (for a family of four) is eligible to fill out an application to be put on a waiting list for a vacancy at project apartments—a list that has more names on it than the 100,000 families already covered by Section 8 assistance. New York City Housing Authority; Committee on Ways and Means, U.S. House of Representatives, *1994 Green Book* (U.S. Government Printing Office, 1994), pp. 814–15; R. Allen Hays, *The Federal Government and Urban Housing* (SUNY, 1995); Malcolm Gladwell, "A Precarious Balancing Act, a Smaller Net: As Social Spending Contracts, Many Fall," *Washington Post*, May 25, 1996, p. A1.

9.   Until the mid-1980s, eligibility for Medicaid coverage was strongly linked to participation in Aid to Families with Dependent Children or Supplemental Security Income programs. States are now required to cover pregnant women and young children whose family incomes fall below 133% of the federal poverty level. Nonetheless, even while many states raise the income ceiling to 185% of poverty and choose to cover other variously defined "medically needy" persons, eligibility for adults and older children remains restrictive and low enrollment rates prevail. In 1992, 38% of those aged 19 to 44 who were officially poor were covered by Medicaid. For those of the same age group whose family incomes fell between 100% and 133% of poverty, the portion covered by Medicaid dropped to less than one-fifth (17%). *1994 Green Book*, pp. 783–89.

10.   Households without an elderly or disabled member are generally eligible for food stamps if family income does not exceed 130% of poverty and counted liquid assets total less than $2,000. For a family of four, the eligibility cutoff is a gross monthly income of $1,555. Benefits are based upon a household's size and its income. For a family of four, monthly allotments range from a maximum of $375 to a minimum—in some states—of just a few dollars for those households that barely fulfill eligibility

requirements. In 1993, the average per-person benefit was $68 per month, a rate made high by the notoriously meager numbers of low-wage earners who actually participate as food stamp beneficiaries. The USDA determined in 1989 that less than two-thirds of individuals eligible for food stamps actually receive benefits. Less than one in ten participants is a member of a household with an income level above the federal poverty level. Like Medicaid, food stamps have traditionally been linked with AFDC participation, so that many families who have never been to the welfare office may not realize that they are eligible for reduced benefits. The food stamp program is still handled by the same welfare offices and personnel that administer AFDC. (Under provisions of the 1996 welfare reform law, state-federal AFDC programs will be overhauled and funded through Temporary Assistance for Needy Families block grants, which will give states more autonomy in fulfilling the legislation's mandate to move welfare recipients off relief roles and into employment.) *1994 Green Book,* pp. 757–82.

11. The Panel on Poverty and Family Assistance, a branch of the National Research Council, recently completed an evaluation of poverty measurement in the United States; see Citro and Michael, eds., *Measuring Poverty.* The panel concluded that the current official measure of poverty needs to be revised for two reasons: it fails to accurately describe differences in the extent of poverty among population groups and across geographic regions (cost-of-living differences for housing and other goods are substantial), and it fails to accurately portray trends over time. They argue that the nation's economy and public policies have changed since the current measure was introduced more than a generation ago. They note, for example, that because the current poverty measure defines family resources as gross money income, it produces a higher poverty rate for families on public assistance and a lower rate for working families not on assistance than would a poverty measure that included the value of cash assistance and some in-kind benefits (such as food stamps) in the determination of family resources. The current measure's reliance on gross money income also neglects the enormous problem of working families who must pay for child care. This issue has grown in importance because of the increasing number of working mothers. The panel recommends that child care expenses, at a capped rate, be deducted from family resources calculations when no adult is at home to provide care. The panel also argues that the nation's poverty threshold ought to fluctuate according to the cost of food, clothing, and shelter.

12. Earl Mellor, "A Profile of the Working Poor" (Report 869, Bureau of Labor Statistics, March 1994), p. 1; Samantha Quan, "A Profile of the Working Poor, 1996" (Report 918, Bureau of Labor Statistics, December 1997), p. 1.

13. Steven E. Haugen and Earl F. Mellor, "Estimating the Number of Minimum Wage Workers," research summary, *Monthly Labor Review* 113, no. 1 (1990), pp. 70–74.

14. Two-thirds of minimum-wage workers are women, and two-thirds work part-time. This is because women are more likely to be part-time workers, and part-time workers are nearly six times as likely as full-time employees to be minimum-wage workers. Ibid, p. 72.

15. Sar A. Levitan and Isaac Shapiro, *Working but Poor: America's Contradiction* (Johns Hopkins University Press, 1987).

16. Raising the minimum wage is a controversial method of improving the lot of the working poor. David E. Card and Alan B. Krueger, *Myth and Measurement: The New Economics of the Minimum Wage* (Princeton University Press, 1993), argue on

the basis of evidence comparing New Jersey and Pennsylvania that modest increases in the minimum wage do not result in job losses. David Neumark and William Wascher, "Do Minimum Wages Fight Poverty?" (NBER Working Paper 6127, 1997), criticizes the database for these optimistic conclusions.

17.   Lawrence Mishel and Jared Bernstein, *The State of Working America 1994–1995* (Economic Policy Institute, 1994).

18.   Richard Wertheimer of Child Trends, Inc., "Characteristics of Working Poor Families and Their Children," report to Foundation for Child Development (1996).

19.   Some scholars have linked these numbers to out-of-wedlock pregnancy among young women, but we should be cautious here. Only 14% of all the children who live in working-poor families in 1994 were born to a teenage mother. Most of the kids in these families were born to women over age 25. Single parenthood would probably be next in line as the obvious explanation for childhood poverty, and there is truth to this, for women earn far less in the labor market than do men. Again, however, the 1994 data tell us that half of the 5.6 million children in working-poor families lived in two-parent households in which at least one parent worked.

20.   Samantha Quan, "A Profile of the Working Poor, 1996" (Report 918, Bureau of Labor Statistics, December 1997), pp. 3–4.

21.   For example, the rate of year-round, full-time young adult (18 to 24) workforce with low annual earnings has increased steadily since 1979. The rate was 23% in 1979 and had grown to 43% in 1990. The "low earnings" threshold is defined as the poverty level for a four-person family. U.S. Bureau of the Census, "Workers with Low Earnings: 1964 to 1990."

22.   Eighteen percent of the 18–24-year-old males who worked full-time in 1979 and 30% of the females of the same age had low wages. By 1990, the numbers had climbed to 40% for men and nearly 50% for women. Although men have always been better off than women in an absolute sense, the direction of change has not been salutary: poverty rates among working-poor men nearly doubled in the 1980s, whereas the increase among women was about 25% (from 20% to 24%). Ibid.

23.   Mellor, "Profile of the Working Poor," p. 2.

24.   Ibid.

25.   Sheldon Danziger and Peter Gottschalk, *Uneven Tides: Rising Inequality in America* (Russell Sage Foundation, 1993).

26.   The racial breakdown of minimum-wage workers is as follows: 68% white, 16% black, 13% Hispanic, and 3% other. Mishel and Bernstein, *State of Working America 1994–1995*.

27.   Mellor, "Profile of the Working Poor," p. 1. Likewise, reemployment rates of displaced workers are higher for whites (76.4% in 1990–91) than for African-Americans (66.6%) or Hispanics (64.9%). Jennifer M. Gardner, "Worker Displacement: A Decade of Change," *Monthly Labor Review,* April 1995, p. 49.

28.   These rates refer to persons in the labor force for twenty-seven weeks or more. Mellor, "Profile of the Working Poor," p. 8.

29.   Ibid., p. 6.

30.   These poverty rates refer to full-time, year-round workers. "Poverty in the United States, 1992," *Current Population Reports,* Series P60-185, Table 14 (Bureau of the Census, October 1993). Racial differences in these rates diminish somewhat when one shifts over to "not year-round full-time."

31. "Institutional racism" is a particularly potent force in hiring decisions. Overt racism, neoclassical economists argue, is costly to firms and therefore readily mitigated by rational market forces. Statistical racism, a concept born in the early 1970s, is much more enduring. The term attempts to distinguish willful participation from reasonable business practice. Statistical discrimination occurs when employers use racial stereotypes not to favor a particular group, but rather to gauge the likely performance of job applicants. Liberal and conservative scholars disagree about the veracity of employers' perceptions of group differences in productivity. Measuring employee productivity is a difficult undertaking, as is measuring racial bias within firms that can influence both productivity and its evaluation. According to the 1990 General Social Survey (National Opinion Research Center, 1991), more than half of whites characterize blacks as lazier and less intelligent than whites. In their study of employment practices of inner-city firms in Chicago, Kirschenman and Neckerman found that employer perceptions of race combined with their notions of an applicant's social class and place of residency in hiring decisions. Employers disfavored inner-city residents and lower-class individuals. Hence, successful black applicants had to overturn expectations and show employers in job interviews that they were not lower-class or from the ghetto. This was accomplished through style of dress and speech, and sometimes by lying about one's home address. See Joleen Kirschenman and Kathryn M. Neckerman, " 'We'd Love to Hire Them, but . . .': The Meaning of Race for Employers," in Christopher Jencks and Paul E. Peterson, eds., *The Urban Underclass* (Brookings Institution, 1991). See also Christopher Jencks, *Rethinking Social Policy: Race, Poverty and the Underclass* (Harvard University Press, 1992), pp. 40–46. For a review of labor market audit studies in which comparably educated and experienced job candidates of different racial or ethnic backgrounds are sent on interviews, see Michael Fix and Raymond Struyk, *Clear and Convincing Evidence* (Urban Institute Press, 1994); Fix and Struyck found that equally qualified African-American and Latino applicants are given proportionally fewer job offers than white applicants.

32. Some studies find that racial differences in test scores and education account for most of the racial differences in average wages. Derek Neal and William Johnson, "The Role of Premarket Factors in Black-White Wage Differences," *Journal of Political Economy* 104, no. 5 (October 1996), pp. 869–72; Frank Levy and Richard Murnane, *The New Basic Skills* (Free Press, 1996). Test scores seem less reliable as a means of predicting employment.

33. Robert B. Reich, *The Work of Nations: Preparing Ourselves for Twenty-first Century Capitalism* (Knopf, 1991).

34. Paul Krugman, *The Age of Diminished Expectations: U.S. Economic Policy in the 1990s* (Washington Post Co., 1990).

35. City of New York, Department of City Planning, *Socioeconomic Profiles: A Profile of New York City's Community Districts from the 1980 and 1990 Censuses of Population and Housing* (March 1993).

36. 1990 Census figures show 99% African-American residents, a classification that probably overlooks the large number of foreign-born black immigrants who live there but often identify themselves as African-American.

37. The ethnic composition of the fast food workforce in Harlem is, not surprisingly, tipped sharply toward minorities when compared to the national population of workers in the fast food industry. Whereas overall, 23% of the nation's fast food

employees are nonwhite, Harlem's fast food employees are basically all members of minority groups; we encountered no whites at all. Ivan Charner and Bryna S. Fraser, *Fast Food Jobs* (National Institute for Work and Learning, 1984); Robert W. Van Giezen, "Occupational Wages in the Fast-Food Industry," *Monthly Labor Review*, August 1994, p. 24.

38. In the late 1980s, Dominicans made up 80% of all immigrants moving into Washington Heights, a neighborhood to the north of central Harlem. New York City Department of City Planning, *The Newest New Yorkers: An Analysis of Immigration into New York City During the 1820s* (1992). While U.S. involvement in Dominican affairs has a long history (early in this century, for example, the United States installed a military government that ruled over the republic), Dominican migration to the United States did not begin in large numbers until after the revolution of 1965, when American visas were issued in order to relieve political tensions. Large migration flows continue because of high rates of unemployment, these being largely related to processes of industrial transformation dominated by American enterprise. Ramona Hernandez and Silvio Torres-Saillant, "Dominicans in New York: Men, Women, and Future Prospects" (unpublished paper, Center for Dominican Studies, City College of New York, n.d.); Alejandro Portes and Luis E. Guarnizo, *Tropical Capitalists: U.S.-Bound Immigration and Small Enterprise Development in the Dominican Republic* (Commission for the Study of International Migration and Cooperative Economic Development, 1990).

39. Puerto Ricans began coming to the mainland United States in small but significant numbers after having been granted citizenship through the Jones Act in 1917. There was a lag in migration from the Depression through World War II. After the war, Puerto Ricans began coming in great numbers, almost 40,000 alone in 1946. Unemployment at home—which was a result of economic restructuring by the United States—inexpensive air flights, and the lure (often facilitated by labor recruiters) of skilled and unskilled work brought Puerto Ricans to New York City, where the vast majority settled. Men usually started work in factories, hotels, or restaurants. Women became domestics or worked as seamstresses in the garment industry. Michael Lapp, "The Migration Division of Puerto Rico and Puerto Ricans in New York City, 1948–1969," in William Pencak, Selma Berrol, and Randall M. Miller, eds., *Immigration to New York* (New York Historical Society, 1991); Alejandro Portes and Ruben G. Rumbaut, *Immigrant America: A Portrait* (University of California Press, 1996), pp. 225–29.

40. Some of which reopened in Puerto Rico itself, taking advantage of lower wages and tax breaks provided by Congress to encourage industrial development and stem the tide of emigration.

41. See Saskia Sassen-Koob, "Changing Composition and Labor Market Location of Hispanic Immigrants in New York City, 1960–1980," in George J. Borjas and Marta Tienda, eds., *Hispanics in the U.S. Economy* (Academic Press, 1985).

42. A study by the New York City Planning Department predicts that Latinos, principally Puerto Ricans and Dominicans, will make up more than half the population of the Bronx by the year 2000. Citywide, Latinos will outnumber African-Americans by the same year. See David Firestone, "Major Ethnic Changes Underway," *New York Times*, March 29, 1995, p. B1.

43. These figures come from Orlando Rodriguez et al., "Nuestra America en

Nueva York: The New Immigrant Hispanic Populations in New York City: 1980–90" (summary of a report by the Hispanic Research Center, Fordham University, August 1995).

44.   Boisjoly and Duncan have found, for example, that lower schooling levels among Latinos, especially immigrants, were an important factor in explaining why they incurred a higher rate of job displacement than other groups in the 1990–92 recession. Johanne Boisjoly and Greg J. Duncan, "Job Losses Among Hispanics in the Recent Recession," *Monthly Labor Review*, June 1994, pp. 16–23.

45.   Rodriguez et al., "Nuestra America en Nueva York," p. 11.

46.   Van Giezen, "Occupational Wages in the Fast Food Industry."

47.   If we consider the dimension of race in the overall U.S. figures, however, the national picture and that of central Harlem begin to converge. According to Charner and Fraser, *Fast Food Jobs*, p. 5, about 41% of the black fast food workers across the country are twenty-one years old and older. Hence, like Harlem's residents, who have even greater difficulty, African-American fast food workers elsewhere who "should" be able to move up to better-paying jobs than these minimum-wage opportunities are, instead, concentrated at the low end of the income distribution even though they are well into their adult careers.

48.   See Table 3 in Appendix I for educational data on central Harlem Burger Barn workers.

49.   In the oldest age group, 45% were high school graduates, 36% were dropouts, and 19% had gone beyond high school.

50.   See Klerman and Karoly, "Young Men and the Transition to Stable Employment," *Monthly Labor Review*, August 1994, p. 35. Through statistical analysis of the National Longitudinal Survey of Youth, Klerman and Karoly estimate that in the early 1980s, the youth population (14–22) was about one-third high school dropouts (36.9%) and one-third high school graduates (35.4%). About 27.7% of males went directly from high school to postsecondary education. Figures in the Charner and Fraser study suggest that fast food workers nationwide are more likely to continue their education beyond high school than our Harlem respondents. Charner and Fraser, *Fast Food Jobs*, pp. 7–11. See Appendix I, Table 4, for the Charner and Fraser data.

51.   Their expectations are somewhat more modest than those of the fast food workforce in the nation as a whole. Charner and Fraser, *Fast Food Jobs*, pp. 10–11, reports that 65% of workers 24 and younger expect to complete at least a four-year college degree.

52.   Forty-two percent of the 19–22-year-olds plan to do the same, a figure that is encouraging given that this is precisely the age when most middle-class children have already taken this step. Almost one-third of those over 23 also plan to attend college as well.

53.   Thirty percent of our full-time respondents have high educational goals, compared to 50% of the part-time respondents.

54.   In 1990, 16.3% of job-holders earned poverty wages; the rate of female job-holders earning poverty wages (23.8%) was twice the rate of males (11.5%). Women outnumber men in all nonagricultural occupations in which the majority of job-holders earn poverty wages (except for miscellaneous food preparation, in which the numbers are about equal). Within each of these very-low-wage occupations, the

percent of women earning poverty wages (the first percent figure cited for each in this list) is generally higher than the percent of men earning poverty wages (the second percent figure cited for each in this list): child-care workers (73.5%, 33.5%), sewing machine operators (64.5%, 32.0%), waiters and waitresses (65.9%, 41.2%), miscellaneous food preparation (59.0%, 59.8%), cooks (67.1%, 45.6%), maids and housemen (62.1%, 34.5%), cashiers (58.1%, 34.9%), and laundering (63.8%, 33.7%). See Kasarda, "America's Working Poor: 1980–1990," table 3.10. While the average wages of full-time, full-year women workers with college degrees have been increasing since 1979, the average wages of full-time, full-year women workers with high school diplomas are only slightly higher, and the wages of full-time, full-year women workers who are college dropouts have declined by 6% since that time. While the wages of these low earners have not fallen as dramatically as for male dropouts (whose average earnings fell 22% since 1979), the wages earned by less-skilled women remain far below those of men. Data through year 1993. See Rebecca M. Blank, *It Takes a Nation* (Russell Sage Foundation, 1997), pp. 60–64.

55. Charner and Fraser, *Fast Food Jobs*, p. 6.

56. See Table 5 in Appendix I for the full data.

57. Half had no high school degree.

58. Fifty-nine percent of these people (whose households receive AFDC support) are female. Forty-five percent are 18 years and under and 33% are 19–22 years old. About one-third of them have children and 12% have kids 6 or under. Thirty percent are in households receiving SSI.

59. Kathryn Edin and Laura Lein make a related point in *Making Ends Meet* (Russell Sage Foundation, 1997). Among the welfare recipients they interviewed, the vast majority had had extensive work experience in exactly these kinds of jobs (an average of 5–6 years). Ultimately they could not afford the cost of child care, transportation, and associated expenses of being in the workplace (e.g., clothing) and "dropped out." *Making Ends Meet* points to a form of integration between work and welfare: a serial or cycling model of work/welfare/work. Here I point to another: the simultaneous integration of work and welfare, principally by mothers on AFDC and their working children.

60. These numbers reflect, once again, the disadvantaged living conditions that prevail in an inner-city ghetto, where the combination of chronic disease (hypertension, diabetes, and the like) and inadequate medical care results in a high proportion of early deaths.

61. Arline T. Geronimus, John Bound, Timothy A. Waidman, Marianne H. Hillemeir, and Patricia B. Burns, "Excess Mortality among Blacks and Whites in the United States," *New England Journal of Medicine* 335, no. 21 (November 21, 1996), pp. 1552–59, provides evidence that African-Americans have very high levels of early mortality.

62. Other low-wage jobs are represented in the mother's employment statistics as well: Factory work and personal services account for 8% each of their employment, and about 6% do janitorial work, including housekeeping.

63. Almost one-fifth of the mothers were unemployed (but not on AFDC) at the time we did this study.

64. Not surprisingly, this growth was also experienced elsewhere—employment in hospitals nationwide rose 10% between 1989 and 1992, with a net gain of 400,000

employees. Barbara Wootton and Laura T. Ross, "Hospital Staffing Patterns in Urban and Nonurban Areas," *Monthly Labor Review*, March 1995, p. 23.

65. Forty-eight percent of the working poor lack health insurance.

66. According to a 1996 General Accounting Office report (GAO/HEHS-96-129), *Health Insurance for Children: Private Insurance Coverage Continues to Decline*, 10 million children were uninsured in 1994. Among children with at least one parent working full-time during the entire year, about one-fourth lacked private health insurance, and almost half of these were not covered by Medicaid or other public programs. According to the National Center for Health Statistics, 2.6 million uninsured children were unable to obtain needed medical care in the past year. See Children's Defense Fund news release, "U.S. Government Survey Finds Millions of Uninsured Children Not Getting Necessary Medical Care" (July 17, 1997). The 1997 budget bill provides for a five-year, $24 billion program—financed largely through an increase in the federal tax on cigarettes and administered through state block grants—to provide medical care for uninsured poor children. Children who live in families whose employers do not provide coverage and whose incomes are too high to qualify for Medicaid but too low to afford insurance will be eligible (the program will be limited to children in families with incomes less than 200–250% of the federal poverty line, in most states). States choose how they will provide child health care for the uninsured from several options: standard federal employee health insurance benefits, enrollment in a health maintenance organization, the standard health plan for state workers, or enrollment in the state's Medicaid program. Estimates of the number of children who will be served ranges from two to five million. In any case, this represents the largest expansion in children's health coverage since Medicaid's creation thirty years ago. Cindy Mann and Jocelyn Guyer, "Overview of the New Child Health Block Grant," Center on Budget and Policy Priorities (August 6, 1997); Hillary Rodham Clinton, "Our Chance for Healthier Children," *New York Times*, August 5, 1997, p. A15; and Douglas J. Besharov, "Beware the Real Agenda," *New York Times*, August 5, 1997, p. A15.

67. Peter T. Kilborn, "Illness Is Turning into Financial Catastrophe for More of the Uninsured," *New York Times*, August 1, 1997, p. A10.

68. More than one million consumers filed for bankruptcy in 1996, an increase of almost 30% from the previous year and a 150% increase since 1986. It is not possible to know what proportion of these bankruptcies is fueled by medical bills, but there is evidence to suggest this is a rising cause of financial dissolution. Kilborn, "Illness Is Turning into Financial Catastrophe for More of the Uninsured," notes that medical bills were noted in half of the bankruptcy petitions they examined in Little Rock, Arkansas, with one in four of those bills exceeding the petitions for other unsecured debts.

69. Rates of asthma prevalence and hospitalization in low-income urban areas, particularly New York City and Chicago, have been increasing rapidly since 1980. Asthma mortality rates in East Harlem are nearly ten times higher than the average U.S. rate. Kevin B. Weiss, Peter J. Gergen, and Ellen F. Crain, "Inner-City Asthma: The Epidemiology of an Emerging U.S. Public Health Concern," *Chest* 101/6 (June 1992), p. 362–7S. The causal pathways between risk factors and asthma incidence are not yet well understood, yet the tendency for deaths to occur either in emergency rooms or outside the health care system altogether suggests that there is inadequate access

to medical care and asthma treatment among inner-city residents. Paul V. Targonski et al., "Trends in Asthma Mortality Among African Americans and Whites in Chicago, 1968 Through 1991," *American Journal of Public Health* 84 (November 1994), pp. 1830–33; Karen M. Kaplan, "Epidemiology of Deaths from Asthma in Pennsylvania, 1978–87," *Public Health Reports* 108, no. 1 (January–February 1993), pp. 66–69.

70.   African-Americans are 1.6 times more likely to have diabetes than the average American. At least two million African-Americans have the disease, which often goes undiagnosed. William Young, "Managing Diabetes," *Los Angeles Sentinel*, April 13, 1995, p. A10.

71.   Infant mortality rates in parts of New York City rival those in developing countries. Central Harlem has an infant mortality rate of 18 per 1,000 live births. In addition, 18% of babies born there have a low birthweight, the highest rate in the city. In Washington Heights, another low-income area north of Harlem, about 13% of mothers receive no prenatal care, which again represents the highest rate in the city. Data are from 1989. Citizens' Committee for Children, *Keeping Track of New York's Children* (1993).

72.   The percentage of women in the paid workforce with school-age children has increased from 27% in 1947 to 76% in 1992. Their ability to care for their sick children, therefore, has declined. According to a Gallup survey, one-third of working mothers say that the last time a parent in their houses missed work for a sick child, it was counted as unpaid time by their employers, costing an average of $139. Four out of five working mothers say that they occasionally send their sick children to child care, a practice with serious public health consequences that has been corroborated by a survey of physicians. Joel Dresang, "Dr. Mom Often Picks Between Pay, Sick Kids," *Milwaukee Journal Sentinel*, November 1, 1996, p. 2. A study from the Harvard School of Public Health, Jody Heymann, Alison Earle, and Brian Egleston, "Parental Availability for the Care of Sick Children," *Pediatrics* 98 (August 1996), pp. 226–30, finds that between the years 1985 and 1990, while more than one-third of families across the nation required more than two weeks of sick leave per year to care adequately for ill children or aging relatives, 28% of mothers in such families had jobs that offered no paid sick leave. The researchers find that the problem is more severe for poor mothers (only 20% of working-nonpoor parents but 38% of working-poor parents lack paid sick leave). Working mothers whose children have chronic illnesses such as asthma, a condition prevalent in many inner-city neighborhoods, had less sick leave than other employed mothers.

73.   These totals include cuts in the following budget areas: (1) patients needing a few hours a week of help cooking and housekeeping, (2) attendant hours for personal hygiene, (3) adult day care, (4) long-term home care, (5) assisted living, (6) protections against "spousal impoverishment," (7) continuing care for former hospital patients, and (8) provider reimbursements for home care and personal care. Estimates by City Comptroller's Office, cited in "Net Loss: Secondary Effects of City Budget Cut Proposals," http://tenant.net/Oversight/Netloss/bctitle.html (June 12, 1998).

74.   Alternatively, we may see those who cannot be accommodated in nursing homes crowd into the hospitals. Since New York City nursing homes have an average 3% vacancy rate (on a base of approximately 42,233 beds), only 1,267 beds would be available for the 19,000 additional patients these cuts are projected to create. Hospitals are the next likely candidate for these patients, though the cost of accommodating

them in these facilities is hardly negligible (estimated at $38 million). Figures from "Net Loss: Secondary Effects of City Budget Cut Proposals."

75. Estimates by the City Comptroller's Office, cited in "Net Loss: Secondary Effects of City Budget Cut Proposals."

76. Quoted in Kirk Johnson, "Medicine in New York Awaits Big Shift in Role of Government," *New York Times,* August 11, 1997, p. A27.

77. Since taking office, Mayor Giuliani has met stiff resistance in his attempt to privatize (by sale or lease) some of New York City's eleven public hospitals. His administration predicts that 8,000 to 10,000 fewer jobs will be created annually in the health care sector if the mayor's budget scenario is fully implemented. Since Giuliani took office, the city's annual direct subsidy to public hospitals has declined dramatically (from $300 million in 1992 to $30 million today). See Blaine Harden, "Long Arm of Social Aid Is Shorter, but Still Touches Many," *Washington Post,* May 25, 1997, p. A23; Pamela S. Brier, "At Risk: Health Care for the Poor," *New York Times,* January 18, 1997, p. 1:23; Elisabeth Rosenthal, "Mayor's Stalled Plans Leave Public Hospitals in Trauma," *New York Times,* May 24, 1996, p. A1; and Thomas J. Lueck, "Giuliani Fiscal Plan Puts Health Care Jobs at Risk," *New York Times,* February 18, 1995, p. A1.

78. See especially Rebecca Blank, "Policy Watch: Proposals for Time-Limited Welfare," *Journal of Economic Perspectives,* 8, no. 4 (Fall 1994), pp. 183–93.

79. Mark Alan Hughes has been one of the strongest voices in pointing out the transportation dilemmas that prevent inner-city residents of central cities, where jobs are scarce, from getting work in suburbs. Mark Alan Hughes and Julie Sternberg, "The New Metropolitan Reality: Where the Rubber Meets the Road in Antipoverty Policy" (Urban Institute, 1992); Mark Alan Hughes, "Over the Horizon: Jobs in the Suburbs of Major Metropolitan Areas" (report to Public/Private Ventures, 1993). Using data on employment and population shifts in Milwaukee, Hughes points out that the county-based administration of the new welfare-to-work programs, as they are now conceived, fragments metropolitan labor markets, isolating central city participants from suburban counties, where there are more jobs. Mark Alan Hughes, "Learning from the Milwaukee Challenge," *Journal of Policy Analysis and Management* 15 (Fall 1996), pp. 562–71.

80. The federally mandated minimum wage increased to $5.15 in September 1997. Its real value is about 14% lower than the minimum wage of 1979. Lawrence Mishel, Jared Bernstein, and Edith Rasell, "Who Wins with a Higher Minimum Wage" (briefing paper, Economic Policy Institute, 1995). Senator Edward Kennedy of Massachusetts and Representative David Bonior of Michigan have introduced legislation to raise the minimum wage to $7.25 by year 2002, but the bill faces strong opposition from conservatives. See "Work Week," *Wall Street Journal,* August 5, 1997, p. A1.

81. Persons leaving welfare will join that portion of the labor market that is already characterized by weak demand and oversupply. Hourly wages of women aged 16–35 with a high school education or less have declined steeply since 1979. Between 1979 and 1993, the hourly wages of those under age 26 fell by more than 15%. Dropouts averaged less than $5 per hour; high school graduates averaged less than $6.50 per hour. Among those between ages 26 and 35, the changes in hourly wages are as follows: white dropouts down 12% to $6.74, white high school graduates down 4% to $8.67, African-American dropouts down 19% to $6.40, African-American high school graduates down 18% to $7.58, Latina dropouts down 14% to $6.11, Latina

high school graduates down 7% to $8.31. Unemployment rates for young women with a high school education or less are highest among those categories that have had the steepest wage declines (the 1993 unemployment rate of African-American dropouts aged 26–35, for example, is 27%, rising from 22% in 1989). The wage and employment trends for young males with a high school education or less are, in general, worse than those for women, especially since 1989. Male wages start from higher levels, but the declines are steeper than for women (between 1979 and 1993, the hourly wages of males age 16–35 with a high school education or less dropped by more than 20%; the wages of white dropouts aged 16–25 declined from $7.53 in 1979 to $5.70 in 1993; the wages of African-American dropouts aged 16–25 declined from $7.10 in 1979 to $5.21 in 1993; the wages of African-American high school graduates aged 26–35 dropped by 29% from $12.04 in 1979 to $8.60 in 1993; wages in 1993 dollars). Unemployment among men with a high school education or less has increased substantially since 1989 (the increases are steepest among African-Americans with less than a high school diploma; the 1993 unemployment rate for those aged 16–25 is 42%, up from 35% in 1989; the 1993 rate for those aged 26–35 is 24%, up from 14% in 1989). See Jared Bernstein and Lawrence Mishel, *Trends in the Low-Wage Labor Market and Welfare Reform* (Economic Policy Institute, 1995).

82.   See especially Michael Hout, "Inequality at the Margins: The Effects of Welfare, the Minimum Wage, and Tax Credits on Low-wage Labor Markets" (Working Paper #111, Russell Sage Foundation, April 1997).

83.   Nationally, 1.25 million children received federally subsidized day care. Since 6.5 million children under the age of 13 live in welfare families, demands for placements in an already overburdened system can only grow as more mothers fulfill the job requirements of local welfare-to-work initiatives. In New York City, both working-poor parents and those assigned to workfare are desperate to find good day care centers, which have become overwhelmed. About 75,000 children participate in day care that the city subsidizes (about 20,000 of these children have parents in welfare work programs), but these 75,000 represent only 14% of those who are eligible under the income guidelines (300,000 children between the ages of 3 and 12 are on public assistance in New York City). According to Child Care Inc., a prominent city child care advocacy organization, the city will need to find a way to provide day care for 35,600 new children this year as welfare changes put more mothers to work. Joe Sexton, "Day Care Center Fills as Working and Welfare Parents Compete," *New York Times,* March 24, 1997, p. B1; Editorial Desk, "The Day Care Squeeze," *New York Times,* March 31, 1997, p. A14.

84.   The vast majority of working-poor parents (62% of mothers, 64% of fathers) earned under $5 per hour in 1989, hence the need for inexpensive child care. Yet the working poor are the least likely of all income groups to receive assistance with child care costs. Thirty-seven percent of nonworking poor families and middle-income families receive direct or tax assistance with child care costs, but only 30% of working-poor families receive such assistance. Sandra L. Hofferth, "Caring for Children at the Poverty Line," *Children and Youth Services Review* 17, nos. 1–2 (1995), pp. 61–90.

85.   The Annie E. Casey Foundation has noted that the working poor face special problems with respect to child care compared to poor families who are out of the labor market: "Children of the working poor [face] an insufficiency of parental time

and a lack of quality preschool or other appropriate day care. . . . The problem of too little time is compounded by their frequent inability to afford adequate child care to compensate for their absence from the home." Annie E. Casey Foundation, *Kids Count* (1996).

86.   Under the 1996 federal welfare law, states are restricted from using federal funds—which now come as block grants called Temporary Assistance for Needy Families grants (TANF)—to provide assistance to most families for more than five years. States may also impose shorter limits. In addition, in order to qualify for the full TANF grant, states must have 25% of recipients engaged in specific work activities in 1997 and must have 50% engaged in year 2002 (exceptions to the mandated participation rates include cases with single parents who have children under age one; the few two-parent families who are eligible have higher mandated participation rates). See Dan Bloom, *After AFDC, Welfare-to-Work Choices and Challenges for States* (Manpower Demonstration Research Corporation, 1997).

87.   Joe Sexton, "Working and Welfare Parents Compete for Daycare Slots," *New York Times,* March 24, 1997, p. A12.

88.   In "Beyond the Street Corner: The Hidden Diversity of High-Poverty Neighborhoods" (forthcoming in *Urban Geography*), Paul Jargowsky reviews a variety of census data to show that urban "high-poverty" neighborhoods are more heterogeneous than is commonly perceived. Researchers generally define a census tract as a high poverty area if more than 40% of its residents are poor. Jargowsky shows that many residents in urban high-poverty tracts are gainfully employed—usually in low-skill jobs with shorter hours and less money than non-high-poverty residents. Jargowsky finds that job earnings account for nearly the same proportion of total income in high-poverty areas as they do elsewhere. In fact, the majority of urban high-poverty households do not receive government assistance.

89.   More than half of today's CUNY community college students have a native language other than English. Karen W. Arenson, "Untimely Degrees," *New York Times,* March 19, 1997, p. B3.

90.   Tuition rates and other costs have risen, but student incomes have declined. While grants have become more limited, the number of students applying for financial aid at CUNY rose from 98,000 to 168,000 in the past seven years. There are about 205,000 students in total. Arenson, "Untimely Degrees," p. B3. These changes mark a nationwide trend in which students are taking on more debt. Since 1993, limits on government-backed student loans have increased and the loans themselves have become easier to get. According to Professor Thomas Kane of the Kennedy School of Government, students and their families are taking on an increasing share of college costs as tuition rates rise and loans supplant outright grants. See Halimah Abdullah, "Credit Lures College Students Down Path to Onerous Debt," *New York Times,* August 24, 1997, p. A20.

91.   This full-time tuition rate is for in-state residents. Full-time tuition for in-state residents at CUNY's senior colleges is $3,200 per year. See Arenson, "Untimely Degrees," p. B3. The real public tuition levels at public four-year and two-year institutions rose 91% and 72% respectively between 1980 and 1995, a period when the proportion of college-age youths enrolled in college grew by one-third. In-state tuition hikes lead to wider enrollment gaps between high-income and low-income youth.

While states provide about $44 billion of financial assistance annually (federal aid accounts for about $13 billion), over 90% of these funds takes the form of across-the-board subsidies intended to lower tuition for all students. Grant aid targeted specifically toward low-income youth has declined. For example, the maximum real value of the federal government's grant for low-income undergraduates, the Pell Grant, has fallen by 35% since 1980. See Thomas J. Kane, "College Costs, Borrowing Constraints and the Timing of College Entry" (NBER Working Paper no. 5164, 1995); Thomas J. Kane, "Beyond Tax Relief: Long-Term Challenges in Financing Higher Education," *National Tax Journal* 50, no. 2 (June 1997), pp. 335–49.

92.   Under open admissions, any New York City high school graduate with a 70 average can go to a two-year CUNY college, and any student with an 80 average can go to a four-year CUNY college. (New requirements have recently been adopted. For example, students at senior colleges are no longer permitted to enroll if they require remedial work. When "open admissions" first began, enrollment jumped from about 20,000 to 35,000 and minority enrollment increased from 9% to 24%. About half the students enrolled would not have been qualified without open admissions. Since that time, critics have argued that open admissions led to lower academic standards and substandard education at CUNY because so many students needed remedial help. See James Traub, *City on a Hill: Testing the American Dream at City College* (Addison-Wesley, 1994). And early studies showed high dropout rates among open-admissions students. A recent study, however, David E. Lavin and David Hyllegard, *Changing the Odds: Open Admissions and the Life Chances of the Disadvantaged* (Yale University Press, 1997), found that while few students finish quickly, more than half the students surveyed do earn bachelor's degrees, sometimes as much as ten years after their first semester. The study estimated that during one year in the 1980s, graduates admitted under open admissions earned $67 million more than they would have had the policy not been instituted. See Karen W. Arenson, "Study Details CUNY Successes from Open-Admissions Policy," *New York Times*, May 7, 1996, p. A1.

93.   In 1993, the poverty line for a married couple with two children was $14,654. Assuming that the wife worked twenty hours per week at minimum wage, the husband would need, after Social Security taxes, a take-home weekly pay of $232 to equal the poverty line. Less than three-fourths of married fathers with a high school degree or its equivalent earn this much or more per week. The 1993 poverty line for a single mother with two children was $11,642. The mother would need, after Social Security taxes, take-home weekly pay of $252 to equal the poverty line. Less than 30% of single mothers with a high school diploma or its equivalent earn this much or more per week. Holding a job, with no other public or private support, is not adequate to escape poverty for many of today's poor families. See Blank, *It Takes a Nation*, table 2.1. See also Edin and Lein, *Making Ends Meet*.

94.   Immigrants have long endured public resentment. But until recently, many economists agreed that immigration is good for the nation's economy and its citizens, and has few effects on most regional labor markets, even those receiving large immigrant flows. See, for example, David Card, "The Impact of the Mariel Boatlift on the Miami Labor Market," *Industrial and Labor Relations Review* 43, no. 2 (1990), pp. 245–57. Shifts in immigrant waves toward less-skilled workers, however, have led some economists to link immigration not only to increased expenditures in public welfare programs such as SSI, but to downward pressure on the wages of the native

low-skilled, accounting for some of the increase in income inequality that began in the early 1980s. In 1980, 13% of workers with less than a high school education were immigrants; in 1990, the proportion increased to nearly 25%. See George J. Borjas, "The Internationalization of the U.S. Labor Market and the Wage Structure," *Economic Policy Review* 1, no. 1 (January 1995), pp. 3–8; George J. Borjas, Richard B. Freeman, and Lawrence F. Katz, "On the Labor Market Impacts of Immigration and Trade," in George J. Borjas and Richard B. Freeman, eds., *Immigration and the Work Force: Economic Consequences for the United States and Source Areas* (University of Chicago Press, 1992), pp. 213–44. See also George J. Borjas, "The New Economics of Immigration," *Atlantic,* November 1996, pp. 72–80.

95.   A supplemental appropriations act passed in Congress in June 1997 gives states the authority to purchase food stamps from the federal government for use in state-funded food assistance programs for legal immigrants. See Stacey Dean, "States Now Have the Option to Purchase Food Stamps to Provide Food Assistance to Legal Immigrants" (Center on Budget and Policy Priorities, August 12, 1997).

96.   The Balanced Budget Act restores SSI and SSI-related Medicaid benefits and eligibility to legal immigrants who were in the country prior to August 22, 1996, and it extends refugees' and asylees' eligibility for SSI and Medicaid from five to seven years. See Dean, "States Now Have the Option to Purchase Food Stamps to Provide Food Assistance to Legal Immigrants."

97.   According to George Soros, founder of the Emma Lazarus Fund, a charity that assists legal immigrants, legal immigrants make up 6% of those on public aid. George Soros, "Legal Immigrants Deserve a Safety Net," *New York Times,* August 22, 1997, p. A23. But the reductions in benefits to legal immigrants account for more than 40% of the savings in the new welfare law. There are currently 1.4 million applicants waiting an average of twenty-one months to become citizens.

98.   Conservatives argue that immigrants ship in their elder relatives who haven't "paid in" and do not deserve to be supported by American taxpayers. Moreover, economists such as Borjas claim that even the children of today's low-skilled immigrants are problematic because they tend to remain low-skilled, so that they are altering the skills of the labor force overall and end up not paying taxes at the rate that better-skilled workers do, though they are providing cheap labor to corporations and to affluent families. George Borjas, "The Welfare Magnate: For More and More Immigrants, America is Becoming Land of Welfare Opportunities," *National Review* 48, no. 4 (1996), pp. 48–51.

Chapter 3: Getting a Job in the Inner City

1.   The Greater Upstate Law Project and NYC-based Housing Works, both welfare rights advocacy organizations, prepared this analysis from Governor Pataki's administrative reports as well as from NYS Department of Social Services and Department of Labor data. These show that 570,100 New Yorkers are unemployed and 618,628 adults are on AFDC or Home Relief (single cases) for a total of 1.2 million potential job-seekers. Department of Labor, *Occupational Outlook Through 1999* (1995), projects that 242,620 jobs will be available every year between 1996 and 1999. The difference between the potential supply and the potential demand is therefore nearly one

million in the state of New York. In New York City alone, there are 282,100 unemployed persons and 442,120 adults receiving public assistance. The difference in number between these potential job-seekers and DOL's projected 90,980 NYC job openings creates a job gap of 633,240, more than half of the state total. See Greater Upstate Law Project Report, "New York State Employment: Job Seekers, Job Gap" (March 1996); and Greater Upstate Law Project Report, "New York State Employment Job Gap, Updated" (June 1996).

2. New York City is experiencing a moderate recovery from a locally severe recession occurring from 1989 to 1992. The City Office of Management and Budget has forecast a net gain of 92,000 payroll jobs from 1995 through 1999. If this forecast is accurate, there will still be a net loss of 200,000 jobs between 1989 and 1999. See "Work to Be Done: Report of the Borough Presidents' Task Force on Education, Employment and Welfare" (August 1995).

3. Drug dealing tends not to be a woman's business. Crime is generally a male enterprise—and an expanding one at that. We know from youth surveys that a large number of young men from poor urban neighborhoods admit that they participate in criminal activity. Richard B. Freeman, "Why Do So Many Young American Men Commit Crimes and What Might We Do About It?" (NBER Working Paper 5451, 1996), argues that the rise in criminal activity among low-skilled young men over the past twenty years is influenced by the job market disincentives of the 1980s and 1990s.

4. Most young students, those in grades six through eight, who hold jobs are from disadvantaged backgrounds. D. C. Gottfredson, "Youth Employment, Crime and Schooling: A Longitudinal Study of a National Sample," *Developmental Psychology* 21 (1985), pp. 419–32. See also Catherine M. Yamoor and Jaylin T. Mortimer, "Age and Gender Differences in the Effects of Employment on Adolescent Achievement and Well-being," *Youth and Society* 22, no. 2 (December 1990), pp. 225–40. Older teenage workers are just as likely to come from middle-class homes.

5. Academics, too, often focus upon adolescents' expanding interests in acquiring consumer goods as a primary motivation for employment; see Ellen Greenberger and L. Steinberg, *When Teenagers Work* (Basic Books, 1986), and Laurence Steinberg, *Beyond the Classroom* (Simon & Schuster, 1996). This is due, in part, to the changing composition of the teenage workforce, once largely made up of youth from lower classes. See Joseph F. Kett, *Rites of Passage* (Basic Books, 1977). The teenage workforce today, which has grown enormously since the 1950s, contains just as many solidly middle-class young people, whose total earnings, in most cases, may be spent on luxuries. Steinberg, for example, found that only 10% of adolescent workers interviewed in his study saved most or all of their earnings for college. Steinberg, *Beyond the Classroom*, p. 167. The majority of earnings are spent on clothes, cars, stereo equipment, and socializing. This prevalence for consumer gratification affects the overall portrait of youth employment, making the enterprise look more like another undifferentiated slice of materialism than anything else.

6. Kathryn Edin's research, based on interviews with 214 AFDC mothers from four cities, makes it exceedingly clear that welfare families cannot make it on state payments alone. Edin found that AFDC, food stamps, and SSI combined make up 63% of the mothers' average total monthly income (which just covers expenses). Contributions from children, family, and friends account for a small but significant 7% of income. See Kathryn Edin, "Single Mothers and Child Support: The Possibilities and

Limits of Child Support Policy," *Children and Youth Services Review* 17, no. 102 (1995), pp. 203–30.

7. See Marta Tienda and Jennifer Glass, "Household Structure and Labor Force Participation of Black, Hispanic, and White Mothers," *Demography* 22, no. 3 (1985), pp. 381–94. Through a statistical analysis of 1980 CPA data, Tienda and Glass found that the number and composition of adults in extended families affects their labor force participation. The extended family arrangement alleviates economic hardships by spreading child care and other domestic obligations among more adults, thus allowing greater proportions of wage earners per household.

8. See Mercer Sullivan, *"Getting Paid": Youth, Crime, and Work in the Inner City* (Cornell University Press, 1989), for an account of Puerto Rican families in Sunset Park, Brooklyn.

9. Very young children in immigrant families are also commonly sent "home" to be cared for by relatives who still reside in the country of origin. Patricia Pessar, "The Role of Households in International Migration and the Case of U.S.-Bound Migration from the Dominican Republic," *International Migration Review* 16, no. 2 (1982), pp. 342–34.

10. For discussion of the cooperative (and strained) structure of immigrant residence and family, see Sarah J. Mahler, *American Dreaming: Immigrant Life on the Margins* (Princeton University Press, 1995); Sherri Grasmuck and Patricia Pessar, *Between Two Islands: Dominican International Migration* (University of California Press, 1991); Lloyd H. Rogler and Rosemary Santana Cooney, *Puerto Rican Families in New York City: Intergenerational Processes* (Waterfront Press, 1984); Nina Glick Schiller, Linda Basch, and Cristina Szanton Blanc, eds., *Towards a Transnational Perspective on Migration: Race, Class, Ethnicity, and Nationalism Reconsidered* (New York Academy of Sciences, 1992); Alejandro Portes and Ruben G. Rumbaut, *Immigrant America: A Portrait* (University of California Press, 1990); Nancy Foner, ed., *New Immigrants in New York* (Columbia University Press, 1987); and Leo R. Chavez, "Coresidence and Resistance: Strategies for Survival Among Undocumented Mexicans and Central Americans in the United States," *Urban Anthropology* 19, nos. 1–2 (1990), pp. 31–61.

11. Nationwide, unmarried female household heads with children have higher labor force participation rates than married mothers. Tienda and Glass, "Household Structure and Labor Force Participation of Black, Hispanic, and White Mothers," p. 391.

12. This motivation for employment is not uncommon. See Arlie Hochschild, *The Second Shift: Working Parents and the Revolution at Home* (Viking, 1989), pp. 128–41.

13. Since 1983, federal employment and training programs for disadvantaged youth have been funded through the Job Training Partnership Act (JTPA). The most effective federal youth program is the Job Corps, a year-long residential program that educates and trains young people and places them in jobs. A typical enrollee is an 18-year-old male high school dropout who reads at a sixth-grade level and stays in the program for seven months. The great majority of participants who complete the program find jobs, join the military, or enter school. Hence, the program is moderately successful, although some recent evaluations are less enthusiastic. See W. Norton Grubb, *Learning to Work: The Case for Reintegrating Job Training and Education* (Russell Sage Foundation, 1996), pp. 33–34. The Job Corps achieves better labor market

outcomes than other JTPA youth programs, which have shown little success in effecting post-program labor market success. Howard S. Bloom et al., *The National JTPA Study: Title II-A Impacts on Earnings and Employment at 18 Months* (*Executive Summary*) (U.S. Department of Labor, 1992); Thomas Smith and Michelle Alberti Gambone, "Effectiveness of Federally Funded Employment Training Strategies for Youth," in *Dilemmas in Youth Employment Programming: Findings from the Youth Research and Technical Assistance Project* (U.S. Department of Labor, 1992). Its residential operation, however, makes the Job Corps very expensive, more than $15,000 per student, which severely restricts enrollment. Sar A. Levitan and Frank Gallo, *A Second Chance: Training for Jobs* (W. E. Upjohn Institute for Employment Research, 1988). Thus, most adolescents who qualify never make it into Job Corps or similar long-term training programs. Nonetheless, 700,000 young people nationwide participate annually in the 25-year-old Federal Summer Youth Employment and Training Program (SYETP), the largest public employer of low-income youth. In 1993, the Clinton administration wanted to expand the program and strengthen its educational components, but the proposal was defeated in Congress, largely because the jobs created have a "make work" reputation. Indeed, in the riotous summers of the 1960s, the program was commonly known as "fire insurance" because it helped keep teenagers occupied and off the streets. Since that time, job quality, training, and assessment have improved. In the summer of 1996, New York Sate received $43 million from the federal government to create about 38,000 short-term jobs. The government allocated $625 million to the program nationwide, 75% of the previous year's level.

Currently there are quite a number of demonstration projects around the country that aim to enrich summer youth programs through classroom learning or work-site education, many of which have improved academic outcomes of participants. See Office of the Chief Economist, U.S. Department of Labor, *What's Working (and What's Not): A Summary of Research on the Economic Impacts of Employment and Training Programs* (1995); Jean Baldwin Grossman and Cynthia Sipe, "The Long-Term Impacts of the Summer Training and Education Program" (Philadelphia: Public/-Private Ventures); Arnold H. Packer and Marion W. Pines, *School-to-Work* (Princeton: Eye on Education, 1996). Typically, however, participants (a third of whom are 14- and 15-year-olds) in summer programs work for minimum wage in much less structured settings. Many of them get placements at government agencies, schools, and community-based associations doing maintenance or office work while receiving some remedial education.

Two out of every three youths who are employed in the summer through SYETP placements would otherwise not have worked at all. Jon Crane and David T. Ellwood, "The Summer Youth Employment Program: Private Job Supplement or Substitute" (Harvard University, March 1984). Evaluations of the effects of SYETP are inconclusive. While young people make modest gains in soft skills and career knowledge, there is little evidence that this translates into increased post-program job market success relative to nonparticipants. By itself, summer work experience, which is necessarily short, has not been shown to improve future employability or earnings. Guidelines of the JPTA, which funds SYETP under a separate provision, now favor year-round or sequential training-intensive programs over summer-only employment. See Andrew Hahn and Robert Lerman, *What Works in Youth Employment Policy* (Committee on New American Realities, 1985), pp. 12, 44–45; Natalie Jaffe, *Summer Employment Pro-*

grams for Disadvantaged Youth: Issues and Options (Public/Private Ventures, July 1985); U.S. Department of Labor, Employment and Training Administration, *Skills, Standards and Entry-level Work: Elements of a Strategy for Youth Employability Development* (1995), pp. 50–51; Howard S. Bloom et al., "The National JTPA Study: Overview: Impacts, Benefits, and Costs of Title II-A" (Abt Associates).

14. Mayor Giuliani has been an enthusiastic supporter of workfare jobs and has been criticized for substituting these sub-minimum-wage workers for union labor. Funding for summer youth jobs has been progressively curtailed over the years. It is possible that the tasks Larry performed in the parks will become workfare jobs as well. This is important because it may limit the availability of entry-level public-sector positions for young people coming into the labor market.

15. Janice Haaken and Joyce Korschgen, "Adolescents and Conceptions of Social Relations in the Workplace," *Adolescence* 23 (1988), pp. 1–14, reports that adolescents from higher-status backgrounds have a better understanding than adolescents from disadvantaged backgrounds about the workplace expectations of employers. See also James E. Rosenbaum, Takehiko Kariya, Rick Settersten, and Tony Maier, "Market and Network Theories of the Transition from High School to Work: Their Application to Industrialized Societies," *Annual Review of Sociology* 16 (1990), pp. 263–99.

16. Using employee referrals in hiring is widespread in the hospitality and food service industries. In a study of thirty-three hotels, restaurants, and fast food establishments in urban and suburban areas of Los Angeles County, Roger Waldinger, "Who Makes the Beds? Who Washes the Dishes? Black/Immigrant Competition Reassessed" (University of California Institute of Industrial Relations Working Paper 246, April 1993), found, for example, that virtually all employers relied heavily upon referrals from current employees to hire new entry-level workers, especially for kitchen jobs.

17. See Mark Granovetter, *Getting a Job* (University of Chicago Press, 1995). Granovetter shows how important connections are for professional, technical, and managerial workers. What my study shows is that the same premium applies in low-wage jobs in the inner city. This comports with Mercer Sullivan's ethnographic study of crime and work in three Brooklyn neighborhoods, two of which are high-crime, high-poverty areas. He found that networks, rather than educational credentials or work experience, explained most of the differences in employment success among teenagers from the three neighborhood groups. Sullivan, *"Getting Paid": Youth, Crime, and Work in the Inner City*, p. 103. A lack of effective networks contributes to the growing problem of joblessness among minority youths. In a statistical analysis of the 1981 and 1982 panels of the National Longitudinal Survey of Youth (aged 16 to 23), Harry Holzer, "Informal Job Search and Black Youth Unemployment," *American Economic Review* 77, no. 3 (1987), pp. 446–52, suggests that young African-Americans are much less successful than whites in job searches involving connections through friends and relatives (rather than formal searches through newspaper advertisements, for example) because their personal contacts are simply less advantageous. Granovetter, *Getting a Job*, p. 133, makes the same point on logical grounds. Jomills Henry Braddock II and James M. McPartland, "How Minorities Continue to be Excluded from Equal Employment Opportunities: Research on Labor Market and Institutional Barriers," *Journal of Social Issues* 43, no. 1 (Spring 1987), pp. 5–39, reports that African-Americans with racially mixed networks are more likely to find better-paying, less

segregated work than African-Americans with exclusively African-American networks. Sanders Korenman and Susan Turner, "On Employment Contacts and Differences in Wages Between Minority and White Youths" (manuscript, Humphrey Institute of Public Affairs, University of Minnesota, 1994), found that among similarly qualified disadvantaged youths who found jobs through contacts in Boston, blacks had lower wages than whites. See also James H. Johnson, Jr., Elisa Jayne Bienenstock, and Walter C. Farrell, Jr., "Bridging Social Networks and Female Labor Force Participation in a Multi-Ethnic Metropolis" (n.d.), pp. 15–19; and Nan Lin, "Social Resources and Instrumental Action," in Peter V. Marsden and Nan Lin, eds., *Social Structure and Network Analysis* (Sage Publications, 1982).

18.   Scholars interested in network analysis would also call William's connection with his mother a "strong tie"; she may have "weak ties"—that is, connections with others that are less intimate, less enduring, or less frequent. A study of white male professional, technical, and managerial workers who had recently changed jobs, Mark Granovetter, "The Strength of Weak Ties," *American Journal of Sociology* 78 (1973), pp. 1360–80, found that those who made use of weak ties earned higher wages. In general, weak ties are thought to be more advantageous than strong ties in job-seeking, for weak ties form bridges into social worlds that might contain resources for new or better job knowledge, whereas strong ties are more likely to carry redundant information. It is not clear, however, that the same principle holds in impoverished communities. As Granovetter himself has pointed out, in *Getting a Job*, p. 137, neither strong nor weak ties will be helpful if the contact network holds no information about job opportunities. When entry-level work is sought and where job knowledge is extremely scarce, the strength of contacts appears less important than the sheer size and diversity of a job-seeker's network. The degree of diversity in the social statuses and activities among network contacts increases the possibility that useful information about jobs can reach the job-seeker. See M. Patricia Fernandez Kelly, "Social and Cultural Capital in the Urban Ghetto: Implications for the Economic Sociology of Immigration," in Alejandro Portes, ed., *The Economic Sociology of Immigration* (Russell Sage Foundation, 1995).

19.   Managers are usually well aware that workers who sponsor new applicants feel responsible for a new hire's performance. See Waldinger, "Who Makes the Beds? Who Washes the Dishes? Black-Immigrant Competition Reassessed," p. 6.

20.   Carol Stack discusses the same kinds of conflicts in her classic *All Our Kin* (Harper & Row, 1974). Reciprocity sounds great and is generally helpful. But it is hard for people to pull away from networks, in terms either of money they can lend or help they can give. They risk being held at arm's length themselves.

21.   Grades and test scores, for example, are almost never used by employers to evaluate applicants. Takehiko Kariya and James E. Rosenbaum, "Selection Criteria in the High School-to-Work Transition: Results from the High School and Beyond Surveys in the U.S. and Japan," presented at the annual meeting of the American Sociological Association, Chicago, 1988, and discussed in Rosenbaum, Kariya, Settersten, and Maier, "Market and Network Theories of the Transition from High School to Work," pp. 276–77.

Chapter 4: No Shame in (This) Game

1.   There are further shades of gray below the line of the employed that distinguish those who are searching for jobs and those that have accepted their fate as non-workers, with the latter suffering the greatest stigma of all. To signal a total lack of interest in work is to place oneself outside the pale of the morally worthy altogether.

2.   The application of efficient, deskilled, routinized work by corporate organizations was made famous through Frederick Taylor's system of scientific management, in which meaningful decision-making is deliberately withdrawn from workers and given over to a small number of managers. Each worker, whose performance is easily supervised and evaluated, repeatedly performs a limited number of well-defined tasks, resulting in very uniform products. Social critics have written extensively on the toll such practices take on workers in manufacturing and clerical bureaucracies. But fast food workers, as well as others in the service sector, are required to interact directly with customers, and in very particular ways, even when customers fail to play by the rules. Counter employees are asked to display warm, sincere smiles whether or not such expressions are authentic. Thus demands to subordinate themselves to the work process extend even further into their on-the-job behavior and self-presentation. Firms rarely achieve exact compliance with these requirements; in fact, workers, both individually and collectively, almost always undermine such efforts in all sorts of ways. But good line managers know that regulating workers' appearance, attitudes, and conduct in the name of proper customer service involves workers' most basic means of self-expression and their profound private feelings, which they are asked to actively deny or suppress on a daily basis. Robin Leidner, *Fast Food, Fast Talk: Service Work and the Routinization of Everyday Life* (University of California Press, 1990), is an incisive study of the social negotiations made among managers, workers, and customers at McDonald's, and how these negotiations shape roles, strategies, and identities at the workplace. See also Arlie Hochschild, *The Managed Heart: Commercialization of Human Feeling* (University of California Press, 1983), which explores the nature of "emotional" labor through an analysis of flight attendants and bill collectors, both of whom are expected to engage in deep acting so as to change the status of their customers (in opposite directions).

3.   Leidner, *Fast Food, Fast Talk.*

4.   In areas experiencing exceptionally tight labor markets—including much of the midwest in the late 1990s—wages for these jobs are climbing above the minimum-wage line.

5.   The steepest increases in inner-city poverty took place in the 1970s as a result of rising joblessness and declining wages, which continue today. Aside from housing and educational policies that contributed to these results, there are a host of interdependent economic reasons for these trends: a shift in demand toward higher-educated workers in higher-wage industries, massive industrial restructuring that was especially pernicious in the urban northeast and midwest, and the increasing suburbanization of employment, taking jobs from downtown to metropolitan peripheries. See William Julius Wilson, *When Work Disappears* (Knopf, 1996). America's inner cities have such incredibly impoverished job bases that they are almost always characterized by slack labor markets. Only when the labor supply outside ghetto walls has tightened down to almost impossible levels do we begin to see this tide lift inner-city

boats. Eventually employers do turn to the workers who are low on their preference queues, as we learned in the 1980s during the Massachusetts miracle. See Richard B. Freeman, "Employment and Earnings of Disadvantaged Young Men in a Labor Shortage Economy," and Paul Osterman, "Gains from Growth? The Impact of Full Employment on Poverty in Boston," both in Christopher Jencks and Paul E. Peterson, eds., *The Urban Underclass* (Brookings Institution, 1991). These analyses show not only that tight labor markets help the employment opportunities in our inner cities but also that the people who live there take full advantage of these opportunities when they arise. These conditions are, sadly, rare and generally short-lived. This is one of the many reasons why increasing the minimum wage is so important. Significant increases in the minimum wage could theoretically lead to raising some employment displacement, especially among youth. One of the reasons for the introduction of the minimum wage in the late 1930s was to lower youth competition for jobs. See Paul Osterman, *Getting Started* (MIT Press, 1980). In an analysis of youth labor markets of the 1970s, Osterman argues that while the minimum wage has modest negative effects on youth employment, it is not a major structural source of youth unemployment. But it is difficult to see how already lean retail firms, such as fast food establishments, could do much more to cut the numbers of front-line employees. What is more, only 15% of minimum-wage earners are teens; 39% are the sole earners in their households; 1994 data, U.S. Department of Labor, "Making Work Pay: The Case for Raising the Minimum Wage" (press release, October 2, 1995). The real value of the minimum wage declined sharply throughout the 1980s (it became so low, in fact, that states began to legislate their own minimum wages that were higher than the federal minimum); this alone was a major factor in the increasing wage inequality at the bottom of the U.S. income distribution, especially for women. See John DiNardo, Nicole M. Fortin, and Thomas Lemieux, "Labor Market Institutions and the Distribution of Wages, 1973–1992: A Semiparametric Approach," *Econometrica* 64, no. 5 (September 1996), pp. 1001–44. John DiNardo and Thomas Lemieux, "Diverging Male Wage Inequality in the United States and Canada, 1981–1988: Do Institutions Explain the Difference?," *Industrial and Labor Relations Review*, 50, no. 4 (July 1997), pp. 629–51, finds that unions and changes in minimum wages account for two-thirds of the differential growth in male wage inequality between the United States and Canada. The new minimum-wage hike (to $5.15 in September 1997), brought the purchasing power of the minimum up to a level that is still 14% lower than the minimum wage of 1979. In time we will see whether these increases lead to reduced turnover and heightened productivity in firms that have trouble holding on to good employees, offsetting higher payroll costs. See Chris Tilly, *Half a Job: Bad and Good Part-Time Jobs in a Changing Labor Market* (Tempe University Press, 1996), p. 181. A now famous examination of the effects of a number of state and federal minimum-wage hikes that took place from 1989 to 1992, David Card and Alan B. Krueger, *Myth and Measurement: The New Economics of the Minimum Wage* (Princeton University Press, 1995), finds that, contrary to what economics textbook models predict, these recent increases did not reduce employment and sometimes had modest positive effects. One of Card and Krueger's main empirical studies considers employment in the fast food industry before and after New Jersey advanced its minimum wage in 1992. They conducted surveys of over 400 restaurants in New Jersey and neighboring eastern Pennsylvania before and after the increase, and found that employment in New Jersey was not negatively affected by the wage hike. Indeed, they learned that employment in New Jersey expanded. In fact, employment growth in New Jersey was higher at those restaurants that had to raise their wages to comply with the law than at those that were already paying more than the new minimum. While Card and Krueger, among others, note that the benefits of a minimum wage are not targeted directly at the poor (workers from nonpoor families also work at minimum-wage jobs), workers who earn the minimum or slightly more than the minimum are disproportionately drawn from families in the lower portion of the earnings distribution. "Minimum-wage earners are primarily women (57.9%), have full-time jobs (47.2%) or work between 20 and 35 hours weekly (33.3%), are disproportionately black (15%) or Hispanic (13.8%), and are concentrated in the low-wage retail sector (44.3%)." Lawrence Mishel, Jared Bernstein, and Edith Rasell, "Who Wins with a Higher Minimum Wage" (Economic Policy Institute Briefing Paper, 1995), p. 1.

6. The fact that Harlem residents rejected for these jobs hold these values is some evidence for the preexisting nature of this mind-set—although these rejects had already piled up work experience, which may have contributed to the sharpening of this alternative critique.

7. Scholars and critics acknowledged many problems and inefficiencies in the WPA's function as a relief agency, but emphasized the psychological superiority of paid work over direct relief. See E. Wight Bakke, *The Unemployed Worker: A Study of the Task of Making a Living Without a Job* (Yale University Press, 1940). For history and analysis of the WPA and other work relief programs of the New Deal, see Michael B. Katz, *In the Shadow of the Poorhouse: A Social History of Welfare in America* (Basic Books, 1986); and Nancy E. Rose, *Put to Work: Relief Programs in the Great Depression* (Monthly Review Press, 1994). Political writer Mickey Kaus writes frequently on the stigma of welfare and the need for a WPA-like jobs program. See, for example, Mickey Kaus, *The End of Equality* (Basic Books, 1992).

8. For families with health problems, the value of Medicaid programs, which usually offer AFDC recipients and their children free doctor visits, hospitalization, and some prescription drugs, can easily exceed the value of welfare cash payments. Kathryn Edin and Laura Lein, *Making Ends Meet: How Single Mothers Survive Welfare and Low-Wage Work* (Russell Sage Foundation, 1997), p. 35. See also Christopher Jencks and Kathryn Edin, "Do Poor Women Have the Right to Bear Children?" *American Prospect* 20 (Winter 1995), pp. 43–52. Nationwide, nine out of ten mothers who rely on cash assistance also receive food stamps. About one in ten lives in public housing and about one in ten receives a subsidy to live in private housing, paying 30% of their cash income for rent. See Edin and Lein, *Making Ends Meet*, p. 36. See also Committee on Ways and Means, U.S. House of Representatives, *Overview of Entitlement Programs (Green Book)* (U.S. Government Printing Office, 1995), table 10–27.

9. Edin and Lein, *Making Ends Meet*, documents this dilemma through extensive interviews in four cities (Chicago, Boston, San Antonio, and Charleston, South Carolina) with 379 low-income single mothers, about half of whom received cash benefits from welfare. They asked each welfare-reliant mother what she felt she would need to earn in order to leave welfare for work. Responses varied according to how many children each mother was supporting as well as the health status and history of each family. About 70% of the mothers gave estimates between $8 and $10 per hour (although, in truth, single mothers leave welfare for wages that are much smaller).

Leaving welfare and entering the labor force means new health costs (since few low-wage employers provide medical plans, and when they do, deductibles and copayments still raise expenses), new transportation costs for traveling both to the workplace and to the daycare provider (commuting to the suburbs is time-consuming and inconvenient—buying and maintaining a used car is a huge goal for many single mothers), and, sometimes, higher housing costs (subsidized housing costs increase when incomes rise) and clothing costs (depending on the job). Using national survey data to approximate some outlays, Edin and Lein found that entering the labor force cost single mothers a huge sum—single mothers who worked spent $2,800 more per year on medical care, transportation, child care, and clothing than did single mothers receiving welfare. They also calculated what the average welfare-reliant mother in the sample would need to earn to maintain the same standard of living she had on welfare. The results agreed roughly with the figures the mothers themselves gave: about $8 or $9 an hour. But the mothers in the sample knew that they could not gain a $9-an-hour job with their skills. Indeed, Kathleen Mullan Harris, "Life After Welfare: Women, Work and Repeat Dependency," *American Sociological Review* 61 (1996), pp. 207–46, shows that throughout the 1980s, women who went from welfare to work earned an average of $6.11 per hour in 1991 dollars. These earnings represent those of the highest-skilled recipients who exit welfare. A full-time, year-round worker with characteristics similar to the average single mother receiving welfare in the 1980s earned just $5.15 in 1991 dollars. Charles Michalopoulos and Irwin Garfinkel, "Reducing Welfare Dependence and Poverty of Single Mothers by Means of Earnings and Child Support: Wishful Thinking and Realistic Possibilities" (Discussion Paper 882–89, Institute for Research on Poverty, University of Wisconsin-Madison, 1989). Single mothers on welfare know that leaving welfare for a low-skilled job will make them worse off than they were on welfare, yet the fact that most recipients receive benefits for brief periods suggests that they prefer work over welfare when at all possible. By looking at their sample of low-wage-reliant single mothers, Edin and Lein found that these mothers experienced special circumstances that lowered the costs of working, such as having only school-age children, receiving timely and adequate child support payments, paying little for rent, child care, or transportation by virtue of social networks and help from kin, or having access to full health coverage for themselves and their children. Most women in this set had been on AFDC before. And despite the fact that they reported heightened self-esteem associated with paid work and consider welfare a very stigmatizing last resort, low-wage work often forces mothers back into welfare when crises arise. According to national data, almost two-thirds of welfare recipients who had left welfare for work return to welfare rolls within six years. Kathleen Mullan Harris and Kathryn Edin, "From Welfare to Work and Back Again" (paper presented at the New School for Social Research conference "After AFDC: Reshaping the Anti-Poverty Agenda," November 16, 1996), cited in Edin and Lein, *Making Ends Meet*, p. 140. See Edin and Lein, *Making Ends Meet*, pp. 83–142.

10.   The size of single-parent families, especially those of teen mothers, is often exaggerated. The average number of children in female-headed households is less than two. In fact, nearly half of all AFDC families have only one child. The proportion of children living in single-parent families has, however, increased dramatically (from 8% percent in 1965 to 22% in 1992), and much of this increase is due to out-of-wedlock births. See Gary D. Sandefur and Tom Wells, "Trends in AFDC Participation

Rates: The Implications for Welfare Reform" (Institute for Research on Poverty Discussion Paper 1116-96, University of Wisconsin–Madison, 1996); June M. Axinn and Amy E. Hirsch, "Welfare and the 'Reform' of Women," *Families in Society* 74, no. 9 (November 1993), pp. 563–72; Donald J. Hernandez, *America's Children: Resources from Family, Government, and the Economy* (Russell Sage Foundation, 1993). Yet while "teenage pregnancy"—often a code word for youth immorality, supposed black licentiousness, ghetto poverty, or all three—became a convenient watchword in our vocabulary on social ills in the early 1980s, few stopped to notice that teenage women were having babies at a slower rate than in the 1950s, and that the probability that an unmarried black woman will give birth has actually declined since that time. The probability that a single white woman will give birth has risen only slightly; Rebecca M. Blank, *It Takes a Nation: A New Agenda for Fighting Poverty* (Russell Sage Foundation, 1997), p. 35. The proportion of out-of-wedlock births is much higher among black women, yet "between 1980 and 1992, when the rate of births outside of marriage increased nationally by 54 percent, it rose 94 percent for whites and only 9 percent for blacks." William Julius Wilson, *When Work Disappears: The World of the New Urban Poor* (Vintage Books, 1997), p. 87. For a discussion on how teenage pregnancy issues have been constructed in our nation's recent public discourse and how they have figured in our past social history, see Kristen Luker, *Dubious Conceptions: The Politics of Teenage Pregnancy* (Harvard University Press, 1996). The meaningful difference is not found in the birthrates; rather, it is that young people are less and less likely to marry. And in inner-city neighborhoods, joblessness among young men has played an important role in the decline of marriage. Wilson, *When Work Disappears*, p. 96. But this trend to not marry cuts across all income levels. Marriage among mothers has declined because women's position in the labor market has improved, especially among educated women; because men's wage rates have dropped, especially among low-skilled men; and because the social stigma of unwed motherhood has declined. See Rebecca M. Blank, "What Are the Causes Behind Declining Marriage Rates and Rising Numbers of Single Mothers?" in R. Kent Weaver and William Dickens, eds., *Looking Before We Leap: Social Science and Welfare Reform* (Brookings Institution, 1995), p. 33. Conservatives argue that welfare payments drive an increase in nonmarital births, but there is no persuasive scientific evidence for such a relationship. Very slight positive associations are found among white women and almost none among black women; for a review of ten statistical studies, see Blank, "What Are the Causes Behind Declining Marriage Rates and Rising Numbers of Single Mothers?" pp. 30–34. In fact, assistance to single mothers in the United States is low compared to that in other industrialized nations, while our rate of single motherhood and teen pregnancy is comparatively very high. The rate of out-of-wedlock teen childbearing in the United States has almost doubled since 1975, despite the fact that during that period the real value of AFDC, food stamps, and Medicaid has fallen. Wilson, *When Work Disappears*, p. 94. When young mothers do enter the welfare system, those with young children and those with three or more children stay on assistance rolls longer. Likewise, those with lower levels of education and no recent work experience spend longer than average on AFDC. While more than half of welfare exits occur when a recipient finds paid work, as many as 40% of these women return to AFDC within one year because of a host of reasons—low pay, poor working conditions, lack of mobility potential, inadequate skills, layoffs and terminations, child care and medical problems, domestic violence, housing instability—most of which are related to their marginal positions vis-à-vis the labor market. LaDonna A. Pavetti, "Who Spends Longer Periods of Time Receiving Welfare? Why Do People Who Leave Welfare for Jobs Return to the Welfare Rolls," in R. Kent Weaver and William Dickens, eds., *Looking Before We Leap: Social Science and Welfare Reform* (Brookings Institution, 1995), pp. 38–47. See also Kathleen Mullan Harris, "Work and Welfare Among Single Mothers in Poverty," *American Journal of Sociology* 99 (1993), pp. 317–52. Education, job skills, and limited child care constraints among young mothers increase the probability for stable jobs, welfare exits, and marriage. Kathleen Mullan Harris, *Teen Mothers and the Revolving Welfare Door* (Temple University Press, 1997).

11.   It is important to note, however, that the misfortunes of many teen mothers, who disproportionately come from lower-income homes and attend lower-quality schools, have at least as much to do with their poverty as with their age. There is increasing evidence that teenage mothers do not face worse employment and wage conditions than other single mothers who come from similar backgrounds; see Blank, *It Takes a Nation*, p. 38. Arline Geronimus and Sanders Korenman investigated outcomes among pairs of sisters living in the same neighborhood, one having had a child in her teens, the other not having children before age twenty. They found that by their mid-20s, those who had children in their teen years earned only slightly less than did, in their mid-20s, their sisters who did not have children in their teens (both groups did poorly). In fact, the teen mothers were only slightly more likely to drop out of high school than their sisters who postponed childbearing, and, on the whole, did no worse than the mothers who gave birth later in life. See Arline Geronimus and Sanders Korenman, "The Socioeconomic Consequences of Teen Childbearing Reconsidered," *Quarterly Journal of Economics* 107 (1992), pp. 1187–1214; Arline Geronimus and Sanders Korenman, "The Socioeconomic Costs of Teenage Childbearing: Evidence and Interpretation," *Demography* 30, no. 2 (1993), pp. 281–96; Arline T. Geronimus, Sanders Korenman, and Marianne M. Hillemeier, "Does Young Maternal Age Adversely Affect Child Development? Evidence from Cousin Comparisons in the United States," *Population and Development Review* 20, no. 3 (September 1994), pp. 585–611; Saul D. Hoffman, E. Michael Foster, and Frank F. Furstenberg, Jr., "Reevaluating the Costs of Teenage Childbearing," *Demography* 30, no. 1 (1993), pp. 1–13. Teenage mothers work less and use more public assistance in their early twenties, but they work more and use less public assistance in their late 20s than non-teenage mothers from similar backgrounds; see Blank, "What Are the Causes Behind Declining Marriage Rates and Rising Numbers of Single Mothers?" p. 35. See also V. Joseph Hotz, Susan Williams McElroy, and Seth G. Sanders, "The Costs and Consequences of Teenage Childbearing for Mothers" (Working Paper 95-1, Irving B. Harris Graduate School of Public Policy, 1995).

12.   Among black families, grandmothers have traditionally served as "kin keepers," especially keepers of grandchilden. This role is a prestigious one, imbued with both moral authority and a sense of resigned hardship. The function of grandmother as kin keeper is emphasized among poor black families and tends to diminish with upward mobility. See Elijah Anderson, "The Black Inner City Grandmother: Transition of a Heroic Type?" in Thomas R. Swartz and Kathleen Maas Weigert, eds., *America's Working Poor* (University of Notre Dame Press, 1995), pp. 9–43. Anderson interviewed inner-city grandmothers, their children, and other residents and found

that economic and social changes in the inner city, especially the expansion of street culture that accompanied the introduction of crack cocaine, have contributed to a decline in authority and an increase in stress for women, often aged younger than 40, who take on this role.

13.   Under the new welfare law, eligibility requirements for legal immigrants' participation in Medicaid, food stamps, cash assistance, and SSI change dramatically. Those elderly and disabled legal immigrants receiving SSI on August 22, 1996, will remain eligible until the Social Security Administration determines whether they qualify under the new rules. Most will not qualify. Legal immigrants entering the United States after August 22, 1996, are ineligible for SSI until they become citizens. Exceptions to this rule are members of the U.S. Armed Forces and veterans, and their spouses and dependent children; certain immigrants in their first five years in the United States who are fleeing oppression; and certain legal immigrants with substantial work histories in the United States, with some of their spouses and children. David Super, "Legal Immigrants' Eligibility for Welfare, Medicaid, SSI, and Food Stamps Under the New Welfare Law" (Special Report Series, Center on Budget and Policy Priorities, January 21, 1997). The Social Security Administration estimates that these changes will take about 500,000 legal immigrants off of SSI roles, reducing expenditures by more than $2 billion in fiscal year 1988. See "Proposals in the President's FY 1988 Budget Affecting Supplemental Security Income [SSI] Eligibility Rules for Certain Legal Immigrants" (Fact Sheet, Social Security Administration, February 1997).

14.   Cash welfare and food stamps covered about three-fifths of the expenses of the welfare-reliant mothers in Edin and Lein's study. The main jobs of the working single mothers in the same study covered 63% of expenses. For details on how both groups of single mothers survived the gap between income and expenses through social networks, cash contributions from family, friends, boyfriends, and absent fathers, supplemental work, and help from private charities, see Edin and Lein, *Making Ends Meet,* pp. 147–91.

15.   The cultural demands on working mothers are, however, fraught with contradictions. As the celebrated "au pair murder trial" in Massachusetts unfolded in the fall of 1997, in which a young foreign baby-sitter was convicted of murdering an infant in her charge while the child's mother worked as an ophthalmologist part-time, a hail of criticism came down on working mothers. This case crystallized the dilemmas of working parents who are supposed to be in the labor force but to stay with their children at the same time. For more on this, see ch. 4, "The Problem of the Moral Mother," in Katherine Newman, *Declining Fortunes: The Withering of the American Dream* (Basic Books, 1993).

16.   The increased cultural importance of work has important ramifications on the way that home and family are lived and imagined by time-starved parents and their children. See Arlie Russell Hochschild, *The Time Bind: When Work Becomes Home and Home Becomes Work* (Metropolitan Books, 1997).

CHAPTER 5: SCHOOL AND SKILL IN THE LOW-WAGE WORLD

1. For a review of the literature, see Bassem N. Kablaoui and Albert J. Pautler, Jr., "The Effects of Part-Time Work Experience on High School Students," in Albert J. Pautler, Jr., ed., *High School to Employment Transition: Contemporary Issues* (Prakken Publications, 1994). A few studies find that limited work experience has no effect on grades and, indeed, is associated with a higher likelihood of school completion. See, for example, Ronald D'Amico and Paula Baker, "The Nature and Consequences of High School Employment," in Paula Baker et al., eds., *Pathways to the Future: A Report on the National Longitudinal Surveys of Youth Labor Market Experience in 1982*, vol. 4 (Ohio State University, Center for Human Resource Research, 1984). In fact, there is some consensus that teenagers who work earn higher wages in later years. The majority of studies, however, point out that whatever benefits work experience brings students (such as developed self-reliance and the adoption of responsible work habits) are paid for by a drop in school performance and attendance when the time spent at work climbs to more than fifteen or twenty hours per week.

2. The emphasis parents place on college is well founded. The futures of students who do not go to college appear dim. A forecast by the Bureau of Labor Statistics, Ronald E. Kutscher, "Projections 2000: Overview and Implications of the Projections to 2000," *Monthly Labor Review*, September 1987, pp. 3–9, predicts that while demands for workers with even a little college will increase, demands for workers with only a high school diploma will decline—and the jobs offered will not likely be permanent. Steady jobs with career prospects are in decline, while part-time, temporary, and contract employment, all of which lack job security, are on the rise. See Eileen Appelbaum, "Structural Change and the Growth of Part-Time and Temporary Employment," in Virginia L. du Rivage, ed., *New Policies for the Part-Time and Contingent Workforce* (M. E. Sharpe, 1992); Arne L. Kalleberg and Kathryn Schmidt, "Contingent Employment in Organizations," in Arne L. Kalleberg, David Knoke, Peter V. Marsden, and Joe L. Spaeth, eds., *Organizations in America* (Sage Publications, 1996). Recent labor market studies characterize young workers with few educational credentials as floundering from one short-term job to another. See Paul Osterman, "The Job Market for Adolescents," in David Stern and Dorothy Eichorn, eds., *Adolescence and Work* (Lawrence Erlbaum 1989). Our nation has no clear policy about what to do with students who will not proceed to college. See Richard H. de Lone, "School-to-Work Transition: Failings, Dilemmas and Policy Options," in *Dilemmas in Youth Employment Programming: Findings from the Youth Research and Technical Assistance Project* (U.S. Department of Labor, Research and Evaluation Report Series 92-C, vol. 1, 1992), pp. 223–91. Funding provided by the Job Training Partnership Act (JPTA), for example, intended to help disadvantaged youth prepare for and find jobs, is very limited in scope, serving only about 5% of the eligible youth population. National Commission for Employment Policy, *The Job Training Partnership Act* (1987). According to National Center on Education and the Economy, *America's Choice: High skills or Low Wages* (Commission on the Skills of the American Workforce, 1990), the United States may have the very worst school-to-employment transition system among developed nations. In recent years, the skills and employability of the non-college-bound has gained attention as the issue has begun to be understood not only as a social problem but, especially in the private sector, as a risk for the nation's competitiveness in a

global economy. See National Commission on Excellence in Education, *A Nation at Risk* (1983). Recommendations to address the problem include increasing business investment in the training of the workforce and developing a national system of training of entry-level workers modeled on European programs. In 1994, Congress passed the School-to-Work Opportunities Act, which aims to improve the skills and productivity of the nation's workforce by better integrating work experience and formal education for the career development of youth. States and localities have begun programs that coordinate learning in high school and the workplace through partnerships of educators and employers, some of which started before the legislation was enacted. See U.S. Congress, Office of Technology Assessment, *Learning to Work: Making the Transition from School to Work,* OTA-EHR-637 (Government Printing Office, 1995); Edward Pauly, Hilary Kopp, and Joshua Haimson, *Home-Grown Lessons: Innovative Programs Linking Work and High School* (Manpower Demonstration Research Corporation, 1994); David Stern et al., *School to Work: Research on Programs in the United States,* Stanford Series on Education and Public Policy, no. 17 (Falmer Press, 1995).

3. The earnings distribution in the U.S. labor market was very stable from the 1940s through the 1960s; in the early 1970s, it gradually widened and became more unstable, a trend that accelerated throughout the 1980s, having devastating effects on the low-skilled. In 1979, among men with less than ten years of work experience, those with a college degree earned 23% more than high school graduates; in 1989, they earned 43% more. The trend is the same among women with less than ten years of experience: they earned 32% more than high school graduates in 1979 and 54% more in 1989. Similar trends are found among workers with many years of experience. Part of this rise in relative earnings of college graduates is explained by supply and demand: in the 1980s, the demand for college-educated workers increased while the proportion of the college-educated workforce grew more slowly. In northern urban areas, in which educational requirements for employment were traditionally low, the change in the education level of jobs and jobholders has been dramatic. In New York City, for example, while the number of working people without high school diplomas declined 26% between 1980 and 1990, the percent of working people who graduated from college increased 54%. This represents a loss of 135,000 jobs in industries with low education requirements and a gain of 30,000 jobs in industries whose occupations require some college. John D. Kasarda, "Industrial Restructuring and the Changing Location of Jobs," in Reynolds Farley, ed., *State of the Union: America in the 1990s,* vol. 1, *Economic Trends* (Russell Sage Foundation, 1995), pp. 215–67. Nationwide, the average real wages of male college graduates rose 8%, but the wages for male high school graduates fell by 40%. The least-skilled workers had greater difficulty in finding jobs with adequate wages. Real wages for young high school graduates at the 10th percentile of the workforce's income distribution were almost 20% lower in the late 1980s than in 1963. See Sheldon Danziger and Peter Gottschalk, *America Unequal* (Harvard University Press, 1995), pp. 116–17; see also Lawrence F. Katz and Kevin M. Murphy, "Changes in Relative Wages, 1963–1987: Supply and Demand Factors," *Quarterly Journal of Economics* 107 (February 1992), pp. 35–78; Chinhui Juhn, Kevin M. Murphy, and Brooks Pierce, "Wage Inequality and the Rise in the Returns to Skill," *Journal of Political Economy* 101 (June 1993), pp. 410–42. By 1990, the number of year-round, full-time workers earning less than $12,195, the poverty level for a four-person family, had grown to over 14 million, representing 18% of the labor force. See U.S.

Bureau of the Census, "Workers with Low Earnings: 1963 to 1990," *Current Population Reports* P-60, no. 178 (Government Printing Office, 1992).

4. See, for example, Amy Saltzman, "Mom, Dad, I Want a Job," *U.S. News and World Report* 114, no. 19 (May 17, 1993), p.68. According to Laurence Steinberg, *Beyond the Classroom: Why School Reform Has Failed and What Parents Need to Do*, (Simon & Schuster, 1996), pp. 164–69, students who work long hours perform worse in school and are less committed to their education than students who work less or not at all. Steinberg reports that working students have less time to devote to schoolwork, and that this gradually decreases students' commitment to education. What's more, he notes that the excitement from earning spending money contributes to daydreaming and a further erosion of commitment—so much so that those students who have worked long hours for a prolonged period are more likely than their non- or less-working counterparts to drop out of school altogether. The negative impact of youth work was first discussed in the book by Ellen Greenberger and Laurence Steinberg, *When Teenagers Work: The Psychological and Social Costs of Adolescent Employment* (Basic Books, 1986), which discussed findings from a body of survey research that began to mushroom in the early 1980s. Social scientists warned then that high school students working long hours, defined variously as ten, fifteen, or twenty hours, were more likely to engage in drug and alcohol use, school misconduct, and antisocial behavior. Researchers argued that because adolescent jobs are almost always stressful and unstimulating, they contribute in making working teens more deviant and cynical, less interested in school, and less involved with their parents. More recently, reports on the effects of adolescent employment have begun to focus more specifically on characteristics of students and their jobs, mechanisms of cause and effect, and, most of all, the amount of work that students engage in. Scholars have begun to speak of a "threshold" of twenty hours of work per week beyond which a typical student's school performance demonstrably suffers. See, among others, Jerald G. Bachman and John Schulenberg, "How Part-Time Work Intensity Relates to Drug Use, Problem Behavior, Time Use, and Satisfaction Among High School Seniors: Are These Consequences or Merely Correlates?" *Developmental Psychology* 29 (1993), pp. 220–35; H. Marsh, "Employment During High School: Character Building or a Subversion of Academic Goals?," *Sociology of Education* 64 (1991), pp. 172–89. Students working long hours are also reported to have lower interests in school and in further educational attainment. See Ronald D'Amico, "Does Employment During High School Impair Academic Progess?" *Sociology of Education* 57 (1984), pp. 152–64; J. Mortimer and M. Finch, "The Effects of Part-Time Work on Adolescents' Self-Concept and Achievement," in K. Borman and J. Reisman, eds., *Becoming a Worker* (Ablex, 1986). For a review of the literature, see Laurence Steinberg and Elizabeth Cauffman, "The Impact of Employment on Adolescent Development," *Annals of Child Development* 11 (1995), pp. 131–66.

5. Indeed, landing an after-school job is much more difficult in places like Harlem. The job market is poor, the students have few connections, and their skills, like those of so many disadvantaged youth, are often perceived by employers to be lacking. See E. R. Reisner and M. Balasubramaniam, *School to Work Transition Services for Disadvantaged Youth Enrolled in Vocational Education* (Policy Studies Association, 1989); Marc Bendick, Charles Jackson, and Victor Reinoso, "Measuring Employment Discrimination Through Controlled Experiments," *Review of Black*

Political Economy 23 (1994), pp. 25–48. Nationwide, survey studies agree that white students are much more likely to be employed than black or Hispanic students. See Kablaoui and Pautler, "Effects of Part-Time Work Experience on High School Students," p. 88. Middle-income students, especially those having a professional parent, are also more likely to participate in the workforce than lower-income students. Black males have the most difficult time finding work and have the lowest rate of student employment. Michael E. Borus, ed., *Tomorrow's Workers* (Lexington Books, 1983). This may have serious consequences. One study, Ronald D'Amico and Nan Maxwell, "The Impact of Post-School Joblessness on Male Black-White Wage Differentials," *Industrial Relations* 33, no. 22 (1994), pp. 184–205, shows that the lack of work experience among young black males accounts for about half of the difference between their wages and those of young white males five years after high school graduation.

6.   Although there is no consensus, some statistical studies show mild positive associations between moderate amounts of part-time employment and school outcomes such as grades. See, for example, Ronald D'Amico, "Does Employment During High School Impair Academic Progress?" *Sociology of Education* 57, no. 3 (1984), pp. 152–64; Larry D. Steinberg and Sanford M. Dornbusch, "Negative Correlates of Part-Time Employment During Adolescence: Replication and Elaboration," *Developmental Psychology* 29, no. 2 (1991); D. E. McNelly, "Does Working Part-Time Enhance Secondary Education?" (paper presented at the American Vocational Association Convention, Cincinnati, Ohio, 1990).

7.   Conservative scholars argue that their "cultural traits" have become deficient, largely through welfare dependency. Liberal scholars, too, discuss culture, but view it as a more immediate and shifting response to structural constraints and opportunities. Elijah Anderson, in *Streetwise* (University of Chicago Press, 1990), an ethnography that explores the social deterioration of an inner-city neighborhood accompanying the decline of city manufacturing jobs and the outmigration of upwardly mobile residents, writes that the underground drug economy appears increasingly attractive to young males, who come to believe that counsel on the traditional pathways of honorable employment offered by some of the neighborhood's remaining older residents is hopelessly fanciful and can lead, at best, and only if one is suitably connected, to a demeaning and dead-end service job. William Julius Wilson, in *The Truly Disadvantaged* (University of Chicago Press, 1987), pp. 55–62, argues that increased joblessness in high-poverty urban areas, along with a host of other impediments, so isolates neighborhood youth from the mainstream working world that the relationship between schooling and employment takes on a different meaning for them. Urban youth from high-poverty neighborhoods are at the greatest risk of dropping out of school. Typically, dropouts are not the least able children in schools. Rather, they reject the paltry educational choices in favor of consumer choices that are more appealing. In overcrowded schools that secure only about half the per-pupil funds that suburban schools receive—see Jonathan Kozol, *Savage Inequalities* (Harper Perennial, 1992)—no one is around to adequately explain the long-term consequences of limited education, which is so often understood only after failure in the job market. See Michelle Fine, *Framing Dropouts* (State University of New York Press, 1991). Even for youth who do not drop out of school, choosing to invest in schooling is often disappointing. A study of an inner-city Chicago school found that many seniors had attainable career goals and could have begun a successful transition to employment if

they had had adequate information, guidance, and resources. Every counselor at the school reported not having the time, materials, and training needed to provide students with effective career counseling. See Wilson, *When Work Disappears*, p. 70. While it is widely believed that career guidance is important to disadvantaged youth, who may well lack exposure to and knowledge of the job market, career guidance is often the lowest priority for school counselors. See de Lone, "School-to-Work Transition," p. 250; Kenneth B. Hoyt, "A Proposal for Making Transition from Schooling to Employment an Important Component of Educational Reform," *Future Choices* 2 (1990), pp. 73–83. For Wilson, the practical solution to urban joblessness is to change the structure of schooling and employment, not to focus on the disillusioned behaviors that result from poor educational and occupational opportunities. For the difficulties in hanging on to mainstream achievement orientations in public schools, see narratives of young residents of central Harlem and East Harlem projects in Terry Williams and William Kornblum, *Uptown Kids* (Grosset/Putnam, 1994), pp. 85–99. For the emphasis on achievement that urban poor parents try to impart in their children in the face of street culture and status-seeking consumerism, see Delmos J. Jones, "The Culture of Achievement Among the Poor: The Case of Mothers and Children in a Head Start Program," *Critique of Anthropology* 13, no. 3 (1993), pp. 247–66; and Mark Robert Rand, *Living on the Edge: The Realities of Welfare in America* (Columbia University Press, 1994), pp. 68–70.

8. According to 1990 census data, 56% of central Harlem residents (Manhattan Community District 10) aged 25 years and older are high school graduates. Department of City Planning, *Socioeconomic Profiles: A Portrait of New York City's Community Districts from the 1980 and 1990 Censuses of Population and Housing* (City of New York, March 1993), p. 295.

9. Less than 30% of the 15,000 children in Central Harlem's District 5 schools read at national grade level. Five of the thirteen schools in District 5 are on New York State's list of chronically failing schools. Early in 1997, School Chancellor Rudy Crew removed the school board in Central Harlem because of its poor performance. Reading scores were at a ten-year low, textbooks were outdated, and basic materials were in short supply. See Somini Sengupta, "School Board in Harlem Is Removed," *New York Times*, February 25, 1997, p. B1; Laura Williams, "Reading Goals to Go in Writing," *New York Daily News*, January 4, 1997, p. 5.

10. According to 1990 census data, 20% of Central Harlem's teenagers aged 16 to 19 are high school dropouts (the number of persons 16–19 years not in school and not high school graduates divided by the number of persons 16–19), far fewer than half graduate within four years, 42% are unemployed, 14% are outside the youth labor force altogether (not high school graduates, not in school, and not looking for work). See *Keeping Track of New York's Children* (Citizens' Committee for Children, New York City, 1993), pp. 97, 161; New York City Department of Planning, *Persons 16–19 Years, Enrollment, Education and Labor Force Employment* (1992)

11. A study by the New York City Human Resource Administration's Office of Employment Services found that women in entry-level jobs in New York City average about $6.50 per hour. Cashiers earn an average of about $5 per hour.

12. A 1982 nationwide survey of almost 5,000 fast-food employees, Ivan Charner and Bryna Shore Fraser, *Fast Food Jobs* (National Institute for Work and Learning,

1984), found that for the majority of school-age fast food employees, there was no connection between their job (or their supervisor or manager) and their schooling (though the proportion of school-to-fast-food-employer linkages may have increased since the time of the study). Charner and Fraser note, however, that the majority of employees had positive opinions of management personnel.

13. It is precisely this kind of integration of school and work that is now being championed as "work-based learning" in many school-to-work initiatives. See U.S. Congress, Office of Technology Assessment, *Learning to Work: Making the Transition from School to Work*, OTA-EHR-637 (Government Printing Office, 1995), which places importance on experiential learning at the workplace, workplace instruction, and mentoring.

14. Harry Holzer, *What Employers Want: Job Prospects for Less-Educated Workers* (Russell Sage Foundation, 1996), finds that fewer than 10% of today's central city jobs require only a high school diploma, even when the diploma is accompanied by previous work experience. Holzer predicts that the overabundance of job-seekers for these jobs will increase in the coming years.

15. Barbara Garson, *The Electronic Sweatshop: How Computers Are Transforming the Office of the Future into the Factory of the Past* (Simon & Schuster, 1988).

16. See also Robin Leidner's account of frustration in figuring out the cash register and working the drive-through window at a Chicago McDonald's restaurant. Robin Leidner, *Fast Food, Fast Talk: Service Work and the Routinization of Everyday Life* (University of California Press, 1993). Leidner concurs that fast food work requires skills and exhausting effort.

17. Roger Waldinger, *Still the Promised City? African-Americans and the New Immigrants in Post-Industrial New York* (Harvard University Press, 1994), based on interviews with Los Angeles County restaurateurs, documents an employer preference for the hiring of immigrants (especially for back kitchen jobs); they are considered to have a willingness to work hard for long hours and are reported to have less turnover than nonimmigrants.

18. It is not surprising that as the number of service jobs increase and the competition for them swells, employers are demanding greater soft skills among employees than they did even five or ten years ago. See Philip Moss and Chris Tilly, "Growing Demand for 'Soft' Skills in Four Industries: Evidence from In-Depth Employer Interviews" (Russell Sage Foundation Working Paper 93, 1996).

CHAPTER 6: GETTING STUCK, MOVING UP

1. For example, the Urban Poverty and Family Life Study included a survey of 179 employers in and around Chicago, in which face-to-face interviews were conducted with managers who were quite candid about their hiring practices and their perceptions of the inner-city labor force. William Julius Wilson, *When Work Disappears: The World of the New Urban Poor* (Knopf, 1996), pp. 111–46. See also Kathleen Kirschenman and Kathryn Neckerman, "We'd Love to Hire Them, But . . . ," in Christopher Jencks and Paul E. Peterson, eds., *The Urban Underclass* (Brookings Institution, 1991), p. 207. About 75% of the employers expressed negative views of inner-city blacks.

Many asserted strong generalized criticisms of inner-city worker traits. Firm representatives voiced concerns not only about the skills of inner-city workers but also about their dependability and honesty. Employers were most suspicious of black males. See also Harry Holzer, *What Employers Want: Job Prospects for Less-Educated Workers* (Russell Sage Foundation, 1996), which reports results of about 800 employer interviews in each of four metropolitan areas: Atlanta, Boston, Detroit, and Los Angeles. He found that less-educated black males appear to face the most significant barriers at the hiring stage not only because of their limited skills and credentials, but also because of discriminatory attitudes of employers.

2. For an analysis of the underlying causes of decline in inner city public schools, see Jean Anyon's new political history of the Newark, New Jersey, school district, *Ghetto Schooling: A Political Economy of Urban Educational Reform* (Teachers College Press, 1997), in which she argues that today's educational reformers in Newark and other cities have little chance of effecting real change in public schools (recent reform efforts have failed to improve schools) until the larger systems of economic opportunity of which they are a part are improved and democratized.

3. Many economists believe that skill demands for U.S. jobs have increased since the early 1980s. There is no clear consensus about skill levels required for jobs, since skills are difficult to measure using survey data. Whether or not technological innovations in the workplace increase skills needed for jobs or actually "deskill" them in aggregate is currently a debated topic. Technical skills are shown to have risen modestly over the past few decades; soft skills—considered to be on the rise—have been given little attention until very recently. See Philip Moss and Chris Tilly, "Growing Demand for 'Soft' Skills in Four Industries: Evidence from In-Depth Employer Interviews" (Russell Sage Foundation Working Paper 93, 1996); David R. Howell, "The Skills Myth," *American Prospect,* Summer 1994, pp. 81–90; James E. Rosenbaum and Amy Binder, "Do Employers Really Need More Educated Youth?" *Sociology of Education* 70 (1997), pp. 68–85. But regardless of the actual skills that are required for work, educational credentials in the form of diplomas are almost always useful in competing against other candidates for jobs (especially in oversupplied labor markets), because they are used by employers not only to gauge skills but as general indicators of an applicant's attitude, dependability, and motivation.

4. Their perceptions are not far off the mark. Declining wage rates over the past two decades are not limited to high school dropouts but are occurring among high school graduates as well. Only college graduates have seen improvements in their earnings opportunities over the past fifteen years. Rebecca Blank, *It Takes a Nation: A New Agenda for Fighting Poverty* (Russell Sage Foundation, 1997), p. 61.

5. Not surprisingly, the poor are five times more likely to be evicted from their homes or apartments than the nonpoor. Twenty-eight percent of poor children move three or more times before their fifth birthday. Fewer than one-fifth of poor single-parent families own their own homes. Maya Federman et al., "What Does It Mean to be Poor in America?" *Monthly Labor Review* 119, no. 5 (May 1996), pp. 3–18.

6. In *Getting Started: The Youth Labor Market* (MIT Press, 1980), Paul Osterman shows that primary firms, those that provide good pay, security, and advancement opportunity, were reluctant to hire workers while they were still very young, but did accept the same applicants when they got older. Wages and employment improved

with age. Osterman also found that early job experiences had little effect on later job experiences. Thus, churning in the secondary sector before entering the primary sector was considered relatively benign. Of course, not everyone had equal access to primary sector jobs—or to secondary jobs for that matter. Even in the 1970s, before the increase in skill demands on the part of youth employers (or the employers' perception of lack of skills on the part of young workers), the unemployment rates for blacks were much higher than those for whites. Osterman's analysis indicated that the situation for young blacks improved dramatically when labor markets tightened. More recently, Osterman has argued that the transition from youth-oriented secondary jobs to quality jobs in the adult labor market has become a serious concern for more young workers, in particular the non-college-bound. The problem has been exacerbated by rising skill requirements of employers. See Paul Osterman and Maria Iannozzi, "Youth Apprenticeships and School-to-Work Transitions: Current Knowledge and Legislative Strategy" (Working Paper no. 14, National Center on the Educational Quality of the Workforce, 1994).

7. See Jacob Alex Klerman and Lynn A. Karoly, "Young Men and the Transition to Stable Employment," *Monthly Labor Review,* August 1994, pp. 31–48.

8. Nationwide estimates of turnover rates among fast food workers run as high as 300% per year. Alan B. Krueger, 1991, "Ownership, Agency, and Wages: An Examination of Franchising in the Fast Food Industry," *Quarterly Journal of Economics,* February 1991, p. 83. According to one recent study, 75% of fast food employees remain on the job six months, 53% stay one year, 25% stay two years, and 12% stay three years or longer. See Robert W. Van Giezen, "Occupational Wages in the Fast-Food Industry," *Monthly Labor Review,* August 1994, p. 24. A survey of nearly 5,000 fast food workers, Ivan Charner and Bryna S. Fraser, *Fast Food Jobs* (National Institute for Work and Learning, 1984), p. 30, found that the length of employment among respondents varied with age: workers 25 years of age or older had worked an average of three times longer than 16- and 17-year-olds.

9. Richard B. Freeman's analyses, "Why Do So Many Young American Men Commit Crimes and What Might We Do About It?," (NBER Working Paper no. 5451, 1996) and "Crime and the Job Market" (NBER Working Paper no. 4910, 1994), illustrate that participation in crime and involvement with the criminal justice system has become a part of normal economic life for many less-skilled men, particularly young black men with little education. The United States has about tripled the number of men in prison over the past twenty years. While no drastic reduction in crime has occurred as a result, a remarkably high proportion of working-age men are now behind bars. By 1993, one man was incarcerated for every fifty in the workforce. Among black men, the number incarcerated was 9% of the work force. These numbers grow more alarming when education is factored in. One-third of black males aged 25 to 34 who lacked high school degrees were incarcerated, and more than half of this young male black dropout population were under supervision of the criminal justice system. Freeman shows that labor market incentives affect the level of crime, and provides evidence that the depressed labor market for less-skilled men in the 1980s and 1990s has contributed to a rise in criminal activity by such men. See Philip Moss and Christopher Tilly, "Why Black Men Are Doing Worse in the Labor Market: A Review of Supply-Side and Demand-Side Explanations" (Social Science Research

Council, 1991), for a review of other studies showing the increased popularity of criminal activity among young urban males in the wake of disappearing jobs.

10. Even here we would applaud the way in which she has "broken the mold" and devoted her life to working hard for a low wage.

11. See Arthur Hertzberg, *The Jews in America* (Simon & Schuster, 1989).

12. Persons from poor families and poor neighborhoods who strive for upward mobility are quite often both praised and resented by those who surround them. Likewise, strivers tend to identify much less with their "nonupwardly" kin and neighbors, and sometimes appear haughty to those around them. This pattern is widespread and well established. See, for example, Joyce A. Ladner's ethnographic account of adolescent black girls (some of whom aspired to middle-class status) growing up in St. Louis's projects and poor neighborhoods during the mid-1960s. Joyce A. Ladner, *Tomorrow's Tomorrow: The Black Woman* (University of Nebraska Press, 1995), pp. 136–58.

13. The outflow of middle-class blacks from deteriorating central city neighborhoods has become a common phenomenon. See, for example, Elijah Anderson's discussions about professional blacks leaving established black urban areas in *Streetwise: Race, Class and Change in an Urban Community* (University of Chicago Press, 1990), pp. 58–65, 159–61, based on his fieldwork from 1975 through 1989 in an eastern city's low-income black neighborhood.

14. In return, men who are employed in jobs that require physical labor have been shown to resent professionals, whose jobs are often viewed as unproductive and therefore not "real" work. David Halle, *America's Working Man* (University of Chicago Press, 1984). A stirring inquiry into the tangled family relationships and internal emotional conflicts arising as working-class children gain higher occupational statuses than their parents possess is found in Richard Sennett and Jonathan Cobb, *The Hidden Injuries of Class* (Vintage Books, 1972). Sennett and Cobb discuss a complex structure of feeling on the part of blue-collar fathers who experience not only pride but also inadequacy and betrayal in the achievements of their children. For their part, upwardly mobile children experience the sacrifices of their parents as a guilt-inducing burden, all in the context of heartfelt, though fragmented, familial love.

15. Typically, surveys ask respondents to name three people they know best and then make inquiries about the labor market status of those individuals. Kyesha would be inclined to think about her friends and not her relatives in answering such a question, a tendency that would represent her as more impoverished in terms of networks than she actually is.

16. In this, Bob was similar to the thousands of other children in poor families who face pressures to fend for themselves even though they live in households where someone else is taking care of the basic costs of living.

17. According to survey data, while the majority of firms across industries hiring for noncollege jobs do require high school diplomas, fewer than half actually check on educational credentials (though urban employers are more likely to do so). Only about half of all employers who hire for noncollege jobs give applicants skills tests for noncollege jobs (again, this is more prevalent in cities than in suburbs), and even fewer firms do so for entry-level sales and service jobs, like those found in fast food restaurants. Harry Holzer, *What Employers Want*, pp. 55–56, 83–84. Analysis of

employer practices in Chicago suggests that skills tests may be less biased than subjective assessments made in interviews: firms that test for skills have a higher average proportion of black workers in entry-level jobs than do nontesting firms (this is true even after controlling for the size of firm, the occupation, and the percentage of blacks in the neighborhood). See Wilson, *When Work Disappears*, p. 133. Holzer's study finds that females are more likely than males to be found in jobs in which tests are given, but gives no evidence that tests help black males. Actually, according to his table on p. 84, black males are slightly less likely to be found in jobs requiring tests.

18.   Some Burger Barn owners have developed tutoring programs for employees who cannot read, an admirable effort but probably not one that will produce many managers.

Chapter 7: Family Values

1.   See Leon Dash, *Rosa Lee: A Mother and Her Family in Urban America* (Basic Books, 1996).

2.   A couple of Rosa Lee's eight children, however, have taken very different paths. In *Rosa Lee: A Mother and Her Family in Urban America*, Dash writes about two of her sons who have never taken drugs or been to prison. Both have worked most of their adult lives, taking care of themselves and their families. One owns his home in a middle-class neighborhood.

3.   In a 1980 survey of urban Santiago (DR) households that had relatives living abroad, about 20% of homes received sustained support from their absent members that averaged about $100 per month. Sherri Grasmuck and Patricia R. Pessar, *Between Two Islands: Dominican International Migration* (University of California Press, 1991).

4.   Indeed, we often look right past the difficulties immigrants experienced in the urban villages of the nation's cities, especially the claustrophobia members of extended families felt when they could not get away from the prying eyes of older generations. One of the major "push" factors that sent previous generations of inner-city dwellers to the suburbs was the desire to get away from the intrusive control of one's elders. See Herbert J. Gans, *The Urban Villagers: Group and Class in the Life of Italian Americans* (Free Press of Glencoe, 1962); and Herbert J. Gans, *Levittowners: Ways of Life and Politics in a New Suburban Community* (Pantheon Books, 1967).

5.   Carol B. Stack, *All Our Kin: Strategies for Survival in a Black Community* (Harper & Row, 1974), even suggests that giving priority to maintaining close family bonds will dissuade ghetto dwellers from moving to better neighborhoods when they have the chance. Part of Stack's explanation lies in the difficulty of forecasting the permanence of good fortune among those poor people who discover that they have the opportunity to "get out." If they are confident that their money will last, then they may decide they can afford to cut the ties and go it alone. But few know for sure that the funds will continue to flow: jobs disappear, divorce may threaten . . . there are a thousand reasons for being skeptical of continuous good luck. And if one cannot be sure that resources will be stable, it may be more prudent to stay in the community where one's ties are strong and the private safety net continues to work. However, Stack also suggests that there is more to the desire to stay close to kin than just an

instrumental need for their help. There is also a high cultural value placed on proximity, and a disdain for those who put mobility ahead of family ties.

6. However, see Judith Stacey, *Brave New Families: Stories of Domestic Upheaval in Late Twentieth Century America* (Basic Books, 1990), for an account of "postmodern" recombinant families, often constructed through remarriages and other agreements, that don't look too different. Our nation's domestic patterns have become increasingly diverse, and no single family model dominates. Only a minority of households in the United States still contain married couples with children. More children live with single mothers than in homes with paid-work fathers and full-time homemaker mothers. See Judith Stacey, *In the Name of the Family: Rethinking Family Values in the Postmodern Age* (Beacon Press, 1996).

7. Poverty has devastating effects, both direct and indirect, on children's well-being. A new set of studies, for example, clearly demonstrates that the negative outcomes for children associated with growing up in single-parent homes are related not only to home environment but to low income. While family disruptions such as divorce and remarriage often contribute to behavioral and psychological problems among children, the studies suggest than the net effects of poverty on cognitive ability and school achievement are at least as large as the effects of family disruptions. See Jeanne Brooks-Gunn, Greg J. Duncan, and Nancy Maritato, "Poor Families, Poor Outcomes: The Well-Being of Children and Youth," and Sara S. McLanahan, "Parent Absence or Poverty: Which Matters More?" both in Greg J. Duncan and Jeanne Brooks-Gunn, eds., *Consequences of Growing Up Poor* (Russell Sage Foundation, 1997), pp. 1–17, 35–48.

8. The experience of parental divorce is often traumatic for children. Research shows that children function better in a single-parent family than in a conflict-ridden two-parent home. James L. Peterson and Nicholas Zill, "Marital Disruption, Parent-Child Relationships, and Behavior Problems in Children," *Journal of Marriage and the Family* 48 (May 1986), pp. 295–307. But there is also ample evidence that children living with only one parent are worse off, on average, than children living with two parents (undoubtedly the quality of family interaction is more important than its form). Divorce has serious short-term effects on children, and, though less is known about adjustment to the separation many years later, many fewer children are thought to suffer long-term psychological harm. Analysis of statistical data from national surveys in Sara McLanahan and Gary Sandefur, *Growing Up with a Single Parent: What Hurts, What Helps* (Harvard University Press, 1994), shows that growing up in a single-parent home (including children born out of wedlock and those who as a result of divorce grow up in a one-parent household) is associated with diminished chances for a successful adult life. Low income—common among both unwed mothers and women divorcées, who almost always experience a sudden drop in income when a marriage breaks up—is by far the most important factor in these children's lower achievement. In fact, low income accounts for about half of the disadvantage. See also Andrew J. Cherlin, *Marriage, Divorce, Remarriage,* (Harvard University Press, 1992); and Frank F. Furstenberg, Jr., and Andrew J. Cherlin, *Divided Families: What Happens to Children When Parents Part* (Harvard University Press, 1991).

9. The high school dropout risks for children with no family disruption, with single parent by divorce, with single parent by death of spouse, and with single parent by nonmarital birth are 13%, 31%, 15%, and 37% respectively. The teen birth risks for

female children with no family disruption, with single parent by divorce, with single parent by death of spouse, and with single parent by nonmarital birth are 11%, 33%, 21%, and 37% respectively. Data come from the 1987 *National Survey of Families and Households*, Cohort 1, consisting of men and women between the ages of 20 and 34. The figures are adjusted for race, sex, mother's education, father's education, number of siblings, and place of residence. The children of widowed mothers probably do better as a group because parental conflict is not an issue and because widowed mothers as a group are more financially secure than other single mothers. McLanahan and Sandefur, *Growing Up with a Single Parent: What Hurts, What Helps*, pp. 65–68.

10.   See Kathryn Edin and Laura Lein, *Making Ends Meet* (Russell Sage Foundation, 1997), for more on this point.

11.   The severe local decline in the formal manufacturing sector has spurred opportunities for small-scale immigrant entrepreneurs, especially in low-wage apparel subcontracting. See Roger Waldinger, *Through the Eye of the Needle: Immigrants and Enterprises in New York's Garment Trades* (New York University Press, 1986). See also Grasmuck and Pessar, *Between Two Islands: Dominican International Migration*, pp. 162–98.

12.   Studies have shown, however, that rapid "informalization" has occurred in several industries in New York City, including construction (in which an estimated 90% of internal work is done without a permit) and the furniture, footwear, and garment industries. In addition, subcontracting of back operations in consumer services (gourmet food stores, custom-made clothes boutiques, caterers, etc.) is expanding into the informal economy. See Alejandro Portes and Saskia Sassen-Koob, "Making It Underground: Comparative Material on the Informal Sector in Western Market Economies," *American Journal of Sociology* 93, no. 1 (July 1987), pp. 30–61. According to Sassen-Koob, the ability of New York City to absorb such a large influx of immigrants from low-wage countries can be understood only by recognizing the profound restructuring of industrial sectors from formal to informal employment arrangements (including subcontracting, sweatshops, and homework). Saskia Sassen-Koob, 1989, "New York City's Informal Economy," in Alejandro Portes, Manuel Castells, and Lauren Benton, eds., *The Informal Economy: Studies in Advanced and Less Developed Countries* (Johns Hopkins University Press, 1989), pp. 60–77.

13.   In 1994, over 1,000 unlicensed sidewalk vendors who crowded along Harlem's 125th Street shopping strip were evicted by the city in a series of police sweeps orchestrated by the Giuliani administration. They were offered an alternative open-air marketplace in an empty lot eight blocks south. While some local Harlem residents and political figures reviled the mayor for the removal, others, including business and development groups, praised the action, since the nontaxpaying vendors were thought to lure customers away from the stores, clogging the sidewalks and littering the street in front of their entrances. Many felt that there were legitimate complaints on both sides. About half the store owners along the strip are white; the street vendors, many of whom have moved to alternative Harlem locations, are overwhelmingly black (many are from West African countries). See Jonathan P. Hicks, "Vendors' Ouster and Boycott Divide Harlem," *New York Times*, October 23, 1994, p. A1.

14.   "Ghetto-related behavior"—overt emphasis on sexuality, idleness, and public drinking; drug abuse, drug trafficking, crime, gang violence; and all the rest—is a term employed in William Julius Wilson, *When Work Disappears: The World of the*

New Urban Poor (Knopf, 1996), pp. 51–86, to describe a set of practices—more prevalent in inner cities but also existent in mainstream society—that result from concentrated, persistent joblessness, poverty, and disconnection from social resources and decent city services. Wilson's survey of Chicago's poor finds an abundance of residents with mainstream norms who vilify those engaging in such behavior but who can, nonetheless, cogently describe how a young male growing up in a barren, impoverished, and dangerous neighborhood can become attracted to this alternative. Wilson's point is clear: ghetto-related behaviors emerge from the structure of opportunity found in marginalized inner-city neighborhoods.

15.   Elliot Liebow, *Tally's Corner* (Little, Brown, 1967), made this point long ago about, poor black men in Washington, D.C. Men who have no money shy away from family obligations because this becomes yet another source of failure, another way they have fallen short of their own images of masculinity. Liebow argues that in this the street-corner men do not differ from the "mainstream" middle-class notions of appropriate behavior.

16.   Working-poor parents rarely have the time, energy, or money to provide environments in which their children can thrive. A great deal of research shows that children from poor families exhibit lower levels of physical development, cognitive functioning, academic achievement, self-esteem, social development, and self-control than do children from more advantaged families. See Thomas L. Hanson, Sara McLanahan, and Elizabeth Thomson, "Economic Resources, Parental Practices, and Children's Well-Being," in Greg J. Duncan and Jeanne Brooks-Gunn, eds., *Consequences of Growing Up Poor* (Russell Sage Foundation, 1997), pp. 190–238. Indeed, the effects of poverty may be more pronounced for younger than for older children, since critical phases in brain cell development and in the capacity to form trusting emotional relationships occur in the first three years of life. Recent studies indicate that stimulation in the home environment can mediate the effects of family income on cognitive abilities, suggesting that less exposure to people and to learning interactions involving toys and books at home is a path toward lower achievement. This also suggests that childhood intervention programs that aim to enrich home environments are well founded. See Judith R. Smith, Jeanne Brooks-Gunn, and Pamela K. Klebanov, "Consequences of Living in Poverty for Young Children's Cognitive and Verbal Ability and Early School Achievement," in Duncan and Brooks-Gunn, eds., *Consequences of Growing Up Poor*, pp. 132–89.

17.   See Katherine Newman, *Falling from Grace: The Experience of Downward Mobility in the American Middle Class* (Free Press, 1988).

18.   According to a statistical analysis of death certificates and census data for the year 1990, boys in Harlem who reach the age of 15 have a 37% chance of surviving to age 65; girls, who are less likely to be the victims of violence, have a 65% chance of surviving to age 65. See Arline T. Geronimus et al., "Excess Mortality Among Blacks and Whites in the United States," *New England Journal of Medicine* 335, no. 21 (November 21, 1996), pp. 1552–58, which finds that the differences in mortality rates before the age of 65 between high-income groups and low-income groups are significant, and that premature death rates among the poor living in central cities are astonishingly high. See also P. D. Sorlie, E. Backlund, and J. B. Keller, "U.S. Mortality by Economic, Demographic, and Social Characteristics: The National Longitudinal Mortality Study," *American Journal of Public Health* 85 (1995), pp. 949–56.

19. See Myron Genel, "Socioeconomic Status, Health, and Health Systems," *Pediatrics* 99 (June 1997), pp. 888–89; Jonathan S. Feinstein, "The Relationship Between Socioeconomic Status and Health: A Review of the Literature," *Milbank Memorial Fund Quarterly* 71 (1993), pp. 279–322.

20. American workers suffer about 6 million occupational injuries and 500,000 occupational illnesses (such as contact dermatitis and carpal tunnel syndrome) each year. Until recently, the construction industry had the highest injury and illness incidence rate, 14.3 per 100 full-time workers, followed by the manufacturing sector, with 13.1 per 100 full-time workers. 1989 data from the Bureau of Labor Statistics, "No Progress on Injury Rates: Statistics on Occupational Injuries and Illnesses," *Occupational Hazards* 53, no. 1 (January 1991), p. 16. While worker compensation cases are still more prevalent among men, assaults, one of the fastest-growing workplace hazards, are the most common in the growing health care industry, which heavily employs women. According to the most recent data, nursing homes are the country's most dangerous worksites, with an occupational injury and illness rate of 17.8 incidents per 100 workers. Fay Hansen, "Who Gets Hurt, and How Much Does It Cost? Workplace Injuries," *Compensation and Benefits Review* 29, no. 3 (May 1997). Repetitive stress injuries on muscles and tendons, once thought to be a problem only for meat cutters, supermarket checkout clerks, and assembly-line workers, are now being reported in a wide range of low-wage industries. More than half of workplace illnesses reported in 1995 were disorders, such as carpal tunnel syndrome, which are associated with repeated trauma. Pat Swift, "On the Job, It's Women Who Are Most at Risk," *Buffalo* (New York) *News*, September 6, 1997, p. 7C; "Workplace Injury, Illness Rates Drop in 1995," *Workers' Compensation Executive* 7, no. 7 (April 9, 1997).

21. Richard Lowry et al., "The Effect of Socioeconomic Status on Chronic Disease Risk Behaviors Among U.S. Adolescents," *Journal of the American Medical Association* 276, no. 10 (September 11, 1996), pp. 792–97.

22. Poor children use only about half as many physician services as nonpoor children after adjusting for health status. And poor children are more than twice as likely to wait more than an hour for consultation at their sites of care. Paul W. Newacheck, Dana C. Hughes, and Jeffrey J. Stoddard, "Children's Access to Primary Care: Differences by Race, Income, and Insurance Status," *Pediatrics* 97 (January 1996), pp. 26–32, concludes that there are significant barriers to the access and use of primary care for low-income children.

23. See Arline Geronimus and Sanders Korenman, "The Socioeconomic Consequences of Teenage Childbearing Reconsidered" (Paper no. 90–190, Population Studies Center, University of Michigan, 1990).

24. Indeed, less-severe fertility problems among healthy middle-class women in their thirties and forties are well known. The medical costs of older mothers' births are often quite high; older first-time mothers are more likely to have babies that are premature and have low birthweights than younger mothers. Kristin Luker, *Dubious Conceptions: The Politics of Teenage Pregnancy* (Harvard University Press, 1996), p. 171.

25. For more on this discussion, see Luker, *Dubious Conceptions*, pp. 134–74.

26. While teenage childbearing has been denounced by liberals and conservatives alike as a cause of social ills, recent studies indicate that teen mothers who come from disadvantaged backgrounds are *not* further disadvantaged by early motherhood. One new study, led by University of Chicago economist Joseph Hotz, used an

extremely rigorous research design. Teen mothers are compared with older mothers who otherwise resemble each other by using a control group of women who as teens had accidental miscarriages and then went on to have their first birth when they were older. The study found that over their adult lives, teen mothers are no more likely to use welfare or to suffer seriously reduced earnings than if they had postponed childbearing. See Arline T. Geronimus, "Mothers of Invention," *Nation* 263, no. 5 (August 12, 1996), p. 6. See also Emory Thomas, Jr., "Is Pregnancy a Rational Choice for Poor Teenagers?" *Wall Street Journal*, January 18, 1996, p. B1; Arline Geronimus and Sanders Korenman, "The Socioeconomic Consequences of Teen Childbearing Reconsidered," *Quarterly Journal of Economics* 107 (1992), pp. 1187–1214; Arline T. Geronimus, Sanders Korenman, and Marianne M. Hillemeier, "Does Young Maternal Age Adversely Affect Child Development? Evidence from Cousin Comparisons in the United States," *Population and Development Review* 20, no. 3 (September 1994), pp. 585–611.

27.   Douglas S. Massey and Nancy A. Denton, in their important work on the historical causes, the ongoing perpetuation, and the dire consequences of our nation's profound racial segregation, in *American Apartheid: Segregation and the Making of the Underclass* (Harvard University Press, 1993), show that many central city ghettos are such vast, densely inhabited, and intensely segregated enclaves that black residents in one neighborhood can walk well past an adjacent neighborhood without ever seeing a white face. Using ethnographic evidence from Chicago's poorest areas, the authors argue that many residents of these hypersegregated enclaves live in extremely circumscribed social worlds, having few if any friendships outside its boundaries and rarely traveling far from their own neighborhoods. Massey and Denton, *American Apartheid*, p. 161; see also Sophie Pedder, "Social Isolation and the Labor Market; Black Americans in Chicago" (paper presented at the Chicago Urban Poverty and Family Life Conference, Chicago, October 10–12, 1991. Thus, concentrated spatial isolation by both race and class contributes to extreme social isolation, which not only has devastating effects when it comes to using social ties and networks for job-seeking—Harry J. Holzer, *What Employers Want: Job Prospects for Less-Educated Workers* (Russell Sage Foundation, 1996), p. 52, notes that many employers who have jobs for noncollege graduates use referrals from current employees to help with hiring; growth in noncollege jobs is much greater in the suburbs—but also has consequences for the well-being and development of children. Very recent studies have investigated the effect of neighborhood income levels on the development of poor children and adolescents. The studies show that after controlling for parental education, age, race, and economic status (using an income-to-needs ratio), living in the presence of affluent neighbors is positively associated with cognitive ability among young children. The studies also show that neighborhood factors affect the parenting of children. Violence, uncertainty, and crowding are stresses that are much more prevalent among parents in poor neighborhoods. See Jeanne Brooks-Gunn, Greg J. Duncan, and J. Lawrence Aber, eds., *Neighborhood Poverty*, vol. 1, *Context and Consequences for Children* (Russell Sage Foundation, 1997); Tama Leventhal, Jeanne Brooks-Gunn, and Sheila B. Kamerman, forthcoming, "Communities as Place, Face, and Space: Provision of Services to Poor, Urban Children and Their Families," in *Neighborhood Poverty*, vol. 2, *Policy Approaches to Studying Neighborhoods* (Russell Sage Foundation, forthcoming); see also Claudia J. Coulton, "Effects of Neighborhoods on Families and

Children: Implications for Services," in Alfred J. Kahn and Sheila B. Kamerman, eds., *Children and Their Families in Big Cities: Strategies for Service Reform* (Cross-National Studies Program, Columbia University School of Social Work, 1996).

28. See Fox Butterfield, *All God's Children* (Knopf, 1995), for an interesting discussion of the origins of the street culture of respect. He argues it derives from long-standing southern white traditions of revenge killing for slights to one's honor.

29. Anderson, *Streetwise.*

30. In Dominican society, for example, to be partly white is to be nonblack. See José del Castillo and Martin F. Murphy, "Migration, National Identity, and Cultural Policy," *Journal of Ethnic Studies* 15, no. 3 (1995), pp. 49–69.

31. Mary C. Waters, "Ethnic and Racial Identities of Second Generation Black Immigrants in New York City," *International Migration Review* 28, no. 4 (1996), pp. 795–817.

32. In 1995, dozens of police officers in Harlem's 30th Precinct were investigated in a corruption scandal in which drug dealers were robbed by police officers. Thirty officers were eventually convicted or pled guilty to crimes including perjury, civil rights violations, and stealing drugs or cash from dealers. John Sullivan, "Ex-Sergeant Is Sentenced in Police Corruption Case," *New York Times,* June 17, 1997, p. B3.

33. Robin Kelly, "Playing for Keeps: Pleasure and Profit on the Postindustrial Playground" (unpublished paper; Department of History, New York University).

Chapter 8: Who's In, Who's Out?

1. The most influential conservative authors trace a faulty inner-city work ethic not only to flawed social welfare policies but to cultural patterns that developed under slavery and Jim Crow. These patterns that impede upward mobility are then compared to the cultural values of successful immigrant groups. Thomas Sowell, *Ethnic America* (Basic Books, 1981); Lawrence Mead, *The New Politics of Poverty: The Nonworking Poor in America* (HarperCollins, 1992); Lawrence E. Harrison, *Who Prospers? How Cultural Values Shape Economic and Political Success* (Basic Books, 1992).

2. We tracked down a representative sample of 93 people (out of a total of about 346) who applied for jobs in two fast food restaurants in central Harlem (where approximately 100 people are actually employed). In order to obtain a fair comparison of the people who were "success stories" (who got minimum-wage jobs) and the people who were rejected, we looked only at those employed who had worked in hourly-wage jobs for less than one year and compared them to those who were turned away. The results from our intensive interviews are weighted in the tables in this chapter to reflect the correct proportions in the total pool of rejected applicants. This method provides us with as accurate a comparison as possible between those people employers chose and those they rejected.

3. Some had found and lost jobs during that year. This figure merely captures at a point in time the proportion of the original population of Burger Barn applicants who were unemployed a year beyond the point of application.

4. See Appendix I, Table 6, for the full details. This relationship holds true controlling for nativity (U.S. vs. foreign-born) and gender.

5. Nationwide, the unemployment rate of 16- to-24-year-olds in July 1996 was 12.6%, the same as the year before. Unemployment among black youths aged 16 to 24 was 25.4%. U.S. Department of Labor, "Employment and Unemployment Among Youth—Summer 1996" (Report 96-360 1996). New York City's youth unemployment rate has been much higher than national figures since the late 1980s. In 1993, the New York City teenage (16 to 19 years of age) rate of unemployment hit 40%. Thomas J. Lueck, "Youth Joblessness Is at Record High," *New York Times,* June 4, 1993, p. A1. It continues at a rate greater than 25%. Robert Polner, "Cuts Vex Young Workers," *New York Newsday,* January 23, 1996, p. A5.

6. This finding is extremely strong in terms of statistical significance. Yet it should probably be treated with some caution because of the way the data were compiled. We asked respondents, "How do you get to work?" and "How far away do you live?" But the answers did not always come back in terms of distance; in some cases it came back in terms of commute times. If they reported distance in terms of blocks, we took this data and converted it to miles. If they reported distance by time, we used their addresses and calculated the distance ourselves. There is obviously room for error here.

7. Philip Kasinitz and Jan Rosenberg, "Missing the Connection: Social Isolation and Employment on the Brooklyn Waterfront," *Social Problems* 43, no. 2 (May 1989), pp. 180–96.

8. Mercer Sullivan, *"Getting Paid": Youth Crime and Work in the Inner City* (Cornell University Press, 1989).

9. Philip Moss and Chris Tilly, "Growing Demand for 'Soft' Skills in Four Industries: Evidence from In-Depth Employer Interviews" (Russell Sage Foundation Working Paper #93, 1996) is based on interviews with managers in retail clothing stores—an industry which, like fast food, emphasizes customer service. Moss and Tilly found that while technical skill requirements for entry-level sales clerk jobs have remained steady or fallen in recent years, employers reported increasing demands for "soft" skills, especially "teamwork, ability to fit in, appropriate affect, grooming, and attire."

10. When we look at those who are 19 and older, the percent local drops down to 70%.

11. Some managers are leery of hiring groups of friends, for fear they will create problems by being clannish, or by goofing off rather than working hard. Others understand that a worker who has friends on the job is more likely to stick with a boring, unpleasant job because he or she is having a reasonably good time. Knowing how managers view a case of this kind will help an applicant decide whether to invoke the connection explicitly or not.

12. William Julius Wilson, *When Work Disappears: The World of the New Urban Poor* (Knopf, 1996). Mark Granovetter, *Getting a Job: A Study of Contacts and Careers* (University of Chicago Press, 1995), pp. 150–51, too, argues that while finding jobs through networks may be one's best option (better than newspaper listings, for example), the quality of the results still rests upon the information one's network can provide.

13. There are other important differences between the native-born and the foreign-born that bear discussion here. The foreign-born applicants are more likely to have a "contact" already in Burger Barn, to have a better network connection to the

employer, and this undoubtedly helps them beat the competition. It suggests as well that foreign-born job-seekers do not bother to try for these jobs unless they have a good reason to think they will succeed—that is, unless they know somebody. But it also suggests that the native-born minorities have weaker networks, which clearly puts them at a disadvantage.

14.   But note that these findings accord with Philip Kasinitz's work, which indicates an employer preference for West Indians over native African-Americans. Philip Kasinitz, *Caribbean New York: Black Immigrants and the Politics of Race* (Cornell University Press, 1992), p. 98. See also Mary C. Waters, "Ethnic and Racial Identities of Second-Generation Black Immigrants in New York City," *International Migration Review* 28, no. 4 (1994), which indicates that West Indians and Haitian-Americans are favored over native African-Americans in employment decisions.

15.   Miscalculation of the costs of living in the United States and New York City is commonplace among poor, undocumented immigrants, who often become mired in debt soon after arrival. See Sarah J. Mahler, *American Dreaming: Immigrant Life on the Margins* (Princeton University Press, 1995), pp. 90–94, which explores this dilemma among Salvadoran and South American immigrants living on Long Island.

16.   It is especially notable that so many people looking for work or holding jobs in the fast food business have industry-specific job experience. About 25% of the applicant pool had previously worked in the business, often in other Burger Barns. And this experience counts: about half the hires came in with job-specific track records. But it does not clinch the deal: 20% of the rejects had also worked in fast foods.

17.   See Appendix I, Table 7, for a full listing of the types of jobs previously held by applicants to Burger Barn.

18.   About 10% of New York City's 300,000 public high school students are now over 18 years of age. In 1995, 48% of students who began high school four years earlier graduated, 18% dropped out, and 34% remained in school. In 1991, 51% of students who began four years earlier graduated, but 20.5% dropped out, with 28.5% remaining in school. Maria Newman, "In New York City High Schools, Path to Diploma Grows Longer for Many," *New York Times,* June 3, 1996, p. B1.

19.   Though this finding washed out when controlling for gender, with older and younger men having an equal chance but older women having an advantage over their younger counterparts.

20.   This finding must be treated with caution, however, as the number of non-natives in my sample of rejects is too small to calculate significance.

21.   Included as well in this category are warehouse workers, delivery boys, and messengers.

22.   Forty-five percent of the "employed rejects" had contacts, 15% used a placement agency, 25% responded to ads, and only 15% were walk-in applicants.

23.   Half the now-employed rejects report that they live five or more miles from their new job. Another 20% live between two to five miles from their jobs. This means that 70% of the employed rejects are "nonlocals," using my original definition.

24.   Based on employer surveys in four metropolitan areas, Harry Holzer, *What Employers Want: Job Prospects for Less-Educated Workers* (Russell Sage Foundation, 1996), pp. 62–66, finds that entry-level credential demands of employers are higher in

central cities than in suburbs. According to the survey, the portion of noncollege jobs that require no high school diploma, training, experience, or references is 4.1% in central cities and 6.1% in suburbs.

25.   The Bureau of Labor Statistics collects data on unemployment and job-seeking each month through the Current Population Survey. Each month about one of every 1,600 households in the United States is interviewed about the employment and job-seeking status of each householder 16 years of age and older. By the bureau's definitions, "unemployed" persons are those who are jobless, have actively looked for work in the prior four weeks, and are available for work. "Discouraged workers," those who want jobs and are available for work, and who looked for jobs within the past year but not in the prior four weeks, are not considered part of the labor force and are not included in the nation's unemployment figures. While the bureau's publication *Employment and Earnings*, based on the survey data, can shed some light on questions such as how many of the unemployed have been seeking jobs for 27 weeks or more, or how many of the unemployed are looking for their first job, or how many persons are too discouraged to look for a job, the results depend on the formal definitions of the categories, some of which were modified as recently as 1994 (at which time surveying methods were also changed). What is more, the sample size of the survey, 60,000 households in all, while reasonable for indicating national trends, is not large enough to produce reliable estimates of unemployment and job-seeking in small geographical areas.

26.   See Kathryn Edin and Laura Lein, *Making Ends Meet: How Single Mothers Survive Welfare and Low-Wage Work* (Russell Sage Foundation, 1997), pp. 83–142. Edin and Lein studied this dilemma through extensive interviews in four cities (Chicago, Boston, San Antonio, and Charleston, South Carolina) with 379 low-income single mothers, about half of whom received cash benefits from welfare. They asked each welfare-reliant mother what she felt she would need to earn in order to leave welfare for work. Responses varied according to how many children each mother was supporting as well as the health status and history of each family. About 70% of the mothers gave estimates between $8 and $10 per hour (although, in truth, single mothers leave welfare for wages that are much smaller). Leaving welfare and entering the working labor force means new health costs (since few low-wage employers provide medical plans, and when they do, deductibles and copayments still raise expenses), new transportation costs both for traveling to the workplace and for traveling to the day care provider (commuting to the suburbs is time-consuming and inconvenient—buying and maintaining a used car is a huge goal for many single mothers), and, sometimes, higher housing costs (subsidized housing costs increase when incomes rise) and clothing costs (depending on the job). Using national survey data to approximate some costs, Edin and Lein found that entering the working labor force cost single mothers a huge sum—single mothers who worked spent $2,800 more per year on medical care, transportation, child care, and clothing than did single mothers receiving welfare. Edin and Lein also calculated what the average welfare-reliant mother in the sample would need to earn to maintain the same standard of living she had on welfare. There results jibed roughly with the figures the mothers themselves gave: roughly $8 or $9 an hour. But the mothers in the sample knew that they could not gain a $9-an-hour job with their skills. Indeed, Kathleen Mullan Harris, "Life After

Welfare: Women, Work, and Repeat Dependency," *American Sociological Review* 61 (1996), pp. 207–46, shows that throughout the 1980s, women who went from welfare to work earned an average of $6.11 per hour in 1991 dollars. These earnings represent those of the highest-skilled recipients who exit welfare. A full-time, year-round worker with characteristics similar to those of the average single mother receiving welfare in the 1980s earned just $5.15 in 1991 dollars. Charles Michalopoulos and Irwin Garfinkel, "Reducing Welfare Dependence and Poverty of Single Mothers by Means of Earnings and Child Support: Wishful Thinking and Realistic Possibilities" (Discussion Paper 882–89, Institute for Research on Poverty, University of Wisconsin–Madison, 1989). Single mothers on welfare know that leaving welfare for a low-skilled job will make them worse off than they were on welfare, yet the fact that most recipients receive benefits for brief periods suggests that they prefer work over welfare when at all possible. By looking at their sample of low-wage-reliant single mothers, Edin and Lein found that these mothers experienced special circumstances that lowered the costs of working, such as having only school-age children, receiving timely and adequate child support payments, paying little for rent, child care, or transportation by virtue of social networks and help from kin, or having access to full health coverage for themselves and their children. Most of the women in this set had been on AFDC before. And despite the fact that the women reported heightened self-esteem associated with paid work and consider welfare a very stigmatizing last resort, low-wage work often forces mothers back into welfare when crises arise. According to national data, almost two-thirds of welfare recipients who had left welfare for work return to welfare rolls within six years. Kathleen Mullan Harris and Kathryn Edin, "From Welfare to Work and Back Again" (paper presented at the New School for Social Research conference "After AFDC: Reshaping the Anti-Poverty Agenda," November 16, 1996), cited in Edin and Lein, *Making Ends Meet*, p. 140. See Edin and Lein, *Making Ends Meet*, pp. 83–142.

27. This figure drops as one goes down the age ladder. The youngest applicants were hoping for $4.56, while the oldest were hoping for $4.71.

28. It is important to note that my discussion of reservation wages is missing an important population: the people who are not looking for work at all. My research design did not include them. To generalize completely from my sample of workers and job-seekers is not entirely justifiable, although the research suggests that they are comparable in many ways to those who are out of the labor force, differing more in their life-cycle situation than their demographic characteristics.

29. William Julius Wilson, in *The Truly Disadvantaged: The Inner City, the Underclass, and Public Policy* (University of Chicago Press, 1987) and in *When Work Disappears*, has argued that living in neighborhoods with high levels of poverty produces just such a culture. This may well be true for families that have no workers and no contact with workers. But we cannot infer this "culture" from the demography of neighborhoods and even households. People like Jervis are quite aware of the difference between their own predicament and the advantages that other families enjoy, because they look around, down the block, across the road, into other enclaves where people are visibly better off. They understand full well that jobs, good jobs, make the difference. There is, however, a huge difference between knowing this is the case and being able to do something about it.

30. See Marta Tienda and Haya Stier, "Joblessness and Shiftlessness: Labor Force Activity in Chicago's Inner City," in Christopher Jencks and Paul E. Peterson, eds., *The Urban Underclass* (Brookings Institution, 1991), pp. 135–54.

31. Tienda and Stier's study was more inclusive than the high-poverty neighborhoods Wilson speaks of in *When Work Disappears*. They included all neighborhoods with poverty rates in excess of 20%, not the 40% cutoff Wilson and others use in designating concentrated poverty areas.

32. During the same year, 21% of parents nationwide were outside the labor force. Tienda and Stier, "Joblessness and Shiftlessness: Labor Force Activity in Chicago's Inner City," p. 139.

33. The authors estimate that between 0.5% and 6% of the respondents were voluntarily idle. Respondents' reasons for not wanting a job considered voluntary include "supported by parents or kids," "supported by public aid," "don't want to work." But nine out of ten respondents who did not want a job reported poor health or family responsibilities. Only about one out of ten respondents who had never worked reported reasons other than family, health, or school for not wanting a job.

34. Elliot Liebow, *Tally's Corner* (Little, Brown, 1967).

35. Nowadays, day laborers are often immigrant men, who, hired on a per-day basis at well-known gathering spots at city's edge, work off the books for contractors and homeowners. While seasonal and short-term arrangements have long been commonplace in some areas of our economy, such as migrant work in agriculture and domestic work in suburban households, unpredictable short-term work has become routine across the country in occupations that were once characterized by steady, full-time arrangements. Kathleen Maas Weigert estimates that as many as 25% to 30% of the civilian labor force may be "contingent" workers—those who are "self-employed," either on or off the books, or those who are employed in leased positions, in at-home work, in involuntary part-time jobs, or in temporary jobs. See Thomas R. Swartz and Kathleen Maas Weigert, eds., *America's Working Poor* (University of Notre Dame Press, 1995), p. 2. The number of temporary workers alone mushroomed 250% between 1982 and 1992. See Chris Tilly, *Half a Job* (Temple University Press, 1996), p. 155. Beginning in the 1970s, especially in the trade and service sectors, firms began replacing higher-wage, full-time jobs with low-wage, part-time jobs that offer little job security and few or no benefits. Over 20 million people, almost 20% of the nonagricultural workforce, worked part-time in 1993. The growth of part-time employment arrangements is largely responsible for growing inequality of incomes. See Tilly, *Half a Job*, p. 160; and Chris Tilly, Barry Bluestone, and Bennett Harrision, "What Is Making American Wages More Unequal?" *Proceedings of the 39th Annual Meeting of the Industrial Relations Research Association* (1986), pp. 328–48. Part-time workers are disproportionately female, but the rate of part-time employment among prime-age (22–44) women has remained steady (about 22%) while the rate of part-time employment among prime-age men (22–64) has more than doubled since 1969 to 8.1% in 1993, suggesting that "family-wage" jobs are surely among those in decline. See Tilly, *Half a Job*, pp. 13–17; and Kathleen Barker, "Changing Assumptions and Contingent Solutions: The Costs and Benefits of Women Working Full- and Part-Time," *Sex Roles* 28, nos. 1–2 (1993), pp. 47–71.

36. The views of my informants are shared by poor Chicagoans quoted in the pages of William Julius Wilson, *When Work Disappears*, an account that shifts public

attention from issues of inner-city poverty to the problem of inner-city joblessness. Some of Wilson's data come from open-ended responses to questions posed in the Urban Poverty and Family Life Survey of Chicago, 1987. The survey responses, reinforced by ethnographic results, revealed that blacks in poor inner-city neighborhoods endorse dominant American attitudes about work, welfare, poverty, and self-worth. Even those living in the most destitute residential areas had internalized a mainstream societal belief: that America is the land of opportunity where anyone can get ahead, where individuals get what they deserve. Wilson notes that the attitudes his research team found bore little resemblance to the magazine articles and television reports asserting that ghetto values undermine American ideas about individualized initiative and responsibility. See Wilson, *When Work Disappears,* pp. 176–82, 251.

37.   The proportion of unemployed persons receiving unemployment insurance declined dramatically in the early 1980s and has remained low (50% of the unemployed received compensation in 1980; 37% received compensation in 1990). This is due to a number of factors: tightening of eligibility requirements (e.g., increasing the minimum earnings required), demographic changes, decline in the manufacturing sector, and decline in unionization. Unemployed full-time workers are almost four times more likely to receive benefits than unemployed part-time workers. See Daniel McMurrer and Amy Chasanov, "Trends in Unemployment Insurance Benefits," *Monthly Labor Review* 118, no. 9 (September 1995), p. 30; Center for Law and Social Policy, "State Reforms to Unemployment Benefits Would Assist Poor Workers" (1992). Calls for an unemployment insurance program began in the height of political progressivism before World War I. Beginning in 1908, the American Association for Labor Legislation, led by institutional economist John R. Commons, stirred the waters for social reform that highlighted programs for worker security, including unemployment insurance. The most important early battles over government-supported unemployment compensation took place at the state level, beginning in 1916, and typically involved conflicts about whether such policies ought to simply compensate workers or compel employers to prevent unemployment in the first place. When the Depression struck, no state had yet successfully legislated an unemployment insurance program. Only two states, Wisconsin and New York, adopted unemployment compensation plans before federal legislation was enacted as part of the Social Security Act of 1935, which provided for a nationwide employer tax. State systems of unemployment insurance became financially attractive, since federal tax credits could be applied against taxes paid to state unemployment compensation funds in each state. The federal-state development of unemployment insurance was intended to sustain industrial workers during layoffs and to provide resiliency to the economy and labor force during our economy's cyclical downturns. While Federal and state unemployment insurance policies have changed over the years—coverage, for example, was extended to many more categories of workers in the 1970s—the fundamental underpinning of eligibility remains: claimants must be strongly attached to the labor market. All states require a minimum number of weeks of employment in a base period, as well as a certain minimal level of earnings, to weed out casual and intermittent workers from coverage, which maintains the integrity of UI as a true insurance policy. In most states, a claimant receives weekly benefits at about half the wages earned during employment in the year prior to the claim for a period proportional to the number of weeks worked, for up to half a year in most cases. Specific

requirements vary from state to state. In New York, a claimant must have worked in at least 20 of the 52 weeks before filing, earning at least $1,600 in "covered" earnings (most employers now participate in UI, although some work circumstances are not covered) during 20 of those weeks. Alternatively, a claimant must have worked in at least 15 of the 52 weeks earning at least $1,200 during 15 of those weeks and also have worked in at least 40 of the 104 weeks before filing, earning at least $3,200 in covered earnings during 40 of those weeks. In New Jersey, a claimant in 1997 must have worked at least 20 weeks earning at least $133 per week (20% of the statewide average weekly wage earnings), and earned at least $8,000 in a base period equal to one year (or $5,100 in a base period equal to three-quarters of a year) prior to filing. See David A. Moss, *Socializing Security: Progressive-Era Economists and the Origins of American Social Policy* (Harvard University Press, 1996); Saul J. Baluster, Wilbur J. Coven, and William Habra, *Unemployment Insurance in the United States: The First Half Century* (W. E. Upjohn Institute for Employment Research, 1993); Tax Foundation, "Unemployment Insurance: Trends and Issues" (Research Publication 35, 1982); New York State Department of Labor, Workforce New Jersey Public Information Network.

38.   The 1994 poverty line for a family of four was $14,763.

39.   Robert Reich, Secretary of Labor in the first Clinton administration, considers incomes between $20,000 and $60,000 to be middle-class. In 1993, 64% of households had earnings between $15,000 and $75,000. The average household income in the United States is about $34,000. Popular definitions of the middle class are very broad—both struggling working families and very wealthy Americans label themselves middle-class. The concept of "middle class" grows more complicated as our nation moves closer to a two-tier society: income distribution in the United States is more unequal than in any other industrialized nation and has become significantly more unequal over the past two decades. In the early 1980s, the poorest, least experienced, and least educated workers began to experience significant declines in their real wages. By the end of the decade, wage declines, which continued for the lesser-skilled, began to affect the better-educated and more highly skilled. While the richest fifth of American families have seen their incomes rise over the past two decades, the poorest two-fifths of families—40%—have seen their real incomes decline by more than 10%. See Sam Roberts, "Fitting In: Another Kind of Middle-Class Squeeze," *New York Times,* May 18, 1997, section 4, p. 1; Michael D. Yates, *Longer Hours, Fewer Jobs: Employment and Unemployment in the United States* (Monthly Review Press, 1994).

40.   The same phenomenon of youth unemployment has developed in most of Western Europe, where the consequences have been disastrous. Attempted suicides have gone up tenfold in the past ten years, according to Stockholm's Center for Suicide Research and Prevention. The study shows that in Denmark, Sweden, and Finland, an estimated 5% of youths under age 20 have attempted suicide, a 500% increase in Denmark over the past 20 years. Cited in "Youth Suicide Rate Said to Rise in Europe," *New York Times,* June 11, 1996, p. A6.

41.   In 1988, federal appropriations for the training and education of AFDC recipients increased to levels not seen since the 1970s. The idea was to reduce relief roles by increasing the work-readiness skills of adult welfare recipients, about half of whom are without a high school diploma or GED. Congress passed the Family Support Act, which included a new program called Job Opportunities and Basic Skills (JOBS), in which about one-fourth of able-bodied welfare recipients without a child under age

three now participate. Reviews of different versions of the program are mixed; some analysts argue for less general education and more emphasis on job search and rudimentary job skills in order to move participants into the labor force more quickly. Others note that wages for the kinds of jobs that can be found through such preparation are too meager to pull one-parent households out of poverty without help. The federal welfare reform legislation passed in 1996, which places firm time limits on the receipt of federal assistance and phases in work requirements for recipients, continues to provide modest education and training support through block grants to states. While the legislation requires that such funds be used only for basic skills (such as literacy), GED and high school diploma preparation, job readiness activities, or training directly related to employment, individual states, which are now restructuring their former programs, may amend such provisions by including some postsecondary education as job training or by extending the time limits on receipt of assistance to women who are making satisfactory progress in school. See Isabel V. Sawhill, ed., *Welfare Reform: An Analysis of the Issues* (Urban Institute, 1997); Dan Bloom, *After AFDC: Welfare-to-Work Choices and Challenges for States* (Manpower Demonstration Research Corporation, 1997).

42.   Jennifer Hochschild, *Facing Up to the American Dream: Race, Class, and the Soul of the Nation* (Princeton University Press, 1996).

43.   They mention, in particular, the Reverend Al Sharpton and his colleague, the lawyer Alton Maddox, who have both claimed to speak for the people of Harlem.

44.   Hochschild, *Facing Up to the American Dream,* notes that racial separatism is more pronounced among educated, middle-class blacks than among those at the bottom of the class structure. One possible explanation lies in the daily experience of different classes. Harlem's fast food workers do not compete against whites, do not see whites on a daily basis, and have little interaction with the white world. Their supervisors, however, are more likely to rub shoulders with whites and see themselves in competition. This may help to account for their greater racial consciousness and more enthusiastic embrace of nationalism.

Chapter 9: What We Can Do for the Working Poor

1.   The 1996 and 1997 minimum wage increases raised the wages of almost 10 million workers, 71% of whom were adults and nearly half of whom were full-time employees. Households in the bottom 20% of income distribution received 35% of the benefit from the increase in the minimum wage. Jared Bernstein and John Schmitt (1997), "Making Work Pay: The Impact of the 1996–97 Minimum Wage Increase," Economic Policy Institute Report available on the web at http://epinet.org/mwsum.html. See also Rebecca Blank (1998), "Enhancing Opportunities, Skills and Security of American Workers," paper prepared for the Aspen Institute conference on "American Workers and the Workplace," July 11–15, 1998, Aspen, Col.

2.   Survey of the New York State Office of Temporary and Disability Assistance. Reported in Raymond Hernandez, "Most Dropped from Welfare Don't Get Jobs," *New York Times,* March 23, 1998, p. A1. This study doesn't track flow into the underground economy, those who left the state, or those working for employers who delay reporting their new payroll entrants, so the study may understate job-finding. Yet it

defines "working" as anyone who earned $100 in the three months following exit from the rolls. This threshold is so low that it probably exaggerates employment.

3. Examining the data from 23 urban areas, the Brookings Institution study concludes that the cities are becoming home to a more concentrated proportion of the welfare population than the nonurban areas of the states. Bruce Katz and Kate Carnavale, *The State of Welfare Caseloads in America's Cities* (Brookings Institution Center on Urban and Metropolitan Policy, 1998).

4. Other public, often state-based agencies have used similarly structured subsidies to encourage private firms to both hire and train welfare recipients and other disadvantaged workers through on-the-job training. Some states may make subsidies to private employers a significant component of the new mandatory work programs under welfare reform. But while subsidized on-the-job training has sometimes been shown to raise welfare recipients' earnings over time, few employers have indicated interest in participating in these programs. Dan Bloom, *After AFDC: Welfare-to-Work Choices and Challenges for States* (Manpower Demonstration Research Corporation, 1997).

5. The Targeted Jobs Tax Credit (TJTC) became available in 1979. It provided employers with a tax credit of 50% of the first $6,000 in wages for the first year of employment of a person from one of several targeted groups and a 25% tax credit for the first $6,000 in wages during the second year of employment. In 1984, about 560,000 people were employed under the program, two-thirds of whom were disadvantaged youth and about one-tenth of whom were welfare recipients. See Paul Osterman, *Employment Futures: Reorganization, Dislocation, and Public Policy* (Oxford University Pres, 1988), pp. 95–98; and John Bishop and Kevin Hollenbeck, *The Effects of TJTC on Employers* (National Center for Research in Vocational Education, Columbus, Ohio, 1985). In 1996, the TJTC was replaced by the Work Opportunity Tax Credit (WOTC), which, for most targeted employees, provides employers with a 35% tax credit on the first $6,000 in wages earned during the first year of employment. Among the groups targeted by the WOTC are individuals on welfare, veterans on food stamps, ex-felons, and high-risk youth in "empowerment zones." See Lawrence F. Katz, "Wage Subsidies for the Disadvantaged" (NBER Working Paper 5679, 1996), for a review of the successes and failures of wage subsidy programs. Katz notes that the TJTC may have modestly improved the employment rates of disadvantaged youth. He suggests a demonstration project to test the effects of a noncategorical wage subsidy for low-wage workers, which might alleviate low employer utilization by avoiding the stigma that arises when groups are targeted.

6. Many have argued that the wage subsidies have been a windfall for businesses, especially those that hire large numbers of low-wage workers. See, for example, Edward C. Lorenz, "TJTC and the Promise and Reality of Redistributive Vouchering and Tax Credit Policy," *Journal of Policy Analysis and Management* 14, no. 2 (Spring 1995), pp. 270–90. Indeed, results from a recent survey of 3,500 participating firms, John H. Bishop and Mark Montgomery, "Does the Targeted Jobs Tax Credit Create Jobs at Subsidized Firms?" *Industrial Relations* 32, no. 3 (Fall 1993), pp. 289–306, suggest that more than 70% of the tax credits granted to employers are payments for workers who would have been hired even without the subsidies.

7. Studies show that employers often have negative views of the categories of workers targeted by the wage subsidies, thereby stigmatizing these job-seekers and

reducing their employment chances when applicants inform employers that they are eligible for the subsidy. See Gary Burtless, "Are Targeted Wage Subsidies Harmful? Evidence from a Wage Voucher Experiment," *Industrial and Labor Relations Review* 39, no. 1 (Winter 1985), pp. 105–14. Nationwide, less than 10% of those firms with eligible employees actually use the subsidies. Rebecca Blank, *It Takes a Nation: A New Agenda for Fighting Poverty* (Russell Sage Foundation, 1997), p. 116. But according to Bishop and Montgomery, "Does the Targeted Jobs Tax Credit Create Jobs at Subsidized Firms?" the TJTC program has a modest effect on generating *new* jobs (about 0.2 new jobs per hire) and induces employers to hire more young workers (under age 25).

8. Edmund S. Phelps, *Rewarding Work: How to Restore Participation and Self-Support to Free Enterprise* (Harvard University Press, 1997).

9. As Kathryn Edin and Laura Lein document in their book, *Making Ends Meet* (Russell Sage Foundation, 1997).

10. A very small credit is available to some low-income persons with no children. See below.

11. In 1996, the maximum credit for families with two or more children, $3,556, begins when income rises to $8,850; the credit begins to decline when income reaches $11,650, and becomes zero when income reaches $28,495. The maximum credit for families with one child is $2,152 (for incomes between $6,300 and $11,650); the maximum credit for childless persons is $323 (for incomes between $4,200 and $5,300). See "Earned Income Tax Credit Worth More Than Ever," *Roanoke Times and World News*, February 24, 1997, Money section, p. 6.

12. The EITC was expanded in 1990 and 1993, and in terms of costs is now about as large as the federal food stamp program. In 1998 nearly 20 million families will qualify for the EITC; total spending for the program is expected to reach about $28 billion by then. Some conservatives have fought unsuccessfully to cut the program, arguing that the EITC, which can carry full-time workers who earn the minimum wage over the poverty line, is really a public assistance program unavailable to middle-income taxpayers. See Congressman Bill Archer, "The Earned Income Tax Credit and Working Families" (Congressional Press Release, July 10, 1997). In current battles over the proposed $500-per-child federal income tax credit, Republicans have only recently compromised by suggesting that low-income families who pay Social Security taxes but no federal income taxes be able to save the child credit for up to three years to offset future income taxes. The original child tax credit proposal in the House would reach fewer than 4% of the 23 million children whose parents earn less than $23,000 per year. Frances Fox Piven, "Helping the Poor as a Last Resort," *New York Times*, July 28, 1997, p. A17.

13. The EITC has a high error and fraud rate—about 20%. This number overstates the problem to some degree because it includes credits paid to the wrong tax filer (to a parent instead of a grandparent sharing the same household, for example), not the net amount the government overpays because of computational errors and fraud Robert Greenstein, Executive Director of the Center on Budget and Policy Priorities, "Understanding the High Error Rate of the Earned-Income Tax Credit," *Washington Times*, May 24, 1997. Recent changes in information requirements are expected to lower the error rate. At the same time, the calculations required to apply for the credit have become so complicated that Michael Graetz, a professor of tax law at Yale,

argues that fewer of the working poor may take advantage of the credit. See David Cay Johnston, "A Tax Cut Your Lawyer Will Love," *New York Times,* August 3, 1997, p. A26; "Prepared Statement of the American Institute of Certified Public Accountants Before the House Ways and Means Committee," House Ways and Means Committee Hearing on the Earned Income Tax Credit, May 8, 1997.

14.   "A Program That Helps the Working Poor Is in Trouble," *New York Times,* July 13, 1995, p. C2.

15.   Richard Caputo makes the same point in "Patterns of Work and Poverty: Exploratory Profiles of Working-Poor Households," *Families in Society,* October 1991, pp. 451–59.

16.   In addition to the jobs moving, residential segregation makes it more difficult for blacks to move to suburbs. Harry Holzer, for example, suggests that spatial imbalances are worse in areas, such as Detroit, where residential segregation is more pronounced. Harry Holzer, *What Employers Want: Job Prospects for Less-Educated Workers* (Russell Sage Foundation, 1996), p. 128.

17.   John D. Kasarda, "Industrial Restructuring and the Changing Location of Jobs," in Reynolds Farley, ed., *State of the Union, America in the 1990s,* vol. 1, *Economic Trends* (Russell Sage Foundation, 1995), pp. 215–67.

18.   David T. Ellwood, "The Spatial Mismatch Hypothesis: Are There Teenage Jobs Missing in the Ghetto?" in Richard B. Freeman and Harry J. Holzer, *The Black Youth Employment Crisis* (University of Chicago Press, 1986).

19.   Using Current Population Survey and National Longitudinal Survey of Youth data from the 1980s, Richard B. Freeman, "Employment and Earnings of Disadvantaged Young Men in a Labor Shortage Economy," in Christopher Jencks and Paul E. Peterson, eds., *The Urban Underclass* (Brookings Institution, 1991), pp. 103–21, analyzes unemployment rates, employment-population ratios, and hourly earnings of out-of-school young men with a high school education or less who resided in areas (metropolitan statistical areas, or MSAs) with tight local labor markets during the 1980s. In 1987, 36 metropolitan areas had unemployment rates lower than 4% (Anaheim–Santa Ana, California; Stamford, Connecticut; and Nashua, New Hampshire had rates lower than 3%)—and about one-fifth of out-of-school young black men with a high school degree or less lived in such areas. Freeman found that local labor market shortages greatly improved the employment opportunities of young men with little schooling, reduced their unemployment rate, and significantly raised the proportion employed, especially for black men. Likewise, he found that labor market shortages increased the hourly earnings of young men with little schooling, especially black men. Paul Osterman, "Gains from Growth? The Impact of Full Employment on Poverty in Boston," in Jencks and Peterson, eds., *Urban Underclass,* pp. 122–34, analyzes poverty and other data for the city of Boston during the period of full employment in the 1980s. Osterman found that the Massachusetts Miracle— which extended into Boston's inner city, drawing minorities, including black men, into employment in large numbers—greatly reduced poverty, especially among blacks. The poverty rate of black families and black unrelated individuals in Boston in 1980, 29.1% and 26.5% respectively, declined to just 13.4% and 5.3% in 1988. Nationally, poverty rates for the same groups remained dismal over about the same time period. The poverty rate of black families and black unrelated individuals in all central cities in 1980, 25.9% and 30.8% respectively, increased to 32.3% and 31.2% in 1987.

20. Mark Alan Hughes, "Employment Decentralization and Accessibility: A Strategy for Stimulating Regional Mobility," *Journal of the American Planning Association 57*, no. 3 (1991), pp. 288–98; Mark Alan Hughes, "Over the Horizon: Jobs in the Suburbs of Major Metropolitan Areas" (Background Paper from Public/Private Ventures, Philadelphia, December 1993).

21. Widespread discrimination was found in Chicago's public housing projects, resulting in a 1976 court order to desegregate public housing. The consent decree that carried the Gautreaux program forward after 1981 expired in 1997, and the program may end before long. Since 1977, about 6,500 families have moved from inner-city public housing to nonsegregated communities. Studies have shown both increased job-holding and educational advancement among participating families. Leadership Council for Metropolitan Open Cities, "Leadership Council for Metropolitan Open Communities Reports That Court Approves Termination of Gautreaux Assisted Housing Program" (news release, Chicago, September 2, 1997); "The Gautreaux Case Isn't Over Yet," Editorial, *Chicago Tribune*, September 3, 1997, p. 18.

22. James E. Rosenbaum and Susan J. Popkin, "Employment and Earnings of Low-Income Blacks Who Move to Middle-Class Suburbs," in Jencks and Peterson, eds., *Urban Underclass*, pp. 342–56; James E. Rosenbaum and Susan J. Popkin, *Economic and Social Impacts of Housing Integration* (Center for Urban Affairs and Policy Research, Northwestern University, 1990).

23. In 1994, the federal government created a small Gautreaux-type program called "Moving to Opportunity" to help a limited number of families in five cities—Baltimore, Los Angeles, New York, Chicago, and Boston—relocate from poor neighborhoods to more job-rich areas. But when officials in Baltimore made plans to move 285 mostly African-American families from city public housing to mostly white suburbs, suburban politicians protested, claiming that the moves would export poverty to middle-class areas. While raucous disputes continue, slowing down initiatives in the other cities, by 1997 about 140 families in Baltimore had been successfully relocated. Larry Gordon, "A Social Experiment in Pulling Up Stakes," *Los Angeles Times*, September 23, 1997, p. A1; James Bock, "Mapping Road from Poverty," *Baltimore Sun*, February 26, 1996, p. 1B; Harold D. Young, "Moving to Opportunity Is a Success, Despite Rare Exception," *Baltimore Sun*, January 25, 1997, p. 11A.

24. Atlanta, Baltimore, Chicago, Detroit, New York City, and Philadelphia–Camden were selected from nearly 300 applications to be the empowerment zones. There is some evidence that the tax incentives may have real effects. For example, early in 1997, Sylvan Learning Systems announced plans to move its world headquarters (expanding employment to 600) from suburban Columbia, Maryland, into a $32 million complex in Baltimore's empowerment zone. Neil R. Peirce, "Baltimore's First Corporate Hit in 20 Years: Harbinger for Empowerment Zones?" *Nation's Cities Weekly*, March 3, 1997.

25. The Upper Manhattan Empowerment Zone has received $550 million in tax credits, grants, and loans from city, state, and federal sources to be used over the next decade, mainly for establishing businesses, creating jobs, and providing job training. So far, about $15 million has been committed for twelve projects expected to create 1,300 jobs. Small projects include the following start-ups: a small business loan program, a credit union, a youth internship program in geriatric care, and a restaurant. The largest project is Harlem U.S.A., a shopping complex to be built on 125th

Street that will have a Gap store and a Disney store. Construction has also begun on a suburban-style Pathmark supermarket at 125th Street and Lexington Avenue. Pathmark will receive wage subsidy tax breaks by hiring workers from within the empowerment zone. Elisabeth Bumiller, "Harlem on Her Mind: Preacher's Daughter Takes Wall St. Sensibility Uptown," *New York Times*, March 28, 1997, p. B1.

26. Others worry about the business climate in the empowerment zones, claiming that crime might threaten it, and that operating expenses are higher in cities than in suburbs. Finally, some charge that the organization of the empowerment zone program, which is administered by the federal Department of Housing and Urban Development through local city agencies and community coalitions, is ripe for bureaucracy, waste, and fraud.

27. Tighter labor markets can also be achieved by limiting immigration, particularly in the low-skill domain. This is a controversial matter that requires much more space to discuss thoroughly. The National Research Council released its definitive report on the impact of immigration in the summer of 1997: National Research Council's Panel on the Demographic and Economic Impacts of Immigration, James P. Smith and Barry Edmonston, eds., *The New Americans: Economic, Demographic and Fiscal Effects of Immigration* (National Academy Press, 1997). It concluded that the nation as a whole benefits modestly from immigration, which adds between $1 billion and $10 billion yearly to the $7 trillion U.S. economy. And while the average immigrant over a lifetime will pay roughly $100,000 more in federal taxes than in benefits that he or she will receive, state and local governments lose a combined average of about $25,000. Particular localities often suffer much more, especially the high-immigration areas in states like California, New York, Florida, and Texas. Immigrants add a great deal to the economy because they work hard, pay taxes, and spend money on goods and services, raising demand. But in some areas they consume public services at high rates and, recent evidence suggests, are at risk for long-term poverty. Recent immigrants from poor countries come with low levels of education and skills, lowering demands for poorly educated native workers. According to the report, wages of native workers without a high school may have fallen as much as 5% over the past 15 years because of competition from immigrant workers. The report suggests, however, that there is no evidence that blacks have been particularly hard hit on the national level.

28. See John J. Sweeney, *America Needs a Raise* (Houghton Mifflin, 1996).

29. According to one survey, about one-third of nonunion private-sector workers would vote for a union "if an election were held today." Joel Rogers, "Talking Union," *The Nation* 259, no. 22 (Dec. 26, 1994), pp. 784–85. But according to a survey by the Commission on the Future of Worker-Management Relations, *Report and Recommendations* (U.S. Department of Commerce and U.S. Department of Labor, December 1994), over three-fourths of nonunions workers believe that it is likely that employees who seek union representation will lose their jobs. Many in the union movement feel that legislative reform must take place if unions are to be strengthened. Site elections for union representation are currently litigious, slow, and risky to workers with pro-union sentiments. Another idea in the current union movement—one that some trade union leaders are skeptical of—is to expand the range of options for worker representation through organizations that focus more attention on work organization and work practice decision-making, so as to form more cooperative

relationships with firm managements. For more on these issues, see Joel Rogers and Wolfgang Streeck, eds., *Work Councils: Consultation, Representation, and Cooperation in Industrial Relations* (University of Chicago Press, 1996); Sheldon Friedman et al., eds., *Restoring the Promise of American Labor Law* (ILR Press, 1994); Thomas A. Kochan and Paul Osterman, *The Mutual Gains Enterprise* (Harvard Business School Press, 1994).

30. Sandra L. Hoffert, "Caring for Children at the Poverty Line," *Children and Youth Services Review 17*, nos. 1–2 (1995), pp. 61–90.

31. The Annie E. Casey Foundation, one of the most respected nonprofit organizations in the field of poverty, has noted that the working poor face special problems with respect to childcare compared to poor families who are out of the labor market: "Children of the working poor [face] an insufficiency of parental time and a lack of quality preschool or other appropriate day care. . . . The problem of too little time is compounded by their frequent inability to afford adequate child care to compensate for their absence from the home." "Overview," *Kids Count Data Book* (Annie E. Casey Foundation, 1996).

32. According to the National Center for Health Statistics, 2.6 million uninsured children were unable to obtain needed medical care in the past year. See Sarah Howe, "U.S. Government Survey Finds Millions of Uninsured Children Not Getting Necessary Medical Care" (Children's Defense Fund news release, July 17, 1997). The 1997 budget bill provides for a five-year, $24 billion program—financed largely through an increase in the federal tax on cigarettes and administered through state block grants—to provide medical care for uninsured poor children. Children who live in families whose employers do not provide coverage and whose incomes are too high to qualify for Medicaid but too low to afford insurance will be eligible (the program will be limited to children in families with incomes less than 200–250% of the federal poverty line, in most states.) States choose how they will provide child health care for the uninsured from several options: standard federal employee health insurance benefits, enrollment in a health maintenance organization, the standard health plan for state workers, or enrollment in the state's Medicaid program. Estimates of the number of children who will be served range from two to five million. In any case, this represents the largest expansion in children's health coverage since Medicaid's creation thirty years ago. Cindy Mann and Jocelyn Guyer, "Overview of the New Child Health Block Grant" Center on Budget and Policy Priorities, August 6, 1997); Hillary Rodham Clinton, "Our Chance for Healthier Children," and Douglas J. Besharov, "Beware the Real Agenda," both *New York Times*, August 5, 1997, p. A15.

33. In pointing attention to what he calls the "anxious class," those less-skilled Americans who are losing both jobs and wages in our increasingly advanced global economy, Reich has made corporate citizenship, education, and job training (especially for the non-college-bound) his mantra in many speeches and articles. Robert Reich, *The Work of Nations* (Knopf, 1991), notes that while the total tax burden (social security taxes, sales taxes, user fees, property taxes, and lotteries) has shifted from wealthier to poorer Americans, public funding that would improve the earnings of the lesser-skilled—through job creation, education, and training—have declined. By the end of the 1980s, Reich writes, federal investment in infrastructure was about the same as it was 30 years before, though the gross national product had grown 144%. Physical capital investment as a percentage of federal outlays decreased from 24% in

1960 to 11% in 1991. During the 1980s, federal support for elementary and secondary education dropped by one-third (with states picking up the tab). During the same period, public funding to train workers dropped by more than 50%, from $13.2 billion to $5.6 billion. Private training, paid for by corporations themselves, is difficult to measure, but it is much more likely to go to college graduates and postgraduates than to high-school-educated workers. See Reich, "The Decline of Public Investment," *Work of Nations,* pp. 252–61. Reich suggests that corporate income taxes could be reduced for those firms that upgrade the general skills of their employees and give them health care and pension protections. He is also a strong proponent of school-to-work initiatives. See Robert Reich, "Building a Framework for a School-to-Work Opportunities System," in John F. Jennings, ed., *National Issues in Education: Goals 2000 and School-to-Work* (Phi Delta Kappa, 1995).

34. Some authors, notably Paul Osterman, have argued that churning—moving rapidly through a series of jobs—is not as much of a liability as we might suppose. The transition from dependent status, as a student and youth worker, to independence from the natal home is filled with stops and starts, he argues, and this is normal in a labor system as comparatively unstructured as ours. The vast majority of American youth settle into jobs eventually. But what of the poor, minority youth of particular concern here? Just over half of black high school graduates are employed at all. The unemployment rates of high school dropouts is "nothing short of catastrophic." More telling, "over 30 percent of 30-year-old [black] minority men and a much larger fraction of 30-year-old [minority] women are in jobs they have held for less than a year." All of this evidence suggests that labor market entry is a stumbling process for minority youth and young adults that does not get much better over time. Paul Osterman, "The Youth Labor Market Problem," in Katherine McFate, Roger Lawson, and William Julius Wilson, eds., *Poverty, Inequality, and the Future of Social Policy* (Russell Sage Foundation, 1995), pp. 387–414.

35. James E. Rosenbaum and Stephanie Alter Jones, "Improving the School-Work Transition: Lessons from Japan and Their Applicability to American Teachers, Employers and Students" (Working Paper No. 20, Center for Urban Affairs and Policy Research, Northwestern University, 1994).

36. Carol Kinney, *From a Lower Track School to a Low Status Job? An Ethnographic Study of Two Japanese High Schools* (Ph.D. dissertation, University of Michigan, 1994).

37. See Osterman, "Youth Labor Market Problem," for a review of American attempts to mimic the German system, and Rosenbaum and Jones, "Improving the School-Work Transition," for the prospects of imitating the Japanese model. Much of the new interest in reorganizing the connection between the American education system and the workplace, especially for the non-college-bound, was generated by the accumulating evidence that the earnings gap between well-educated and lesser-educated workers widened dramatically during the 1980s, and by the belief that schools were not meeting the needs of students who do not continue to college. See William T. Grant Foundation Commission on Work, Family, and Citizenship, *The Forgotten Half: Pathways to Success for America's Youth and Young Families* (1988); Keith F Allum, *Finding One's Way: Career Guidance for Disadvantaged Youth* (U.S. Department of Labor, 1993); Thomas R. Bailey and Donna Merritt, *The School-to-Work Transition and Youth Apprenticeship: Lessons from the U.S. Experience* (Manpower Demonstration Research Corporation, 1993). In addition, many analysts have

begun to argue that skills for entry-level jobs have increased or will increase, especially for those firms that are responding to increased global competition with "high-performance" workplace reforms. National Center for Education and the Economy's Commission on the Skills of the American Workforce, *America's Choice: High Skills or Low Wages* (1990). High-wage employers increasingly look for new workers with strong basic skills (such as mathematics, problem-solving, reading ability, the ability to work in groups, and computer literacy), sometimes bypassing those with only a high school degree out of a belief that high school graduates with no further education or training lack these skills. See Richard J. Murnane and Frank Levy, *Teaching the New Basic Skills: Principles for Educating Children to Thrive in a Changing Economy* (Free Press, 1996). For more on how work-based learning pedagogy and school-to-work linkages can be made more effective, see Sue. E. Berryman and Thomas R. Bailey, *The Double Helix of Education and the Economy* (Institute on Education and the Economy, 1992). Edward Pauly, Hilary Kopp, and Joshua Haimson, *Home-Grown Lessons: Innovative Programs Linking Work and High School* (Manpower Demonstration Research Corporation, 1994), reporting research on sixteen early school-to-work projects in twelve states, shows that it is feasible to operate innovative programs that combine school-based and work-based learning.

38. Rosenbaum and Jones, "Improving the School-Work Transition," p. 11.

39. The Wisconsin Regional Training Partnership has developed an innovative program designed to connect teachers to the workplace. The forty metalworking firms that belong to the partnership have "committed to a series of 'take the teacher to work' days, involving 300 Milwaukee Public School teachers, for youth apprentices and co-op students. Given the high level of employer involvement, the effort promises to move several hundred young people into manufacturing youth apprenticeships in the next few years." Laura Dresser and Joel Rogers, "Rebuilding Job Access and Career Advancement Systems in the New Economy" (unpublished paper, Center on Wisconsin Strategy, Madison, Wisconsin, prepared for the "New Employment Policies for the Emerging Post-Industrial Market" conference, sponsored by the William T. Grant Foundation and the Teacher's College Institute on Education and the Economy, May, 1997).

40. Quoted in "Youth Apprenticeship in Consumer Service Management—Executive Summary," available from the McDonald's Corporation Public Information Office, Oak Park, Illinois.

41. Indeed, research has shown that attracting employers to participate actively in school-to-work programs is sometimes slow and difficult. See U.S. Congress, Office of Technology Assessment, *Learning to Work: Making the Transition from School to Work,* OTA-EHR-637 (U.S. Government Printing Office, 1995). Some analysts question whether it is possible to gain enough participating employers to make school-to-work initiatives broadly successful. See Thomas R. Bailey, "Incentives for Employer Participation in School-to-Work Programs," and Paul Osterman, "Involving Employers in School-to-Work Programs," both in Thomas R. Bailey, ed., *Learning to Work: Employer Involvement in School-to-Work Transition Programs* (Brookings Institution, 1995), pp. 14–25, 75–87. Bailey discusses three kinds of employer motivations: (1) philanthropic; (2) individual self-interest (good public relations, source of low-cost labor, source of future workers); and (3) collective interest (a strengthened industry-wide or occupational labor pool. Bailey does not rate the strengths of different incentives.

He does note that employer incentives are weak, and he suggests an industry- or occupation-oriented approach, founded on more collective than individual motives, to work-based education. He suggests that encouraging employers to act together may be more effective than subsidies or other policies directed at individual interests.

42. James E. Rosenbaum and Amy Binder, "Do Employers Really Need More Educated Youth?" *Sociology of Education* 70 (January 1997), pp. 68–85, reports recent interviews of managers of 51 diverse firms in and around Chicago. Thirty-five of the 51 managers said that basic academic skills in mathematics (such as arithmetic and adding fractions) and English skills (such as reading and spelling) are needed for *entry-level* jobs they are seeking to fill. Even more managers said that basic academic skills are needed for higher-level jobs. Managers' assessments of these skill requirements were based largely on experiences they had had with poorly skilled workers in these positions. Many managers complained about the difficulty in finding high school graduates with adequate math or English skills. Holzer, *What Employers Want,* suggests that the great majority of jobs for non-college graduates require the daily use of major cognitive skills, such as reading/writing paragraphs, doing arithmetic, or using computers. Only 5–10% of jobs in central-city areas for non-college graduates require few cognitive skills or work credentials. See also Nurnane and Levy, *New Basic Skills.*

43. A recent survey of nearly 3,000 employers found that while 71% of the firms gave some training to employees, only about 3% provided basic training in academic skills. David Boesel, *BLS Survey of Employer-Provided Formal Training* (U.S. Department of Labor, Bureau of Labor Statistics, September 23, 1994).

44. "Youth Apprenticeship in Consumer Service Management—Executive Summary," p. 1.

45. The nationwide court-mandated school desegregation that took place in the 1970s, for example, is quietly being reversed. Because of releases from court-ordered desegregation busing orders as well as the school choice movement, schools across the nation since the late 1980s have been consistently resegregating into isolated middle-class white schools and poor black and Latino schools. Gary Orfield et al., "Deepening Segregation in American Public Schools" (Report from the Harvard Project on School Desegregation, 1997). See also Gary Orfield and Susan E. Eaton, *Dismantling Desegregation: The Quiet Reversal of Brown v. Board of Education* (New Press, 1995). However, Reynolds Farley has suggested that 1990 census data show a decline in residential segregation. Reynolds Farley, ed., *State of the Union: America in the 1990s* (Russell Sage Foundation, 1995).

46. The Summer Youth Training and Education Program, a summer jobs program for at-risk youth, funded since 1982 through the Job Training Partnership Act.

47. Most participants (a third of whom are 14- and 15-year-olds) work for minimum wage for a month or two during the summer at government agencies, schools, and community-based associations. They often do maintenance or office work while receiving some remedial education. Evaluations of the federal summer jobs program are inconclusive. While young people make modest gains in soft skills and career knowledge, there is little evidence that this translates into increased post-program job market success relative to non-participants. Thomas J. Smith and Michelle Alberti Gambone, "Effectiveness of Federally Funded Employment Training Strategies for

Youth," In U.S. Department of Labor, *Dilemmas in Youth Employment Programming: Findings from the Youth Research and Technical Assistance Project,* vol. 1, Research and Evaluation Report Series 92-C (U.S. Department of Labor, 1992) pp. 15–67.

48. In 1992, New York City received $57 million from the federal government, which, along with about $3 million from city sources, was used to create over 50,000 summer youth jobs. *The Mayor's Management Report* (City of New York, September 1993), p. 469. In 1996, New York City received about $35 million, which, along with about $2 million from city sources and $1 million from private sources, was used to create about 27,000 summer jobs. *The Mayor's Management Report,* vol. 1 (City of New York, September 1996), p. 174.

49. The 125th Street BID, now three years old, is currently researching an expansion plan that would be aided by the Upper Manhattan Empowerment Zone. Jane H. Lii, "Neighborhood Report: Harlem: Business District to Stretch its Boundaries," *New York Times,* March 23, 1997, section 13, p. 6.

50. See Katherine S. Newman, "Dead End Jobs—a Way Out," *Brookings Review,* Fall 1995, pp. 24–27.

51. According to a number of studies, African-Americans face more negative employer perceptions than any other racial or ethnic group. In a survey of 179 Chicago-area firms, Wilson, *When Work Disappears,* p. 111, finds that many employers consider inner-city workers, and in particular black males, to be "uneducated, unstable, uncooperative, and dishonest." The survey results indicate that racial stereotyping is greater among employers with lower proportions of blacks in their workforces. See also Kathryn M. Neckerman and Joleen Kirschenman, "Hiring Strategies, Racial Bias, and Inner-City Workers," *Social Problems* 38 (November 1991), pp. 433–47; and Holzer, *What Employers Want.*

52. Indeed, in areas like Milwaukee, with unemployment rates at less than 2%, we are seeing very little overall wage growth, but many frustrated employers who are losing their people to new opportunities. Laura Dresser, Center for Wisconsin Strategy, personal communication.

53. That said, it is true that suburban wages for entry-level workers at Burger Barn are considerably higher than they are in Harlem. Does this mean that Harlem owners could, in fact, afford to pay more for their labor? One would have to look carefully at the profit margins (factoring in differential rents, pricing policies, and the like) to answer this question.

54. Consortiums would also appeal to the civic spirit of minority business owners, who often choose to locate in places like Harlem rather than in less risky neighborhoods because they want to provide job opportunities for people in their own community. They endure a certain amount of frustration because they cannot provide for much upward mobility. Participating in a consortium would make that easier.

55. Demonstration projects could experiment with various sorts of financial incentives for both sets of employers.

56. This program is described in detail in the pamphlet "Career Ladder Program," available from the Hospital Workers Union Local 767, Service Employees International Union, 94 Main Street, Hyannis, MA 02601.

57. Twelve first-class hotels are members of this partnership, as are two unions, which together represent 90% of the unionized hotel workforce in these hotels, for a

total partnership membership of 5,000 people. The hospital industry is the largest private-sector employer in San Francisco, and hotels are the largest unionized private-sector employer.

58.   For more details, see Stuart Korshak, "Negotiating Trust in the San Francisco Hotel Industry," *California Management Review* 38, no. 1 (1995).

59.   The Wisconsin partnership is a variation on the theme of "sectoral strategies," which link local/regional/state government and private industries in particular sectors (defined as a group of employers who share a common market, produce a common product, or share basic labor force, infrastructure, or technology requirements). For more on this promising approach see Beth Siegel and Peter Kwass, "Jobs and the Urban Poor: Publicly-Initiated Sectoral Strategies" (Mt. Auburn Associates, Somerville, Massachusetts, 1995).

60.   Laura Dresser and Joel Rogers, "Rebuilding Job Access and Career Advancement in the New Economy" (paper prepared for the "New Employment Policies for the Emerging Post-Industrial Market" conference, sponsored by the W. T. Grant Foundation and Teacher's College Institute on Education and the Economy, 1997).

61.   See Julia Lopez et al., "Connecting Inner City Residents with the World of Work: Pilot Tests of New Approaches" (Discussion Paper, Rockefeller Foundation, 1996).

62.   New Hope's control group seems to be doing very well in terms of employment as well, reflecting the surging job market in the Milwaukee area. Greg Duncan, personal communication. It will take time and further research to sort out the impact of New Hope's interventions as opposed to the impact of a better job market.

63.   Paul Osterman and Brenda Lautsch, "Project Quest: A Report to the Ford Foundation" (1996).

64.   Ibid., p. 4.

65.   Rather than merely responding to criminal incidents when they occur, community policing efforts and community-based prosecution attempt to better serve a neighborhood's daily needs by tackling specific local problems in concert with social agencies and private citizens. Community policing represents an interventionist police strategy that focuses on order maintenance. Thus, despite community policing's fundamental connection to communities and their conflicts, the strategy, now being undertaken in one form or another in several major cities, is ironically but by its very nature more aggressive than traditional "911" policing. Indeed, while very real reductions in crime have been attributed to community policing, a significant problem in implementation has been shaping and controlling line officers' discretion in their daily work. For a review of findings of community policing efforts in several cities including New York City, see George L. Kelling and Catherine M. Coles, *Fixing Broken Windows* (Free Press, 1996).

66.   Michael Porter, "The Competitive Advantage of the Inner City," *Harvard Business Review*, May–June 1995, pp. 55–71.

67.   The same might be said of many welfare recipients, who have had plenty of experience at the low-wage end of the labor market, only to discover that they could not keep body and soul together for themselves and their children on the strength of a Burger Barn income.

Index

NOTE: *Individuals identified by first names only are interview subjects.*